GODDESS UNMASKED

GODDESS UNMASKED

The Rise of Neopagan Feminist Spirituality

PHILIP G. DAVIS

SPENCE PUBLISHING COMPANY · DALLAS
1998

Published in the United States by
Spence Publishing Company
501 Elm Street, Suite 450
Dallas, Texas 75202

Library of Congress Cataloging-in-Publication Data

Davis, Philip G., 1950-
    Goddess unmasked : the rise of neopagan feminist spirituality / Philip G. Davis
        p. cm.
    Includes bibliographical references and index.
    ISBN 0-9653208-9-8
    1. Goddess religion.   2. Feminist spirituality.   I. Title.
BL325.F4D38   1998
291.1'4—dc21   97-47378

Printed in the United States of America

For Catrin

*whose love and support
have given me the best of life.*

Contents

Preface

WHEN I EMBARKED on my academic career, I never imagined I would write a book like this one. In the 1970s, I, like most people, had never heard of the Goddess movement. I expected to write specialized books and articles that would bring me into debate with other scholars without having much direct relevance outside the university. When I first encountered Goddess spirituality, I was mildly bemused; it seemed self-evidently outlandish, but no more than many other new religions of modern times. As I discovered that the Goddess was being taken seriously in religious institutions and that her myth was being taught as factual history on campus, my informal collection of rebuttals grew larger, more elaborate, and more rooted in my concerns for the health of contemporary society. These concerns grew as the influence of the Goddess movement became more and more apparent.

This book is an historical critique of Goddess spirituality: a description of its claims, an examination of those claims measured against the available evidence, an account of its true origins and sources, and an assessment of its place and significance in society. As is evident from the title of the book, I do not believe that the assertions of the Goddess movement stand up to scrutiny; indeed, it is perplexing that claims so easily disproved are nevertheless in wide and increasing circulation. An important lesson of this book is the ease with which patent falsehoods may clothe themselves in the garb of scholarship and masquerade as truth.

Goddess spirituality makes dramatic claims about anthropology, archaeology, ancient and modern history, social organization, psychology, art, and human biology, as well as religion. Any account of this burgeoning movement must address most of these disciplines. There is no one academic specialty which deals with all of the major issues raised by the Goddess movement, and this book is accordingly the work of a generalist. There is, in fact, rather little in this book that is new; most of what I have to say is known to specialists in various fields and is dependent on their work. As far as I know, however, the sum of the knowledge of the particular disciplines I address has never been brought to bear on Goddess spirituality. The reason this book needed to be written is, quite simply, that the wide range of facts necessary to understand and assess the Goddess movement has not previously been made accessible to those who might encounter the movement in one of its many manifestations.

THERE ARE MANY PEOPLE to whom I have cause for gratitude arising from this work. I wish to thank the Senate Research Committee at the University of Prince Edward Island, former Dean of Arts Robert Campbell, and the former acting Dean, John Crossley, for making available the funding to allow my research to proceed. Many individuals read parts or earlier versions of this study, and I am sincerely grateful for all the advice and information offered by the following people in particular: Dr. Ruth Gruhn (Department of Anthropology, University of Alberta); the late Dr. Barry Gross (Department of Philosophy, City University of New York); Dr. Graeme Hunter (Department of Philosophy, University of Ottawa); Dr. Mary Lefkowitz (Andrew Mellon Professor of the Humanities, Wellesley College); two anonymous reviewers for the *Journal of the History of Ideas*; the Rt. Rev. Dr. Geoffrey Rowell, Bishop of Basingstoke; and some present and former colleagues at UPEI, Dr. Kenneth Butler (Philosophy), Dr. Ian Dowbiggin (History), and Prof. Lothar Zimmermann (Modern Languages). I am especially thankful to Dr. David F. Buck (Classics, UPEI) and Dr. Anthony O'Malley (International Studies, Dalhousie/ St. Mary's) for reading and commenting on virtually the entire manuscript, and above all to Dr. R. David Smith of Toronto for encouraging me to proceed with the entire project in the first place as well as providing detailed and thought-provoking suggestions at every stage along the way. My editor at Spence Publishing, Mitchell Muncy, is also responsible for several major improvements to the book. Obviously, any errors of fact, judgment or expression which have persisted into the final text despite all this assistance are entirely my own.

On the personal side, I wish to record my appreciation for the fellowship and encouragement received from the clergy and my fellow parishioners at the Cathedral Church of St. Peter in Charlottetown. It was partly the Goddess project which led me there, finding a lively community of like-minded people, and the warm welcome accorded to our family is something we value deeply. I also want to thank our children—Jonathan and his lady Sarah, Trevor, Andrew, and Konika—for the interest, support, and practical help which all of them provided in their own different ways, even though the writing of the book took so much of my time and attention away from them. To our various foster children as well, I am grateful for the stimulating dose of reality which they provided on an ongoing basis. The encouragement of my parents, George and Agnes Davis, and my parents-in-law, Dr. Desmond and Peggy Little, is also much appreciated.

Finally, I must try to put into words the depth of my gratitude towards my wife Catrin. She established and maintained the warm home environment which I require for my own wellbeing and productivity; she gave unfailing support throughout the period of research and writing, encouraging me in difficult times, cautioning and advising me on the handling of some of the more sensitive areas of my critique. Moreover, she arranged to have the entire manuscript read aloud to her, owing to her visual impairment, and offered valuable ideas and insightful comments which have left a definite imprint on the final product. The bulk of the writing took place during the year of our twenty-fifth wedding anniversary, and as an all-too-small token of appreciation for everything that these years have meant to me, I dedicate this book to her.

GODDESS UNMASKED

The Pagan Revival
and the Problem of Modernity

A S THE SUNLIGHT FALLS gently through the canopy of leaves to daub mottled patterns on the floor of the glade, the intense little group is reaching a pinnacle of high emotion. They have cast the circle, they have evoked the spiritual powers, they have chanted and sung. Now the librarian, the counselor, the artist, the entrepreneur, and the others within the circle grasp each other's hands. Eyes locked together, the women whisper the joyous affirmation. "Thou art Goddess!" "Thou art Goddess!"

As the traffic builds and the smog rises from the streets up the walls of the office towers, the driver searches in vain for a place to pull over. With a wry smile on her face, she calls whimsically to the Goddess of Parking: "Hail Asphalta, full of grace, help me find a parking space!" A few minutes later, the car safely deposited, she goes about her business.

As the two thousand delegates to the conference listen and applaud, one speaker after another points towards their shared vision of a beautiful new world. It is an ecumenical church conference, and the audience contains Presbyterians, Methodists, Lutherans, Roman Catholics, and members of almost a dozen other denominations, eager to take the vision home with them and pass it on. "We are here together in order to destroy this patriarchal idolatry of Christianity," they hear. "We invoke Sophia, Divine Wisdom, who chose to play with all the people of the world. Her voice has been silenced too long . . . Our maker Sophia, we are women in your image." And they applaud again, cheer, and weep for sheer emotion.

As the twentieth century comes to a close, the search for meaning in life is on again in earnest. Mainline churches continue to wither, but new religious movements are flourishing, and even forcing traditional denominations to adapt to a changing spiritual and political agenda. For a growing number of people, the search has not been in vain: they have found the Goddess. But who is she, and where did she come from? Do they really know what they have found?

THIS BOOK IS AN EXPLORATION of one of the striking religious success stories of the late twentieth century. In 1950, no one had heard of Goddess spirituality; now, as we approach the end of the millennium, the Goddess is being proclaimed and celebrated in important sectors of modern society, and she shows no sign of retreating to her previous state of obscurity. On the contrary, we are likely to meet her more often and in a greater variety of places as the new millennium begins. It is time to tell her true story.

I intend to accomplish two things in this book. My immediate purpose is to describe, analyze, and critique the contemporary Goddess movement and its claims. Part I introduces the major writers and devotees of the Goddess and critically examines the message of the movement—particularly its account of its own past, its origins, and development. In addition, however, I seek to outline the broader significance of this movement and its place in the current "culture war"; the debate over the nature and future of Western society itself. This second task requires that I locate the movement itself, and the key elements of its message, in the wider context of recent Western history. Part II provides the broad, general background, while Part III deals with the more direct forerunners of today's Goddess phenomenon and Part IV covers the rise of the movement itself. In the Conclusion I address Goddess spirituality's place on the spectrum of contemporary religiosity and its relevance to some pressing social issues.

Goddess spirituality is a new religion. Like most religions, it is meant to be much more than a weekly break from the hectic routine of work, workouts, and socializing which constitutes life in the cities of the modern West. An effective religion shapes its believers' understanding of reality as a whole, of their own place in the scheme of things, of those values which are worthy of upholding, and of the course of human history. The Goddess movement makes provocative assertions in Welds as diverse as theology, anthropology, ancient history, sociology, psychology, and art history. If we hope to understand what it is all about, we need to examine its claims in all these areas. So far as I am aware, there has not yet been a critical look at the Goddess movement that deals comprehensively with its many facets.[1]

Pursuing the Goddess will lead us down quite a few paths and alleys in the history of the West. Some of those byways can be tricky for the traveler because they are not the main routes by which Western civilization reached its present position, and so they are not well marked in regular history books. In the rest of this introduction, I provide some general orientation which will help us keep our destination in focus.

The Problem of Modernity

As many writers of all shades of opinion have noted, we live in paradoxical times. By most obvious standards of measurement, life has never been better. Never have so many people lived such long and healthy lives, with more access to information and goods, than those of the West in the late twentieth century. The scourge of smallpox, for instance, is a fact of history rather than a fact of life, and the struggle against other diseases has witnessed similar remarkable victories. My wife's grandmother often marveled that man had progressed from Kitty Hawk to moon landings within her lifetime, and the same story could be told of the development from telegraph to telephone to telecommunications, and of many other fields of technological accomplishment. More people, and more kinds of people, have access to education and the ownership of property than ever before.

Other standards of measurement tell a different story, however. We live in a time of widespread personal alienation and social dislocation. Even in the West, where we have so far been spared the actual collapse of nations (such as occurred in the former USSR and Yugoslavia), we have witnessed a long-term pattern of steadily decreasing trust and participation in political and religious institutions. The legal definition of "family" is being readjusted, simply because the traditional definition fits too small a percentage of contemporary households—including those where children are being raised. The increasing rates of homelessness, addiction, suicide, and various forms of violence add to the unease with which many of us face the present and the immediate future.

As foster parents of many years' standing, my wife and I have often encountered this paradox face-to-face in the form of an anguished young person desperately adrift in one of the wealthiest and most comfortable societies ever to appear on the face of the earth. We ourselves happen to live far from the urban ghettos, in a small rural Canadian province which is known to the world at large as the tranquil home of Anne of Green Gables. It is a place "safe" enough that people still commonly leave their cars and homes unlocked. Nonetheless, we have seen at first hand the devastating effects of violence and abuse, drug addiction, and family breakdown. The fact that we Westerners can now broadcast vivid images of wealth and leisure into the homes and communities of places like Bangladesh only heightens the paradox of our apparent "prosperity."

How did we come to this? That is the larger question which interests me, and it is indeed too large to be encompassed within this book. Clearly, though, if something that looks as improbable as the Goddess movement can experience such striking success, we must acknowledge that large numbers of people are ready to turn away from established patterns of life and thought and embrace truly radical alternatives. This is not, as it turns out, an entirely new situation: it has been developing for several generations. Accordingly, we cannot understand the Goddess phenomenon fully or properly without understanding this larger pattern and paradox, the simultaneous attraction and revulsion which modern Western civilization inspires.

MODERNITY AND THE ENLIGHTENMENT

Historians of the West often trace our present circumstances back to the eighteenth century, the age of "Enlightenment." This period witnessed European civilization's decisive rejection of much of its own tradition. The intellectual, social, political, and religious spheres of life underwent dramatic changes; with later refinements and elaborations, these forces are still driving many of the developments in our culture.

As its well-known name suggests, the Enlightenment was above all an intellectual event. In the generations that immediately preceded it, scientists and philosophers like Francis Bacon, René Descartes, Copernicus, Galileo, Isaac Newton, and John Locke had firmly established the basics of the modern scientific method: meticulous empirical observation, experimental testing, and the rational explanation of natural phenomena. Their successes and persuasively logical arguments pointed the way to dramatic new possibilities— could the free exercise of human intelligence lead to an understanding of the world that would allow us, through deliberate planning and calculated action, to remake human life?

The major Enlightenment thinkers of the 1700s, for all their differences, were those who answered "Yes!" and set themselves to the task, at least in theory. They shared the belief that there was a natural order in the universe which could be discovered and grasped by the rigorous application of human intelligence. This natural order, once fully understood, would provide the blueprint for an ideal human society, one in which each would be free to develop his talents for the benefit of all. Because the natural order was objectively real and not just imaginary, it guaranteed that free human beings would eventually achieve agreement and harmony in their social arrangements—as long as they had the opportunity to redesign them apart from the burdens of entrenched tradition. If these changes could be made freely and completely, without interference from the old ways, the self-interest of individuals would naturally coalesce into the common good.[2]

The first step, as many saw it, was to wipe the slate clean. Skepticism toward traditional ideas and customs was essential to begin the total reformation of society. Religious dogma, social structure, anything that stood in the way of improving the conditions of life must be subjected to a thorough rational critique; if something made no obvious pragmatic contribution to human advancement, it was to be relegated to the scrap-heap of history. The new and modern had to replace the old and traditional, and we can begin to discern an ideological commitment to "modernism."

René Descartes' famous formulation, "I think, therefore I am," underscored the importance of systematic doubting. Nothing outside the self should be taken for granted; nothing should be accepted simply because it was already believed or done. Everything must be "proven," or else shown to be useful in a practical way. Under the rubric of the "social contract," some Enlightenment theorists envisioned a social structure designed entirely according to rational principles. This entailed a harmonious division of labor to ensure the prosperity of all, freely adopted by the consent of the individuals involved.

One immense roadblock to the project of the Enlightenment was the traditional principle of authority. Intellectually, to accept definitive authorities in philosophy was to stifle the free-ranging originality which was the lifeblood of Enlightenment thinking. Reason could not accept such restrictions and still be true to itself. Politically, to submit to monarchs and aristocratic hierarchies was to leave humanity divided between the idle rich and the miserable poor, neither of whom could unleash their talents for the betterment of their fellows. Reason could not justify the notion that human status and value were determined by the accident of birth.

Most of all, to bow to the authority of the church seemed to mean abandoning the project altogether. It was not only that the church was a traditional hierarchy in itself, allied to the other hierarchies of the day; not only that it was the purveyor of a whole range of dogmas and creeds which, by their very existence, were an affront to the free exercise of reason. Even more importantly, Christianity was home to the doctrine of original sin. This crucial teaching cut to the heart of

Enlightenment thinking because it meant that human beings, individually and generically, cannot ever be perfected by their own efforts independently of the grace of God. Inevitably, some of the choicest invective from Enlightenment writers like Diderot and Voltaire was targeted at the church.

The greatest advances of the Enlightenment were made primarily in England and France. Despite the political rivalry between these two nations, there was an active commerce of ideas across the English Channel. Thomas Hobbes and Descartes were personally acquainted, and shared a skeptical approach to philosophy and politics. John Locke's articulation of the natural rights of man influenced both French thinkers and American revolutionaries. But the richest concentration of the great minds of the Enlightenment was to be found in Paris. Through the middle of the eighteenth century, the likes of Montesquieu, Voltaire, Diderot, Rousseau, d'Holbach, Turgot, and Condorcet proposed and argued their theories to each other and, more importantly, to the glittering but brittle social order headed by the Bourbon monarchy.

In the midst of this thorough critique and reassessment of Western civilization, the modern movement for women's rights took root. With the Enlightenment's emphasis on individuality and the removal of age-old restrictions on life and thought, it was inevitable that traditional sex roles would be reconsidered. In France, Turgot and Condorcet expressed humanitarian concern and pity for the women of their time, and the latter especially argued that freedom for women would improve the lives of men as well.[3] England witnessed the landmark publication of Mary Wollstonecraft's *Vindication of the Rights of Women* in 1792; she argued that individual women should hold the same legal and educational rights as individual men. This marks one of the origins of what Christina Hoff Sommers has called "equity feminism," the idea of reducing or eliminating the social and political differences between men and women so that individuals of both sexes are freer to chart their own courses in life.[4]

As we might expect, Enlightenment principles were put into revolutionary practice by the two nations which had developed them most fully: the British colonists of North America and the French at home.

REVOLUTION AND REPRESSION

Although it is of minor significance to our topic, the American Revolution of 1776–84 is notable as the first and most durable political achievement of the Enlightenment. Notions typical of the Enlightenment permeate the American experiment, from the very idea of casting off colonial and monarchical rule to the famous "self-evident" truths of the American constitution and the canonization of "life, liberty, and the pursuit of happiness" as the goals of individual human beings' existence. "Manifest Destiny," the ideal of United States hegemony over all of North America, crowned the optimistic vision of the revolutionary generation and its immediate successors.

Despite violent revolution and political separation, as well as a largely inconclusive rematch in the War of 1812, the United States was in many ways a product of the English Enlightenment. Although there was some extremist rhetoric to be found on both sides of the Atlantic, practical considerations led quickly to the recognition of common interests between the two nations, and the Anglo-American "special relationship" was already developing before 1820.[5]

France, however, had a much more turbulent experience. The French Revolution of 1789 was not a blow for independence by a group of remote colonies. It was a violent uprising of class against class which intended to destroy the entire social fabric of a centuries-old system and replace it with something radically new—so radical that a formal "religion of reason" was designed to replace Christianity, and even the calendar was completely revised with new names for the months. Despite the popular slogan "liberty, equality, fraternity," there was no effective consensus on what the new social structure should be, and the French nation was launched on a dizzying course of events for the next several decades.

Even a brief summary of those events gives some indication of the heights and depths which France experienced. The Revolution itself culminated in the bloodshed of the Reign of Terror, 1793–94, until Robespierre was overthrown by the conspiracy of Thermidor (the new "month" during which the coup occurred). The Directory ruled from 1795 to 1799 and conducted foreign wars to spread the Revolution, while it was plagued from within by insurrectionists like Babeuf's "Conspiracy of Equals." The Directory's greatest general, Napoleon Bonaparte, took over himself as Consul in 1799 and made himself Emperor in 1804, going on to conquer and dismantle dozens of old European states and principalities. Finally, coalitions of other powers defeated and exiled him in 1815.

This series of cataclysmic events had a lasting effect on French thought, political and otherwise. It was almost as traumatic for the other European powers. Their established regimes were threatened by the events in France, both philosophically and militarily, and Napoleon's brief reign over most of the continent showed how real the threat could be. The Treaty of Vienna, signed in 1815 by the victorious powers, restored several of the monarchies overthrown by Napoleon and established the Holy Alliance to suppress liberalism and revolution all over Europe.

For our purposes, the significance of these events lies in the fact that the Enlightenment's political agenda seemed to be discredited in Europe. While the American Revolution was a fairly straightforward war with a clear and successful conclusion, the shifts and lurches of European events and the enormous bloodshed and social disruption which resulted were far more disruptive experiences for all concerned. By 1815, conservative forces and resurgent monarchies seemed to have won the day. They failed to extinguish the underlying dissatisfactions of individuals and peoples, however, driving them instead to other forms of expression which often drew on the new fashion of Romanticism.

The Romantic Reaction

Romanticism was a more complex phenomenon than the Enlightenment; it encompassed both an extension of some principles of the Enlightenment and a reaction against others. This complexity was always part of its nature. Even during its heyday, a year-long attempt by two French scholars to work out an acceptable definition of Romanticism ended in failure.[6]

Romanticism began as a German literary movement but became, in effect, an international ideology. In place of cold, analytical reason, Romantics reveled in their emotions and regarded dramatic experiences as the real color and purpose of life. In place of dead materialism, they sought the "life-force" and the heights and depths of the spirit. In place of the rationally organized state, they longed for the organic community of shared blood, language, and ethnicity. Groups as large as the Germans and as small as the Welsh conducted "revivals" of their indigenous cultures in opposition to the homogenizing forces of modernity and industrialization. In both of these cases, as in others, many Romantics came to believe that the "purest" Germanness or Welshness lay in the primeval origins of the respective races, before Roman soldiers and Christian missionaries from the alien Mediterranean world overran the north and west of Europe. They also came to feel (whereas modernists "think," Romantics "feel") that the future of the politically fragmented Germans and the culturally threatened Welsh depended on rediscovering and revivifying their distinctive ancestral gifts.

Very broadly conceived, Romanticism represented the claims of the heart, soul, and blood over the intellect. But in keeping with the Enlightenment, Romanticism looked to nature rather than to supernatural revelation as its ultimate source of truth. For the Romantic, however, nature was not just a physical mechanism governed by rational laws that could be discovered and adapted to the human social order. Rather, nature was wild and free, colorful and dramatic; it was life itself in all its splendor and horror. Some Romantics regarded civilization itself as artificial, a human deviation from the true and natural way.

The Romantic approach to ethnic nationalism and social order was mirrored in its impact on the movement for women's rights. The emphasis moved away from the establishment of equality among individuals of both sexes, and highlighted instead the differences between males and females as biological groups. Now, the liberation of women came to mean the celebration and empowerment of everything that could be regarded as distinctively female, over against what was considered essentially male. The stereotypical view of the female as emotional, intuitive, and instinctively loving coincided so well with the basic values of Romanticism that women were idealized to the point of worship among some Romantics. Here we can recognize some crucial elements of what Sommers has labeled "gender feminism," as opposed to "equity feminism."

From one angle, Romanticism represented the evolution of Enlightenment individualism into a more extreme form, a virtual narcissism. Romantics often cultivated a devotion to the uniqueness of the inner self and of personal experience. This nurtured and deepened the sense of rebelliousness against established norms and structures that the Enlightenment had already encouraged.

From another, the focus on the inner self prompted a reaction against rationalism with its arid, abstract generalities. The stereotypical Romantic prized instead the depths of feeling and dramatic experiences which seemed to give vibrancy and excitement to life.

From yet another, the Enlightenment's success in discrediting the traditional systems of church and state demanded new ways of establishing community and solidarity. A frequent Romantic response was to turn away from such seemingly artificial notions as membership in the church or citizenship in the state, and to seek the supposedly deeper unities of blood, ethnic kinship, and the affinities of shared language and culture.

One of the great paradoxes of Romanticism was its ability to combine and stimulate both narcissism and tribalism. Romantics proclaimed the invaluable uniqueness of individual experience; Romantics also hymned the overriding claims of biological and cultural communities, the groups to which individuals belong by nature (not by rational choice), in which they find their true selves, and to which they owe ultimate allegiance. Such paradoxes are to be expected, perhaps, in a movement which was dedicated to the primacy of the irrational.[7]

THE RISE OF NEOPAGANISM

This tension between the Enlightenment and Romanticism in styles of thought and life has carried on, in different forms and under different banners, into our own time. On the one hand, we have the modernistic worldview based on materialism, empiricism, and rationalism, offering the lure of individual freedom and the benefits of science and technology. On the other, we see a somewhat nostalgic appeal to the heart and the spirit, offering emotional fulfillment and the comfort to be drawn from intimate connection with one's own kind. It is from the latter that today's "revived" paganism, including Goddess spirituality, draws its sustenance and support.

Thinkers of the Enlightenment had devoted a good deal of their intellectual energy to attacks on the church. Their critiques were sufficiently impressive that traditional Christianity seemed to be discredited as an option for many intelligent and educated people. When some of them started having second thoughts about modernism and began looking for alternatives, they bypassed the Christian heritage altogether and sought renewed inspiration from the pagan religions of antiquity. "Pagan" derives from a Latin word which originally meant someone who lived in the countryside; because the rural populations of Europe were often the last to be reached by Christian missionaries, "pagan" became a common designation for the practitioner of a pre-Christian religion. Romanticism encouraged the rise of "neopaganism," the idea of looking to this distant past for guidance to a better future. This sort of future would not be the result of modernist progress, building on the recent growth of science and technology; rather, it would represent a fundamental change in the way we think, act, and work. Thus we encounter the term "New Age" as the conventional label for the fulfillment of neopagan hopes.

But why the continued resistance to modernity, which has brought so many advantages to so many people? It is still true that the benefits of modernism—primarily physical and materialistic—have offered very little for the soul and spirit. Beauty, joy, and love are among the fulfilling but intangible elements of experience which a thoroughgoing modernism downplays. Such intangibles lose their dignity when they are regarded as nothing more than chemical reactions in the brain. A purely rational and materialistic world seems, in some ways, a cold and clinical world in which the most dramatic and inspiring moments of human life have little significance. Indeed, if human beings are ultimately nothing more than temporary combinations of molecules—or, in keeping with evolutionary theory, complicated descendants of pond scum—what is the real value of individuals, of communities, of life itself?

This is essentially a religious issue; the crucial problem is the ultimate value to be ascribed to human beings and their experiences. The Goddess movement of today is proving to be one of the more popular attempts at offering new answers to these questions. It is, therefore, not only an interesting phenomenon in itself; it is also an effective point of entry into some larger questions about the present direction of Western culture.

PART I

GODDESS SPIRITUALITY TODAY

I

The "Return" of the Goddess

Our sweet Sophia, we are women in your image.
"Blessing over Milk and Honey,"
The Reimagining Conference

I T'S ON T-SHIRTS AND BUMPER STICKERS; it is said, chanted, and sung in spirituality groups, in covens, and between friends. "The Goddess is alive, magic is afoot!"

Something is certainly afoot. We have always known that polytheistic religions of all times included various goddesses as well as male gods, but only in the last three decades have we begun to find thoroughly modern people—even trendy ones—who profess their allegiance to "the Goddess." And we find them in a striking variety of places.

GODDESS RELIGION TODAY

The closest thing there is to a formal Goddess religion is Wicca, or modern witchcraft. As a recognizable movement, Wicca dates back to the 1950s. This contemporary witchcraft has little in common with the witches familiar from Halloween and Hollywood. It includes both men and women, and presents itself as a religion of nature which emphasizes life, growth, and joy. The real heart of Wicca is not in its doctrine but in its rituals and ceremonies, which are designed to encourage spiritual insight and personal bonding with the other celebrants and with the forces of nature itself. Rituals are typically celebrated in small groups on a regular basis; there are sometimes larger ceremonial gatherings on "earth holidays" like the solstices and equinoxes.

While many versions of Wicca feature a God/Goddess couple, it is common to give priority to the Goddess over the God, and to the high priestess over the priest. There are also all-female witch covens devoted exclusively to the Goddess.[1] In fact, the largest umbrella organization for Wiccans is called the Covenant of the Goddess; its official acronym is COG (which is not to be confused with the late David Berg's Children of God). This body is rapidly achieving recognition alongside older, traditional religions—it was one of the sponsors for the second Parliament of the World's Religions held in Chicago in 1993, and it has its own frequently-patronized homepage on the Internet.

From organized witchcraft, word of the Goddess has spread to other sectors of the New Age movement, the neopagan revival which has been accelerating in Western societies in recent times. People who were dabbling in esoteric traditions like Gnosticism, or attempting to rediscover the spirituality of the ancient Egyptians, Norse, or Celts, frequently came face to face with female images of the divine. These goddesses or female symbols from the past seemed to offer stimulating new insights into modern life. *Gnosis*, one of the most "academic" of New Age journals, devoted its entire Fall 1989 issue to the Goddess.

With its focus on a female divinity, Wicca naturally came to the attention of the "second wave" feminists of the 1960s and onwards. One of the early radical groups called itself WITCH (Women's International Terrorist Conspiracy from Hell), at least partly tongue-in-cheek, but soon there was a more serious interest in the actual content of modern witchcraft. As the campaign for inclusive language got underway, the traditional practice of referring to God as "He" was no longer allowed to function in a generic and non-sexual way; instead, the Bible's "male" image of God was identified as yet another way of excluding the female from proper recognition and of oppressing actual women. The quest for "female" ways to talk about God led inevitably to Wicca, the only contemporary Western religion which comfortably and habitually talks about the Goddess.

By the 1970s, there was a full-blown feminist spirituality movement which took the practice of "consciousness-raising" in a specifically religious direction. Books appeared with titles like *Womanspirit Rising: A Feminist Reader in Religion* and *The Politics of Women's Spirituality: Essays on the Rise of Spiritual Power within the Feminist Movement*.[2] These are collections of articles by feminist writers from various religious backgrounds; the contributors to *Womanspirit Rising* include Roman Catholics (Rosemary Radford Ruether, Mary Daly, Elizabeth Schüssler Fiorenza), Protestants (Sheila Collins, Eleanor McLaughlin), and Jews (Rita Gross, Judith Plaskow, Aviva Cantor), as well as Wiccans (Starhawk, Zsuzsanna Budapest) and other writers on the Goddess (Merlin Stone, Carol P. Christ). This particular collection concludes with Carol Christ's essay "Why Women Need the Goddess," an influential argument for the Goddess which has since been reprinted in numerous other settings. This offer of a religious identification which would lend a special sanctity to being female obviously struck a chord with many. Sessions and displays on witchcraft and goddess worship are now common at radical feminist gatherings.[3]

Studies of the membership in Wicca, feminist spirituality groups, and other alternative religions are beginning to appear, and it is interesting that both English and American observers are reporting similar findings. Tanya Luhrmann's study of ritual magic in England includes a brief section entitled "Portrait of the Practitioners." She found that the attraction of magical groups, including those practicing feminist witchcraft, seems to reach an audience quite different from the economically disadvantaged strata which commonly gravitate towards sectarian movements. She noted that the magical circles she encountered were dominated by middle-class members and that computer workers, for some reason, were especially well-represented. Luhrmann offered the following composite character sketch: "The sort of person who takes the relatively dramatic step of initiating contact with magicians and then enjoys the practice well enough to continue with it, may well be imaginative, self-absorbed, reasonably intellectual, spiritually inclined, and emotionally intense. He also may be rebellious and interested in power, possibly dreamy or socially ill at ease. He may be concerned on some level with issues of control—controlling himself, or the world, or the two in tandem. This is a descriptive, not a causal, account." She also observed that people are most often recruited into witch covens or other magical groups by reading books and following up on advertisements in occult bookshops.[4]

Cynthia Eller's American study *Living in the Lap of the Goddess* is specifically focused on feminist spirituality, which is a more visible presence in the United States than it is in Great Britain. Many of her observations are the same, however. Members of Goddess groups are very likely to be white, middle-class, reasonably well educated, and in their thirties and forties. There seem to be several common predisposing factors: a general inclination towards spiritual endeavors; personal experience with apparently psychic or paranormal phenomena; and a sense of alienation from society at large, especially the traditional religious institutions.

Eller's narrower focus turned up some specific features of Goddess devotees which did not appear in Luhrmann's broader inquiry. She found, of course, that most members of feminist spirituality groups are women. More particularly, she documented the strong representation of women from Jewish and Christian backgrounds rather than from other traditions, and a distinctly high proportion of lesbians, with a correspondingly low profile for confirmed heterosexuals. She substantiated Luhrmann's findings on recruitment, however. The single most important factor in leading women to the Goddess is literature, the kind of books which we shall survey in Chapter 2.[5]

Before long, this growing movement came to the attention of the media. Feature stories on the witchcraft revival appeared on newspapers' religion pages or in the soft news sections, while television talk-shows of varying degrees of seriousness often found Wiccans and feminist spirituality spokespersons to be lively subjects for interviews. Weekly news magazines have run more and more cover stories on religion and spirituality as the end of the millennium approaches, with witches receiving at least their share of attention.

Maclean's, the Canadian weekly, led its April 8, 1996 edition with a cover story titled "Is God a Woman?" The cover itself featured a controversial statue of a nude female in crucifixion pose. First unveiled without warning during a worship service at Bloor Street United Church in Toronto, the statue now stands in a secluded spot on the University of Toronto campus (although *Maclean's* started its own small controversy by printing her image on its cover, with her pubic area encircled by the "o" of the word "God"). The story contained typical anecdotes about women who are dissatisfied with patriarchal religion and traditionalists who are uncomfortable with the theological implications of inclusive language.

In addition, *Maclean's* noted that New York's *Publishers Weekly* had recently "hailed women's spirituality as one of the fastest-growing categories in the business." Across the continent, alternative bookstores have opened and flourished by purveying books on magic, divination, witchcraft and paganism to an increasingly interested public. Major chains have followed suit and often feature "New Age" sections as extensive as the standard "Religion" offerings. The phenomenal success of the neopagan novel *The Celestine Prophecy*, which led the bestseller lists for a period of months over the past couple of years, illustrates the vast marketability of New Age literature at the present time; witchcraft, and Goddess books continue to multiply in an environment of spiritual questing, amplifying their crucial role in recruitment to these new religious movements.

The media have played a significant role in spreading the word of the Goddess—strikingly so in Canada. For five episodes in January 1986, the Canadian Broadcasting Corporation's highbrow radio program "Ideas" ran a series entitled "Return of the Goddess," introducing thousands in Canada and abroad to a movement which still had a relatively low public profile at that point. Even more of a success was the National Film Board of Canada's epic "Goddess Remembered." This was a product of the NFB's Studio D, which billed itself as " . . . the first publicly funded feminist production unit of its kind in the world ... Designed to engage audiences, spark discussion and raise consciousness, [Studio D productions] are conceived as tools for social change and empowerment."[6] (Incidentally, Studio D was one of the casualties when Canadian government funding to the NFB was slashed in 1996).

"Goddess Remembered" became one of the NFB's most popular productions ever, and has been a featured and controversial presentation during pledge campaigns by public broadcasting television stations in the United States as well. Its 1993 appearance on KQED-TV in San Francisco prompted Robert Sheaffer to produce an on-line critique of the film, "The Goddess Remembered—A Case of False Memory Syndrome."[7] The following summer, when it was featured on WNED-TV in Buffalo, New York, it elicited a deluge of protesting telephone calls from offended viewers until the station's on-air staff turned it into an issue of free speech.

Clearly, the Goddess is still in the ascendant. Wicca and its spin-offs in feminist spirituality continue to grow, and it seems that public exposure and recognition of Goddess religion can only increase in the foreseeable future. More surprising is the extent to which the Goddess has made her presence felt outside the small circles of witches and radical feminists, in some of the most influential institutions in contemporary society: mainstream churches, universities, and hospitals.

The Goddess and the Churches

Not all feminists, even gender feminists, are so radical that they are willing to abandon their previous religious identities in favor of recently established witch covens or consciousness-raising groups. In Catholic, Protestant, and Jewish circles, the quest for inclusive language has led many, among both the leadership and the regular members, to familiarize themselves with the Goddess and to use Goddess-talk to "balance" traditional God-talk. As they seek to apply more female imagery to the biblical God, they often need a greater supply of raw material than the Bible itself offers, and the witches' Goddess is ready to hand with a wide range of ritual and symbolism to offer. As a result, neopagan and Wiccan themes are now surprisingly prominent within older religious establishments.

In many cases, one small but influential religion served as the bridge between Wicca and feminist spirituality on the one hand, and mainstream religious organizations on the other. This is the Unitarian Universalist Association (UUA), which resulted from the 1960s merger of two older liberal religious organizations. Since the early 1800s, Universalists had been denying the biblical notions of hell and damnation, while Unitarians denied the doctrine of the Trinity and, therefore, the uniqueness of Jesus as the incarnate Son of God. In both cases, the original decision to reject one particular traditional doctrine led gradually to a freethinking approach to religion in general. Individual members are at liberty, and indeed encouraged, to choose and develop their own beliefs (prompting their old joke that Unitarians believe in one God, at most).

This dogma-free approach to religion proved to be fertile ground for the Goddess movement. In 1977 the UUA passed a Resolution on Women and Religion which, among other things, called for educational materials dealing with gender issues in the history of religion. One outcome was the appearance, several years later, of *Cakes for the Queen of Heaven*. This is a ten-session workshop in feminist "thealogy" (a term coined to describe women's relationship with the Goddess, as opposed to man's relationship with God). The first four sessions are subtitled "Why Women need the Goddess" and include Carol Christ's essay as required reading. The next four deal with feminine imagery in Judaism and Christianity, while the last two fall under the rubric "Contemporary Feminist Spirituality" and deal with witchcraft and "Future Fantasies" respectively. The UUA's actual membership is so small that this development, by itself, would be merely curious. In actual fact, however, *Cakes* has been circulated through the major denominations and adopted for use in numerous mainstream churches.[8]

At the same time, the UUA has developed something of a special relationship with the Covenant of the Goddess. A COG press release of December 10, 1993 announced that the two groups would hold a joint celebration of the winter solstice in New York City; the UUA's

Reverend Darrell Berger was quoted as saying that "it represents the convergence of similar approaches to spirituality. It's also a way of getting to a more universal expression of the spiritual meaning of this season," a comment presumably directed at the Christian feast of Christ's birth rather than at the annual commercial extravaganza. On May 25, 1996, the Toronto *Star* ran a story on witchcraft rituals in the Ottawa Unitarian Church; its senior minister, Rev. Brian Kopke, told the reporter that witchcraft "is a way in which, using pagan sources, women own their own strength. It's a form of feminism, if you will. As Unitarians, we don't shy away from these things." One member of the Ottawa group said she preferred to engage in the witchcraft experience within a Unitarian setting precisely because "it is safe and without what she calls 'the oddballs who call themselves pagans.'"

There is now a special organization for UUA witches, known as the Covenant of Unitarian Universalist Pagans (CUUPS), with its own Worldwide Web cite on the Internet. Further, the UUA's active and well-known publishing house, Beacon Press, has produced a significant proportion of the current Goddess literature which we shall survey in Chapter 2. Unitarianism provides a fascinating illustration of the dynamic we saw in the Introduction: its immediate forebears were orthodox Protestants; its earlier generations were defined by their rationalistic critique of traditional Christianity; and now it is heavily involved in the neopagan revival. Moreover, despite its small size, the UUA has made a major contribution to the credibility and acceptance of Goddess spirituality in more conventional religious circles.

The Goddess is increasingly visible in those circles. When God the Father is supplemented by God the Mother, it seems that the Mother Goddess is rarely far behind. Her appeal crosses many boundaries. In the larger denominations today, it is not only women in small groups who welcome her. Male theologians with international reputations have spoken up in her cause; some of the more prominent names include Rev. Matthew Fox, OP, of "creation spirituality" fame, and Professor Harvey Cox, the erstwhile secular theologian of Harvard Divinity School. It appears to make little difference where a church stands on the ordination of women; the Goddess has found an equally warm welcome in mainstream Protestant denominations which have been ordaining women to the ministry for decades, and in the Roman Catholic Church which continues to restrict the priesthood to males.

Among Protestants, recent reforms of liturgies and hymnals have made feminine imagery and God the Mother metaphors increasingly familiar. On the grassroots level, *Cakes for the Queen of Heaven* and "Goddess Remembered" have become staples for study groups in some major denominations. My own first encounter with the Goddess was the enthusiastic recommendation of a United Church of Canada minister that I see "Goddess Remembered," then being shown as the centerpiece in a local ecumenical event. *Cakes* has been in use for years.[9] The UCC's new hymnal, *Voices United* (1996), has generated controversy not only for its neutered versions of old hymns ("This is my Father's world" has become "This is God's wondrous world"), but for its new hymns with explicit Divine Mother imagery. In addition to demasculinizing God the Father, one hymn goes so far as to invoke the "Mothering Christ."[10] The new hymnals being prepared for the Presbyterian and Anglican churches appear, from current indications, to be following suit.

Donna Steichen's *Ungodly Rage* documented the dramatic spread of Goddess spirituality into American Catholicism. Focusing on a number of specific conferences and institutions, she pointed out that Wicca was being imported wholesale into liberal and radical reform movements within the Catholic Church. Influential figures like Dr. Rosemary Radford Ruether, professor of applied theology at Garrett-Evangelical Seminary, and Sr. Madonna Kolbenschlag, HM, have been preaching the specific tenets of Goddess spirituality through their writings and their participation in church conferences and workshops, even though these tenets deviate in almost every detail from traditional Catholic teaching. Support comes not only from radical Catholic groups like Women-Church, but from seemingly mainstream official organizations such as the Leadership Conference of Women Religious. The latter body, which speaks for at least 75 percent of American nuns, has promoted the writings of prominent non-Catholic Goddess devotees like Jean Shinoda Bolen, Carol Christ, Judith

Plaskow, and Starhawk, all of whom we shall meet in the next chapter.[11]

Catholic Church authorities have taken some steps to curb the Goddess. A Canadian Press story in April 1992, reported that the Roman Catholic diocese of Toronto had refused for the second consecutive year to allow the annual "Celebrate Women" festival to be held on church premises, because the program had been permeated by Wiccan notions. In 1993, Pope John Paul II warned American bishops against precisely that sort of gender-polarizing feminism which infiltrates the church by substituting an essentially non-Christian mythology and nature worship for Catholic teaching and sacramental worship.[12] By all accounts, however, such interventions have done little to stem growing interest in the Goddess.

For bringing the Goddess to public awareness in the churches, the most dramatic event was the Reimagining Conference held in Minneapolis in November, 1993. This gathering of some 2000 participants, almost all of them women, won fame and controversy for its emphasis on—and worship of—Sophia. *Sophia* is the Greek word for "wisdom" and is, in the Greek language, grammatically feminine. Drawing on biblical references to the wisdom of God, the conference leaders developed full-blown prayers and liturgies addressed to Sophia as a specifically female divinity. Most controversial was the "Blessing over Milk and Honey," a Sunday ceremony reimagining the Eucharist. "Our sweet Sophia," they recited, "we are women in your image. With nectar between our thighs we invite a lover, we birth a child. With our warm body fluids we remind the world of its pleasures and sensations." Other sessions featured a contemptuous rejection of the doctrines of the incarnation and atonement, a standing ovation for "out" Christian lesbians, and a call for "sex among friends as the norm . . . valuing genital sexual interaction in terms of whether and how it fosters friendship and pleasure." Interspersed with it all was a constant, bitter hostility towards "this patriarchal idolatry of Christianity."

Sensationalism aside, the striking thing about Reimagining was the fact that it was initiated, sponsored, and attended by representatives of the major American churches. The Presbyterian Church USA and the United Methodist Church each had approximately four hundred members in attendance and provided major funding. Lutherans, Roman Catholics, Episcopalians, Baptists, and members of the United Church of Christ and United Church of Canada were also present in significant numbers. When the conference was told that "Christianity as practiced in today's world demonstrates more a nightmare than a vision," the speaker was none other than Rev. Dr. Lois Wilson, a minister and former moderator of the United Church of Canada, and a past president of both the Canadian and the World Councils of Churches. Reimagining was an unprecedented event: an interdenominational assembly of Christians openly bent on destroying the historic Christian religion root and branch, and steering the churches into wholesale neopaganism.

When reports of the conference appeared in the mainstream press, some clergy and members of the denominations involved raised objections to this church-sponsored attack on Christianity; the subsequent General Assembly of the Presbyterian Church U S A reportedly received more overtures of protest about the Reimagining Conference than on any other issue in its history. Most of the institutions involved, however, refused to take formal action of any kind. Conference participants themselves reacted to the criticism as an "attack on women . . . spiritual rape." Reimagining has, on the other hand, given rise to an ongoing movement which continues to pursue its objectives.[13]

THE GODDESS AND THE UNIVERSITY

The Goddess's credibility has been greatly enhanced by her rising profile in another institutional setting, arguably more authoritative with the general public these days than the churches—higher education. As a group, professors have proven more sympathetic to the Goddess than an average cross-section of the population.

There are good reasons for this. An essential purpose of the modern university is the free and untrammeled exploration of new ideas to promote the extension of knowledge. Of necessity, this means that seemingly-outlandish ideas must be entertained, at least for a while, by some academics; ideally, as they work out the implications of their new insights and hunches, scholars will discard the erroneous and unproductive lines of thinking in favor of more accurate and fruitful conceptions. In such a setting, the Goddess was assured of getting a hearing.

Goddess spirituality soon found favor in many quarters of the academy. One factor here is probably the generational composition of many faculties. There was an enormous growth in the professoriate during the 1960s, as institutions expanded to accommodate the huge numbers of late baby-boomers. Many of those who filled the new positions, being recent graduates or dropouts of doctoral programs, were imbued with the radical consciousness of the 1960s campus and carried this sensibility into their professional careers. The result was the so-called "tenured radical" who is now, frequently, of such age and seniority as to be a dominant influence in institutions of higher education.[14]

As the academic job market dried up in the 1970s and 1980s, this group continued to constitute a large proportion of many teaching staffs, unleavened by a natural and gradual influx of new scholars. Today, new graduates are often the students and protégés of precisely this group, which further enhances the receptivity of academia towards radical ideas. The rise of affirmative action policies has strengthened this trend even more, by ensuring that the groups which benefit from these policies—particularly feminist women—are more likely to get jobs, and thus make up a larger proportion of faculties.

Some key individuals in the early promotion of Goddess spirituality were professors, many of them from the boomer generation. *Womanspirit Rising* and *The Politics of Women's Spirituality*, to take only those two examples, included Goddess-oriented contributions from professors Carol P. Christ (Women's Studies and Religious Studies, San Jose State University), Mary Daly (Philosophy, Boston College), Marija Gimbutas (Archaeology, UCLA), and Naomi Goldenberg (Religious Studies, University of Ottawa). Academic conferences often feature sessions and seminars on Goddess religion; both Religious Studies and Women's Studies programs sometimes include the Goddess in the curriculum. A brief Internet search for the film "Goddess Remembered" reveals that it has been adopted in universities across the continent and beyond: it appears, for example, in Women's Studies course outlines at UCLA, Northern Arizona University, and even Massey University in New Zealand; it is stocked in the libraries and media centers at the University of Maine, the University of Colorado, the University of Virginia, and Berkeley; and it is being given public showing at the University of Utah, Louisiana State University, and the College of Charleston.

Far from being confined to the specialized research interests of individual professors, the Goddess now appears in the mundane world of textbooks. In 1995, Prentice-Hall, a major publisher of university texts, produced Marianne Ferguson's *Women and Religion*. Despite its bland title, the book is actually a recitation of the tenets of the Goddess movement, from its opening section on "Early Goddess Cultures" to its concluding comments on innate differences between men's and women's spiritualities. Along the way, Ferguson cites Wicca as the only contemporary Goddess religion, and she dismisses critiques of the modern Goddess phenomenon as the work of jealous, threatened male clergy who wish to maintain their control over women's sexual activities.[15] This little-noticed event is actually a striking development: after the long modern struggle to free higher education from church control, the doctrines of a new religion are being packaged and promoted as factual material for use in publicly funded and accredited institutions of higher education.

THE GODDESS AND THE HOSPITAL

The rising tide of Goddess devotion in churches and universities may not worry people outside of those institutions, but the Goddess has established a strong and growing presence in another field which affects everyone—health care, and particularly nursing. The extent to which radical feminists in the nursing profession have made common cause with Wiccans and the Goddess comes as a surprise to many outside the field. For a speedy introduction to this situation, let us compare two quotations:

> Women have always been healers, and the knowledges of healing—of aura work, colors, herbs and homeopathy, reflexology,

midwifery, massage, crystals and trance states—have always been
part of the goddess' [*sic*] mysteries. Healing in the matriarchies
was women's work, connected to birth, death, and the life force,
and this only changed with the submergence of women's culture, women's political, religious, and personal power, under patriarchy.[16]

Women's wisdom is ageless and timeless, and passes from generation to generation primarily by oral tradition. Women's wisdom is all too often the hidden foundation of patriarchal
scholarship throughout academic, religious, and philosophic literature—without credit to the origins of the ideas. These origins are grounded in women's experiences, female symbolism,
and the spiritual roots of the Triple Goddess.[17]

The first, as one might guess, comes from a book on women's spirituality by a thriving purveyor of neopagan literature, Llewellyn Publications in St. Paul, Minnesota. The second, however, is from a product
of the publishing wing of the National League for Nursing (NLN),
the New York–based accrediting agency for nursing schools.

To a degree, the Goddess's arrival in nursing schools may have
been an inevitable development. At least three factors are probably
involved in preparing the nursing profession for the Goddess. First,
the advances in health care in modern society often prompt strong
reactions against science and technology. For all the spectacular successes of medical science, it ultimately fails—human beings are still
mortal, and some illnesses remain terminal. Moreover, the great
medical advances in the treatment of disease and injury have not always been matched by progress in alleviating distressing chronic conditions such as back problems. In this context, the New Age
movement has made alternative and psychic medicine of various sorts
much more available to the general public and, inevitably, to health
care professionals as well. When mainstream medicine has done its
best and run out of options, there often seems to be little reason not
to try something different, no matter what the source, especially if
the techniques seem both harmless and inexpensive.

Second, the rapid progress of medical technology has given health
care the image of cold, clinical service where patients' feelings, emo-

tional states, and spiritual concerns are marginalized. This tendency has been magnified with the rise of supposedly cost-effective "managed care systems," which usually increase the caseloads of medical personnel. The burden of coping with and comforting distressed patients tends to fall upon the nurse more often than the doctor, forcing nurses to find ways of addressing emotional and spiritual matters. Not all, needless to say, can or will look to the mainstream religions for guidance. The direct human contact which many New Age therapies entail, combined with their relative inexpensiveness, can provide significant incentive for the exploration of alternative medicine.

Finally, gender issues have become prominent concerns in nursing. While women have made great inroads into traditionally male occupations, the reverse is not the case, and nursing retains the identity of an overwhelmingly female profession. Here, the general feminist resentment of male domination is magnified by the real and significant power differential between doctors and nurses—so much so that "the oppression of women and nurses" reads like a cliché in some nursing publications.[18] It is interesting to note, however, that feminist stridency in nursing has increased just as the number of practicing female doctors has reached unprecedented levels in the Western world.

All this comes at a time when nursing has become more professionalized. This has led to the establishment of many new university-level schools and faculties of nursing, with accredited degree programs up to the doctoral level. With the rapid expansion of the field, defenders and practitioners of alternative therapies have sometimes been able to move into commanding positions and propagate their views—nursing's version, perhaps, of the tenured radical.

For instance, "therapeutic touch," the practice of passing one's hands over a patient's body without actually touching it, has reportedly been taught to thousands of nurses in eighty North American nursing programs. It purports to be a way of manipulating auras and energy-fields (non-scientific New Age notions loosely based on traditional Asian medicine and metaphysics) so as to restore a healthy balance of forces within the suffering individual. In fact, this particular technique was developed by the team of Dolores Krieger, a nurse, and her mentor Dora Kunz, a professional psychic and former president of the Theosophical Society of America—the influential occult group which we shall encounter again in Chapter 9. Therapeutic Touch (TT) closely resembles a healing ritual which is well known in Wiccan circles; its next of kin, such as "Reiki" and "Healing Touch," rely explicitly on the New Age practice of channeling messages from beings who supposedly exist on other planets or dimensions.[19]

Along with this general New Age influence has come the Goddess. Jean Shinoda Bolen, MD, a Jungian psychologist and professor of psychiatry at the University of California San Francisco, is best known for her book *Goddesses in Everywoman*. Here she takes seven goddesses from Greek mythology and uses them to represent seven different female personality types.[20] These ideas have actually been put into practice in nursing schools. Kathleen Heinrich, RN, PHD, published an article in *Nurse Educator* entitled "The Greek Goddesses Speak to Nurses," apparently based on her classroom work with nursing students at the University of Hartford and then the University of San Diego. She encourages the students to identify themselves with one or more of the archetypes in Shinoda Bolen's scheme, in order to create better self-understanding and stronger rapport with other women. Heinrich concludes by discussing "strategies for integrating goddess literature into nursing courses," and includes literature from the Goddess movement in her bibliography.[21]

Of more recent vintage is an article by Valerie Abrahamsen of the Massachusetts General Hospital Institute of Health Professions. Her reported qualifications are not degrees in medicine or nursing, but a doctorate in theology in New Testament and Christian origins from Harvard Divinity School. Entitled "The Goddess and Healing: Nursing's Heritage from Antiquity," the article touches briefly on the healings attributed in the ancient world to Asklepios and Jesus before surveying several goddesses of healing, arguing that "the female principle . . . was primary." She concludes, "To recapture the spirit of the goddess is to be allowed to heal every kind of wound—physical, mental, and spiritual."[22]

More prominent and influential still is Jean Watson. Watson is Distinguished Professor of Nursing and former Dean of the School of Nursing at the University of Colorado, as well as founder and director of the Center for Human Caring. In her 1985 book *Nursing: Human Science and Human Caring*, she argues for a vision of "transpersonal caring . . . within a metaphysical context." By this she means not merely empathy and compassion, but actual spiritual union between nurse and patient. In 1994 she published an article entitled, "A Frog, a Rock, a Ritual: Myth, Mystery, and Metaphors for an Ecocaring Cosmology in a Universe That Is Turning Over," in which she evokes Sophia and the Mother Earth Goddess, and celebrates her belief that "the Goddess is emerging from the dark side of the moon."

This is, apparently, no private sideline for Watson. "A Frog, a Rock, a Ritual" was published as one chapter in *Exploring our Environmental Connections*, another collection of essays published by the National League for Nursing Press.[23] Moreover, Watson assumed the presidency of the NLN itself in June 1995. This proved an unhappy step, however; she resigned in August 1996, with her term little more than half over, while the U.S. Department of Education investigated administrative irregularities at the NLN. Nonetheless, the Center for Human Caring continues its work, and the Goddess continues to ride the wave of New Age enthusiasm into the education and practice of new generations of nurses.

There will likely always be some patients with chronic or terminal conditions who seek out alternative and unorthodox therapies, and few would deny them the freedom to do so. The inclusion of Goddess spirituality and New Age therapies in accredited nursing programs is another matter. Again we encounter the paradoxical fact that these new religions are gaining entry into the curriculum, despite the continuing effort to ensure that no influence of traditional religion makes its way into state-supported institutions. In the case of nursing, a largely female profession in a largely feminist environment, Goddess spirituality is clearly one of the beneficiaries of these developments.

How do actual patients react to the neopagan, occult ideas behind some of the care they receive? For those who seek out alternative therapies deliberately and consciously, healing and symptomatic relief are likely the sole criteria by which such matters are judged.

Increasingly, however, we may expect to encounter New Age beliefs and practices in the course of regular care in mainstream hospitals and clinics. Indeed, it seems that techniques like therapeutic touch are often performed on patients who are not only uninformed about its neopagan background, but actually unconscious or asleep when it is practiced.[24] There appears to be an increased blurring of the distinction between scientific medicine (which most people expect to receive when they enter hospital) and the essentially mystical New Age therapies which now sometimes accompany it. This phenomenon serves as a further illustration of why and how the Goddess is becoming more visible in some of our major institutions.

SINCE THE SECOND WORLD WAR, the Western world has witnessed an amazing reorientation of its religious life. As immigration has increased, traditional religions from Asia, Africa and the Caribbean have established themselves in many of the major centers of Europe and North America. Even more strikingly, new religions and "cults" have sprung up and flourished, and the New Age Movement has grown to embrace a significant proportion of the population in at least some of its attitudes and practices. Social and political issues ranging from poverty and war to the status of women have changed the inner life of the older religious organizations.

In all of this, the Goddess movement stands out in a number of ways. It is the only new religion which has made sexuality and gender politics, two of the dominant social concerns of the late twentieth century, central to its very existence and claims. It has ridden the new wave of feminist scholarship to a position of credibility in the academic world, where the thinkers and leaders of the next generation are now absorbing the principles which will guide them for life. And, it has had unique success in spreading frankly pagan images and ideas within traditional, biblically-oriented religious organizations, as well as in such seemingly secular fields as health care. For all these reasons, and more which will emerge, Goddess spirituality deserves close investigation.

We begin, in Chapter 2, with an examination of the major representatives of the Goddess movement and the story they tell.

2

The Story of the Goddess

The Earth is our Mother; we must take care of Her.

Gen Huitt

O N A FIRST ENCOUNTER with Goddess spirituality, it is not always immediately clear what is involved. For those familiar
with hearing God described as "Father," a notion like God
the Mother may prompt a variety of reactions. Women who are happy
as females, and men who feel positively about the opposite sex, may
be attracted to the possibility of imagining the divine in feminine
terms. Victims of paternal abuse may have trouble with the whole
notion of a loving father. Others may conclude that, out of sheer
fairness, female imagery ought to be used as often as male imagery.
Still others, comfortable with traditional language, may find something disconcerting in the new terminology, but have trouble expressing what that "something" is without sounding anti-female.

Traditionally, the God of the Bible has been described in largely
masculine terms, partly for grammatical reasons and partly because
of the frequent biblical affirmation of his fatherhood. In theological
terms, however, the import of this masculine language is muted by
the doctrinal insistence on God's transcendence and pure spirituality; he is described in masculine terms but he is not male in any literal or biological sense. Once one has taken the first step of addressing

the biblical God as Mother, however, there arises the question of whether "she" can or should be distinguished from the Goddess of the witches. There is no doubt that this Goddess is specifically and exclusively female.

A New History of Religion

As we have noted already, the bulk of specifically female divine imagery did not originate within the biblical religions, lying unnoticed in the scriptures until modern theologians discovered it. Rather, it came in from the outside, from the radical feminists and witches who already emphasized the priority of their Goddess over their God (if they had one at all). Goddess spirituality is an alternative religion; in its pure form it is fully distinct from, and implacably hostile to, the biblical religions. When the Goddess comes, she comes with all the trappings of her origin in the revived paganism of the post-war Western world.

The tenets of the Goddess religion are to be found in an extended narrative in which the entire history of religion is played out as a gender struggle between an original, positive, affirming religion of the female deity and a later, usurping, oppressive and patriarchal set of religions and philosophies based on the Judeo-Christian and Greco-Roman traditions. In this story, the God of the Bible is not joined by the Goddess or even subordinated to her. He is, instead, reduced to being the villainous self-image of sexist, racist oppressors who have supposedly dominated most of recorded history, bringing suffering and degradation to women, children, and the earth itself. The returning Goddess is meant to *replace* God the Father; this, according to her devotees, is an essential step towards curing the social and environmental ills of our times.

The story of the Goddess is told as follows. During the Stone Ages, particularly between 40,000 and 3500 BC, humanity first achieved civilization. The earliest human religion was worship of the Great Goddess who, being female, symbolized the life-forces of birth and nurture, growth and fertility, death and rebirth. Since the male role in the conception of children was not yet understood, social organization centered on the female, giving women in general a high status and value. Over time, an almost utopian Goddess culture developed, which spanned the vast territory between Britain and South Asia, at the least. Life was peaceful, with weapons and fortifications rarely to be found because they were not needed. Life was prosperous, because the Goddess was closely identified with the fertile earth, resulting in a natural, positive approach to ecology. Life was harmonious, because women loved all their children equally, and therefore they discouraged the development of social hierarchies or the hoarding of wealth by the few.

Tragically, we are told, these peaceful and harmonious societies were defenseless against the onslaught of roving barbarians. The Indo-Europeans of the northern steppes and the Semites of the southern deserts were wandering tribes of herdsmen who fought over cattle, turf, and anything else which came their way. Their violence is taken as proof that these groups were patriarchal; men must have ruled by force, with women and children reduced to being mere possessions. As cattle-breeders, they knew about paternity and imposed patrilineal systems of inheritance on their offspring. As nomads, they were patrilocal, with the men deciding where to live, and when and where to move; ecology, moreover, would be of minor concern to people who never stay settled. Naturally, they invented and worshipped powerful and violent male gods, more associated with stormy skies than with the earth.

Beginning about 5000 BC, these tribes began large-scale migrations, destroying the settled cultures in their path. Adopting whatever elements of civilization they saw as useful, they supposedly forced their patriarchal social systems on the conquered Goddess peoples, paying special attention to the destruction of her religion. New mythologies were invented which either celebrated the defeat and destruction of the Goddess or, worse, ignored her altogether. Hierarchies of sex, class, and race were imposed, and the earth was treated as a mere object of exploitation. Goddess cultures survived longest in remote outposts like Crete and Ireland, but even these eventually fell to the patriarchal systems which came to full flower in the Roman Empire and then the Christian church.

Under such vicious persecution, we are told, the Goddess religion had to go underground. It supposedly became the sacred custody of secretive groups who passed it on from generation to generation, particularly from mother to daughter, keeping as much as possible out of sight of the oppressive family, social, and religious authorities. Occasionally these loyal folk were discovered; the witch-hunts which raged from roughly AD 1500 to 1700 were really, we are now to believe, a war of extermination against the Goddess religion. Modern devotees claim that as many as nine million people, at least 80 percent of them women, perished during the so-called "burning times."

Today, however, the destructive forces of patriarchy have run amok to the point that they have undermined the system itself. Goddess spirituality holds out the assurance that the current crisis of Western civilization is a sign that the male God's reign is coming to an end, and that the Goddess is waiting to lead us into a New Age of peace and harmony if we will only follow her. We must jettison patriarchy and all its supportive institutions: male-god religions, monogamous patrilineal families, and all hierarchies of power and authority. If we fail to do this, the alternative we are said to face may be the end of civilization, and even of life on earth.

This is the story of the Goddess. It is both *descriptive*, claiming to reveal the true history of culture and religion, and *prescriptive*, showing us the way to a supposedly brighter future. This underlying pattern is not new or unique to the Goddess movement; it has seen much broader applications in modern neopaganism as a whole. Many individuals and groups who claim to have revived or rediscovered ancient truths and practices have idealized the ancient times in which those truths and practices allegedly held sway. This often leads them to demonize the intervening religion and culture—usually the Judeo-Christian, Greco-Roman core of Western civilization—which supposedly obscured and suppressed them. For convenience, I use the phrase "neopagan paradigm" to identify this scheme of an ancient utopia, interrupted and attacked by malevolent powers, which is re-emerging to lead us into a glorious New Age.

In the Goddess movement we see a specific application of the neopagan paradigm, with several distinctive characteristics. Obviously, issues of sex and gender are dominant. Unlike the biblical God, who is grammatically masculine but too formless and transcendent to be truly male, the Goddess is emphatically and exclusively female. Goddess spirituality, though favorably disposed towards polytheistic religions, actually espouses a form of monotheism by insisting that religion began as veneration of a single Great Goddess. The multiple goddesses of later times are supposed to be mere aspects or local adaptations of the one original Goddess, whose unity and supremacy fragmented under the blows of the patriarchs. The ancient utopia, further, is defined in its essence through sex roles. Some form of matriarchy, or at least a radically different relationship between the sexes, is supposed to be typical of the Goddess cultures. More than that, it is the very source of their other glories: egalitarianism, peacefulness, creativity, and harmony with nature.

With matters of sex assuming such a commanding role, sexuality itself serves as the driving energy behind the Goddess cultures, embracing both natural fertility and human community. The Goddess's power emerges specifically from her female sexuality, as expressed in the explicit sexual symbolism and rituals of ancient times. By the same token, the suppression of women in Western culture has allegedly gone hand in hand with the suppression of sexuality itself; thus, the return of the Goddess is inextricably linked to the sexual revolution, the liberation of those innate creative forces.

The tale of the Goddess is a story almost no one had heard of thirty years ago, but it is readily available in any trendy bookshop now. We must tour that bookshop to discover who has been telling this story and how they put it together.

THE STORYTELLERS

We begin with a book in which the Goddess herself is not highlighted, but which contains many of the other assertions we find in Goddess spirituality. This immediate forerunner is Elizabeth Gould Davis's *The First Sex*, which appeared in 1971. Davis was a librarian and adorned her book with an impressive array of quotations and references from sources both ancient and modern. The book presents itself as a history of society and culture, emphasizing the priority and superiority of matriarchy—actual female rule—over patriarchy. Religion plays only a supporting role in *The First Sex*; Davis does argue that the preponderance of female figurines in the art of preliterate cultures indicates Goddess-worship as the first religion, but she tends to treat this as a secondary reflection of the high social status of women as such, the inevitable religious expression of real-life matriarchy.

Davis's title is meant quite literally. She argues that women were once the only sex—all humans were female. The Y chromosome developed as a mutation of the X: "The first males were mutants, freaks produced by some damage to the genes . . . the male sex represents a degeneration and deformity of the female."[1] By the time men appeared, women had already created all the worthwhile arts of civilization, and they remained in control for several millennia. Males were bred selectively for female enjoyment, and men who failed to display proper subservience were exiled to the wilderness.

Eventually, male resentment of this treatment broke out in violence. Out in the wilderness, the Indo-Europeans (the ancient "Aryans") and the Hebrews developed their patriarchal social systems and then proceeded to impose them by force on the rest of the world. Although they are usually considered to be Indo-Europeans too, Davis claims that the Celts somehow preserved many of the features of the primeval matriarchies until they also fell before the combination of "Teutonic barbarism and Semitic Christianity." Problems ranging from the oppression of women to the destruction of nature followed directly from these events. The only workable remedy is, in her words, a matriarchal counter-revolution. "Only masculine ego . . . stands in the way of a decent society."[2]

Biologists, anthropologists, and ancient historians discounted Davis's book almost as soon as it appeared. As her notes make clear, she read widely but indiscriminately. Her general understanding of history was shaped by the catastrophe theories of the eccentric but then-popular Immanuel Velikovsky. Alongside the works of reputable historians, she set books like Lewis Spence's *History of Atlantis*, which is exactly what it sounds like—a reconstruction of the course of events on the mythical lost continent. Several times she appealed to Robert Eisler's *Man into Wolf*, a Jungian survey of werewolf mythology; the fact that Eisler himself was relying on such dubious sources as Margaret Murray's books on witchcraft, and even the famous anthropological hoax of Piltdown Man, failed to diminish Davis's enthusiasm for his work. Eisler was her authority for the claim that the early patriarchs practiced selective breeding to produce women with hymens, and that sexual guilt then developed among men as a consequence of spilling women's sacred blood during first intercourse.[3]

Davis relied heavily on several figures whose dubious credibility will be the focus of later chapters. The most important of these is Johann Jakob Bachofen. Bachofen, whose work we will explore in detail later, was, in 1861, the first to propose the idea that a matriarchal stage of civilization had preceded patriarchy all over the Mediterranean world. Portions of his writings were first published in English translation in 1967, and the quotations from Bachofen which adorn several of the chapter headings in *The First Sex* show how decisively Davis's work was inspired by her discovery of this book.

As we shall see in the next chapter, both her selection of evidence and her interpretation of it were fatally distorted according to the normal standards of research. Her extraordinary assembly of information and misinformation, and the extravagance of the argument founded upon it, ensured that her book would be largely ignored by conventional scholars. Even a great proportion of committed feminists conceded that the book was so heavily flawed as to be useless.[4] It found a home, however, among the radicals who were involved in the nascent feminist spirituality movement—in fact, an Elizabeth Gould Davis Coven was formed in Florida.[5]

The true founding document of Goddess spirituality was produced by Merlin Stone. An art historian, she published *The Paradise Papers* in 1976 (intentionally echoing the controversial Pentagon Papers); the book was later renamed *When God was a Woman*.[6] Although she abandons Davis's biological speculations, her history of civilization is essentially the same, ranging from the peaceful gatherers on the face of Mother Earth to the cultured and harmonious matriarchies of preliterate urban civilizations and on to the Indo-European invasions.

Unlike Davis, however, Stone emphasizes religion. She argues that worship of "the Goddess" both supported and reflected the high socio-political status of women in ancient societies. The Goddess herself was One—despite the differences of language, ethnicity, and specific religious vocabulary and ceremony, all the peoples of Europe and the Near East supposedly worshipped the same female deity. The patriarchs, therefore, had to make the Goddess a primary target for destruction if they hoped to make their revolution permanent. In the biblical story of Eden, for instance, Stone sees sheer anti-Goddess propaganda: the Goddess herself is reduced to the misled and misleading Eve; her sacred serpent, symbol of her divine wisdom, is transformed into a demonic tempter; and the trees of knowledge and life, those free gifts of the Goddess, are put off-limits by a jealous God. The resulting hierarchy of God-man-woman-earth, distorting the interconnected web of existence, serves to justify and facilitate all forms of exploitation and violence. Only a return to the Goddess can undo the damage in time to salvage the earth and human society.

Perhaps knowing that much of her intended audience has been predisposed to regard ancient paganism as either primitive or positively evil, Stone sets about redeeming primeval religious practices. Human sacrifice, for instance, she traces back to the Mesopotamian story of the goddess Inanna and her slain lover Dumuzi. Following Sir James Frazer, the turn-of-the-century anthropologist who wrote the highly influential *Golden Bough*, she interprets this myth as proof that ancient and primitive societies actually sacrificed their chiefs, kings, or other virile males on a regular basis. Frazer regarded such ritual sacrifices as fertility rites, meant to renew the earth with blood while avoiding the problem of aging leadership. Stone, however, argues that these ritual executions were object lessons—Dumuzi died "at Inanna's command," reinforcing female control over both males and the very powers of life and death.

Stone also devotes a chapter to the ancient Near Eastern practice of temple prostitution, which she calls the "sacred sexual rites" of the

Goddess religion. She supposes that these early urban cultures (unlike the nomadic herdsmen) were unclear about the biological facts of paternity. She also cites the report of the ancient Greek travel-writer Herodotus, who claimed that Babylonian women normally sacrificed their virginity in the temples as sacred prostitutes before going on to marry. Stone concludes that the mature Goddess cultures saw ceremonial sex as an especially potent way to celebrate and share in the life-giving powers of the Goddess. In addition, promiscuous sexual activity was encouraged for the specific reason of confusing the lines of paternity, and thus reinforcing matrilineal inheritance of property and power—fathers could not bequeath power and property to their sons if they did not know who their sons were. Patrilineal monogamy, she says, is just another aspect of the later oppression of women, and hence sexual liberation today is an essential component of the liberation of women.

As with *The First Sex*, *When God was a Woman* has been routinely ignored by historians. One of its most striking features is Stone's willingness to twist evidence, and even to ignore obvious facts, in the service of her argument. She is committed to Davis's view that the Indo-Europeans devised and spread patriarchy, because only by attributing it to a specific group of conspiratorial innovators can she portray it as essentially unnatural. But then she finds herself somewhat hard-pressed to explain how patriarchy arose among the Semitic Hebrews as well—although she must insist that it did, so that she can attack the Bible on that account.

Her solution is a far-fetched linguistic speculation. She knows that the Hittites were an Indo-European kingdom at the time of Moses, situated in what is now Turkey, and that a group called the Luvites or Luwites was either part of the Hittite nation or closely related to it. With these facts in hand, she makes the bold claim that ancient Israel's priestly tribe, the Levites, were not ethnic Hebrews at all, but Indo-Europeans—Aryan migrants who imposed their rule and their patriarchal system on the Semitic Israelites.[7] The Luwite/Levite connection actually has no basis whatsoever in established historical fact; the two words are drawn from completely unrelated languages, and it is most likely a pure coincidence that they sound alike. The German word for God sounds almost exactly like the past tense of the English verb "to get," and these two languages are much more closely related than Hebrew and Hittite, but no useful conclusion can be drawn from this coincidence either.

In the most ludicrous single paragraph in her book, Stone tries to establish a connection between the Levites, whom she associates with the Hittites and therefore with "Aryans"—and Hitler's Nazis. She invites the reader to speculate that the term "Nazis" was not simply an abbreviation of *Nationalsozialisten,* but was somehow related to the Hittites' name for their own language, *nasili,* and also to the Hebrew word for prince, *nasi.* She actually suggests that the would-be Führer invented the surname "Hitler" to replace Schickl-gruber—*lehren* is the German verb "to teach," so the name Hit-ler would supposedly have given him the aura of a Hittite teacher.[8] Only a few minutes of research in almost any library will confirm, of course, that Adolf was born a Hitler; his birth registration in the name of "Adolphus Hitler" still exists. It was his father who made the switch from Schicklgruber upon being recognized as the legal son of a member of the Hitler/Hiedler family.[9] As she perpetrates this astonishing assault on well-known facts, Stone argues that the holocaust was "not only . . . tragic but ironic"—patriarchal Aryans exterminating patriarchal Aryans on the pretext of racism.

On the whole, respectable and responsible historians have not deemed such assertions worthy of rebuttal; outside their purview, however, *When God was a Woman* laid the foundation for Goddess spirituality, a dynamic new religious ideology with far-reaching consequences. At this early stage, we have seen two closely similar but distinct expressions of feminist spirituality: Davis's socio-historical approach, emphasizing the matriarchy-patriarchy conflict; and Stone's religious orientation, focusing on the Goddess as opposed to God. These two streams can be detected separately for most of a decade, before blending almost beyond distinction in the late 1980s.

The matriarchal theme is perhaps most evident in our next example, Mary Daly. She began as a Roman Catholic theologian, and her early book *The Church and the Second Sex* was an expression of inside-the-church reformist feminism. *Beyond God the Father* marked a major transformation, moving her away from the traditional standards of orthodoxy, although not into the Goddess camp as such; as a professional philosopher, she developed her own religious vocabulary, preferring to use "god" as a verb.[10]

In *Gyn/Ecology* (1978), she elaborates her version of the matriarchy theory.[11] Here, she presents polemical descriptions of five atrocities suffered by women in the course of history: suttee (the burning of live widows on their husbands' funeral pyres in traditional India); footbinding (the crippling technique of "beautification" practiced in the last dynasties of imperial China); genital mutilation (the "female circumcision" found in some areas of Africa and the Near East); the witch hunts of 1500-1700 in Europe and North America (citing the supposed nine million victims); and gynecology as practiced in America today. All these she interprets as religious rituals. Mythically, she says, they represent the murder and dismemberment of the Goddess; practically, they serve to maintain the hold of the oppressive patriarchs over the minds and bodies of generations of women. All this is founded on the assumption that matriarchy preceded patriarchy, and that patriarchy requires a high level of violence to maintain its present and essentially unnatural position. Her subsequent book, *Pure Lust* (1982), emphasizes the role of sexual liberation in the liberation of women, particularly the vital importance of lesbian relationships to strengthen solidarity among females.[12]

Meanwhile, the specifically religious version of matriarchy theory was fuelling itself from the resources of Wicca. As early as 1972, Zsuzsanna Budapest published *The Feminist Book of Lights and Shadows*, adapting witchcraft and the Hungarian folk customs she had learned from her grandmother to the concerns of the contemporary women's movement. She published a fuller version of *Lights and Shadows* in 1989, *The Holy Book of Women's Mysteries: Feminist Witchcraft, Goddess Rituals, Spellcasting, and other womanly arts* . . .[13] Budapest offers a version of witchcraft for women only, a "wimmin's religion" which includes lesbian ritual sex magic and a matriarchal coming-of-age ceremony for witches' sons, who must pledge their allegiance to "life and the Carriers of life, women." Women's wisdom and power must not be shared with men until men have given up their patriarchal claims, status, and modes of thought.

According to a popular story among Wiccans, Miriam "Starhawk"

Simos, who was already both a feminist and a witch, was wondering why the two movements had not come together when she happened upon Budapest's shop, named "Feminist Wicca." They met and worked together, and Starhawk went on to become probably the most prominent feminist witch in North America. In 1979, she published her first book, *The Spiral Dance: A Rebirth of the Ancient Religion of the Great Goddess*.[14] It develops her claim that there was an historic continuity between the ancient Goddess-worshipping utopias, the victims of the witch-hunts, and the plight of women and the earth today; it also offers a series of ritual instructions which will be useful when we discuss the antecedents of feminist Wicca. She followed it up in 1982 with *Dreaming the Dark: Magic, Sex and Politics*, a call to a spiritually nourished activism in the cause of women's liberation, sexual liberty, and the defense of nature.[15] Starhawk has also been in wide demand as a speaker and workshop leader in neopagan and radical feminist circles, as her Internet web page indicates.

The first edition of Margot Adler's *Drawing Down the Moon*, an informative and witty inside account of "Witches, Druids, Goddess-Worshippers and Other Pagans in America Today," in the words of the subtitle, was also published in 1979. Adler, a Wiccan priestess, has also pursued a successful and influential career in radio journalism; she is a longtime reporter and New York bureau chief for National Public Radio. Her articulate advocacy of Wicca has occasionally made her an object of media attention herself. She was, for instance, the featured interviewee when the Canadian Broadcasting Corporation's religious affairs program "Man Alive" examined modern witchcraft. A second edition of *Drawing Down the Moon* appeared in 1986 and remains in high demand.[16]

The distinction between matriarchy theory, an account of the history of civilization which is held with religious fervor, and feminist Wicca, a religion which took the ancient gynocentric utopia as an article of faith, was in some ways so subtle that it could not last for long. In *Womanspirit Rising* (1979) and *The Politics of Women's Spirituality* (1982), as we saw previously, Wiccans and matriarchalists staked a significant claim to credibility by writing alongside more orthodox Jewish and Christian feminists. By the mid-1980s, Goddess spirituality had established itself as a presence in New Age and radical feminist circles. Its essential content was a fusion of Wicca with matriarchy theory, but it had taken on a life of its own, ready to enter into debate with the "patriarchal" structures of academia, the church, and public life at large. The National Film Board of Canada's "Goddess Remembered" was able to assemble Merlin Stone, Starhawk, Carol Christ, and Charlene Spretnak (editor of *The Politics of Women's Spirituality*) together with several other spokeswomen of the Goddess, showing how the different streams of feminist spirituality had come together.

Riane Eisler's *The Chalice and the Blade: Our History, Our Future* (1987) typifies the new breed.[17] While essentially affirming the ancient Goddess cultures, she is in some ways less extravagant in her claims than earlier writers. The Goddess civilizations, she writes, were not entirely utopian—people then had their frustrations too— but they were, at least, more equitable than modern Western society. She specifically refuses to use the word "matriarchy," since it makes female domination sound like the mirror image of male rule under patriarchy. Instead, Eisler coined the term "gylany," using syllables from the Greek words for "woman" and "man," to describe what she called a "partnership" pattern of social organization. Patriarchy, on the other hand, is an example of the "domination" pattern. As both Daly and Starhawk had done, Eisler followed up with a sequel emphasizing sexual liberation as crucial to both women's liberation and the psycho-physical health of society as a whole: *Sacred Pleasure. Sex, Myth, and the Politics of the Body* (1995).[18] Eisler and her husband, David Loye, have established the Center for Partnership Studies to propagate her ideas and, like Starhawk, she is in widespread demand for lecture tours and workshops.

A strikingly high proportion of the Goddess literature has come from artists and art historians. Like Merlin Stone, they rely heavily on the art of preliterate cultures to generate speculative visions of the entire value systems and social structures of those times. Michael Dames approaches this task on a rather grand scale with respect to prehistoric Britain. In his books *The Silbury Treasure. The Goddess Rediscovered* (1976) and *The Avebury Cycle* (1977), he attempts to link

Stonehenge and other megalithic sites to the supposed religion of the Great Goddess.[19] His central argument is that the builders had designed their works in such a way that they would blend with the natural setting to form huge earth-portraits of the Goddess. Silbury Hill, for instance, represents her swollen, pregnant womb, while moats and ditches complete the outline of the Goddess's figure. He went on in the second book to an imaginative reconstruction of the Goddess rituals performed at Avebury and other sacred spots, rituals which supposedly emphasized the female life-cycle.

Elinor Gadon's *The Once and Future Goddess: A Symbol for our Time* (1989) follows the now-familiar historical outline and advocacy of societal and religious reform, but gives overwhelming emphasis to visual art in all ages as an index of social and sexual relations. She decries the image of women presented in media like *Cosmopolitan* magazine, not to mention male-targeted pornography. At the same time, however, she notes that the female genitals have been essentially off-limits as subjects of Western art, and celebrates the symbolism in the depiction of the vagina in the works of Judy Chicago and other feminist artists. Inevitably, sexual liberation is a major theme.[20] Other artistic explorations of the Goddess myth are pursued by Hallie Inglehart Austen in *The Heart of the Goddess: Art, Myth, and Meditations of the World's Sacred Feminine* (1990), by Anne Baring and Jules Cashford in *The Myth of the Goddess: Evolution of an Image* (1991), and, emphasizing drama and ritual rather than visual art, by Donna Wilshire in *Virgin, Mother, Crone: Myths & Mysteries of the Triple Goddess* (1994).[21]

One of the more extreme treatments of the theme was produced by European artist Monica Sjöö with Barbara Mor, in *The Great Cosmic Mother: Rediscovering the Religion of the Earth* (1991). Sjöö is more explicit than most Goddess writers in her reliance on radical leftist political thinkers, particularly Karl Marx, Friedrich Engels, and Michel Foucault. Among her claims are the assertions that "the original witch was undoubtedly black, bisexual, a warrior, a wise and strong woman, also a midwife, also a leader of her tribe"; that Celtic cultures were matriarchal, and Roman legionaries undermined them by ridiculing the manhood of their Celtic captives; that abortion, when preceded by dream-conversations with the fetus, "is indeed a participation ritual"; and that woman is "designed by evolution itself as the *link* between sexuality and spirit . . . the leading edge of earthly evolution," whereas males, even the greatest mystics, are biologically incapable of achieving "true fusion."[22] Clearly, Davis's claims for the organic superiority of women over men live on in the Goddess movement.

The field of psychology is also well represented in the Goddess literature. Naomi Goldenberg, a professor of Religious Studies at the University of Ottawa, published *Changing of the Gods: Feminism and the End of Traditional Religions* (1979), which owes a great deal to her background of training in Jungian analysis with its gender-related archetypes.[23] Jean Shinoda Bolen, the previously mentioned professor of psychiatry at the University of California San Francisco and another participant in "Goddess Remembered," contributed *Goddesses in Everywoman: A New Psychology of Women* (1984). This survey of goddess myths aims at assisting contemporary women to "reclaim" the powers associated with female deities in the past.[24]

Conspicuous by their absence in the catalogue of Goddess books are specialists in those fields where some of the movement's claims can actually be tested: anthropology and ancient history. The story of the utopian matriarchal Goddess cultures of preliterate peoples is emphasized repeatedly within the movement because it is more than a matter of historical curiosity. It provides the blueprint for contemporary social change, and the necessary precedent which supposedly proves that such change can succeed and flourish. Thus, the informed opinions of experts on ancient cultures should be of special interest.

Only one notable professional from these disciplines truly entered the ranks of the Goddess movement. This was Marija Gimbutas, the late professor of archaeology at UCLA who specialized in the neolithic cultures of the Balkans, which she titled "Old Europe." Gimbutas had done valuable field work in the Balkans earlier in her career. In her last years, she published interpretations of these finds which corresponded exactly with the Goddess myth, particularly as it was propounded by Riane Eisler.[25] As we shall see in the next chapter, however, Gimbutas's professional colleagues essentially parted company with her when her interpretation of the recovered artifacts was pressed into the service of the Goddess movement; in professional circles, she stood virtually alone in her support for the Goddess.

Goddess spirituality is not a tightly organized, centrally governed system; on the contrary, it is largely a grassroots movement composed of small local units. In such a movement, as Luhrmann and Eller have shown, literature is one of the primary ways of circulating information and ideas, recruiting new members, and reassuring them that other like-minded people are to be found in other places. Books by writers such as those we have been considering are, to a great degree, the vital links in the movement as a whole. As such, they deserve close attention and careful assessment. While no one can deny the massive exertion in reading and research which the Goddess literature embodies, the fact remains that scholars in the fields best equipped to assess the historical claims of the movement have almost unanimously discounted those claims.

How likely is it that these utopian, matriarchal Goddess cultures actually existed? We must attempt to ascertain what is really known about the ancient societies which the Goddess writers are asking us to imitate.

3

A Search for the Ancient Goddess

Remember. Make an effort to remember. Or, failing that, invent.

Monique Wittig

T HE TENETS OF GODDESS SPIRITUALITY entail a radical departure from the understanding of human history which is familiar to most educated people. Even so, this new religion has experienced astonishing success in propagating its central myth in influential sectors of modern society as though it were actual fact, or at least a well-founded new theory about the development of civilization. With active support in places like universities and even churches, the Goddess is beginning to permeate Western culture. While this development is still in its early stages, it is imperative to take a close and critical look at the specific content of the Goddess's story.

Although we have noted a few individual oddities in some of the Goddess books, the focus here is different—we must deal with the central claims of the entire movement. Did gynocentric Goddess cultures really exist, and were they as happy and enlightened as we are told? To merit the answer "yes," an ancient civilization must pass several tests: (1) a single, unquestionably female deity must reign supreme over its religion and culture; (2) women must be prominent in

53

its public life, exhibiting the high social status which would justify such terms as matriarchy or "gylany"; (3) the predominance of feminine values must manifest itself in concrete, practical benefits such as an equal sharing of wealth among social classes, a healthy and constructive relationship with the environment, and especially in a relative absence of interpersonal violence and warfare.

If the story of the Goddess is an accurate reflection of history, and not simply the devotional narrative of a specific religious movement, we should expect to find more than just a few isolated Goddess civilizations here and there. Goddess spirituality typically assumes a sort of female monotheism shared across continents and centuries, with only superficial differences of language and ethnic flavor. This supposed unity of culture, all the way from Ireland to India, is a central part of the story, and thus it is also at issue here. We must begin, however, by seeing how many actual Goddess cultures we can find; if we have enough of them, we can go on to investigate whether or not they are really just different local varieties of the same basic civilization.

Before we proceed to examine specific cases, one general consideration must be noted. We do not, in fact, possess a single translated text from any of the most important Goddess cultures to tell us what these ancient peoples actually believed or how they went about their lives. Most of the civilizations which are claimed for the Goddess existed before the invention of writing (Paleolithic Europe; Çatal Hüyük in Turkey; "Old Europe" in the Balkans; the megalithic culture of Malta; pre-Celtic Britain), while a few used forms of writing which we still cannot decipher (the Indus Valley script; Cretan "Linear A"). To put it another way: not a single ancient civilization which has left us readable records was a Goddess culture.

The genuinely helpful evidence we possess about the religion and social structure of these preliterate peoples consists primarily of archaeological remains, particularly their art and architecture and their burial customs. Some use is also made of the myths and legends of later peoples like the Sumerians and Greeks, and of analogies drawn from the non-literates of modern times. Nevertheless, physical remnants from the early cultures themselves obviously carry the greatest weight.

The major Goddess writers tend to emphasize three periods of cultural development in their attempted reconstruction of the ancient utopian societies. They typically begin with the cave-dwellers of the "upper Paleolithic" period in Europe, extending from forty thousand to ten thousand years ago. Second, they highlight several neolithic cultures featuring agriculture and urbanization, genuine civilizations which existed perhaps from 6000 to 1500 B C with some regional variations. Finally, ancient Crete is hailed and mourned as the last and greatest of the Goddess cultures, the shining example of what we lost when we fell into patriarchy. This is the path trodden by those who seek the Goddess. We must tread it too, if we wish to understand what today's Goddess movement is offering us.

PALEOLITHIC EUROPE

The general problems associated with the study of preliterate cultures are magnified when we look as far back as the Paleolithic ages. The scale of time and space is immense. To address the claims of the Goddess writers, we must deal with a period which lasted approximately thirty thousand years, and ended one hundred centuries ago. The evidence is drawn from an area reaching from Gibraltar to the Urals, from Scotland and Scandinavia to Turkey, and pertains to a time when there were no artificial means of transportation or communication whatsoever. A fascinating array of relics has been recovered, but it is unfortunately sparse when set within these enormous temporal and geographic dimensions. When the finds come from so many times and places, we cannot be sure that they belong together and display a single, unified worldview.

In general, Paleolithic or "Old Stone Age" culture was characterized by a hunting and gathering style of subsistence; surviving artifacts are typically made of chipped stone, bone, or antler. The evidence which concerns us here is of several distinct types.

First, Paleolithic living quarters in the entrances of caves have been excavated by anthropologists. This work has revealed stone tools and the bones of the animals which were hunted and eaten, and also some intriguing artistic objects. A significant number of these, particularly from eastern Europe, seem to represent the female anatomy in whole or in part; in both statuettes and wall carvings, the figures of women tend to be very rounded, emphasizing the breasts and the belly. Other objects appear to be phallic symbols.

Second, there were burials of the dead located in or near the living quarters, and the remains show suggestive indications of ritual. Skeletons are sometimes found in the fetal position, accompanied by assorted possessions, arrays of cowrie shells, and stains of red ochre.

Third, we have the famous cave paintings, which have been found only in France and Spain. These impressive works are not on open display. They are normally located deep in the caves, reached only after a long and sometimes dangerous passage; this again suggests to anthropologists that at least part of their purpose may have been associated with ritual of some kind.

The basic question is to what extent we can extrapolate from these relics to the worldviews of the people who created them. One of the most painstaking attempts to interpret the Paleolithic remains as evidence of a unified Mother Goddess culture was Gertrude Rachel Levy's *The Gate of Horn* (1948). Levy was a professional archaeologist who had previously worked on Mesopotamian sites. Her finds there led her to wonder whether the religious conceptions on display in Sumer and Babylonia had roots extending back to the Stone Age. She visited a number of the Paleolithic sites just before the Second World War, and familiarized herself with accounts of modern preliterate peoples.

She proposed that the female statuettes and the burial customs of the cave-mouth dwelling areas pointed to a conception of "a life-substance . . . conceived already in the human form of maternal fecundity."[1] The statuettes' emphasis on female reproductive anatomy, the fetal position of the buried dead, and the blood-red ochre stains were interpreted by Levy as signs of a belief or hope in some sort of afterlife, which was portrayed by these symbols of (re)birth. The fact that the graves were located in the living quarters suggested to her that some notion of ongoing communion between the living and the dead was prevalent even in these early days.

As for the cave paintings, Levy relied heavily on the cave rituals of the modern Australian aborigines as analogies. On this basis she suggested that the animal paintings were the totems of a hunting people, and that the long cave journeys could have had the ritual significance of initiation and rebirth. Themes such as this, she speculated, could have been passed on to the later neolithic cultures, which would combine the "feminine" notions of the cave-mouth with the "masculine" pursuits of the deep caverns. Cave, tomb, and womb would coalesce into a grand vision of the earth as Mother Goddess, and themes of initiation and immortality through rituals of rebirth were thus, in her reconstruction, permanently implanted in the religious thought of the West.

Levy offered her hypothesis in appropriately restrained language; her phrasing often incorporates such careful words as "could," "would," and "it seems reasonable to imagine." Her theory held sway for a time with the support of prestigious scholars like Glyn Daniel and O. G. S. Crawford, who tended to interpret all sorts of abstract designs and asexual human figures as Goddess symbolism.[2]

Andrew Fleming's 1969 article "The Myth of the Mother Goddess" proved to be a watershed for professionals, however. He presented convincing arguments on three crucial points: first, that there was no scholarly justification for assuming that female carvings and statuettes represent a Goddess; second, that abstract artistic patterns do not constitute self-evident Goddess symbolism; third, that the phallic symbols and other representations of masculinity cannot be explained away as representing the son or consort of the Goddess.[3] Once the scaffolding of unsupported assumptions was removed, the Mother Goddess theory collapsed and was discarded by the vast majority of practicing anthropologists and archaeologists.[4] Interestingly, although she was a female scholar writing about the Mother Goddess, Levy receives surprisingly little attention from contemporary Goddess writers; Gadon cites her once and Eisler not at all.

Their preference is for the much more radical theory of Alexander Marshack. Marshack is described by Gadon as "a scientific writer interested in theories of cognition"; Eisler reports that he "was not an archaeologist, hence not bound by earlier archaeological conventions."[5] Marshack's contribution is primarily twofold. First, he reinterprets some of the painted scenes in the cave art—where most scholars see hunters' spears and arrows, for instance, he sees tree branches or tufts of grass. By turning hunting scenes into vegetation, he shifts the focus from masculine pursuits to female fertility symbolism. Second, he argues that the patterns of scratches found on some cave walls and bone carvings were actually records of the phases of the moon. By suggesting that the people of the Stone Age knew and used a sort of lunar calendar, he invites the customary analogies between the lunar cycle and the menstrual cycle, between nature and woman, between earth and Goddess. This female-oriented vision, with fertility at the center and hunting relegated to the periphery, comes much closer to the peaceful, matrifocal utopias of the Goddess myth than the more conventional and cautious interpretations of mainstream anthropology. Everything else can be brought into line with Marshack's theory: the red ochre evokes menstrual blood as the blood of life; the cowrie shells become vulva symbols; everything speaks of the Goddess.

There are other and more persuasive ways to interpret many of the Paleolithic data, however. With respect to the burials, we must note first of all how few have been found—according to Ronald Hutton, even if we extend the scope of our search to cover a period of seventy thousand years, we still have only thirty-nine burial sites found in all of Europe. Further, the "fetal" position appeared in fewer than half of the Stone-Age burials which have been excavated, so it is not likely to be a major indicator of Paleolithic belief. Even if it were, we cannot necessarily presume that the Paleolithic peoples had accurate knowledge of the child's posture in the womb. Burial in a crouched position may reflect a normal sleeping posture, and thus symbolize eternal rest rather than rebirth.[6] On the other hand, it may simply be the most compact way to inter an entire body.

The cowrie shells are usually found positioned in such a way as to indicate that they were originally threaded together as garments or caps; while they may resemble the vulva to a vivid imagination, any visitor to a tropical tourist center knows how easily they lend themselves to being strung. The red ochre could represent menstrual blood, the blood accompanying childbirth, the lost lifeblood of the person being buried, or something else we have not imagined—inanimate artifacts were sometimes coated in it as well.

Finally, there are two crucial facts noted by Hutton but never reported in Goddess literature. First, these burials are so rare as to suggest that there was some process of selection involved. Since the vast majority of Paleolithic individuals were not included in these cave-mouth interments, is it not possible that those who did receive ceremonial burial held some sort of elite social status? Second, a clear majority of those individuals found in the graves were adult males—a serious problem to any gynocentric interpretation of these finds.[7] In short, the evidence of the Old Stone Age burials indicates the probability that Paleolithic peoples had religious beliefs of some kind, but it is virtually impossible to know what they were, and the Goddess myth is especially unlikely to be the correct explanation.

What of the female statuettes and reliefs, the prehistoric "Venuses"? We do not and cannot know, in fact, whether the carvings represent real individual women, one or more spiritual beings, or abstract concepts of some sort. While they do not seem to be just casual productions of Stone-Age whittling (much less ancient erotica, as some have occasionally suggested), it is generally agreed by prehistorians that they lack the sort of features which suggest divinity or majesty in any obvious way.[8] One female art historian suggested to me in conversation that, based on her own experience of pregnancy, many of these figures are not even necessarily pregnant as the fertility theme demands. They may be merely fat—as fattened as we should expect of someone who planned to survive an Ice-Age winter. Moreover, the figurines may represent only a thin slice of Paleolithic culture. All of the datable statuettes have been assigned to the comparatively short period of 25,000 to 23,000 BC, the beginning of the last Ice Age.[9] Even if we knew what they stood for, it would be overstepping the boundaries of scholarship to extrapolate from them to the supposed belief system of the entire Stone Age.

Most Paleolithic art is much more recent than these particular figurines. Thousands of carved reliefs, as well as the cave paintings, have survived from the later Old Stone Age. They include representations of humans, animals, and seemingly abstract designs. Most of the artistic remains which could be considered as possible religious symbols are found inside the caves. As Hutton notes, the female representations on cave walls tend to be nude, with emphasis on the genitals, and in passive or reclining poses; the males are in active postures suggesting dance, sometimes with erect phalli, but almost always wearing animal heads and skins. The character of this apparent sex-role distinction seriously weakens any suggestion of a gynocentric culture. Various explanations of late Paleolithic art, ranging from hunting magic to totemism, have been proposed and examined without any one of them coming to dominate the field.[10] As archaeologist Sarunas Milisauskas put it, "all these interpretations are only speculations."[11]

The upshot is, then, that the Paleolithic evidence is far too sparse and flimsy to support a theory as elaborate as the story of the Goddess. Goddess writers themselves, in attempting to explain their beliefs, often appeal to later cults of the Great Goddess and read them back into the cave art; only thus does their interpretation gain a degree of plausibility. We shall now consider the major examples of those later cultures to see whether the Goddess myth has a firmer foundation there.

NEOLITHIC CULTURES

Mesolithic Silence and Neolithic Civilization

The term Mesolithic, or "Middle Stone Age," refers to the transitional period between the long Paleolithic era of the cave-dwellers and the rise of actual prehistoric civilizations. In Europe and the Near East, the Mesolithic period is said to have begun around 8300 BC, the end of the last Ice Age; it lasted until the development of agriculture and animal domestication, which marks the Neolithic or "New Stone Age," and which spread across the region between 5000 and 3500 BC.

Mesolithic remains are much less plentiful than those of the ages before and after, but some general features of life in this period can be discerned. As the climate warmed and trees grew over the previous stretches of steppe and tundra, the human diet shifted from large herd animals to solitary forest-dwellers like deer, as well as to seafood. Mesolithic people cleared large tracts of woods by means of fire; in some cases, the destructive impact on the environment was such that the forests never recovered, leaving heaths and bogs in their place. Cattle and deer may have been penned in some of the clearings, but only dogs seem to have been fully domesticated. Higher-quality stone tools, particularly small implements with blades of chipped flint, distinguish the Mesolithic from the Paleolithic.[12]

On matters of religion, we know even less of the Middle Stone Age than we do of the preceding millennia. No burials have been found which can be dated to this era with any certainty. Art is almost equally absent, with only some rock paintings in Spain to fill the void. Interestingly, these paintings indicate a clear separation in sex roles: women are gathering plants, while men hunt and fight with spears. As Hutton comments, "The Middle Stone Age art leaves no doubt that warfare was now a part of the human record."[13]

The "Mesolithic silence" is not just the relative scarcity of archaeological evidence—strikingly, the whole period is utterly invisible in Goddess literature. In part, this is understandable, since there is simply nothing in the relics which bears directly on religion. Nonetheless, this lack of evidence for a Mesolithic Goddess raises a serious challenge to any idea that there was continuity between the Paleolithic female carvings and the goddess figures of later civilizations. Even if there were Goddess cultures in more recent times, these can hardly be projected back onto the Paleolithic remains when the intervening millennia are so completely devoid of supportive evidence. Even more importantly, we do have clear evidence of Mesolithic sex-role differentiation, the commemoration of lethal combat between coordinated groups, and ecological despoliation on a large scale, all at this very early stage of human cultural development. The supposedly idyllic past of sexual partnership, peace among people, and harmony with nature is as startling in its absence as the Goddess herself.

Beginning about 5000 BC, several cultural advances mark the onset of the Neolithic period. "New Stone Age" cultures often featured improved methods of producing stone tools, particularly ground and polished stone. The invention and use of pottery indicate another practical advance which is typical of the period. Most striking is the change in food production—the beginnings of agriculture and the domestication of animals for meat and milk. This appears to have been a Near Eastern innovation. The staple crops of wheat and barley, and the sheep and goats which made up a large proportion of the domesticated animals at this stage, were native to western Asia and reached Europe only in their domesticated form.

Many Neolithic sites have been discovered and excavated by amateurs and professionals over the past two centuries. It is from these finds that some of the strongest arguments in favor of the Goddess have been erected. As noted above, we must consider several of them individually before we can even ask if they formed parts of a unified network of Goddess cultures.

Çatal Hüyük

Discovered in the late 1950s and partially excavated in the 1960s, the town of Çatal Hüyük in modern Turkey has become a cornerstone in the Goddess myth. Until very recently, only one archaeological team had worked the site; accordingly, anyone who has discussed Çatal Hüyük in print was entirely dependent on the published reports of James Mellaart, who led that team. He dated the ruins as far back as the seventh millennium BC, which would make Çatal Hüyük one of the oldest urban sites ever excavated.

Mellaart's discoveries have been celebrated in virtually every account of the ancient Goddess cultures. Indeed, when he first wrote, Levy's Mother Goddess theory was still in vogue among archaeologists, and Mellaart's early books seem to take it for granted.[14] As a result, Elizabeth Gould Davis hailed Çatal Hüyük as "not only a matriarchal but a utopian society." Claiming Mellaart as her authority, she announced that "there had been no wars for a thousand years . . . vegetarianism prevailed . . . there is no evidence of violent deaths . . . [women] were reverently buried, while men's bones were thrown into a charnel house. Above all, the supreme deity in all the temples was a goddess." Eisler and the others have followed suit, usually in more muted language.[15]

Mellaart issued his final account of Çatal Hüyük in 1975; probably aware of the declining credibility of the Mother Goddess, he concentrated on a detailed description of the actual finds.[16] If we compare the Goddess writers' accounts with this report, some disconcerting questions emerge. In fact, of all the key characteristics of Goddess cultures, not a single one can be applied to Çatal Hüyük with any confidence. What we see in the Goddess literature is a striking display of disregard for the actual evidence, arguments from silence, and imaginative speculation.

Was a goddess the central deity of Çatal Hüyük? There are various representations of humanoid females in images and reliefs, ranging from girlish running figures to birthing mothers and perhaps aged crones. These might depict one goddess, several separate goddesses, or no actual goddesses at all; Goddess monotheism is merely one of several logical possibilities, and not the most self-evident among them. Mellaart identified several structures as shrines, and female representations play a prominent role in them, along with the bulls' horns which are usually understood as phallic symbols. In both wall carvings and statuettes, females in the act of giving birth have been discovered. Given the absence of written texts, however, we have no way of knowing what they represent beyond the obvious general connection with fertility. Even this minimal observation is hedged about with questions, however—Çatal Hüyük imagery included women giving birth to horned animals, female figures associated with predators and vultures, and wall-models of human breasts where hooked beaks or fanged jaws protrude in place of the nipple.

As for matriarchy or "gylany," the evidence as to how the town was governed is negligible. To judge by funerary arrangements, individual women were regarded positively by those who buried them, and some seem to have been priestesses in the neighborhood cult. By the same token, however, some men seem to have been priests, and they were not buried in charnel houses after all. Ian Hodder, who is now leading the renewed excavations at the site, has pointed out that women tended to be buried with ornaments and cosmetic boxes while men are accompanied by tools and weapons, suggesting a fairly standard distinction in sex roles. The same impression emerges from Çatal Hüyük art, since males are usually portrayed in hunting scenes painted on walls, while female representations tend to be nude figurines.[17]

Mellaart also reported that women seem to have had larger bed-platforms than did the men. Eisler and Gadon take this as proof that women had preeminent status in Çatal Hüyük families, without considering the simpler possibility that the extra space was needed for practical purposes like the nursing of infants.[18] We still lack the sort of clear evidence which permits definitive pronouncements, although the Goddess writers invariably report their speculations as firm discoveries.

When we turn to the question of the general social character of this ancient community, however, a serious problem of distorted evidence emerges. It is true, for instance, that the houses Mellaart found differed very little in their overall size. Eisler and Gadon emphasize this observation, and take it as proof that Çatal Hüyük embodied an egalitarian society with minimal class stratification.[19] They completely ignore Mellaart's clear statement that he excavated only a small portion of the town, amounting to less than 4 percent of the entire mound. Thus, his reports deal with the houses of perhaps just a single neighborhood. This crucial and obvious piece of information destroys the entire argument. Until the entire city is excavated, no one can be sure that the other 96 percent of the mound contains absolutely no palaces or hovels.

Even within the small area he worked, Mellaart was able to identify a few high-status burials, accompanied by some prize artifacts. The majority were interred with no more than some basic personal possessions; as noted above, these artifacts varied according to the sex of the individual. Both social class distinction and sex-role differentiation make their appearance at Çatal Hüyük, but Goddess writers take little notice of the fact.

Most strikingly, Goddess literature presents Çatal Hüyük to us as a community free of weapons and fortifications, proof of the peaceful character of the gynocentric cultures. Mellaart's reports clearly indicate the contrary. It is true that he found no defensive wall surrounding the town. Rather, the outermost houses were attached to each other like row houses—they formed a blank external wall which served the purpose of fortification just as well, without additional expenditures of labor and material. It is also true that the excavation turned up no sign that the town was ever sacked by invaders. This may mean only that the inhabitants never lost a war, not that they never fought one. On the other hand, Mellaart did describe evidence of an active weapons industry, pointing out that some of its products were clearly designed for human conflict rather than for hunting, and that fine weapons were included in the burials of high-status males. He even noted with surprise the number of skulls he found showing evidence of head wounds, a most unlikely circumstance in a nonviolent society.

Çatal Hüyük is a critically important test case for the Goddess. It is one of the best-preserved Neolithic urban sites ever excavated, and it dates from precisely the period when the Goddess culture should have been at its purest and most undefiled, long before any Indo-European incursions could possibly have complicated the picture. It is also one of the easiest to test—Mellaart's books are widely available, and they remain so far the only first-hand expert account of the site. Further, Mellaart wrote as a genuine scholar, distinguishing clearly—particularly in his last book—between the actual evidence and his own hypotheses.

As a result, the distortion embodied in the Goddess literature stands out clearly. We are in the realm of religious mythmaking, not historical reporting. Imaginative speculation about female figurines and women's beds, arguments from silence about the absence of fortifications and burnt ruins, and misleading or even false reports about burials, weapons, and the size of the excavation itself add up to a massive fabrication of the life of this ancient town. We have found no Goddess culture at Çatal Hüyük.

Malta

Goddess writers frequently appeal to the impressive art and architecture of Neolithic Malta in support of their story. Maltese builders constructed some of the first megalithic structures in the Western world, cutting and arranging huge stone blocks into round-walled

temples which are as old as the first Egyptian pyramids and the earliest cities of Sumer. Some of the temples are laid out as five circular
rooms, and feature large statues which some excavators have nicknamed "fat ladies."

The significance of all this seems obvious to the Goddess writers. The real "fat lady" is the Goddess herself, ample in her nurturing
power. The fivefold temples are symbols of her body, presumably her
head, breasts and hips. Thus, to enter the temple was to enter through
the birth channel into the Goddess herself, and perhaps to undergo
an experience of spiritual connection and rebirth. Gadon dismisses
any difficulties in this interpretation, asserting all these claims in the
first three sentences of her chapter on Malta.[20] Her most prized
authority is Sybille von Cles-Reden's *Realm of the Great Goddess*, which
dates from 1962, several years before Fleming laid Levy's Mother
Goddess theory to rest.

The actual fact, here as well, is that close examination of the evidence does more to undermine than to confirm the Goddess myth.
David Trump's chronological study of the Maltese temples shows that
they began on the model of tombs cut into the living rock, which
were round because of their tendency to utilize and perhaps imitate
natural caves. Once temples were being built above ground, they
developed from three-chambered structures to larger efforts with four,
five, or six round rooms. There was, thus, no standard plan which
conformed to the shape of a woman's body; instead, there was a general style of circular building which was adapted and elaborated over
a lengthy period of time.[21] As for the large statues, most of them are
fragmentary, and all of them lack specific sexual characteristics—that
is, none of them is necessarily female at all, let alone a goddess. The
only definitely female sculptures are small statuettes which betray no
clear indication of majesty or divinity. Phallic symbols, on the other
hand, are decidedly present.[22]

Gadon casually remarks that we know almost nothing of Neolithic
Malta's socio-economic structure.[23] This restraint may arise from
the fact that professional anthropologists and archaeologists see signs
of a distinctly unmatriarchal society behind the production of the
temples. The most common and likely suggestion is that monument-

building cultures like Neolithic Malta fall somewhere between the relatively egalitarian pattern one might expect among people totally preoccupied with subsistence, and the organized urban states like ancient Egypt and Sumer. Colin Renfrew proposed the term "chiefdom societies" for such cultures.

"The essential feature of chiefdom society is the marked social hierarchy," he wrote, noting that the chiefdoms observed in recent times have had male chiefs and a patrilineal pattern of rank and succession.[24] Such a hierarchy would be capable of mobilizing hundreds or even a few thousands of people, making possible the construction of large stone monuments where materials permit. It is quite evident that chiefdom societies produced the large structures made of smaller stones which have been found in Zimbabwe, as well as the *marae* of Polynesia and the stone sculptures of Easter Island.[25] Thanks to the geological character of their island, the early Maltese had large, rectangular blocks of stone ready for the taking, which allowed them to erect their distinctive temples once they were able to mobilize sufficient labor and expertise.[26]

How does the Goddess movement respond to this suggestion of a hierarchical, patriarchal society behind the temples of Malta? "Goddess Remembered" features an unnamed aficionado of the temples who cheerfully informs us that, by sitting in the ruins and opening his mind, he can sense how content and happy were the people who lived around these structures—an instance of the intuitive approach to archaeology which we shall encounter again in our quest.

Early Britain

Pre-Celtic Britain, the series of cultures which produced such marvels as Stonehenge, the huge Avebury stone circle, and the conical, artificial hill at Silbury, is often claimed as another part of the ancient network of Goddess-worshipping matriarchies. Once again, professionals advise us that very little is reliably known of the religious and social systems of the early inhabitants of Britain. Only two Neolithic statuettes have been found, and only one of them is definitely female. On the other hand, carved phallic symbols abound in ritual deposits at the monuments, often accompanied by chalk balls to complete the male imagery.[27]   The famous large figures cut onto chalk hillsides generally portray horses or humanoid males, not females, and are notoriously difficult to date—some may be only a few hundred years old.   The long barrows of the inland and the round barrows of the coastal regions were certainly burial sites, but have not produced enough artifacts to provide reliable answers to our key questions.   The sheer scale of the larger monuments, and the fact that part of Stonehenge was built of stone quarried as far away as Wales, point once again towards a hierarchical chiefdom society capable of mobilizing the necessary resources and labor.

In actual fact, when the Goddess writers add ancient Britain to the list of gynocentric utopias, they rely almost entirely on the books of the English artist Michael Dames.   Starting from the unquestioned assumption that all the ancient peoples worshipped the Great Goddess, Dames developed corresponding visual interpretations of the major sites.   As we saw in Chapter 2, he portrayed Silbury Hill as the swollen womb in a huge earth-portrait of the pregnant Goddess, with the quarry and ditch marking the outline of the rest of her figure. The fact that no royal corpse or treasure was found buried within the hill was supposed to demonstrate that it was the work of an egalitarian, harmonious society.   In his second book, Dames went on to an imaginative reconstruction of festivals celebrated at Avebury.   In keeping with his theory, they are said to revolve around the analogies between female physiology and natural fertility.

The blunt fact is that there is no actual evidence whatsoever in support of Dames's interpretation of the monuments.   While it is true that the builders of Silbury Hill did not bury rich rulers inside it, this tells us only that burials were not the purpose of the hill—not that the builders had no such rulers at all.   The notion of Silbury as an earth-portrait is intriguing, but, unlike most of the chalk figures, Silbury has no earthly vantage point from which the whole can be viewed; one would need to be airborne, in the tradition of *Chariots of the Gods*.   Even so, the whole exercise is like a game of join-the-dots on a map; as Hutton reports, "I myself produced a perfectly nice unicorn by the same means, and I thank Mr. Dames warmly for the sheer childish pleasure of that experience."[28]

In fact, even Goddess devotees cannot agree on what Silbury represents. In "Goddess Remembered," the hill is not her pregnant womb but her nurturing breast; as we are shown evocative scenes of the site bathed in the golden glow of evening, the narrator recites a hymn to Inanna, the fertility goddess of distant Mesopotamia.

The Balkans

Perhaps the most formidable argument on behalf of an ancient Goddess culture appears in Marija Gimbutas's descriptions of what she called "Old Europe," the Neolithic urban culture of the Balkans from the period 7000–3500 BC. As we saw in the previous chapter, Gimbutas was a professional archaeologist who herself worked on some of the sites which figure in her books. "Old Europe," in her reconstruction, conforms perfectly to the egalitarian, peaceful utopia we have been told to expect in a Goddess-worshipping, woman-centered civilization. Her last major book began with an extended discussion of the nature of civilization, attributing "artistic creation, aesthetic achievements, nonmaterial values, and freedom" to this "gynocentric" culture. On the other hand, "a hierarchical political and religious organization, warfare, a class stratification, and a complex division of labor" appear only with the "androcratic" Indo-European groups which invaded the region later.[29]

While there is no disputing the importance of the artifacts Gimbutas and her colleagues brought to light, her description of the culture which produced them is quite another matter. Part of the problem, again, is the difficulty of interpreting artistic relics. As classical historian Mary Lefkowitz has pointed out (specifically in connection with Gimbutas's findings), we have no extant texts to tell us what the Old Europeans actually thought and felt about their artifacts; a statuette of a pregnant female could be anything from a Great Goddess ruling the powers of life to a mere votive offering to some indeterminate being or force.[30] Brian Hayden highlighted the fact that Gimbutas freely attributed Goddess symbolism to objects and abstract designs which might easily be considered asexual or even phallic; in her books, "nowhere is there even a mention of methodology, testing, statistics, chance variation, assumptions, or rigor."[31]

If one considers her work chronologically, it becomes clear that Gimbutas, towards the end of her career, was far from being a purely disinterested scientific scholar—she evidently became something of a believer. In an early book which predates the Goddess movement, *The Goddesses and Gods of Old Europe* (1974), we find that she described Old European religion as polytheistic, although the relative prominence of goddesses led her to infer "a society dominated by the mother."[32] Even at this point, her fellow scholars were concerned at how glibly she assumed that humanoid figures and statuettes must be divinities, and presumed to divine the inner meaning of abstract and geometrical patterns in the decorative arts.[33]

In *The Language of the Goddess* (1989) and *The Civilization of the Goddess* (1991), however, we see a significant change. Gimbutas now espoused the Goddess myth in full-blown, utopian form; as the books' titles suggest, this included a virtually monotheistic religion of the Great Goddess. Indeed, *Language* concludes with what must be considered a neopagan confession of faith: "now we find the Goddess reemerging from the forests and mountains, bringing us hope for the future, returning us to our most ancient human roots."[34] The change of view which Gimbutas displayed between *Goddesses and Gods* and *Language* arose not from new field work—that part of her career was essentially over—but from a change in her own perspective. Here we begin to see the true import of Hayden's remark that Gimbutas's claims "seem to be verifiable only with the eye of faith."[35]

In Gimbutas's case, that faith seems to have had at least two significant components. First, in her efforts to interpret the silent Balkan relics as testimony to the Goddess, Gimbutas relied heavily on Jungian psychology. Her bibliographies include a significant number of Jungian authorities, including Erich Neumann, Robert Eisler, Marie-Louise von Franz, and Karl Kerényi, in addition to the master himself. The foreword to Gimbutas's watershed book, *The Language of the Goddess*, was written by Joseph Campbell, the famous comparative mythologist who actually began his career at Jung's Bollingen Institute. Campbell commented that Gimbutas had hit on some fundamental Jungian archetypes in her archaeology, and that she recognized the need for a transformation of consciousness in the modern world. He also linked Gimbutas's work to the heritage of J. J. Bachofen, the nineteenth-century pioneer of matriarchy theory whose works were partially translated into English at Bollingen.[36] As we shall see in Chapters 11 and 12, both Bachofen and Jung made vital contributions to the development of the Goddess myth in the first place; the use of Jung to confirm elements of that myth today is a frequent feature in Goddess literature generally.

A second component in Gimbutas's change of perspective appears to be her contact with the Goddess movement itself. Both *The Language of the Goddess* and *The Civilization of the Goddess* were written when the movement was well underway, and they include references to some typical representatives like Merlin Stone, Naomi Goldenberg, and Michael Dames. Particularly important is Riane Eisler—both *The Chalice and the Blade* and Eisler herself are celebrated in the later books, and Gimbutas even adopted Eisler's neologism "gylany."[37] Moreover, in an interview with the Canadian Broadcasting Corporation's radio program "As It Happens" on the occasion of Gimbutas's death in 1994, her colleague Ernestine Elster commented on how much Gimbutas had enjoyed participating in Goddess rituals and being fêted by "her groupies" in the movement.

It seems inescapable that contact with the Goddess movement, rather than contact with the evidence, accounts for much of this change in Gimbutas's writing. As a result, her later Goddess books must be considered alongside those of other believers like Stone and Eisler, rather than those of more objective archaeologists like Mellaart, Trump, and Hutton. As Hayden noted, faith—faith in the Goddess—is the key to Gimbutas's final books.

The Indus Valley Civilization

There is another Neolithic culture which seems at first glance to meet the criteria of a Goddess culture, although it generally receives only passing mention in the literature. This is the Indus Valley culture, the earliest known civilization in South Asia, which flourished in what is now Pakistan between 3000 and 1500 BC.[38] This should be a textbook case for the Goddess. Once again, we encounter an essentially neolithic, urban/agricultural society which left us no decipherable written records. It was a strikingly advanced civilization—the remains of the major Indus cities, Harappa and Mohenjo-Daro, featured indoor plumbing and sewage systems superior to those of some nineteenth-century European cities. Such amenities of life as domesticated chickens and cotton appear to be Indus innovations.

As possible evidence of their religion, the Indus cities left us a large quantity of clay female figurines, with breasts and hips emphasized. Other typical fertility symbols, including stone pillars set into stone rings and carvings of bulls and trees on small clay seals, are in ample supply. There are no personal monuments or signed works of art, which Goddess writers sometimes interpret as signs of the rampant male ego. The few weapons found in the cities seem to be made for ceremonial rather than practical use. Best of all, the standard explanation for the decline of the Indus Valley culture has always been that it really was destroyed by marauding Indo-Europeans—specifically, the tribal Aryans who went on to produce Hinduism's most holy scriptures, the Vedas. Even scholars who wrote before the rise of the Goddess movement alluded to the "feminine" spirit which seems to animate the Indus remains.[39]

So why does the Indus culture play such a small role in Goddess books? Perhaps it is too little known in the West, although one would expect that writers diligent enough to familiarize themselves with prehistoric Malta and Çatal Hüyük would encounter it sooner or later (particularly Gadon, who has published articles on Bengali art). On the other hand, perhaps the underlying weakness of the case for an Indus Goddess culture is so obvious that no one wishes to raise the subject and invite instant refutation.

Was this a Goddess-worshipping culture at all? The argument here would rest largely on the myriads of female figurines. These are subject to the same difficulties of interpretation as those found elsewhere. The problem is compounded this time because the Indus female figurines are of distinctly crude quality by comparison to the other artifacts, which is something we should hardly expect if they are representations of the Great Goddess. Some archaeologists have suggested that they represent the devotional activities of the lower classes only, but this presumes a social hierarchy which is supposed to be out of character for a pre-Aryan Goddess culture.   On the other hand, these figures may be good candidates for Peter Ucko's observation that most small figurines around the world are simply dolls, are intended for girls, and tend to be in female form themselves.[40] Of the finer artistic pieces which have been found, the majority actually have male subjects. One of them has been dubbed "the priest-king" for the aspect of authoritative tranquillity it seems to convey. Some of the illustrations on the clay seals appear to represent mythological or cultic scenes; most of these center on male figures.[41]

Still other features of this culture seem to contradict the utopian character which is supposed to pervade a Goddess civilization. Excavation has shown that the Indus cities were repeatedly ruined by floods; each time, they were rebuilt according to exactly the same town plan as previously. Further, the bricks with which the two cities—hundreds of miles apart—were built are all of the same, standardized dimensions. Such features betray a surprising degree of inflexibility, and this strongly suggests an authoritarian structure capable of imposing the necessary regulations. The dwellings are, in fact, not all the same size; some class distinction was present.

Even though it generally passes unnoticed, the Indus Valley civilization provides yet another example of the pattern we find when we investigate the alleged ancient Goddess cultures. The usual superficial signs are there, from the masses of female figurines to a destructive Aryan invasion. Once again, however, a close look at the facts is every bit as damaging to the story of the Goddess as any marauding tribe was to Harappa.

CRETE

Lastly, we come to Crete, the capstone of the Goddess's tale of ancient glories. It is not only the Neolithic culture of Crete which is claimed for the Goddess, as in our preceding examples, but also the mature Bronze Age civilization nicknamed for the legendary King Minos. The "Minoans" flourished from approximately 3000 until

1100 BC, when Indo-European Greeks from the mainland decisively imposed themselves and their culture on the island. For the true believers, Minoan Crete clinches the argument that Goddess-worship promotes egalitarian prosperity, sexual equality, and peace; moreover, it gives us a moving insight into what we lost when we fell into patriarchy. Here, "the great universal civilization of the ancient world reached its apogee" (Davis); Crete illustrates the "essential difference" when the Goddess reigned supreme over a war-free society (Eisler); it was the "fulfillment and flowering" of woman-centered culture, "a free, joyous society, where people lived in peace and in harmony with nature" (Gadon).[42]

There can be little doubt that the Cretan finds are entrancing; many writers on the subject, of various ideological stripes, describe with evident enthusiasm the extraordinary quality of the sculpture, murals and architecture, and the image of a pleasant and comfortable life which they conjure up. Still, we must remain prosaic enough to measure the claims of the Goddess movement against the actual evidence one more time.

This time, the evidence is abundant. Crete has been subject to sustained archaeological investigation for a century now; indeed, one is tempted to think that nowhere other than the Holy Land has there been a higher density of archaeologists per square mile than in this Mediterranean island. As a result, a fairly standard scheme has been established for ancient Cretan history: first, an "Early Minoan" period beginning with the mining of copper and the smelting of bronze, perhaps as far back as 3000 BC; then a "Middle Minoan" era, marked by the construction of great palaces in cities like Knossos, Phaistos, and Mallia, from about 2200 BC; and finally, a "Late Minoan" stage, beginning between 1500 and 1400, in which Greek influence is clearly present, although a good deal of continuity in Cretan culture remains apparent. The transition from Middle to Late seems to have been marked by a double calamity. There was widespread devastation caused by tidal waves from the volcanic explosion on nearby Thera around 1500 BC, and this was followed by the successful invasions of the Mycenaean Greeks.

The great advantage we have in Crete as opposed to our previous cases is the fact that, in addition to a wealth of physical remains, we do possess some written sources of information. Crete was not an isolated outpost; it was part of the busy world of the Aegean region, and it figures numerous times in early Greek literature. Moreover, there are readable documents from Crete itself. Tablets inscribed in a form of writing known as Linear B were recovered from the "Palace of Minos" in Knossos, dating from the Late Minoan period. Eventually, it was discovered that the Linear B tablets were written in an early form of the Greek language; this was confirmed by the later discovery of more Linear B documents in Greece itself. The Linear B symbols are derived from an earlier Minoan script known as Linear A; this probably represents the native Cretan language, but it remains undeciphered.

So, what does this wealth of evidence tell us? We must acknowledge at the outset that some conventional scholars have indeed interpreted the Cretan relics in ways which support some of the claims of the Goddess movement. In *The Gate of Horn*, Rachel Levy portrayed Minoan Crete as a crucial channel through which her neolithic Mother Goddess cult was preserved and passed on, to become the foundation of Greek mystery religions. Jacquetta Hawkes followed this up with *Dawn of the Gods* (1968), an in-depth application of Levy's theory to Crete and Mycenaean Greece.[43] Less extreme examples occur in sources like R. F. Willetts' *Civilization of Ancient Crete*, which, with appropriate reservations, ultimately leans towards interpreting Minoan culture as a goddess-worshipping matriarchy.[44] Can we, however, accurately identify Crete as a Goddess culture in the sense that Eisler and Gadon do? They assume that the original settlers of Crete brought the Goddess with them from the mainland; since we have not found her there, however, we must consider the Cretan evidence as much as possible on its own.

For the Early and Middle Minoan periods, we face the same situation as we did in our previous examples. There are many statuettes of female figures, seals and signet rings featuring women, and the famous mural in which rows of men, some raising their arms and others bearing vessels, converge on a single woman. There are, however, no decipherable written records to indicate what any of these images mean. The same is true of some male representations, including a diminutive masculine figure who appears to be descending from the sky on some seals and signet rings: child of the Goddess, dwarf god, god in the distance? No one knows.

The images themselves tell us much less than we might wish. Except for the occasional nude, the female figures are always dressed like ordinary Cretan women, with long skirts, tight jackets, and bare breasts; no clear signs of majesty or divinity mark one off from another. The lady in the center of the famous mural could be a goddess, a priestess, a queen, or a warehouse manager; there is no way to know. The even more famous statuettes of women holding snakes are just as resistant to our questions—we cannot even be sure whether the woman or the snake was the more important element in the mind of the artist, let alone whether the figurine is a goddess image, a votive offering, a magical implement, or a decoration.

When we turn to the written records, the evidence becomes more complex. The Greek sources attribute Cretan origins to, not one, but several distinct goddesses. Willetts demonstrates that the goddesses Britomartis, Diktynna, Eileithyia, and Leto had distinctive attributes and cult centers in Crete, and in some cases on the mainland as well. Ariadne, the Cretan princess who aids Theseus against the Minotaur in the Greek myth, may well have been modeled on a native Cretan goddess cult. Finally, according to Homer, the goddess Demeter and her Eleusinian mysteries originated in Crete; certainly Demeter was a popular goddess during the post-Minoan, Greek era on the island.[45] Gods figure as well, although less commonly. The most striking example is Hesiod's story of Zeus's birth on Crete, which again may reflect an earlier, native Cretan cult. Cretans also apparently believed that Zeus died and was buried on the island, which further suggests that the Cretan "Zeus" was not originally the same deity as the Olympian king at all.[46]

The Linear B tablets, our only written evidence from Crete itself, also attest a polytheistic system of gods and goddesses. Besides being residences for heads of state, Cretan palaces were great storage centers for agricultural produce and other goods; no other palaces in the world at this time gave over so much of their space to warehousing. The tablets are essentially records of receipts, inventories, and disbursements. They do, however, mention a number of divinities, male and female, by name and with indications of rank. This is intriguing information, because the divine roster includes gods and goddesses familiar from the Greek pantheon—including Poseidon, Zeus, Athena, Hera, and Ares—as well as others who may have been native to Crete.[47] Both the god Poseidon and the goddess identified as Potnia were titular owners of large estates with employees and slaves.[48] Thus, the Linear B records confirm that Cretans worshipped goddesses, and may strengthen the possibility that some goddesses in the Greek pantheon had Minoan origins. On the other hand, the plurality of goddesses and the presence of powerful gods militates against the sort of monotheistic Goddess religion which we have been told to expect.

This situation highlights the particular difficulty posed by the written sources. Precisely because the Linear B records, Homer, Hesiod and the others are all Greek, their usefulness in the reconstruction of Minoan religion is open to debate. If we assume that these writings provide fundamentally accurate descriptions of Minoan religion, we must conclude that the Cretans were polytheists, with many gods and goddesses rather than one supreme Goddess. In the story of the Goddess, however, the Greeks have been assigned membership in the villainous Indo-European tidal wave, the moral equivalent of the Thera explosion. If we therefore dismiss this written evidence as the work of patriarchal Greeks, Minoan religion recedes into the same opaque mist as that of Çatal Hüyük. Either way, we are left once again without a solid foundation for the claims of the Goddess.

So we turn to our next question: was Minoan society a paragon of sexual and social equality? For its time, and by conventional standards, it may have been. On the evidence of Cretan art, particularly those murals which show groups and community activities, there is no doubt that women participated extensively in public life. In some cases we see groups of women dancing in public; in others, priestesses, in the company of male priests and/or attendants, officiate at sacrifices.

One particular mural features a sort of grandstand scene in which most members of the crowd are male, but one small section is made up of women, and another group of females occupies what appears to be a front row of balcony seats. It is, of course, impossible to discern whether this arrangement is analogous to the elite box seats of modern arenas, to the women's balcony at the back of an Orthodox synagogue, or simply to the voluntary aggregation of same-sex friends. Since the men and the women are each grouped together, some sex-based differential may be present, but we do not know what it was. On the other hand, the conventions of Minoan art dictated that men's skin was painted in a ruddy shade and women's in white; given this rule, the grouping of the sexes may simply have been the easiest and tidiest way to portray this particular crowd scene.

Against this artistic evidence we must set the remarkable discovery and excavation of a Middle Minoan temple by Yannis Sakellarakis and Efi Sapouna-Sakellarakis, as described in *National Geographic*'s issue of February 1981.[49] The temple was apparently destroyed by an earthquake; from the pottery found in the ruins, the archaeologists were able to date the destruction around 1700 BC, too early for any patriarchal influence from the Greek mainland. This report has been controversial, primarily because the earthquake seems to have caught the temple personnel in the midst of a human sacrifice: the bones of a young man were found on an altar, in a position indicating that he had been bound, with an ornate bronze blade still in place. This grisly discovery has been difficult to accept for those who celebrate the Minoans, including Riane Eisler.[50]

More important to us here, however, is the fact that not only the victim's bones were found—three other people were caught in the temple's collapse. The remains of one are too badly damaged to permit identification. Of the other two, one is male and one female. Nothing distinctive was found with regard to the female, who was probably a temple functionary of some kind, but the male carried two badges of office: a silver and iron ring (iron, as the authors remark, was rare and precious in the Bronze Age) and a finely worked seal, bearing a scene of a man poling a boat. Inescapably, the report concludes that this was the officiating priest who had actually conducted the sacrifice. The relevance of their find to our inquiry is equally inescapable: even with a woman present, a male priest was in charge of this desperate Middle Minoan ceremony, and a male was the victim. Human sacrifice was not common in Crete, and we must presume that it was something of a last resort with much at stake. Nothing would be left to chance in such circumstances, least of all the credentials of the officiant and the appropriateness of the victim.

We are left with compelling evidence for a male priesthood in Crete, perhaps independent of priestesses, prior to patriarchal Greek influence from the mainland. This evidence is a critical blow to any theory of a matriarchal or gynocentric character in Minoan culture. We must not extend the implications of a single site too far, but to find four Minoans "caught in the act" probably tells us much more about real life in Crete than any number of artistic creations do. The fact that both priest and victim were men suggests not a matriarchy, but a selective valuation of the male, at least in time of crisis.

Do we know any more of the social hierarchy generally? Eisler argues that no known Minoan relics point to cases of abject poverty (which, almost by definition, are unlikely to leave much physical evidence in any case). Crete may well have had an unusually high level of prosperity, however. As Renfrew has pointed out, the addition of the grape and the olive to Crete's agricultural repertoire brought new tracts of land under cultivation and produced large crops for a relatively small investment of time and labor, providing a strong economic base for the entire island.[51]

On the other hand, excavations have indeed revealed indications of class stratification. Such stratification is often said to be typical of Bronze Age societies as such. Bronze itself, an alloy of tin and copper which required significant advances in metallurgy, could never be produced in sufficient quantities for all; it therefore became something of a status symbol, as well as prompting a small-scale arms race.[52] In general, Bronze Age societies seem to exhibit a fairly strong degree of craft specialization, a further indication of social hierarchy.

Class stratification in Crete is confirmed by the many excavations of Minoan living quarters. These differ substantially in size; even for the Early Minoan period, Hawkes could refer to the "well-to-do" who lived in multi-roomed dwellings with plaster walls, patronized the craftsmen who produced specialty items and decorative luxuries, marked their personal property with seals, and were buried in family tombs accompanied by prized possessions.[53] By the Middle Minoan period, Cretan houses varied from the great palaces of Knossos, Phaistos, and Mallia to the villas of a landowning nobility, the "upper-class" urban homes adjacent to the palaces, and the smaller dwellings of towns and rural areas.[54]

The function of the Cretan palaces demands further attention here. As we already noted, the major palaces were not only elite dwelling places but warehouses for the collection and redistribution of agricultural produce and manufactured goods. Producers marked their contributions with seals, and palace bureaucrats tracked the arrival, storage, and disbursement of the goods on the clay tablets mentioned above, even noting some cases of arrears. The whole system is an impressive display of centralized authority over economic life.

The Linear B tablets tell us, therefore, a certain amount about who was who in Late Minoan society (just as the Linear A records probably would for the Middle Minoan, if we could read them; they appear to have served the same purposes). What we discover is, in essence, a well-developed form of the typical chiefdom society, highly stratified, with priority given to the male. As Hawkes reports, the chief or king was identified by the term *wanax* and his queen by the feminine derivative *wanassa*. The wanax held a large estate of his own, and let out other land for the use of nobles known as *telestai*; he also had a "Leader of the War Host" and a circle of court retainers at his disposal. In addition, there were groups of lower-class collective landowners who, according to the tablets, could and did assert their rights when necessary.[55] Interestingly, the Linear B tablets found at Pylos in mainland Greece confirm the high status of males in the system now in force: the official allocation of wheat was given to men, women, and children in a ratio of 5:2:1.[56]

The pressing question is, again, how much of this information from the Late Minoan period can be applied to the earlier, pre-Greek stages of Cretan civilization. The layout of the Middle Minoan palaces and the close similarity between the Linear A and Linear B tablets present a strong case that the essential socio-economic system was not altered greatly between the Middle and Late Minoan periods; even if the identity of the people at the top of the hierarchy had changed, it is unlikely that the basic structure itself had been radically transformed. This would indicate a chiefdom society with male rulership for at least the Middle Minoan period as well.

The contrary view, held by the Goddess movement and by some Minoan experts, is that before the incursion by mainland Greeks, Crete was an actual matriarchy. There is, in fact, very little evidence for or against this claim; the Minoans were, by all indications, utterly uninterested in recording the names, faces, or exploits of their leaders. Those who argue in favor of a Cretan matriarchy, rule by a queen or queen/priestess, do so primarily by extrapolating from those artistic remains in which one or more female figures are prominently featured, and by assuming that a supreme Goddess would require a female representative at the top of her earthly hierarchy.[57]

If we leave out the Linear B material and Greek literature, the evidence against a Cretan matriarchy is almost equally soft (although hard evidence *against* something is notoriously difficult to produce). No identifiable portrait or monument of a ruler of either sex has been found. The main line of argument here is simply that a matriarchy would be such an extraordinary exception to what we know of the ancient world that we need more than just inferences from art to support it. All the other Bronze Age cultures and chiefdom societies we know had male rulership as the norm; other civilizations had prominent goddesses without conferring ultimate practical authority on actual women. Why, in the absence of clear proof, should we believe that Crete was so very different?

The nearest possible analogue to Minoan society, if we wish to pursue that approach, appears to be ancient Egypt. There was trade between the two nations from the Early Minoan period onward, and similarities between their artistic traditions and the economic role of the palaces have prompted debate over which culture influenced the other. Goddesses, notably Isis, figure strongly in Egyptian religion. Women are prominent in Egyptian art, including scenes of public events, and some forms of matrilineal inheritance in Egyptian society have been conclusively proven. At certain points in Egyptian history, the throne itself was passed through the female line. The actual Pharaoh, however, was almost always a man; typically, he inherited by marrying the crown princess, thus grounding the tradition of brother-sister marriages in the Egyptian royal house. The most famous female Pharaoh, Hatshepsut, dressed as a man for formal occasions and was so portrayed in her iconography. Again, despite some interesting details on sex roles, we find no sign of anything approaching either matriarchy or an equal interchange of male and female rulers.[58]

In the absence of conclusive evidence one way or the other, it seems most advisable to side with the typical rather than the unprecedented, or simply to confess our ignorance.

Finally, we turn to the question of war and peace. It is clear beyond doubt that the Minoans were not the creators of a warlike culture. Their towns and cities were truly unfortified, open to entry. Prior to the Late Minoan and Greek periods, we find evidence of weapons being used for hunting rather than fighting, and the artistic relics contain virtually no commemoration of battle whatsoever. Cities and palaces were destroyed several times between 2200 and 1500 BC, but such devastation seems to be the result of earthquakes rather than human conflict.

This impression changes by the Late Minoan era. The destruction of the palaces between 1500 and 1400 BC, and again later, does appear to be deliberate. The Linear B tablets identify military retainers of the king and list inventories of war supplies; Greek-style warrior graves in Knossos date from this period as well. All this appears to indicate that the introduction of a warrior society coincided with the ascendancy of mainland Greek influence on the island, probably as a result of invasion and conquest. Beforehand, however, it seems certain that Minoan Crete comprised an uncommonly peaceful society, largely free of both internal strife and the threat of external invasion.

The Goddess myth ascribes all this to her. A civilization worshipping a Mother Goddess, ruled by actual mothers who loved their children, is presumed to be almost incapable of creating a culture of conflict. An egalitarian society in which wealth was shared on a non-competitive basis would provide no grounds for envy and no reward for conquest. What could be more natural than to assume that a Goddess culture would be at peace? We have found, however, no compelling evidence for either the Great Mother Goddess or a matriarchal political system. We must ask, therefore, whether Crete's peaceful character can be explained in some other way.

As it happens, this is not difficult. Crete benefited from several fortuitous factors which other cultures did not share. Internally, it was large enough and fertile enough to support a growing population for an extended period of time, so that conflict over land seems not to have been an issue. The relatively homogeneous population probably minimized the risk of local conflict, as did a well-entrenched tradition of communal living dating back to the neolithic.[59]

Externally, Crete spent much of the Minoan period in a comparative power vacuum. Its nearest neighbors were much smaller islands. The mainland cultures of Egypt, the Levant, Anatolia, and Greece, all of which traded with Crete, were for political reasons either uninterested in or incapable of mounting a serious threat to the island. Several ancient sources testify to an impressive Cretan navy, which could have prevented any major incursion without difficulty. According to one widespread theory, the Greek invasion in the Late Minoan period succeeded at least in part because it followed the devastation created by the explosion of Thera. Prior to these catastrophes, it seems, Crete was peaceful primarily because, in terms of geography, demographics, and politics, it was lucky.

Attractive and evocative as it is, Minoan Crete fails to provide us with a utopian Goddess culture. Even if it did, this would now have to be viewed as exceptional, as an anomaly of history, given the outcome of our earlier investigations. As it is, however, this long search for the Goddess in antiquity has come to an end empty-handed.

THE FINDINGS OF OUR INVESTIGATION in this chapter indicate that none of the societies most often cited as authentic ancient Goddess cultures actually conforms to our expectations. Not a single one provides clear evidence of a single, supreme female deity; not a single one exhibits the signs of matriarchal rule, or even of serious political power-sharing between the sexes; not a single one displays with any surety the enlightened attitude towards social egalitarianism, non-violent interpersonal and interstate relations, and ecological sensitivity which we have been led to anticipate. In each of these cases, the story of the Goddess is a fabrication in defiance of the facts.

The further question—whether these civilizations located in such different times and places are really manifestations of a single Goddess culture—is now moot. There may well be some common features linking some of these societies, but these features have nothing to do with the Goddess. On the other hand, most recent findings reinforce the contrary view: civilizations tended to arise independently of each other in the ancient world, and generalizations about them should be avoided unless the evidence is truly compelling.

It is now the Goddess movement itself which needs to be explained, not the ancient civilizations. How, in the absence of archaeological evidence which would suggest it, did the modern idea of the Goddess ever arise? What accounts for its increasing popularity among non-specialists when specialists have long since turned their backs on it? And how do the more authoritative Goddess writers cope with such uncooperative evidence as they propagate their movement?

Questions like these will occupy us for the remainder of this book. Clearly, our approach to them must be guided by the recognition that the tale of the Goddess is neither an established fact nor a credible hypothesis, but a myth, a normative story imbued with the worldview and values of a particular religious orientation. The line between scholarly theory and religious belief has clearly been crossed, for instance, when Riane Eisler describes the Paleolithic female figurines as "important psychic records" and goes on to claim that the identification of the earth with the Mother Goddess "was central to our lost psychic heritage," all in the first three pages of *The Chalice and the Blade*. This psychic historiography is what permits the leaps of imaginative speculation and the arguments from silence which permeate so much of the Goddess literature. Goddess writers themselves are fond of quoting French feminist Monique Wittig's advice: "Remember. Make an effort to remember. Or, failing that, invent."[60] The full import of this guidance is now becoming apparent.

That being the case, we must inquire further into the nature and dynamics of the contemporary Goddess religion. As I suggested in the Introduction, Goddess spirituality appears to be a recent flowering of the Romantic reaction to the rationalistic materialism of the Enlightenment, which nevertheless borrows and builds upon the latter's assault on the Judeo-Christian tradition. In the next chapter we shall explore more fully the implications of our findings and observations so far.

4

The Foundations of "Thealogy"

> Goddess, *then, can become our broom, our flying Night-mare, carrying Wild wanderers beyond the dulling day-dreams programmed by the perpetual soap operas of the sado-state.*
>
> Mary Daly

FROM ONE POINT OF VIEW, it might seem that this book could conclude right now. If the story of the Goddess were just one academic theory competing with others to explain the origin and development of Western religion and culture, considerations like those raised in the previous chapter might be enough to eliminate it as a serious contender; it would be nothing more than a minor curiosity in the history of scholarship. It has been clear from the outset, however, that Goddess books are not simply about the history of religion and culture; they are, in and of themselves, expressions of a particular religious mindset which shapes both their presuppositions and their conclusions. Assessing their claims against our current knowledge of ancient history, therefore, is only the first step in the full examination of the significance of this new religion. Once we recognize the Goddess books as religious literature rather than historical scholarship as it is normally understood, we must seek to clarify the implications of the religion these books are intended to propagate. Only then may we embark on the larger quest to assign to Goddess spirituality its proper place in the unfolding history of the modern West.

GODDESS BOOKS AS RELIGIOUS LITERATURE

The centrally religious (or at least ideological) character of the Goddess books is clearly evident in a feature we noted earlier: the Goddess myth which they express is both descriptive and prescriptive. The purpose of going to such great lengths in portraying the ancient matriarchal utopias is, quite explicitly, to use them as models for contemporary social reform. As Sjöö expressed most clearly, "it is necessary for all of us to conceive that this female-oriented creative-collectivism existed."[1] This statement of the necessity of belief is almost creedal; Goddess books, accordingly, should be seen as professions of faith, and their authors as neopagan evangelists. Innovative terms like Eisler's promotion of "cultural transformation theory" bring a more neutral vocabulary to the cause, but the issue remains the same.

Now that we have seen how the alleged Goddess cultures have been fabricated from the scant existing, often falsified, evidence, the relationship between these two themes appears in a new light. It is not, as might first appear to be the case, that the Goddess writers' descriptions of the past generate and sustain their prescriptions for the future; on the contrary, their designs on the future have shaped and skewed their presentations of the past. Factual accuracy in the writing of history is sacrificed to the demands of contemporary cultural politics. While there is always a likelihood that a writer's immediate concerns will inadvertently influence what he or she writes about other times, the Goddess literature is marked by the pervasive and systematic way in which the past is made to serve the needs of the present, even when the actual evidence is highly uncooperative. It is not a matter of sloppy research, but of a precise and deliberate stance on the nature of truth and historical methods.

Guided by a faith which blatantly overrides facts, the Goddess writers often seem impervious to criticism on factual grounds. Their response to such criticism can be illuminating. On the one hand, we sometimes encounter the gender feminist variation on the *ad hominem* argument, which we might designate the *ad virum* argument: any criticism coming from a man must automatically be an exercise in gender politics, and therefore is not to be taken seriously. Marianne Ferguson's textbook *Women and Religion* contains the brief subsection entitled "Critique of Contemporary Goddess Religions," in which all such critique is dismissed as the hostile reaction of male clergy and academics eager to preserve their elite status and power over women.[2] In the same vein, Riane Eisler condescendingly suggests that a male, non-feminist archaeologist—even one as amenable as James Mellaart—could not really be expected to grasp the significance of his own discoveries from the Goddess cultures.[3]

A second defense is more prominent among Wiccans and other actual practitioners of Goddess religion. Some of these writers are willing to concede the factual weakness of the arguments in favor of ancient Goddess cultures, on the grounds that such issues are beside the point in any case. As early as 1979, Margot Adler was writing that many neopagans had already given up on the idea that the ancient matriarchies really existed.[4] She recited some of the basic arguments in a tone of amused tolerance, but emphasized that the real criterion by which to judge witchcraft and its sister faiths is the quality of religious experience they provide to their members today, and the stimulus to contemporary social reform which the Goddess myth can provide.[5] Virtually none of the Goddess books deals directly with the factual challenges which can be made to their story. Instead, we are most likely to encounter one or both of these defenses of the Goddess: the irrelevance of men and their opinions, or the irrelevance of truth itself.

Since Goddess literature is essentially prescriptive, clothing a political agenda in the language of historiography, it is no surprise to discover that its real purpose is not intellectual persuasion but personal conversion. Even Ferguson's book is well designed to serve as a tool of recruitment. Discussion questions following its chapters include such entries as these: "Compose a two-sentence prayer addressed to the mother goddess. How does it resemble or differ from a prayer addressed to a male deity?" "Create your own religious ritual to commemorate a rite of passage for a woman," and, "How can women work together to ensure the benefits of salvation in this world for one another?"[6] We do well to recall that this is a textbook for religion courses in universities—and to wonder how easily an orthodox Jew or Christian, or a male for that matter, could pass such a course.

The Goddess is more than just a female replacement for the biblical God—she represents, as her followers often affirm, a fundamentally different approach to religion and life. As Cynthia Eller noted, the Goddess is "not just God in a skirt."[7] What, then, are the primary features of the religion which is being propagated in Goddess literature?

The Goddess as Divinity

In Goddess literature, two qualities of the Goddess stand out starkly. First, of course, the Goddess is female; this is the crucial element in the movement as a whole. The point needs to be emphasized, however, that it is the Goddess's exclusively female features which define her. Menstruation, childbirth, and lactation are some of the central images through which the Goddess is linked to human women and to nature as a whole with its cycles of growth. Female physiology is the essential, irreducible manifestation of the Goddess, as any survey of vaginal symbolism in the work of Goddess-oriented artists will amply demonstrate.[8]

Does this mean that Goddess devotees are against belief in male gods? Not entirely. Certainly, the overthrow of ancient Goddess cultures is attributed to patriarchal tribes who worshipped masculine deities. Today, however, pagan male gods often find a place within Goddess circles. These gods are really, in an exclusive and limiting way, male—they have phalli, and they can relate to the Goddess as consort, son, or subject.[9]

The god who is opposed by the Goddess movement today is specifically the God of biblical monotheism. As Gadon says, "Monotheism, the belief that there is only one deity, was to prove an even more implacable foe of Goddess religion than the polytheism of the sky gods."[10] The kind of monotheism claimed by the Goddess movement itself is not absolute; even as they insist on the singularity of the Goddess, the major authors affirm the pagan polytheistic deities as valuable images or representations of the one true Goddess herself.[11] On the other hand, Goddess writers attack the absolute monotheism of the biblical tradition, the insistence that there is one God and no other.

This attack is motivated in part by the traditional descriptions of the biblical God in masculine terms. Languages which make gender distinctions generally refer to God in the masculine, and "Father" is one of his most prominent epithets. This does not make the biblical God male in the sense that phallic gods like Pan are. Biblical Hebrew, like French, has only two grammatical genders. When referring to persons, it commonly uses the feminine exclusively for females, and the masculine for everything else—not only males, but mixed groups and indeterminate entities. Nonetheless, according to most feminist writers, the fact that the one and only God is designated by masculine terminology means that the feminine has been excluded from the divine. This exclusion is held to be the basis and rationale for sexual inequality in society; in the words of Mary Daly's famous non-sequitur, "If God is male, then the male is God."[12]

The second issue goes beyond gender parity in the Godhead. Both advocates and opponents agree that Mother-Goddess imagery produces a substantially different understanding of the divine than Father-God imagery. The crucial difference is rooted in the biological facts of parenthood. A human father's role in conception is momentary, and his relationship with his children may be somewhat abstract; in some situations, he cannot be certain whether or not a particular child is his. A mother's role, on the other hand, involves a more direct physical relationship with the child, whom she carries and nurtures through pregnancy, bears, nurses, and usually raises.

Applied to theology, this biological parent symbolism undergirds different understandings of the relationship between the divine and the natural world. The Father-God of the Bible created by speaking; the physical universe came into existence at his behest and according to his will, but he remains essentially distinct from it. The Mother-Goddess gives birth to life and remains organically and tangibly connected to the earth; she is within all, not beyond all. Here, the Goddess movement firmly aligns itself with the conception of the divine as naturally immanent within the physical universe.[13]

In doing so, Goddess devotees reject not one but two alternative conceptions: both the transcendent God of the Bible and the thoroughgoing materialism which would deny the divine altogether. On the one hand, the monotheistic affirmation of God's transcendence means that the world is not God—it is no more, and no less, than the contingent object and outcome of his creative power. On the other, the materialistic rejection of God's very existence means that the physical universe is simply the chance result of random forces and accidents, an object with no maker.

In contrast to both of these, the Goddess represents the notion that the world is intrinsically divine, because the Goddess herself is immanent in all existing things. From here, it is but a short step to the "eco-feminist" contention that Mother Earth is alive, a concept commonly expressed through the name for the ancient Greek earth-goddess, Gaia. The underlying disposition here is to regard the physical world not as a mechanism (with or without a maker) but as an organism, a living being in which each individual element is an intrinsic part of the whole. These basic presuppositions of immanence and organicism shape the Goddess writers' stances on other salient issues.

The Goddess and Human Beings

The notion of divine immanence has a fairly specific and direct application to human beings—we ourselves are all divine, inasmuch as the Goddess is already present within us. We are not merely the accidental outcome of random natural processes, as the popular materialistic understanding of evolution suggests; nor are we merely the image of God, the approximate and finite likeness of an infinite being (even though marred by sin), as the biblical tradition has it (Genesis 1:26; 5:1-3). No: "Thou art Goddess!" and nothing less, they tell themselves and each other. After giving instructions for a ritual of Self-Blessing, Zsuzsanna Budapest writes, "This is what the Goddess symbolizes—the Divine within women and all that is female within the universe. We *must not* underestimate the importance of this concept."[14] The thousands of participants at the Reimagining Conference cannot be accused of underestimating this particular point.

If we dwell on it for a moment, however, some of its implications become clearer. The idea that humans are ultimately divine is simply the logical outcome of a full-blown commitment to divine immanence. The version of immanence preferred within the feminist spirituality movement, however, focuses particularly on the organic and biological processes of life, as we have just seen; matching the cycles of nature with the cycles of female physiology is fundamental to an understanding of the Goddess. Our divinity is within our biology.

The logical outcome of this notion is an emphasis on biological distinctions. Because the Goddess is both immanent and specifically female, it is only to be expected that women will be more attuned to her than will men. The more moderate members of the Goddess movement do not draw this conclusion consistently; Riane Eisler coined her term "gylany" as a way of sidestepping this issue, even as she celebrated the advocacy of "feminine values" by a few exceptional men like Pythagoras and Jesus.[15] Budapest, on the other hand, opposes "teaching our magic and our craft to men until the equality of the sexes is a reality." What she is willing to teach is a ritual in which young men pledge their service to "life and the carriers of Life, women"; they recite to their mothers, "You are truly the Goddess manifest among us."[16] In *Gyn/Ecology* and *Pure Lust*, Mary Daly adopted a similar, radical stance of female separatism. Monica Sjöö followed Elizabeth Gould Davis's argument that women's biological characteristics make them spiritually superior to men.[17]

Either way, this emphasis on the organic basis of the divinity within, along with the organic nature of the physical world as a whole, suggests that our biological characteristics are the most important things about us. It follows that any worthwhile community must be defined and structured in biological, organic terms—either precise gender parity, on the assumption that femaleness and maleness are distinctive and specific forces which must be held in balance, or outright matriarchy, assigning functional supremacy to those who are best suited to it. In a context other than the Goddess movement, such considerations could be applied to other biological categories, such as race or ethnicity.

Once again, the Goddess movement sets itself apart from both the biblical tradition and pure materialism. Although the Bible frequently describes differences in sex roles, the notion of human beings reflecting the divine "image" is applied to both sexes (but to no other species) in Genesis 1:27. In Genesis 2, the bifurcation of the original *'adam* (human being) into two sexes (*'ish*, man, and *'ishshah*, woman) who belong together as "one flesh" makes the same point in a different way—their common humanity is ultimately of more significance than their sexual differentiation. It is their humanity, their shared likeness to God, that distinguishes their high status in the created order. The basis of the covenant community in the Old Testament is kinship, loosely defined as descent from Abraham by means of sexual procreation (although other people are incorporated at various points). In the New Testament, the essential community is the Church, open to voluntary affiliation by both sexes and by all races and nations.

Between the lines of their polemic against biblical religion, it is clear that Goddess writers reject the stance of secular materialism as well. Both materialists and neopagans share the view that humanity is part of nature and the product of natural processes, and not distinct from the rest of creation. A purely materialistic reading of the situation suggests that humanity is, like all life, an accident—an unusually complicated form of pond scum. Goddess spirituality insists that the natural processes which produce life are themselves the life cycle of the Goddess, and that all who live are innately divine as a result. Materialists might form practical alliances to achieve common goals—the "social contract" theory of statecraft being one example—but they would logically tend towards individualism rather than organic connection.

Goddess writers typically attribute this materialistic denigration of humanity and the physical world to the aftereffects of the Judeo-

Christian tradition. By asserting the transcendence of God, they say, the Bible made the world into an inanimate object, a machine; then, when belief in the biblical God retreated in the face of scientific progress, the soulless machine with its individual cogs was all that seemed to remain.[18]

The Goddess and the Truth

The belief that the divine is immanent in the world at large, and in ourselves in particular, has some direct implications for issues of truth and knowledge which we noted earlier. While this is not the place to explore the specifics of sensory perception or philosophical episte-mology, we can once again identify some basic issues which distin-guish the Goddess movement from biblical religion and secular materialism.

If we begin by supposing that the Goddess is immanent, it seems only sensible to conclude that she is most accessible to us within ourselves. The whole point, for many in the movement, is to discover divinity within the self and to encounter it in female form. Gadon highlights the appeal of this approach by titling one of her chapters, "The Goddess Within: A Source of Empowerment for Women." To focus on the Goddess within is, at the same time, to affirm a distinc-tive approach to knowledge of the divine. Essentially, the Goddess is to be encountered through intuition and spiritual experience, and to be known intimately rather than factually and logically.

There are two general ways in which this knowledge, or state of awareness, are typically pursued. Most prominent are the collective rituals practiced within small groups. Goddess rituals tend to focus on natural "holy days" (solstices and equinoxes, for example), and on the biological events of female life (childbirth, menstruation, and menopause). The vast majority of feminist spirituality groups adapt their rituals directly from Wicca, with the books of Zsuzsanna Budapest and Starhawk being the most widely accessible sources.[19] Although the language and techniques of traditional Western magic are often involved in these ceremonies, the emphasis in both Wiccan and Goddess circles tends to be upon the subjective effect of the rituals as they are performed, rather than any concrete results which might be expected from them afterwards. The spiritual experience brought about by the ritual itself is its own purpose and justification. Secondarily, the strengthening of the bonds within the ritual group, enhancing its organic sense of solidarity, is a frequently cited benefit.

Individual practice is also encouraged, however. In addition to ceremonies which are specifically designed to be celebrated alone, the inward quest is pursued through such mental techniques as visualization and meditation. Here, it is said, the Goddess can be encountered in her abode within the "Deep Self."[20] This insistence that the Goddess is within, and that she is best known through inward experience, illustrates the close affinity between the belief in divine immanence and the emphasis on personal experience, particularly of an emotional and intuitive type.

Once again, some distinguishing features of the Goddess movement become apparent. The paramount emphasis given to experiential, intuitive knowledge is very much at odds with an empirical, rationalistic approach to truth. A fully materialistic outlook would ascribe "reality" to those things which are physical enough to be counted and measured. The whole thrust of value-free science is that notions like justice and beauty do not physically exist in and of themselves, and are therefore not directly the business of the scientific endeavor. As we shall see, the Goddess movement's emphasis on immanence and intuition ties in with some broader feminist critiques of the "male" scientific orientation towards step-by-step logic, dissection, and analysis, as opposed to the "female" perspective, which focuses on holistic thinking, analogy, and synthesis.

If feminist spirituality is uncomfortable with empiricism and rationalism, it is even more hostile towards the biblical understanding of revelation. This understanding is rooted in the idea that a transcendent God is, by definition, largely unknowable through the sensory perceptions, rational speculations, and experiential intuitions of finite creatures. Both the "mind" and the "heart" may be involved in responding to revelation, but the revelation itself has its origin and source outside the created order—most especially, outside the self. The different neopagan and biblical approaches to ultimate knowledge reflect the difference between immanence and transcendence as the operative mode of the divine.

The Goddess and the Good

The same sort of distinction arises with respect to the question of moral standards. It might be expected at the outset that a perspective which emphasizes immanence and intuition would encourage a subjective approach to issues of right and wrong. This does turn out to be the case, to a large degree. Part of the liberation of women involves freeing them to make their own moral decisions on their own grounds, without interference from abstract laws and principles or from the men who supposedly invent and enforce them. As Starhawk writes, "The immanent conception of justice is not based on rules or authority, but upon integrity, integrity of self and integrity of relationships."[21]

In matters of sexuality, for instance, Goddess writers encourage the individual to seek a broad spectrum of sexual experience as an exercise in freedom. More than that—since sex provides some of the most potent and explosive experiences many people ever undergo, it is one of the most highly prized routes to the encounter with the Goddess within. In Wiccan circles, the "Great Rite" of ritual intercourse is featured as the logical conclusion of this line of thinking.[22] Lesbianism and bisexuality are specifically encouraged in several Goddess books. Love of a woman, by either sex, is seen as a concrete experience of the love of the Goddess as well as a general broadening of sexual experience and power. Mary Daly has attracted criticism even from moderate feminists for her insistence that a woman who refuses to engage in lesbianism is in some way a token woman who cannot achieve a loving affirmation of the female. On the other hand, some strippers have dignified their profession by aligning themselves with the Goddess and her ancient temple prostitutes.[23]

There is a socio-political dimension to the sexual ethics of the Goddess movement as well. Daly's *Pure Lust*, Budapest's *Holy Book of Women's Mysteries*, Starhawk's *Dreaming the Dark*, and Eisler's *Sacred Pleasure* all emphasize two particular benefits they ascribe to sexual

liberation: that shared sex creates intimate bonds within the immediate group, reinforcing their organic unity; and that free sex strikes
a powerful blow against one of patriarchy's most repressive institutions, monogamous marriage. Thus, women's liberation is closely
linked to—and perhaps even dependent upon—the sexual revolution.

In the West, the institution of marriage is explicitly associated
with biblical religion. Judeo-Christian moral standards are held to
originate in the conscious will of God the transcendent creator. As
such, they are absolute rather than relative; right is right and wrong
is wrong, no matter how individuals happen to feel about it. In the
case of sex, it is held to be right and good within the institution of
monogamous heterosexual marriage, and to be wrong outside it, on
the grounds that the God who created humans as sexual beings willed
it so (Genesis 2:24; Exodus 20:14; Matthew 19:4-7). Interestingly,
after presenting her argument for sexual liberation, Starhawk offered
a somewhat defensive explanation of her own monogamous relationship.[24]

A more secular and materialistic approach to morality tends, like
the Goddess movement, towards relativism. Denial of the transcendent essentially eliminates any foundation for absolute moral standards. "Situation ethics," a sort of objective relativism, has been
characteristic of secular morality for at least the past generation. In
essence, it calls for individuals to calculate rationally the potential
benefits and harms which would likely result from any given course
of action at any given time.[25]   Sex is typically regarded as a physical
appetite to be satisfied according to the desires and tastes of the people
involved, with no larger issues at stake. "We hold the view that man's
personal self-interest is natural and good . . . [and] the belief that
morality should be based upon reason . . . Sex can be one of the most
profound and rewarding elements in the adventure of living . . . The
attempts at its suppression, however, are almost universally harmful,
both to the individuals involved and to society as a whole." So wrote
one of the most widely influential advocates of recreational sex and
freedom from religion, Hugh M. Hefner of *Playboy* magazine.[26]

While those involved in feminist spirituality agree with secularists in their opposition to transcendent moral absolutes, they tend to see this unspiritual and trivializing approach to free sex as demeaning and often exploitative. What, then, is the actual goal of the sexual revolution as Goddess writers see it? Starhawk, Eisler, and Gadon call for the full and free expression of what they consider a healthy eroticism to energize and humanize the process of social change. Budapest and Daly, on the other hand, insist that the first step must be the sexual liberation of women from men; this requires the restriction and elimination of patriarchal sexual expression, ranging from monogamy to pornography, from the public sphere at least.

Here, the Goddess movement is experiencing the same conflict as feminism generally. There has been a raging debate over whether feminists should side with the "religious right" in opposing pornography, or with the libertarians who oppose traditional restrictions on sexual activities of all kinds. On the one hand, Betty Friedan can give an interview to *Playboy*, welcome its support on issues like the legalization of abortion, and even pronounce the monthly centerfold "harmless."[27] Catharine MacKinnon, on the other hand, castigates the *Playboy* empire as the epitome of the co-optation and exploitation of women for male sexual gratification, all the more insidious because it is considered relatively respectable over against *Hustler* and its ilk.[28]

The Goddess and History

The Goddess movement is based on a distinctive view of history. Goddess literature posits a sort of three-stage scheme: a golden age of gynocentric Goddess cultures at the origins of human history; a relatively recent fall from glory into barbarous patriarchy; and an imminent New Age in which the true and foundational values of the Goddess civilization will be reasserted, saving us from violence and ecological disaster. The New Age represents a radical change from the present system, with new beliefs and values, and even new forms of awareness and spiritual perception.

This scheme, which I call the neopagan paradigm, allows us to make yet another set of comparisons. Secularism is usually wedded to belief in human progress—if we permit science to go its untrammeled way, it will gradually remove the greatest obstacles to human fulfillment and provide us with more and better goods and techniques as we proceed, although in and of itself progress has no fixed goal. Biblical religion is founded on the view that God does have an ultimate end in store for the universe as a whole and for every individual in particular; the timing and the manner of the end, however, are entirely his prerogatives.

All three points of view look for a happier future. They differ on whether we will reach it by continuing to progress on our present course, by adopting a revolutionary change in our beliefs and values, or by orienting ourselves towards a transcendent being who will achieve his own purposes in his own time.

WE HAVE NOW IDENTIFIED several characteristics of Goddess spirituality which distinguish it from biblical religion and from secular materialism. The Goddess movement espouses divine immanence, an intuitive and experiential approach to truth, a subjective style of moral relativism, and a view of history which I have dubbed the neopagan paradigm. It sets itself against traditional biblical religion, which affirms a transcendent creator and the consequent need for revelation, moral absolutism founded on the revealed will of the creator, and an eschatological view of the course and destination of history. Though the opposition is not always so sharp, the Goddess movement also presents itself as an alternative to secular materialism, which is characterized by a denial of the spiritual, an emphasis on empiricism and rationalism at the expense of feeling and intuition, an objective and value-free moral relativism, and a goal of continued progress in the same vein as we have come to know over the past two centuries.

At this point, it is clear why our quest for the origins of the Goddess must lead us to Romanticism. As we saw in the Introduction, the modern Western cultural world was created in two steps: the eighteenth-century Enlightenment, which unleashed the powers of modern science and relegated the Judeo-Christian religious perspective to the background; and the Romantic reaction, which sought new ways to restore the meaning, color, and significance to life which the rationalists—with their theories and their machines—seemed to have destroyed. The principles and values we have uncovered in the Goddess literature correspond in most respects to the Romantic worldview. Goddess spirituality, then, reveals itself as a new expression of the ongoing tension amongst the Biblical, rationalistic, and Romantic approaches to life and the social order.

Even before Romanticism, however, many of the threads which would be woven into the Goddess's tapestry were already in evidence. The Goddess movement speaks openly of its interest in magic and points to witchcraft as its forebear. Accordingly, we must go back even before the Enlightenment to familiarize ourselves with the Western occult tradition, if we wish to understand fully what today's feminist neopaganism actually entails.

PART II

MAGIC AND ROMANTICISM

5

European Magic and Occultism

*That which is above is like that which is below
and that which is below is like that which is above,
to achieve the wonders of the one thing.*

The Emerald Table of Hermes Trismegistus

OUR SEARCH for the real historical origins and forebears of
Goddess spirituality takes its cues from the movement itself. Goddess devotees look not only to primordial cultures
but, in more recent times, to witchcraft and the magical heritage as
precursors of their beliefs and practices. Now that we have seen the
general relationship between feminist neopaganism and Romanticism, we should also recall that neopaganism was a strong element in
Romanticism itself, and that this prompted a significant revival of
interest in traditional occultism during the nineteenth century. This
patrimony of occult thought and technique, often designated "the
esoteric tradition" by its modern partisans, is therefore a logical point
of entry into the history of those Western religious developments
that have borne fruit in the Goddess movement.

MAGIC AND THE OCCULT

The term "occult" often carries strong emotional overtones. It is frequently used to produce shivers in the hearer—shivers of fear and horror, or shivers of enticement and anticipation. The word itself means, quite simply, "hidden." Although there are many things which are hidden, "the occult" has come to be identified specifically with hidden matters of the mind and spirit, and secretive practices involving extraordinary powers.

This conventional notion of the occult overlaps, to a great extent, with the idea of magic. Most scholarly definitions of magic focus on the central idea of attempting to manipulate unseen forces to accomplish practical goals. In one classic formulation, the anthropologist Bronislaw Malinowski argued that "science" means achieving practical results through direct physical action (e.g., making water boil by heating it); "magic" means seeking practical results through indirect, immaterial, and sometimes supernatural means (e.g., making crops grow by chanting spells and invoking spirits of fertility); and "religion" means seeking fellowship with the divine, totally apart from practical results of any kind.[1]

From a more theological perspective, a certain amount of common ground between magic and religion has been recognized from the beginning. The invocation of unseen beings and forces is characteristic of both, and some magicians see their art as simply a practical application of religious principles.[2] Moreover, religious people often do expect some concrete benefits from their faith and allegiance—this is why there are prayers of petition and intercession. Some explanations of the Christian sacraments can sound remarkably similar to the rationale for magical spells. On the other hand, who would ever perform a Black Mass unless they thought that the real Mass was actually powerful and effective?[3]

From this perspective, the difference between religion and magic is the difference between asking God or the gods for some favor, and trying to compel the unseen world to do one's bidding. Prayer is a request, and leaves the outcome to God's decision. Magic is the attempt to exert power and establish control, sometimes even over forces regarded as demonic. A religious person might say, "The Lord answered my prayer; thanks be to God!" A magician will more likely say, "I did it correctly; it worked!" Even the strongest view of the sacraments stops short of this; sacraments are believed to be effective because of the reliable grace of God, which operates regardless of—not because of—the personal qualities and abilities of the celebrant.

Together, the notions of magic and the occult cover a huge assortment of human activities, and we cannot even attempt to touch upon them all in this book. The roots of the Goddess movement are to be found in a fairly specific setting, a particular range of occult and magical notions. Another definition which is helpful at this point is the distinction between "low magic" and "high magic." Low magic is the sort most people will encounter from time to time, in circus sideshows and psychic fairs if nowhere else—magic which purports to deal with very specific and concrete details of practical life. The use of spells to find a new job or a new lover, the use of crystals to improve one's health or mental state, the use of the Ouija board to make weekend plans or simply as a parlor game, are all examples of low magic.

High magic, on the other hand, aspires to the status of a spiritual discipline. In its classic forms, high magic entails a long process of mastering the hidden forces which supposedly control events in this world, and learning to manipulate them according to one's own will. Magical lore of this sort deals with the mystical powers and meanings of all sorts of natural things: numbers, colors, chemical elements, heavenly bodies, personality traits, and bodily organs, among others. By learning to understand and control the forces behind all these phenomena, the high magician aspires to ever greater spiritual status and power. The ultimate goal of high magic, its logical conclusion, is perfect knowledge and complete power over the universe. In effect, this means the deification of the magician. While the religious person seeks fellowship with God, the high magician—the real "occultist"—seeks to match and even to become God.

Principles of Magical Thought

In his pioneering and highly readable accounts of the occult tradition, Richard Cavendish has explained some of the basic principles which lie behind the enormous variety of magical practices, giving them their inner logic and unity. Cavendish singles out two key notions: polarity and correspondence.[4]

Polarity plays on the fairly obvious fact that many of our everyday experiences involve pairs of opposites. We habitually think in terms of opposites such as up and down, light and dark, warm and cold, wet and dry, male and female, life and death. In magical traditions, these polarities are believed to function in a particular and consistent way—they are not mutually exclusive opposites, but more like two sides of the same coin. Any physical object has both an up side and a down side, both a light side and a shadow side. Male and female seem designed for a reciprocal relationship. Life and death make up an alternating cycle of growth and decay, in which each individual has its chance to flourish and then must make way for others.

The notion of polarity which is employed in occult traditions typically emphasizes this close relationship between opposites. They are not antagonistic and mutually exclusive—indeed, we cannot have one without the other. Concepts like warm and cool, or wet and dry, make no sense in isolation; each can be established only by comparison with its opposite. This difference may be highly subjective, a fact known to any family where there have been arguments over room temperature. Accordingly, the goal of high magic is not the total victory of one side over the other; this would mean mastery of only half of reality. Instead, the ultimate aim is to establish a perfect balance between the poles, which is supposed to blend their distinctive energies and produce a power which is greater than the sum of its parts. Magical polarities do not cancel each other out; properly manipulated, they combine into a larger whole.

One obvious corollary of this principle is moral relativism. The ultimate goal of balancing all the contrary energies of the universe means that there cannot be any absolute distinction between opposites, even between good and evil. Like warm and cool, good and evil are merely the subjective opinions of individuals. Nothing can be off-limits to a high magician—if he cannot experience and master all the forces of the universe, without exception, he cannot achieve his ultimate goal of deification.

Correspondence is, in some ways, a more complex version of polarity. The basic idea behind magical correspondence is the notion that reality is made up of many parallel dimensions: physical elements, numbers, colors, heavenly bodies, spiritual beings, virtues, and so on. These dimensions are all interconnected, not just generally, but very specifically—each element correlates exactly to a particular number, color, spirit, bodily organ, and heavenly body. Thus, for example, the planet Mars, with its reddish appearance, corresponds to the color red; red evokes blood and bloodshed, linking it to warfare and, with its astrological symbol of shield and spear, to the male sex; iron, the ancient world's great achievement in military technology, is Mars's corresponding metal. Red is a "hot" color, so Mars is associated with fevers as well as "hot" tempers. Much of the sacred knowledge of the occult tradition consists of these schemes of correspondence, which can obviously become exceedingly complex. The practice of magic in many forms is conceived and planned in accordance with these principles.

Again, there is a broader corollary which arises from this basic idea. Just as polarity lends itself to moral relativism, so correspondence has a logical affinity with the idea of spiritual immanence. Magical practice, by and large, operates on the assumption that nothing exists outside the web of correspondences. Anything that did so would be, by definition, beyond the reach of human manipulation and control. The Western occult tradition has emphasized the notion that the divine or supernatural dimension exists within the natural world and permeates it; only thus can it be included among the correspondences and manipulated by the magician. This is the real import of the common maxim derived from *The Emerald Table of Hermes Trismegistus*, a twelfth-century magical text: "As above, so below."[5]

This is particularly striking as it is seen in the customary magical belief that man is a microcosm or miniature version of the whole universe, the macrocosm. All the varied phenomena of the cosmos, from the stars to the spirits to the metals and numbers, correspond to specific physical parts and character traits of the human being. There is nothing outside us which is not also, at the same time, within us— even God. Thus, high magicians who pursue self-deification do not need to seek God outside themselves; rather, they focus on discovering and empowering their own inner divinity.

The notion that one can experience deification leads to a further observation on the nature of magical "thought" itself. Such an experience is not said to be the logical conclusion drawn from certain observations and exercises. Rather, it is presented as a breakthrough in consciousness, a moment of supreme enlightenment which leaves everyday rational thought far behind. Discovering that God is already within oneself would have to be a momentous, even shattering, experience.

Accordingly, magical thought naturally inclines toward the intuitive rather than the rational. The notion that the light and the shadow can be reconciled into something higher and more powerful than either one by itself, or that the health of a particular bodily organ can be affected by colors, numbers, and planets, is obviously the product of a symbolic and poetic form of thinking—not of empirical observations and logical inferences. Belief in spiritual immanence rather than divine transcendence fits naturally with a preference for intuition over reason.

OCCULT PRACTICES AND TECHNIQUES

There are far too many different ways of practicing magic for us to attempt a complete survey here. Instead, we will acquaint ourselves with some of the more typical and pervasive techniques relevant to our inquiry. This section will illustrate how traditional occultists have gone about seeking the two major goals of high magical practice: knowledge of the hidden mysteries and forces of the cosmos; and power to express and enhance one's inner divinity.

Numerology

The process of seeking wisdom through numbers is one of the simplest of occult techniques, and it provides us with easy examples of magical thinking before we proceed to some of the more complex practices. The basic idea of numerology is that numbers constitute a distinct dimension of reality which corresponds in precise ways to all the other dimensions. Each individual number correlates to specific forces, characteristics, and types of events. Therefore, by learning the number which applies to a particular person or circumstance, one has access to valuable inside knowledge.[6]

Numerology was so easy in ancient times that it probably came naturally. The Hebrews and Greeks, for instance, did not have a separate set of written symbols for their numbers; instead, they used the letters of their alphabets. Basically, they used the first nine letters to represent the numbers one to nine; the next nine letters stood for the tens, ten to ninety; and the rest served to make up yet higher numbers. This meant that any name, or any word at all, could be read as a series of numbers and used for calculations.

Now that we use Latin letters for our words and Arabic numerals for our numbers, several systems have been developed to assign numerical value to the letters. One of the most common is to equate each letter with a single-digit number, so that A to I correlate with numbers 1 to 9; J to R repeat the pattern, 1-9; and S to Z are assigned values of 1 to 8. The number value of a person's name can then be added up (Philip George Davis = 101). The individual numbers in the total are then added together as many times as necessary to arrive at a single digit (1 + 0 + 1 = 2). The single digits, being the building blocks of all other numbers, receive most of the attention when it comes to establishing correspondences with other aspects of reality.

Many further variations are possible. Adding up the vowels of one's name is supposed to produce the number of the inner self, while the consonants correlate to the outer self, and the entire name indicates one's overall character and destiny; if these seem less than ideal, one can change one's fate by changing one's name. The digits in one's birth date can be added up to produce further insights into one's basic character, while the number of one's most recent birthday may tell a person what to expect in the coming year.

The point of all this is the assumption that the numbers will convey important information once their correspondences are known. In Cavendish's example, a person like myself whose number is 2 will be characterized by feminine traits and a soft, sweet nature. "They are *even*-tempered, lovers of peace and harmony. They tend to play *second* fiddle and make excellent subordinates, conscientious, tidy and modest."[7] By contrast, a 5 (the number of my "professional" name, Philip G. Davis) is "restless and jumpy, clever, impatient . . . Fives are jacks of all trades and masters of none, attracted by everything but held by nothing . . . quick tempered, sometimes conceited and sarcastic."[8] Differences like this are supposed to reveal various aspects of one's character and the changing personas one might assume with the different roles in one's life. Similarly, an examination of the individual numbers which make up my name reveals a large number of 7s ("the number of the scholar, the philosopher, the mystic and the occultist") and 9s ("the number of high mental and spiritual achievement . . . large-minded, visionary, idealistic").[9]

The extent to which I do or do not exhibit these qualities in real life is best left to readers' imaginations. These examples, however, should serve to illustrate the basic objections to numerology, which have been around almost as long as this pseudo-science itself. First, the huge variety of human characteristics and behaviors which we see in ourselves and others is too complex to be reduced to nine categories in a widely satisfactory way. Second, most human individuals share qualities which are assigned to most, if not all, of the numbers. Thanks to a simple error in arithmetic, I thought for several years that my number was 6 and used it thus as an illustration in the classroom. With its characteristics of domestic harmony, interest in teaching, and lack of business sense, it seemed to fit me at least as well as any of those mentioned above. The advantage to numerologists, on the other hand, is that anyone who wants to will find something believable in their reports. The human will to believe is a great asset to magicians of all sorts.

Astrology

As even the most infrequent reader of newspaper horoscopes knows, astrology entails the quest for knowledge by means of observing the movement of the heavenly bodies and correlating them to events and conditions on earth. The vague, terse comments of horoscope writers barely hint at the complexity of astrological lore, which has developed considerably since its origins in ancient Babylon.[10] Correspondence is the key to astrology. Rather than one set of numbers, however, astrology has several areas of inquiry with which to work—the planets, the constellations, and the "houses."

Like the numbers, the planets are said to correlate with specific human traits and tendencies. Traditional astrology knew seven heavenly bodies which seemed to move freely against the backdrop of the fixed stars: the sun, the moon, Mercury, Venus, Mars, Jupiter, and Saturn. Mercury is associated with intelligence, Venus with love and beauty, Mars with aggression and belligerence, Jupiter with rulership and achievement, and Saturn with justice, retribution, and disaster.[11] The sun correlates with light, heat, energy, and creativity, while the moon symbolizes change, flux, passivity, and the depths of night and the soul.

The signs of the Zodiac are named for the twelve constellations through which the sun, moon, and planets appear to pass when seen from the earth. Although the constellations themselves vary in size and spacing, the system of signs is used to divide the heavens into twelve equal parts. Again, each sign has its correspondences: Aries with creativity and energy, Virgo with quietness and dependability, Scorpio with intensity and passion, and so on.[12] Further, the signs have been linked to the traditional four elements (earth, water, fire, and air) and all their associations.

Third, there is the system of houses. This is another division of the sky into twelve sections but, unlike the Zodiac constellations, the houses do not move; rather, both the signs and the heavenly bodies move through them. The twelve houses represent different aspects of life—prosperity, character, relationships, career, and so on. For instance, the first house, which begins where the Zodiac and the eastern horizon meet, governs personality and appearance.[13] Clearly, the process of correlating heavenly bodies, Zodiacal signs, and houses opens up correspondences of almost infinite complexity.

Natal astrology, as the name suggests, begins with the most precise possible identification of one's place and time of birth. An astrologer determines which signs of the Zodiac and which heavenly bodies were in which houses at the moment of birth, and from the visual standpoint of the place of birth. Once all these positions are determined, the influences of each of these items on all the others can be measured and balanced, resulting in a comprehensive picture of the forces shaping the character and destiny of the person born.

Predictive astrology works by calculating the position of the signs and heavenly bodies at some given moment in the future, and drawing conclusions about the interplay of cosmic influences which will bear upon that moment. The same process can be used looking backwards to interpret events in the past; for example, Mary K. Greer's *Women of the Golden Dawn* is an extensive astrological biography of four female members of a Victorian magical order, and correlates significant events in each of their lives with the astrological circumstances which obtained at the time of those events.[14] Mundane astrology is the application of this same art to nations as a whole and to the course of history.[15]

The Tarot

The Tarot is vaguely familiar to millions as a set of fortune-telling cards. Practitioners of Tarot divination are commonly found at carnivals or other spots where large numbers of people may congregate for recreational purposes. Its origins are, for the most part, lost in history, but the earliest surviving Tarot cards may date from the late 1300s.

The conventional Tarot deck, as known in recent centuries, contains seventy-eight cards. There are four suits, resembling an ordinary deck of playing cards. Each suit contains cards numbered 1 to 10, and then four "face cards," often designated King, Queen, Knight and Page. The four suits are Swords, Cups, Pentacles or Coins, and Wands or Staffs. In addition, the Tarot deck contains a further 22 cards known as the Trumps, or the Major Arcana. These feature symbolic figures such as the Empress, the Fool, the Tower, and the Sun. Although most modern versions of the Tarot follow this general pattern, there is a wide variety of actual designs. The pictures on each card contain important symbolism, and therefore different decks with different illustrations have been developed by individuals and groups for their own purposes.

Each of the suits and, indeed, each of the individual cards has specific themes and implications associated with it. According to one standard Tarot manual, the Wands suit is associated with "Enterprise & Glory," and with the element fire; Cups correspond to "Love & Happiness," and to water; Swords represent "Strife & Misfortune," and air; Pentacles betoken "Money & Interest," and earth.[16] For example, the nine of Wands represents preparedness; the ten of Cups, a happy family life; the six of Swords, success after anxiety; and the eight of Pentacles, apprenticeship.[17]

The Major Arcana, as the name suggests, are said to be much more significant than the suit cards. "Their symbolism is a type of shorthand for metaphysics and mysticism. Here are truths of so subtle and divine an order that to express them baldly in human language would be a sacrilege. Only esoteric symbolism can reveal them to the inner spirit of the seeker."[18] The Empress corresponds to marriage, material wealth, and fertility; the Lovers represent not only attraction and harmony but the struggle between sacred and profane; the Hanged Man, suspended upside-down, symbolizes the reversal of behavior which follows an encounter with "a higher Being."[19]

Tarot divination is performed by shuffling the deck while the inquirer is in a state of mental receptivity, with a specific question in mind. Then cards are laid out in one of the patterns prescribed by tradition (the "Ancient Celtic" method and the "Tree of Life" method both call for ten cards). Each position in the layout has a defined signification. In the Ancient Celtic pattern, the fourth card identifies "influence that has just passed," while the eighth refers to "opinions of friends and relatives."[20] A Tarot reading, then, involves correlating the meanings of the cards with the position in which the cards appear; a card dealt upside-down generally signifies the reverse of its normal interpretation.

With seventy-eight cards available to fill ten positions in a layout, each with a whole range of meanings which can be all reversed if the card appears upside-down, the complexity of serious Tarot card use is nearly a match for astrology.

Ceremonial Magic

Numerology, astrology, and the Tarot, employed individually, are supposed to provide the seeker with special knowledge hidden from the world at large; they share this focus with other divinatory techniques such as scrying in mirrors or crystal balls. Knowledge, however, is generally meant to be used, not merely hoarded and gloated over. High magic finds its fulfillment when this knowledge is employed to gain mastery over the universe.

Once again, there is an enormous variety of schools of thought and actual techniques found in the old manuals, the *grimoires*, and their modern adaptations. What lies behind almost all of them, however, is the pair of notions we encountered above: polarity and correspondence. The ultimate goal of high magic is to act—to control, manipulate, and balance the unseen forces of the world, essentially creating the world one wants. To wield such power entails mastery over all the elements and dimensions of reality. The actual exercise of magical power typically takes place in the context of a ritual or ceremony.[21]

Commonly, a serious high magician will prepare for his work with a period of abstinence and "purification." This is supposed to preserve the individual from accidental contamination by elements which might undermine his activities, as well as to heighten his spiritual power by conserving and damming up his energies. He must also prepare the site of his workings, and the theme of correspondence comes into operation here. The point of a traditional magic ritual is to evoke, and then master, a specified spirit, force, or energy; accordingly, the setting and implements to be used in the ritual must correspond as exactly as possible to the object of the ceremony.

> Suppose a magician wishes to obtain knowledge of some obscure occult science, a matter which is traditionally one of the attributes of the god Hermes (Mercury). His task then is to supplement his psychic hermetic (that is, mercurial) deficiencies by drawing upon the hermetic qualities of the universe as a whole—to use the terminology of the magician, he must "in-

voke the god Hermes." He carries out this ceremony by surrounding himself with things, numbers and substances traditionally associated with Hermes. The number of Hermes is eight, so he has an eight-sided altar standing in an octagon; his temple is illuminated by eight lights; he has eight dishes of burning incense and he eats fish and drinks white wine, foods associated with Hermes since classical times. Having designed his ceremony with the appropriate correspondences, the magician uses his willpower to send up a "ray" which extends into other planes and taps the hermetic energies of the macrocosm, thus giving himself the qualities appropriate to gaining a knowledge of obscure sciences.[22]

There are numerous other considerations. Astrology will inform the magician as to the best time to perform the ceremony, whenever the planet Mercury is in the most advantageous position in the sky. The element mercury would likely be used in some form—"quicksilver," the dry liquid, is a favorite substance in occultism because it possesses qualities which seem to be mutually exclusive.

Traditionally, the ceremony begins with the demarcation of the site of the operation, usually by the drawing of a circle. The magic circle creates sacred space and provides protection from the spirits which are to be invoked. The circle may be drawn with chalk, or simply delineated with the magical knife or wand. In the more complex ceremonies, it may be inscribed with magic words; some of these are names of protective spirits while others are not words at all, but simply the sounds which correspond to the matter at hand. Such utterances are also used in the invocations and incantations which invest the circle with magic power, and which, later on, evoke the spirit in question. The circle must at all costs remain unbroken, so that annoyed or malevolent spirits cannot gain entry and threaten the magician.

The actual ceremonies vary greatly, depending upon the resources used and the goals in mind. Incantation and chanting generally play a large part; since sound is believed to be one of the fundamental elements of the universe, great care is taken to pronounce each syllable in the most potent way possible, activating unseen vibrations.

The use of stimulants, gesture and dance, and even animal sacrifice play a part in some magical rituals. Ritual sex, which taps into one of the strongest inner energies known to most people and which seems to enact the ultimate reconciliation of all polarities, has assumed increasing importance in the last hundred years, but it is far from new. All in all, traditional ceremonies were designed to compel the chosen spirit to reveal itself, then to overcome it, and to bind it to the magician's will. The rituals are steps by which the individual gains knowledge and mastery of those hidden forces which exist both within and outside himself.

The actual summoning takes place following the extended period of purification; it often proceeds in the midst of burning incense, and consists largely of long, repetitious chants calling on the spirit to appear and invoking protective energies so that the magician will remain in control of the proceedings. All the while, the magician himself is in an intense state of anticipation, and perhaps fear. As Cavendish notes, "there is not much doubt that the procedures of ritual magic are likely to cause hallucinations."[23] Among modern magicians, it is often the ceremonial experience itself which is the true value of the exercise. As Alan Richardson puts it:

> The modern era with its indulgence in projected two-dimensional entertainment, electric lighting, double-glazed and centrally heated lives has forgotten the impact of the great rites which were once part of our heritage. We have forgotten the effect of candle light and shadow, chanting, incense, ritual and invocation, when each member is unknown, a pair of glittering eyes, an expression of Power in a throbbing room. Used to the cult of the personality we have forgotten the awe that such obliteration of the face can bring, forgotten the way that we ourselves when cloaked in anonymity can become something other than our normal selves, momentarily greater, immeasurably truer to our higher natures . . . each man becomes a true lightbearer, and stands in an energy field of almost tangible weight, feeling as though his mind is peeling open like a bud, revealing the glowing jewel within, glowing with the Spiritus Mundi that dwells inside, awaiting its call.[24]

FOUNDATIONS OF THE ESOTERIC TRADITION

The more thoughtful practitioners of high magic have not been content to use a random set of techniques on an ad-hoc basis. Rather, they see their task as the expression of a profound and coherent understanding of the nature of reality; this is what makes occultism into a kind of philosophy or religion. Since the fundamental principles of magical practice differ in crucial ways from the essential teachings of mainstream Judeo-Christian religion, occultists have long turned, in neopagan fashion, to ancient modes of thought which seem to validate their activities. For the sake of what comes later in this book, we must identify a few of these archaic systems of thought.

Neoplatonism

The rise of Neoplatonism as a distinct form of philosophy is credited primarily to the work of Plotinus, a third-century A D native of Egypt who spent most of his career teaching philosophy in Rome. As the name of the school suggests, this was a new departure in the tradition of philosophy which traced itself back to Plato, and it included notions from a number of other ancient sources as well. Neoplatonism had a significant influence on some major early Christian thinkers, notably St. Augustine, and it was also well known in certain Jewish and Muslim circles.

Plato's legacy to Western thought includes a dualistic approach to philosophy. It emphasizes the contrast between the temporary, changeable physical world which we perceive with our senses, and the ideal, eternal realm of changeless "ideas" or "forms," which can be known only through the educated and disciplined efforts of the mind and spirit. The objects and qualities of this world are shadows or reflections of eternal principles, but only those principles themselves qualify as absolute truth. By contrast, the things our senses reveal to us are merely appearances.

Neoplatonism featured a very complex conception of the relationship between the spiritual and the material.[25] Rather than a basic dualism, Plotinus taught of a sort of cosmic hierarchy. It began with the One, the unknowable supreme God, and descended through various forms and spiritual beings to the *animus mundi*, the so-called universal soul which resides throughout the entire cosmos. Then, moving from the invisible to the visible realm, we encounter the celestial bodies and their divinities, the earth, and matter. In the middle is man, the microcosm in which matter and spirit are most equally balanced. The human being is composed of a physical body, a rational soul, an "astral body" which can exist separately from its physical counterpart, and the "higher mind" which corresponds to the eternal spirit itself. At its incarnation, the human soul descends through the heavens to the earth, acquiring along the way some characteristics from the stars and planets which it passes.

The higher mind still holds some awareness of the eternal truths from our heavenly home, but our conscious mind tends to be captivated and distracted by our sense impressions of the physical world. To escape the trap of endless reincarnation, the higher mind must be purged and purified through meditation and "practical" exercises—like out-of-body experiences with the astral body—to make it fit and free to ascend to the One.

The cosmic hierarchy is not one-dimensional; all physical things have their own, appropriate spiritual counterparts. As David Stevenson put it, "the Neoplatonist universe was drenched in the spiritual."[26] This teaching gave a philosophical explanation and rationale for the polarities and correspondences of high-magical activities, and stimulated leading scholars of Europe to explore the potential of these techniques.

Hermeticism and Gnosticism

A second ancient philosophy which became fundamental to the esoteric tradition was known as Hermeticism.[27] Unlike Neoplatonism, it was once completely forgotten, but in the late 1400s, the collection of books known as the Hermetic literature was rediscovered by Western scholars. The books themselves claim to come from Hermes Trismegistus ("thrice-greatest Hermes," known to the Romans as Mercury), the ancient Greek messenger god. Hermes was also a god of knowledge—he could hardly be a messenger without a message. Accordingly, the ancient Greeks had equated their god Hermes with the Egyptian god of wisdom, Thoth. The Hermetic literature, though composed in Greek, shows signs of Egyptian influence in its phrasing and content.

Since it shows signs of Christian influence as well, experts today agree that the Hermetic literature was written in the second or third century AD. Before this was recognized, however, readers of the Hermetic books presumed that they really were what they appeared to be on the surface—a set of religious and philosophical texts from ancient Egypt, the oldest, most glorious, and most mysterious civilization then known, a priceless link to the very origins of civilized wisdom.

The teaching of the Hermetic literature is usually understood to be tied more or less closely to Gnosticism. By this term, which also found favor in the esoteric tradition, I mean the post-Christian group of religious philosophies which taught that salvation comes by knowledge rather than by faith; that saving knowledge was offered through a series of initiations into higher and higher ranks of the movement.[28] The Hermetic books contain some fairly typical Gnostic ideas which were well suited to the magical tradition. The text called "Poimandres," for instance, presents a version of dualism in which spirit is essentially good and matter is evil. The physical world was created, not by the true God, but by an evil Demiurge who himself was created by mistake. A further error accounts for the existence of human beings. Our souls are divine and belong with God, but they are trapped in physical bodies, a tragic fact which makes them subject to pain, suffering, and death. In addition, the world of mortals is surrounded by a hierarchy of hostile spirits, the "archons," who block the soul's ascent to the divine realm. Only secret, divine knowledge holds the key to the soul's escape from travail, its victory over the archons, and its eternal reunion with God. This emphasis on a salvation which comes about through initiatic knowledge and which makes one like God is fundamental to the magical quest; the Egyptian trappings added enticing mystery and the sense of being in touch with the primeval origins of human wisdom.

Kabbalism

The Kabbalah (also spelled Cabala or Qabalah in English) is a set of Jewish mystical and magical traditions. Its roots probably reach back to the late biblical period, drawing on the spiritual disciplines and visionary experiences of both Gnosticism and the apocalyptic litera- ture. A Kabbalistic style of thought is clearly present in the *Sepher Yetzirah* ("Book of Formation," dated between AD 200 and 600). The movement achieved much of its current shape in the 1200s with the publication of its key text, the *Sepher ha-Zohar* ("Book of Splendor"). It is of interest to us here, not because of its considerable role in the development of medieval and modern Judaism, but because some of its distinctive ideas proved almost irresistible to philosophers and practitioners of high magic.[29]

To give it a brief and simplified description, Kabbalism is founded on a cosmology which, although it centers on the Bible, clearly draws on other sources, with special methods of interpretation. Essentially, God in himself is supposed to be completely unknowable as far as the inhabitants of this world are concerned. To escape the constraints and limitations of this world and come to know God truly, one must first know how the world came about. Kabbalism generally teaches that God did not create the universe as an object separate from him- self; rather, it is the outcome of a series of emanations which some- how came forth from the very being of God. The physical world of our sense experience is the end result of the interplay among these emanations, and it constitutes the lowest dimension of reality, fur- thest removed from the divine source. Despite this "distance," God is omnipresent, and there is a spark of divinity within each of us, waiting to be discovered, nurtured, and unfolded. Various strains of Kabbalistic thought have been recognized as pantheistic, or at least panentheistic.[30]

The best known visual symbol in Kabbalism is the "Tree of Life." This is a sort of chart which maps out the ten emanations, or *sephiroth*. The pattern of the Tree of Life is held to be the pattern or map of the universe itself, showing the way back to God. It is also a diagram of

Adam Kadmon, the ideal type of the human being, man as microcosm. The top nine of the ten sephiroth are arranged in triangles; in each case, the sephira on the right side is masculine and positive, that on the left is feminine and negative, and that in the middle is the androgynous balance. The tenth, isolated at the bottom, is this world.

The sephiroth are joined by lines or "paths." Mystical Kabbalism included a sort of astral travel by which one could journey spiritually along the paths, ultimately seeking the highest sephira and virtual union with God. In this pursuit, the sephiroth were pictured as worlds or realms, each with its own guardians, inhabitants, and symbols. Each path also had its own distinct characteristics, opportunities, and risks. Naturally, Kabbalistic thought generated its own set of correspondences founded on the sephiroth and the paths.

The top triangle, for instance, has *kether* ("crown") at the peak; this is the first sephira, representing God as the initiating force in creation. It is said to be guarded by the four "living creatures" of Ezekiel 1, and its magical symbol (the mental image to be used as a focus for meditation) is an old king. Down and to the right is *hokmah* ("wisdom"). This is the second emanation and, like all those on the right side of the Tree, is characterized as positive and masculine (even though *hokmah* is grammatically feminine in Hebrew). It represents God's creative wisdom, and is therefore connected with creativity, growth, and male sexuality; its symbol is a mature, bearded man, and phallic pillars and lines are associated with it as well. Third, on the left, is *binah* ("seed"), which is feminine and negative like all the sephiroth of the left side. Binah is passive and receptive understanding, responding to active wisdom. It is represented by a mature woman, and features vulva symbols like cups and circles. The fertile interaction between Hokmah and Binah produces the other sephiroth, and thus the world itself. On the other hand, Binah is also associated with its polar antithesis, death.

On classic diagrams of the Tree, the paths between the sephiroth are twenty-two in number—the same as the number of letters in the Hebrew alphabet. Since the Jewish scriptures had been revealed and preserved in Hebrew, this was believed to be God's own alphabet. It therefore contained, if fully understood, all the wisdom of the universe. Each path corresponds to a particular letter, and can be interpreted according to all the letter- and equivalent number-symbolism available. Kabbalists made great use of numerology in the form of *gematria:* converting the letters of a word into their numerical equivalents to unlock secrets in the Scriptures. Since, in Hebrew, the words "Shiloh" and "Messiah" both add up to 358, the phrase "until Shiloh shall come" in Genesis 40:10 was taken as a veiled reference to the coming of the Messiah.

There were two other related techniques. *Notarikon* meant building a new phrase out of a single word, by treating each letter in the word as the first letter of an individual word--or, conversely, taking the first or last letters from each word in a phrase to form another word. Thus, the first word of the Hebrew Bible, *berashit,* could be converted into the sentence, "In the beginning God saw that Israel would accept the law."[31] *Temurah* involved letter-substitution schemes of various kinds, such as replacing the first letter of the alphabet with the last and so on, to arrive at new statements and revelations.

Kabbalism contained a wealth of scriptural and mystical lore in which the notions of correspondence and polarity are quite prominent. Moreover, it embraced such key concepts as man-the-microcosm, the immanent presence of divinity within creation, and the ascent to God through human discipline and effort. No wonder, then, that it became such an alluring resource for occultists of the Western world who, in some cases, had only antipathy for other aspects of Judaism.

One other component of Kabbalistic thought is relevant to our inquiry. Thanks to the biblical commandment restricting the use of God's name, Jewish tradition developed many ways of referring to God without naming him. Of the various terms which could be used as synonyms for God, one was the word for "presence": *shekhinah.* In early Kabbalism the "presence" of God was essentially the same concept as the Holy Spirit.[32] The sexual symbolism which is evident in the Tree of Life also took account of the fact that *shekhinah* is grammatically feminine in Hebrew, and sometimes the divine presence was personified in female form. Modern Goddess devotees who have a Jewish heritage now look to the *shekhinah* as a major symbol of the "divine feminine" within the Judaic tradition.[33]

Alchemy

Alchemy is commonly regarded as the spurious effort to get rich by turning base metals into gold. Its sincere practitioners, however, regarded it as a serious and strenuous spiritual discipline.[34] The gold they sought was not simply a metal; they embarked on a quest for personal transformation which would confer upon them the brilliance, enlightenment, and incorruptibility which gold symbolized. I have chosen to discuss alchemy here, as a sort of applied philosophy, because its main contribution to modern occultism is its distinctive set of ideas and symbols rather than its actual laboratory techniques, which have largely fallen into disuse.[35]

Traditional alchemical theory was founded on the speculative physics of the ancient Greeks. Briefly, the idea was that all physical objects are made up of "first matter," an almost insubstantial essence. First matter has no characteristics of its own, but it can acquire, display, and cast off such observable traits as color, density, and liquidity. The differences we perceive between wood and oil, or between stones and leaves, are differences of external characteristics; at bottom, however, all are constituted of first matter. This theory made the alchemists' belief in transmutation possible—if lead and gold are both made of first matter, and differ only in superficial traits like color and weight, surely those traits can be altered in such a way as to change the element itself.

Thanks to the theory of correspondence and the influence of Neoplatonism, alchemists tended to assume that metals had their corresponding spirits and character traits (as well as numbers, planets, and so on). To master the process of transmutation was, therefore, to control the spirits and to magnify one's own self through the acquisition and enhancement of selected virtues and powers. Some alchemists appear to have believed that they were engaged in a devotional and mystical activity, approaching God through participation in his own mysteries; for others, the goal was clearly self-deification—this time by learning to control the processes by which the universe itself was made.

The desired product of alchemical work was not gold, but the

"Philosophers' Stone." The Stone was not necessarily a rock; sometimes it was described as a powder or liquid. It was, however, the true goal of the process, the substance which encapsulated the powers of creation and could bring about any chosen transformation—sickness into health, lead into gold, death into life. In Cavendish's words, it was "the divine spark or Holy Spirit in tangible form."[36]

The specifics of practical alchemy are still, to some extent, unknown. Most alchemical writings followed the occult principle of concealing powerful truths from the inept and ill-motivated masses, and therefore expressed themselves in highly symbolic form. Some texts suggest there were seven steps to the quest, others twelve or more. Basically, one had to start with some selected raw material and, through various procedures of burning, melting, boiling, distilling, and blending, reduce the raw material to first matter and then impregnate it with the characteristics of the desired product of the process. "Impregnate" is often the operative term; sexual symbolism abounds in some alchemical writings and pictorial images, along with astrological and other motifs. "Marriage" or "union" was a common way of designating the high goal of reconciling the opposites and blending contrary elements into a single, greater whole.

The crucial observation for our purposes is this: alchemical laboratory work did not stand on its own; it was the external aspect of a work which was supposed to go on, with equal intensity and effectiveness, within the individual soul. As one changed the characteristics of the substance in the vial, one was also casting off personal impediments, acquiring new virtues and powers, and extending the reach of one's ability in all spheres. Long after practical alchemy had been largely abandoned with the rise of scientific chemistry, spiritual alchemy would continue to be a practice of magicians and occultists of many stripes.

These beliefs and techniques make up the main conceptual and practical elements of the Western esoteric tradition. Immanence and pantheism, intuition and experiential "knowledge," and the neopagan nostalgia for Greece and Egypt left their stamp on this tradition from the beginning and confirm that this is where the ancestry of the modern Goddess is to be found. The magic which is said to be afoot among the Goddess devotees descends directly from the occult tradition described here. In Chapter 6, we acquaint ourselves with some of the individuals and groups whose contributions to the esoteric tradition paved the way for the modern New Age movement in general and for Goddess spirituality in particular.

6

The Western Esoteric Tradition

For what we do presage is not in grosse,
For we be brethren of the Rosie Crosse:
We have the Mason's word and second sight,
Things for to come we can foretell aright.

Henry Adamson, *Muses Threnodie*

OST OF THE OCCULT IDEAS and magical practices we have considered are very old. Individually, some of them can be traced back to the early civilizations of Sumer and Egypt, and similar activities have been found among tribal peoples in modern times. When we speak of the Western esoteric tradition, however, we mean more than just the sum total of these practices. In actual fact, the worldview we now associate with high magic appears to have coalesced about five hundred years ago, during the Renaissance. While it has been affected by various developments since then, there is a certain continuity which stretches from the 1400s to the present day in the typical approach to the hidden arts and arcane wisdom that go to make up "the occult."

We do not find Goddess worshippers here. We do, however, find much of the actual content of Wicca and Goddess spirituality in its earlier forms. The most distinctive mark of Goddess spirituality, its insistence on the feminine nature of the divine, does not appear much before the rise of Romanticism in the late 1700s; to understand that later development, however, we must familiarize ourselves with some of the individuals and groups who make up the esoteric tradition and trace their paths through the Renaissance, the Reformation period, and the Enlightenment.

THE RENAISSANCE

As the word itself suggests, the Renaissance (approximately 1400–1600 AD) was a period of "rebirth" in at least two senses. First, it marked a new departure in Western culture, an important transition from the Middle Ages to modernity. Renaissance culture tended to be more humanistic and less theological than the medieval philosophy which came before it. Artistic styles achieved new heights of realism; political theory became more mundane and practical (leaving us the term "Machiavellian" from the name of its greatest Renaissance proponent); investigations into nature were increasingly empirical and rational. At least among the educated classes, confidence in our human ability to figure out the workings of the world around us took great strides forward.

The Renaissance was a time of rebirth in another sense. It witnessed the revival of knowledge and interest in a wide variety of ancient ideas and beliefs. There was a streak of neopaganism in some influential Renaissance figures as they sought to rediscover the cultural treasures of ancient Rome, Greece, and even Egypt. Realism in art was not simply a new style or technique; it was also a deliberate imitation of the best Classical art. Old philosophies experienced a revival, sparking new intellectual developments as they meshed with the discoveries of Renaissance thinkers and investigators. Egypt, the oldest civilization then known, with its overwhelming monuments and enigmatic hieroglyphics, acquired a special allure for those who were attempting to penetrate the mysteries of the universe.

The role of the Islamic world in stimulating the Renaissance demands recognition. The European Renaissance followed shortly after the golden age of Islamic civilization under the Abbasid Caliphate in Baghdad. The literature and knowledge of the ancient Greeks and the Byzantines had been preserved and developed among the Muslims when much of it was lost to Western Europe. Then, through the late Middle Ages, Western contact with Islam increased considerably. During the Crusades, Europeans spent a hundred years in the Holy Land fighting with—but also learning from—Islamic culture at its peak. When the Mongols overran the Near East in the 1200s, Muslim scholars scattered with other refugees to North Africa and Europe. Spain, with its large Christian population, remained under Muslim rule until the late 1400s.

From the Islamic world, the West recovered lost writings of figures such as Aristotle, which stimulated the philosophical and theological achievements of St. Thomas Aquinas and others like him. The introduction of Arabic (originally Indian) numerals made modern mathematics possible—doing calculus in Roman numerals is almost inconceivable, and the very word "algebra" is adapted from the Arabic. Many similar cases occurred in other fields of knowledge; indeed, the Islamic world had universities before Oxford, the Sorbonne, and Bologna. This influx of knowledge from Muslim civilization, much of it bearing a pedigree reaching back to ancient Greece, contributed to the neopagan tendencies of the Renaissance. In many cases, the key to advancing knowledge seemed to be the ability to go back, to reach outside the medieval Christian heritage to ancient or foreign sources of wisdom. This is the cultural atmosphere in which the foundations of the high magical tradition were laid: confidence in human beings' ability to penetrate and master the mysteries of the universe, and inspiration from the non-Christian lore of other times and places.

In some ways, high magic was almost indistinguishable from the rudimentary science of the time. Magic and science shared the confidence that human beings could gain knowledge through their own effort and ingenuity, and could use this knowledge to control their environment in practical ways. It is not our concern here to explore how modern science separated itself from magic and developed out of the Renaissance matrix, but only to note the progress of occult thinking as it progresses towards modern times.

The Renaissance itself began in Italy, and the esoteric tradition started to acquire its mature form there as well. It was in 1439 that a visiting scholar introduced the newly translated Hermetic literature to the ruler of Florence, who became a powerful enthusiast of these new/old ideas. Then Marsilio Ficino (1433–99), afire with the idea of gaining access to the secret wisdom of the ages, made new translations of numerous Classical sources—Plato, Plotinus, Pythagoras, and "Hermes" among them. His short-lived disciple, Giovanni Pico della Mirandola (1463–94), became one of the first Christian experts in Kabbalah and added it to the mixture; as Cavendish notes, he thus "created the synthesis which has been the foundation of high magic ever since."[1] Pico opened his *Oration on the Dignity of Man* with the claim that, in all the world, nothing is more worthy of wonder than the human being. Affirming the man-as-microcosm theory, he drew the conclusion that human beings need not accept any limits—all qualities and potentialities exist within each of us. "We have made you a creature neither of heaven nor of earth, neither mortal nor immortal, in order that you may, as the free and proud shaper of your own being, fashion yourself in the form you may prefer."[2] Pico, in fact, narrowly escaped being condemned as a heretic.

Germany proved to be fertile ground for the new ideas. Germanic Europe already had a strong heritage of myth and mysticism, ranging from the Holy Grail legends of Wolfram von Eschenbach to the spiritual illuminations of Meister Eckart. Heinrich Cornelius Agrippa (1486–1533), a well-traveled soldier and diplomat, mastered Pico's philosophical synthesis as well as a broad range of magical techniques. His book *Occult Philosophy* is considered one of the clearest and most influential books on high magic in Western history. He defended the practice of magic, arguing that this is how the biblical Magi found their way to the Christ child. A strong proponent of the man-as-microcosm philosophy, he also developed a medical theory based on correspondences amongst herbs, metals, bodily organs, and heavenly bodies.[3]

The medical application of occult philosophy was a hallmark of Agrippa's German contemporary, Philippus Aureolus Theophrastus Bombastus von Hohenheim, better known as Paracelsus (1493–1541).[4]

A prodigious traveler in his early life, he made stops at several universities and eventually claimed to hold a medical degree from the University of Ferrara. He declared that universities had no monopoly on knowledge, and professed to have mastered the lore of gypsies and other mysterious groups. From all this he developed a holistic medical theory based on the idea that body and soul are intimately linked to each other, and both must be treated at the same time to achieve harmony and health. Paracelsus taught that illness occurs when we are attacked by the "seeds" of disease which come from outside us. Careful examination of physical symptoms is necessary to recognize and diagnose a patient's condition; then, Paracelsus commonly recommended a combination of rest, dietary alterations, chemical medicines, and a change of attitude to restore health.

Paracelsus' concept of medicine was, in fact, primarily alchemical. He espoused a theory of three elements: salt, representing solidity; sulfur, correlating to fire and action; and mercury, corresponding to spirit. Through practical experimentation, he apparently produced effective painkillers and sleeping potions. He also left behind recipes for the production of the Philosophers' Stone, the Elixir of Life, and a *homunculus* or artificial man. His supreme goal, however, was to cure people by restoring the celestial harmony between the patient and the cosmos. The microcosm principle was central to his whole system; health depends on the interplay between the patient's physical condition, his mental and spiritual state, and the cosmic forces which surround him. Linking all these things together is the "universal spirit," the world-soul of Neoplatonism.

Much of Paracelsus's teaching sounds strikingly modern, and there are Paracelsian holistic healers frequenting New Age circles even today. Not everyone is equally impressed by him, however; even the tolerant Cavendish notes that "he was rarely sober and reading him is like groping through a pitch-dark room lit by occasional flashes of blazing lightning."[5]

The Reformation

The Protestant Reformation of the 1500s had a limited impact on the developing esoteric tradition. Roman Catholics and Protestants, even when they agreed on little else, shared an antipathy towards magic and sorcery, and both hunted witches. The conflicts of the sixteenth century made religious deviance of any kind a more dangerous pursuit, and self-publicizing magicians like Paracelsus appear less often.

In Roman Catholic southern Europe, the most important figure to emerge in the occult tradition during this period was probably the philosopher Giordano Bruno (1548–1600).[6] Although Bruno paid lip service to the transcendence of God, his thought was heavily imbued with pantheism; he emphasized the role of the world-soul as the inner dynamism of all things. Bruno came close to rejecting Christianity altogether. He supported Copernicus, and went on to argue that an infinite number of stars and worlds exists in the universe. Since he still believed that man is the microcosm of that universe, this conferred an enormous degree of significance upon the individual human being. Bruno clearly fits the definition of a neopagan—he regarded Christianity as a fall away from the truth, and he hoped to restore the true "Egyptian" religion he thought he saw in the Hermetic literature. He antagonized both Catholics and Protestants, and died at the stake in Rome.

In Protestant England, these years witnessed the career of John Dee (1527–1608).[7] A renowned Cambridge scholar of philosophy and mathematics, with a personal library of over four thousand books, Dee was jailed early in his career for his Hermetic, alchemical, and astrological interests. He met the future Queen Elizabeth 1 while she was under house arrest during the reign of her Roman Catholic half-sister, Queen Mary. Pleased by his prediction that she would gain the throne and enjoy a long reign, Elizabeth appointed him court astrologer when the first part of it came true; one of his initial tasks was to choose the date for her coronation.

One of Dee's most influential writings was a book called the *Monas Hieroglyphica* (1564). The monas is a symbol very similar to the astrological sign for Mercury, and Dee interpreted its symbolism in such a way that it served as his key to the unseen world. The book has been described as "a combination of Cabalist, alchemical, and mathematical disciplines through which the adept believed that he could achieve both a profound insight into nature and vision of a divine world beyond nature."[8]

In 1582, Dee began working with the disreputable Edward Kelly, who had already been convicted of forgery and necromancy. Together they performed alchemical experiments and produced long accounts of Dee's discussions with angelic beings whom he supposedly contacted through his crystal ball, with Kelly serving as the medium. These alleged spirit communications, some of which were recorded in an otherwise unknown language called Enochian, have served as raw material for occult speculations ever since. At one point, Kelly informed Dee that the angels had commanded the two men to share their wives; although the young and attractive Mrs. Jane Dee protested tearfully, her learned husband could not refuse a directive from the spirits.

Kelly and Dee later traveled to the court of the Holy Roman Emperor Rudolf II in Prague. He was a keen student of the occult sciences and evidently wanted them to put their famous alchemical talents to work, but here Dee and Kelly had a falling out, and the latter never returned to England. Dee lost his greatest defender when Queen Elizabeth died in 1603. King James I, with his great fear of sorcery and witchcraft, would have nothing to do with him. Dee gradually sold off his great library just to survive and died in poverty, but his books and exploits continue to provoke heated discussion in occult circles even today.

MAGICAL ORDERS

These individuals, and others of the Renaissance and Reformation eras, seem to have worked alone or in very small groups. We have no reliable evidence that there were organizations of high magicians prior to about 1600, and for a century after that the evidence is unreliable. On the whole, it centers on two movements: Rosicrucianism and Freemasonry.

The Rosicrucian Riddle

The entry of Rosicrucianism into European history is easy to identify, but more difficult to explain.[9] Between 1614 and 1616, three books were published in northwestern Germany which launched the entire phenomenon. The first two were called *The Proclamation of the Praiseworthy Order of the Rosy Cross* (nicknamed the *Fama* from the original Latin) and *The Confession of the Fraternity*. They told the story of a German sage named Christian Rosenkreutz ("Christian Rosy-cross" in German) who supposedly lived from 1378 to 1484. He traveled to the Near East and north Africa, and was initiated into the secret wisdom and healing techniques of various mysterious groups. After trying in vain to spread his new-found knowledge in Spain, he collected a small group of disciples in Germany and established the Fraternity of the Rosy Cross, with its headquarters in a so-called House of the Holy Spirit.

The Fraternity allegedly carried on secretly for 120 years after Rosenkreutz's death. Then, in 1604, the next generation of disciples discovered and opened Rosenkreutz's burial vault. They found a seven-sided room full of mystical implements and symbols, ranging from an artificial sun to a book by Paracelsus (even though Rosenkreutz supposedly died before Paracelsus was born). The opening of the vault was taken to be a sign that the Fraternity should now go public with its message. The *Fama* and the *Confession* both called for a social reformation to follow and complete Luther's religious reform; they seem to express the vision of a utopian society in which all oppositions—Catholic and Protestant, religious and scientific, mundane and esoteric knowledge—would be reconciled under the umbrella of a Hermetic type of wisdom. The books called on high-minded persons to join with the Fraternity in pursuit of its goals, but the appeal gave no indication as to how responsive readers might contact the Fraternity. Since no one could find them, the Rosicrucians were soon reputed to have mastered the art of invisibility.

The third book, *The Chemical Wedding of Christian Rosenkreutz*, was written in quite a different style. It is a densely symbolic story of the wedding of a King and Queen attended by Rosenkreutz. The trip to the wedding site is a pilgrimage full of encounters with mysterious beasts, magical operations, and ordeals which were sometimes fatal to the prospective wedding guests. As the title suggests, much of the imagery has strong alchemical connotations.

The three books caused a major sensation at the time and stimulated a whole series of books arguing both for and against the Fraternity and its goals. In Germany, Julius Sperber claimed that Rosicrucianism drew on the primordial wisdom which was first given to Adam, but which had been lost long ago in Christendom; Michael Meier, a leading alchemist and practitioner of Paracelsus's teachings, reinforced the link in the public mind between Rosicrucianism and traditional alchemy. In England, Francis Bacon made use of the Rosicrucian manifestos in his utopian book *New Atlantis*, while the learned physician Robert Fludd published detailed defenses of Rosicrucianism.

The reaction in Catholic France was more negative, and the Rosicrucians were accused of heresy and diabolism. The philosopher Descartes heard about the Order in Germany and tried unsuccessfully to locate the sages in person. When he returned to Paris, he encountered a poster campaign claiming that the Rosicrucians had arrived there in invisible form; to avoid accusations that he was in league with devil worshippers, Descartes made a point of visiting friends and acquaintances to prove that he was, indeed, perfectly visible. In these days, with Catholics and Protestants often at war and both sides hunting heretics and witches, such precautions were certainly advisable.

Episodes like this occurred in the 1620s, but there was never any concrete evidence that the Fraternity of the Rosy Cross actually existed. Invisible it remained, and historians are divided over what was actually happening. One point is clear: Johann Valentin Andreae (1586–1654) was involved in it. Andreae's grandfather had been one of Luther's major supporters during the Reformation; his father was also interested in alchemy. After the father's death, the family moved to Tübingen in 1601. Andreae studied and then taught at Tübingen University until 1614, when he left to take up other responsibilities as a Lutheran pastor. He was also a prolific writer, turning out everything from plays modeled on English drama to a utopian tale called *Christianopolis* (1619), portraying a place "in which science and religion would flourish and in which men of all creeds and races would be respected."[10]

In his autobiography, Andreae claimed that he himself was the author of the *Chemical Wedding*, and that he originally wrote it during his student days, in 1604. He referred to it as a *ludibrium*, a Latin term which can mean joke, comedy, or theatrical play. Here and in some of his other works, he actually mocked those readers who believed that the Rosicrucian order really existed. What are we to make of this?

Christopher McIntosh presents what seems to be the most widely accepted explanation. He indicates that Andreae, during his student days, was part of a circle of Tübingen students who were fed up with the religious strife of the day and yearned for a "second reformation" which would establish religious and social peace and unity. Influenced by the esoteric tradition in general and the works of John Dee in particular, they saw the Hermetic wisdom, alchemy, and Dee's blend of mathematics and angelology as the umbrella under which competing sects and societies could be harmonized. The original *Chemical Wedding* would have reflected these interests, as the later published version does.

According to this theory, members of that group eventually wrote the *Fama* and *Confession* as fictions designed to stimulate the reform they sought. They used Andreae's character Christian Rosenkreutz (the rose and cross were part of the Andreae family's coat of arms) as the hero of the tales. They also included, with the *Confession*, two other documents: a summary of John Dee's philosophy; and an extract from an Italian satire which suggested that the only true and successful reform is one which starts in the hearts and minds of individuals, not in organizations or social structures. To Andreae's chagrin, suggests McIntosh, readers of the first two manifestos took the Rosicrucian order literally and either tried to join it or sought to stamp it out. He then published his own *Chemical Wedding* to indicate the fictitious character of the order, while still promoting the values he supported. Since this tactic did not work, he was even more explicit in denouncing would-be Rosicrucians in his later writings.

McIntosh notes that the mature Andreae did belong to at least one actual secret group: the Fruit-Bringing Society, which was founded in 1617 to promote German nationalism and the German language. He goes on to point out that this group had links to an older society, the *Unzertrennlichen* or Inseparables, which had been established as early as 1577 and pursued interests in mineralogy, mining, and alchemy. It is possible that Andreae belonged to this group as well, and even that it was the real-life model for the Rosicrucian Fraternity.[11] At any rate, most historians treat the original Rosicrucian episode as a roundabout attempt to stimulate religious and social reform by means of symbolic, fictitious tales—tales which, contrary to their authors' intentions, took on a life of their own.

Frances Yates presented a much more precise interpretation, arguing that the manifestos were part of a specific political campaign. In the early 1600s, the German area of Europe was constituted as the Holy Roman Empire; though there was an actual emperor, political power was fragmented among the scores of small states which divided up the territory, and the hegemony of Catholics or Protestants still hung in the balance. The original Rosicrucian activity took place in two small Protestant principalities located in western Germany near the Belgian border, Württemberg and the Palatinate.

The Palatinate was a lively center of esoteric and occult activity; some major publishers of Hermetic and alchemical books were located there. The idea that the truths of the esoteric tradition could bring together the rival Lutherans and Calvinists, and perhaps the Roman Catholics as well, seems to have been widespread. This principality also had close ties to Protestant England. Its ruler, Frederick v, had been made a Knight of the Garter by Great Britain's King James I and then married James's daughter, the Princess Elizabeth, in 1613.

This was the year after the Holy Roman Emperor Rudolf II, the supporter of John Dee, had died; political maneuvering over the succession was intense. As head of the Union of Protestant Princes in Germany, and allied by marriage with the most powerful Protestant monarch of all, Frederick was the focus of Protestant hopes in central Europe. When the Protestant population of Bohemia revolted against their Catholic ruler, they offered their throne to Frederick and he accepted. The result was disaster. Frederick and Elizabeth took up residence in Prague during the autumn of 1619, but their German and British allies failed to provide practical help, and their forces were destroyed by Catholic armies in November 1620. The Palatinate itself was invaded and sacked by Spanish armies from the Netherlands, and Frederick and Elizabeth spent the rest of their lives as fugitives.

Yates's argument, in essence, is that the Rosicrucian manifestos were a form of propaganda for Frederick and promoted a utopian vision which was meant to be accomplished in practical terms when he achieved supreme power. After the failure of the so-called "Winter King," the Rosicrucian furor quickly evaporated as well.

McIntosh and Yates agree that there was no actual Rosicrucian order in the early seventeenth century; the manifestos were designed to stimulate reform on a broad scale, although the means by which this was to happen remain unclear, and the plan seems to have been unsuccessful in any case. By the time we do finally find actual Rosicrucians, in the eighteenth century, they bear the marks of an older and entirely real movement: the Freemasons.

Freemasonry

The true origins of today's Freemasonry are as difficult to sort out as those of the Rosicrucians, although for somewhat different reasons. We know for a certainty that there were guilds of stonemasons during the Middle Ages and the Renaissance, when the great stone structures of Christendom were erected. We know that during the 1600s "speculative" masonry appeared, first of all in Great Britain, using the terminology, tools, and lore of the stonemasons to teach moral uplift and charitable fellowship. The argument is over how these two phenomena were connected. The usual answer is to suggest that the guilds of practical stonecutters, during a period of intense social and religious change, changed course themselves and were transformed into the fraternal organization known around the world today. David Stevenson's *The Origins of Freemasonry* (1988) gives a succinct summary of this answer and attempts to identify the time and place in which the actual transition may have been made.

Stevenson points out that stonecutting had several features which distinguished it from other trades.[12] Coppersmiths, for example, could live in the same place all their lives, buying metal, working it, and selling it. They could inhabit neighborhoods of their own, and their guilds could reign over the entire communal life cycle of apprenticeship, career, marriage, family life, religion and community festivals, and care of the ill and aged. The skills needed for copper work were precise and significant, but limited in their scope. Copper work, on the other hand, was relatively safe for both producer and consumer; a poorly-made bracelet might fall off, but only rarely could anyone be seriously endangered.

Stonemasonry was different in almost all of these respects. A man building a cathedral could not take his work home with him—he had to go to where the work was. Masonry was often a job for travelling workers, so their need for accommodation and fellowship gave rise to the masonic lodge as a sometimes temporary substitute for the guild neighborhood. Moreover, stoneworking was an extraordinarily difficult and dangerous profession. To design and erect cathedrals and other such structures required extensive and precise knowledge in many fields: geology and the properties of different types of stone; advanced mathematics for accurate measurement and for an understanding of what sort of an arch can support how much roof; and the practicalities of cutting stone to fit and to decorate, and of getting the cut stone to its intended location, however high off the ground that might be. The stakes were high—faulty stonemasonry could mean the collapse of the structure and the death of anyone present, whether during construction itself or in the years afterwards.

Anyone who has visited Europe and seen the results of the masons' work can grasp how demanding a profession this was. Small wonder, then, if some masons may have thought themselves to be an elite group, possessing knowledge and abilities which no outsider could match. Small wonder, too, if they were jealous of this knowledge and wanted to be able to discern who truly possessed it and who did not. A man who joined a worksite without the proper training endangered everyone else on the job.

In those days of low literacy when written tests would have served little purpose, other ways of examining a new workman would have been necessary to distinguish a truly qualified mason from an amateur carver with a persuasive manner. Two general methods seem to have been implemented. First, along with the practicalities of the trade, a masonic education included a craft legend which traced the profession back at least to the days of Solomon's temple, if not to the days of Enoch before Noah's flood; this created a body of lore shared among true masons which no imposter could figure out for himself by experimenting with a chisel and a rock in his garden. Second, the famous series of passwords and secret handshakes, known collectively as the Mason's Word, simplified the task of telling an outsider apart from the three ranks of accepted masons—the Entered Apprentice, the Fellow Craft, and the Master Mason.

The common explanation of the rise of "speculative" masonry suggests that in the 1600s the construction of great stone projects was in decline, but the search for the hidden meaning of existence was on in earnest. In this environment, the masonic lodges started attracting upper-class men who had no intention of working as stonecutters but who were drawn to the mystique and symbolism which the masons had developed. Stevenson's particular contribution is to isolate the evidence that points to seventeenth-century Scotland as the place in which this transformation first occurred and from which it spread.

Writers sympathetic to the claims of the esoteric tradition argue a more dramatic case than this, however.[13] The practical needs of the stonecutters' trade, they suggest, fail to account for several prominent characteristics of Freemasonry, including the excessively bloodcurdling punishments a mason calls down upon himself if he reveals the craft secrets. These writers also consider it implausible that British aristocrats could have been enticed into intimate fellowship with real, scruffy workingmen, no matter how impressive the lore and ceremony which went along with it all.

Instead, they suggest, speculative Freemasonry owes its existence to the Knights Templar. This, the most famous of the medieval orders of monastic knights, became almost an independent power during the Crusades, when it was responsible for protecting the Holy

Land from the Muslims. The Knights were driven out of Palestine in 1291, however, and became a target of suspicion and persecution at the hands of the Church and of King Philippe IV, "Le Bel," of France. The Templars had been directly under papal authority, independent of bishops and kings; the order was also rich, with its Paris head-quarters serving as a major financial center, and it was very secretive about its internal doings. Philippe, probably coveting their wealth as a resource to finance his own ambitions, initiated action against the Templars in 1307 and had the Inquisition extract confessions from them. These confessions were very similar to those the Inquisition had wrested from the Albigensian sect in previous years: denying Christ, spitting or stepping on the crucifix, worshipping the devil and an idol called Baphomet, and practicing homosexuality, ritual sex, child sacrifice, and the Black Mass. The Templars' leaders were sent to the stake in 1316, the order disbanded, and its possessions in France turned over to the King.[14]

In recent centuries, occultists have been fond of regarding the Templars as initiates of the arcane mysteries and as martyrs for the esoteric tradition; a certain amount of Templar lore has been absorbed into both Rosicrucianism and Freemasonry. The alternative expla-nation for the origins for Freemasonry, then, is this. Refugee Templars fled from the wrath of King Philippe and the Pope and landed in Scotland, where they helped Robert the Bruce drive off an invading English army at Bannockburn in 1314. The Templars, now incognito, established a continuing tradition of esoteric teaching and fellow-ship which, in the sixteenth and seventeenth centuries, took over the stonemasons' guild as its public face. Crucial to this theory is a badly eroded carving on Rosslyn Castle in Scotland which, it is claimed, depicts the typical masonic initiation of an Entered Apprentice, com-plete with a tow-rope around his neck, in the hands of a figure in Templar regalia.[15]

At any rate, it is becoming generally accepted that speculative Freemasonry has a Scottish origin. The earliest surviving record of a speculative masonic lodge is the one which was joined by Sir Robert Moray in Edinburgh in 1641. The better-known case of Elias Ashmole, the Oxford antiquarian, dates his admission to October

1646. Ashmole was a pivotal figure in the English esoteric tradition; a devoted student of John Dee's work, he was also fascinated enough by the Rosicrucian manifestos to make his own translations of them, complete with a letter asking the Brothers to admit him to their membership.[16]

The first known Grand Lodge established to govern masonic practice dates from 1717, in London. By the 1720s there were lodges in France, and another Grand Lodge was established in Paris. Germany and other parts of Europe were not far behind; neither were the inhabitants of the British colonies around the world, for whom a masonic lodge was often a tangible link to the old country.

THE EIGHTEENTH CENTURY

Freemasons and Rosicrucians

The Enlightenment, the age of reason, was also the age in which occult and spiritualist movements became firmly established. Campaigns to reduce the authority of church and state opened the way to much more than just the rise of science and democracy. Individuals and groups began exploring ideas, practices, and techniques of all sorts. For those interested in plotting radical social change, the Rosicrucian/Freemason model of a secret society possessed an undeniable attraction. Conspirators could adopt structures of secrecy which were already well established.

The Scottish influence on Masonry remained strong. Many early French masons were actually Scottish refugees, supporters of the exiled Stuart dynasty. One such Scot, the Chevalier Michael Ramsay, served as Chancellor of the Paris lodge. In 1737 he made the claim that Masonry had been involved in the Crusades, with the masons hoping to recover the site of Solomon's great temple; in this capacity they had formed a working relationship with a lesser-known order of military monks, the Knights of St. John. McIntosh suggests that this statement "led later and even more fertile imaginations to associate Masonry with the suppressed Order of the Templars"—a claim which does not seem to have been made until years later.[17]

The Grand Lodge of Paris was not able to maintain control over continental Masonry to the degree that the London Lodge could in Great Britain, and deviant forms of Masonry were quick to spread. They often justified their existence by claiming Scottish origins, an indirect testimony perhaps to Scotland's role as the first home of speculative Masonry. Of particular interest to our quest is a German variant known as the Strict Observance rite. Founded by Baron von Hund in 1764, it had a strong alchemical component in its teachings. It also made the Templar connection explicit—von Hund claimed that the Templar tradition had been preserved most purely in Germany and found its full expression in the Strict Observance. He also seems to have insisted that the Strict Observance worked in the service of a group of unseen superiors, reminiscent of the invisible Rosicrucians.[18]

It may be no coincidence that eighteenth-century Germany also gives us our first "real" Rosicrucians. In 1710, a book was published in Breslau titled *The True and Complete Preparation of the Philosophers' Stone of the Brotherhood, from the Order of the Golden and Rosy Cross*, by one Sincerus Renatus ("Genuine Reborn"). This was probably Sigmund Richter, a Protestant pastor with a deep interest in Paracelsus and the mystic Jakob Boehme. The book provides some alchemical recipes and also some rules and regulations for the Order. McIntosh points out that Richter had studied his theology in Halle, which was also an important center for alchemy and had a lodge of the Inseparables, the alchemical fraternity to which Johann Andreae may have belonged. The Inseparables had several grades of initiation and employed astrological and Gnostic motifs in addition to their alchemy. McIntosh speculates that the Golden and Rosy Cross may have been a spin-off of the Inseparables; not only that, but the Inseparables may be the actual link between Andreae in the early 1600s and the operative Rosicrucian orders of a century later.[19]

Other Golden and Rosy Cross manuscripts have been found elsewhere in Germany, demonstrating that by this time there was a real organization with chapters around the country. At some point in the course of the century, a structural blending of the Rosicrucian and masonic streams took place: by 1767, initiation into the Golden and

Rosy Cross was granted only to individuals who were already Master Masons. Rosicrucianism thus begins to look like an occult "graduate school" for masons who were not satisfied with mere symbols of fellowship and wanted a real, first-hand encounter with the powers of the universe.

The Golden and Rosy Cross offered further degrees of initiation beyond Master Mason. The 1767 record gives a list of nine grades, which were to become standard in European occultism afterwards. Beginning with the entry rank, they are:

9. Junior
8. Theoreticus
7. Practicus
6. Philosophus
5. Adeptus Minor
4. Adeptus Major
3. Adeptus Exemptus
2. Magister
1. Majus

Each grade has its own corresponding number, color, word, and sign; it also has a secret chief, a special topic of study, and a cost of initiation. Entry into the Junior grade cost three gold marks. The rank of Majus was priced at ninety-nine marks, although McIntosh points out that this would present no deterrent to those who were truly qualified, since they would already have mastered enough alchemy to make themselves gold from any substance at all.[20]

The Golden and Rosy Cross had a brief moment of power. The crown prince of Prussia had joined the order, and in 1786 he took the throne as King Friedrich Wilhelm II. His close advisors included Johann Rudolf von Bischoffswerder and Johann Christoph Wöllner, who were both members of Strict Observance Masonry as well as the Golden and Rosy Cross. Friedrich Wilhelm managed to combine a disreputable private life (he committed bigamy twice and kept mistresses) with a repressive religious policy under which Wöllner hired other Rosicrucians to police the theological opinions of pastors and professors. The great Rosicrucian experiment came to a final and generally welcome end with the death of Friedrich Wilhelm in 1797.[21]

This episode, along with Yates's argument linking the original manifestos to the political career of Frederick v of the Palatinate, shows Rosicrucianism involved with the aspirations of princes. In broader terms, it does seem to be the case that Rosicrucianism served as a vehicle for establishment and conservative agendas, particularly in Germany, while Masonry—especially its French variants—tended towards the more liberal ideas of equality and tolerance.[22] Either way, there was an almost natural affinity between these secret societies and the need of political conspirators to recognize and communicate with each other undetected by the world at large.

Sometimes mystical orders did indeed serve as seedbeds for radical plans on both the left and right wings of the political spectrum. At the same time, the fear of these secretive groups, which was so much in evidence when the Rosicrucian manifestos appeared, led to the propagation of a whole series of conspiracy theories which are still with us today. Central to many such theories are the Illuminati, an order founded in Bavaria by Adam Weishaupt in 1776. Intensely secretive, it infiltrated other masonic groups to promote Weishaupt's political agenda, which was said to include the overthrow of existing states, the abolition of private property, free love, and the legalization of drug use, suicide, and abortion. Conspiracy theorists commonly attribute the French Revolution itself to masonic conspirators influenced by Weishaupt, a charge which was first made almost immediately after the Revolution itself. Be that as it may, the order was broken up by the Bavarian government in 1794.

Swedenborg and Mesmer

In addition to the various Masonic and Rosicrucian organizations, the eighteenth century was still producing individuals who put their personal stamp on the development of the occult tradition. Flamboyant charlatans like the Count of Saint-Germain and Count Cagliostro left their marks, but to tell their highly entertaining stories would not advance our particular inquiry. Emanuel Swedenborg and Franz Anton Mesmer made much more durable impressions on the esoteric tradition, and we shall conclude this chapter by considering their contributions.

Swedenborg (1688-1772) spent the first part of his professional life doing scientific and technical work for the Swedish board of mines. By all accounts a brilliant man, he "formulated an atomic theory of matter, was the first to correctly identify the function of the cerebral cortex and the ductless glands, introduced the first Swedish textbooks on algebra and calculus, founded the science of crystallography, and designed and oversaw the construction of what is still the world's largest drydock."[23]

In 1745, while he was trying to pinpoint the location of the soul in the human body, Swedenborg had a spiritual crisis. He claimed afterwards that Christ had given him a mandate to explore the spiritual realm. His route to the other worlds lay deep within his own mind. He cultivated altered states of consciousness and wrote vast accounts of his conversations with angels and spirits, as well as his journeys to various heavens and hells. Modern accounts of the "inner planes," other dimensions of existence which can be perceived through changes of consciousness, owe much to Swedenborg's pioneering efforts. Swedenborg wrote of his paranormal experiences in the common-sense scientific style to which he was already accustomed; this alone accounts for some of the popularity of his work, since it made spiritual teachings seem much more credible in the Enlightenment era and afterwards. Moreover, he described the next life in very concrete terms: hells are made up of deserts, caves, or slums, and even the highest heaven features "angelic homes, parks, clothes, meals, and sexual relations."[24]

Interestingly, the key to Swedenborg's teachings is nothing else than the doctrine of correspondence. He claimed that reality is composed of many dimensions, arranged in hierarchical fashion from the spiritual down to the material.[25] Knowledge of the correspondences increases one's spiritual power, especially in view of the fact that he also espoused the doctrine of man as microcosm: "it is through our own humanness that we have access to the divine . . . we find evidence of the divine by looking within ourselves."[26] Maintaining a claim to Christian orthodoxy, Swedenborg advocated and practiced a technique of Bible study which emphasized the search for hidden meanings in the text, a search to be guided by the doctrine of correspondence. Several movements were founded on the basis of his teachings, including the General Church of the New Jerusalem, and his visions of the community of heaven influenced several of the utopian philosophers and colonists. Two representatives of the Swedenborgian church were, in fact, invited guests at the 1997 investiture of Frank Griswold as Presiding Bishop of the Episcopal Church U.S.A.

The lifework of Franz Anton Mesmer (1734-1815) had a much less happy outcome.[27] An Austrian who knew Mozart personally, Mesmer trained in law, philosophy, and medicine. It was his fate to live at a time when scientific inquiry as we know it was just beginning, but before some of its most basic findings had been established; this left the way open for wild new speculations to explain natural phenomena, and Mesmer's became one of the best known and most controversial.

Gravity, magnetism, electricity, and life itself seemed to be self-evident proof that there were invisible forces operating in the world. Many thinkers during the Enlightenment preferred to think of these forces as natural rather than supernatural, but explaining them in any detail was still next to impossible. Like many of his contemporaries, Mesmer speculated and experimented in an attempt to identify and harness this hidden power of nature. Unlike most of them, his eventual theory led him first to fame and then to humiliation. Mesmer asserted that the animating force behind various natural processes was an ethereal, imperceptible fluid which he called "animal magnetism." Mesmer further claimed that he had learned how to channel this force in a way that could cure people of various ills and ill-humors. Sometimes he touched his patients directly; sometimes they formed chains to transmit the energy through a group; sometimes he just gazed at them; sometimes they gathered around the *baquet*, his special tub studded with iron rods, and took hold to receive a transmission of the healing force.

Through a combination of his own personal charisma and the heightened suggestibility of jaded aristocrats, Mesmer met with great success when he brought his practice to Paris in 1778. Some patients undoubtedly felt better after their mesmeric sessions than before, and went out to proclaim Mesmer's healing power to the world. For many others, at least part of the attraction was the great variety of side-effects which his techniques produced. The moment of healing was normally the "crisis," a state of collapse and convulsion which often resulted from mesmeric treatment; Mesmer kept a crisis room lined with mattresses at the ready. In some cases, however, patients went into a form of trance. They would return telling of visionary experiences and conversations with the dead and various other spirits. It was a group of Mesmer's disciples, practicing this variant of his technique, who stumbled onto the phenomenon which we now call induced hypnosis.[28]

Almost immediately, the academic and medical establishments in Paris came out in force against Mesmer. Mesmerism became a favorite topic of public debate, and the pamphlets and cartoons through which some of the arguments took place probably engaged more members of the reading public in the 1780s than did the brewing political storm. The major turning point came in 1784, with the establishment of a royal commission to investigate Mesmer's claims; the commission included both Benjamin Franklin, who was already famous, and a Dr. Guillotin, whose name would later become notorious. The commission concluded that Mesmerism was fraudulent, and that all its effects could be attributed to the overheated imaginations of those who participated in it.

Mesmer's disciples and defenders established their own organization, the Society of Universal Harmony. Since Mesmer's French was not fluent, the founding chapter in Paris was effectively dominated by Nicolas Bergasse and Guillaume Kornmann. Both of these individuals were to play significant roles in the French Revolution; several other prospective revolutionaries at least dabbled in Mesmerism, including Jacques-Pierre Brissot and, in a minor way, his friend Jean-Paul Marat. Part of Mesmerism's appeal to people like this was precisely its anti-establishment character, which was reinforced each time Mesmer's claims were rejected and ridiculed by those professional doctors whose own primitive healing methods still emphasized purging and bloodletting.[29]

Founder and movement eventually went their separate ways. Mesmer apparently saw himself as a scientist ahead of his time, persecuted by the old guard who had too much to lose if his ideas won the day. Belying its name, the Society of Universal Harmony fragmented after a few years, and Mesmer left Paris to pursue his dream in other locations; he eventually died penniless, not far from his birthplace. The Society itself did, however, succeed in spreading and popularizing Mesmerism. Chapters were established in major French cities, and travelling mesmerists found even more enthusiastic audiences in small towns and rural areas where there was neither enough entertainment to compete with a mesmerist demonstration nor enough education to challenge its claims. This form of popular Mesmerism spread across Europe and as far as North America. There, it helped prepare the way for American seers and psychic healers like Andrew Jackson Davis and Edgar Cayce, as well as for the rise of Spiritualism in the mid-century.

In urban centers, Lyons and Strasbourg especially, Mesmerism appealed strongly to those who were already interested in the paranormal and the occult, since it seemed to offer the sort of scientific validation which was so desirable during the Enlightenment. As Robert Darnton noted, the Lyons chapter "blossomed with Rosicrucians, Swedenborgians, alchemists, cabalists, and assorted theosophists," many of whom had a background in unorthodox Masonry.[30] In 1787, as a matter of fact, a Swedenborgian group in Stockholm had written to Mesmer suggesting that these two groups of spirit-communicators should combine their efforts to enlighten the world.[31] The Society's own activities took on some distinctly masonic trappings, but the organization as such did not survive the Revolutionary period.

Mesmer's attempt to formulate a universal science survived primarily among the aficionados of the esoteric tradition. Those disciples who were also politically active based their arguments for equality and freedom on the belief that all living beings share in the same single life-force; their insistence on this interconnection amongst all living things is another expression of the organic view of existence, particularly since animal magnetism was very nearly equated with the presence of God himself in the world. Political Mesmerism even developed tones of neopaganism. If animal magnetism was the force animating all life, it was clearly at its purest form in nature. People and societies which existed in close harmony with nature must, therefore, be most in tune with it. According to Bergasse and others, primitive cultures must become the models for social reconstruction when the crass materialism of modernity is finally swept away.[32]

As Darnton suggested, Mesmerism appears to be one of the bridges which led from the Enlightenment to Romanticism. Beginning as a scientific theory, it appealed to popular interest in the extraordinary and the paranormal, and it was rejected by both the Church and the scientific establishment. The changing fortunes of the mesmerist movement reflect the larger cultural recoil from Enlightenment materialism and rationalism. Its survival was guaranteed by those people who, one might suspect, were of least interest to Mesmer himself—the denizens of heterodox masonic lodges and the heirs of the magical tradition. The coming of Romanticism would stimulate all these interests in ways which would have been difficult to foresee.

In the next two chapters, we shall trace these developments as they appeared in Germany and then in France. In both cases, Romanticism was to add a crucial new element to the esoteric tradition—the idealization of the female. This, as we shall see, is the first crucial step on the path which leads directly to the Goddess.

7

Romantic Neopaganism in Germany

The Eternal Feminine draws us on high.

Johann Wolfgang von Goethe

R OBERT DARNTON'S STUDY of Mesmer bears the intriguing title *Mesmerism and the End of the Enlightenment in France*. The transformation of Mesmerism itself from a putative scientific theory into a rudimentary religious movement foreshadows much of what we are about to see. By the end of the eighteenth century, the Enlightenment had done much of its critical work, discrediting traditional systems of religion and statecraft in the eyes of many; but neither Mesmerist theory nor the political visions of the French revolutionaries succeeded in bringing about a new, harmonious and prosperous state of affairs. Previous sources of human inspiration and aspiration were effectively overthrown without being substantially replaced. Growing out of the Enlightenment but reacting against its deficits and failures, Romanticism swept across European culture. Here we can begin to discern the faint outline of the Goddess herself.

Appropriately enough, Romanticism seems to have begun spontaneously in several places at once and not as a rationally calculated response to events and trends. England's Joseph Wharton and France's

Jean-Jacques Rousseau, for instance, have both been regarded as precursors of Romanticism, but they seem to have worked in ignorance of each other.[1] The real driving force, however, appears to have come from Germany; the international discovery of German literature is said to be one of the critical developments which stimulated Romanticism in Europe and beyond.[2]

At this point in history, there was still no "Germany" as we think of it today. The 1700s were the last years of the Holy Roman Empire, a network of small principalities, dukedoms, and bishoprics under a figurehead emperor. As the historians' joke goes, it was neither holy nor Roman nor an empire. It was an affront to the neat and tidy thinking of the Enlightenment philosophers, but the Enlightenment had rather less impact there than in England and France. It was also an affront to Napoleon. After he won a decisive victory over the Prussian army in 1806, he dismantled the Holy Roman Empire and attempted to reorganize the political structure of central Europe. The fact that he did it along French, rational, Enlightenment-style lines provoked resistance and resentment among many patriotic and nationalistic Germans.

The Germany of the eighteenth and early nineteenth centuries was a cultural entity rather than a political one. From the Baltic Sea to the Austrian Alps and the Rhine Valley, German-speaking people knew themselves to be distinct from the Slavs, Italians, and French. They shared not only a language and ethnic kinship, but a glorious heritage. Germans had made, and were making, monumental contributions to European art, music, literature, and scholarship. This seemed to be their special excellence, and thus it is not surprising that much of the energy of Romanticism can be attributed to its German exponents.

THE PHILOSOPHERS

Some of the crucial underpinnings of Romantic thought emerged from German idealistic philosophy. The pivotal work of Immanuel Kant (1724–1804) helped to tilt the direction of philosophical inquiry away from the external world of objects and motion, and towards the functioning of the mind itself. Kant argued that the human mind is more than just the passive receptacle of sense impressions, which it must then analyze and organize. Rather, there are structures and patterns in the mind itself which shape our perceptions of reality and, thus, help to shape reality itself. Kant, it seemed, set the mind free from its bondage to the external, cause-and-effect mechanism of Enlightenment thought; we can, and therefore we must, create for ourselves the world we wish to inhabit.[3]

Kant himself was no Romantic, but it has been suggested that German Romanticism was heavily influenced by a misunderstanding of three of his central ideas.[4] First, the Romantics seized on his theory of the mind as being an active force which actually creates knowledge, but which does not directly perceive the objective facts outside of ourselves. From this, they developed the notion that human thought could be a law unto itself, absolutely free from external restrictions—including even the rules of logic and the limitations imposed by factual evidence.

Second, Kant argued that empirical observation and rational theorizing, those crucial components of Enlightenment thought, were not capable of uncovering the metaphysical order of reality. When he emphasized the active role of the mind in the creation of knowledge, he correspondingly minimized the possibility that our knowledge of the world outside ourselves can ever be absolutely certain. Romantics accepted this cautionary advice up to a point, but typically claimed that they had found one crucial exception which permitted absolute knowledge of the world after all. Instead of empirical facts and rational explanation, Romantics would sometimes argue that the source of truly certain knowledge was some kind of semi-spiritual force which we could experience within ourselves, as well as observe in the world around us. The primary route to truth was inward.

Third, Kant himself allowed one exception to his general argument that we can never possess absolute knowledge: morality. We cannot be sure that our impressions of the world are strictly accurate, but we can indeed know in any given situation what we ought to do. This knowledge comes from within the individual, so it is not subject to the problems which afflict our attempts to observe and make

sense of the outside world. While Kant maintained a basically rational approach to morality, Romantics took his affirmation of innate
moral knowledge and applied it to the whole realm of feeling, intuition and imagination. The result was a worldview in which the
individual's source of certainty, of meaning, and of ethical direction
lay in the subjective realm of the emotions.[5]

Further features of Romantic thought come into view in the work
of Kant's student Johann Gottfried von Herder (1744–1803).[6] Herder
had wide-ranging interests which included the Middle Ages, the plays
of Shakespeare (many of which were being introduced to Germans
for the first time), folklore, and the newly emerging study of the cultures and religions of Asia. Herder's contribution to Romanticism
revolved around his espousal of the pre-Enlightenment theme of organicism. He held that natural human groups should be understood
as unified organisms, cohesive living things, and not as contractual
arrangements made by individuals. Herder opposed rationalism and
defended the significance of individual subjective experience. In particular, he objected to the idea that human life in its teeming variety
could be organized on crisp rational principles.

To Herder, a real nation was not created when free people agree
to live together under a mutually accepted social contract. On the
contrary, a nation was a group with a shared racial or ethnic identity,
a shared language, and a shared heritage shaped by their geographical setting and historical experience. A nation was an organism which
would grow and develop over the generations; if free to unfold naturally, each nation would do so differently, in a way which was true
only to itself. The Germans, for instance, must not copy the ways of
the French or anyone else, but must develop customs and institutions
which expressed and enhanced their national distinctiveness. Herder
helped to popularize the notion of the *Volksgeist*, the National Spirit,
a non-empirical reality which defined the basic character of each individual within the nation or race. In a sense, it can be understood as
a nationalistic version of the Neoplatonic world-soul.

Romantics thus helped to preserve the idea of organicism as a
way of understanding human life and society in terms of biology.
Contradictory though it may seem (and Romanticism, no friend to

logic, is full of contradictions), the Romantic exaltation of the individual was often accompanied by a similar exaltation of the natural, biological group, whether it was a nation, a race, or even a sex.

Herder was still something of a forerunner to, or perhaps an elder statesman of, Romanticism. The great generation of Romantic-era philosophers and scholars in Germany included Johann Fichte (1762–1814), Friedrich Schleiermacher (1768–1834), Georg W. F. Hegel (1770–1831), Friedrich von Schelling (1775–1854), and Friedrich Karl von Savigny (1779–1861). Most of these historic figures were colleagues or successors of each other at the University of Berlin after its founding in 1810, and they shared and elaborated upon the sorts of ideas we have just noted.[7]

Fichte first made his mark as a Kantian, and went on to develop his own theory of knowledge which emphasized the importance of feelings and the mastery of the irrational. To Fichte, knowledge was anything but passive observation; he saw it as the means by which the ego imposed itself upon the world. The ego, in fact, was his key to the universe. He postulated a Universal Ego which drove and guided all of human development; the individual ego derived all its real energy and significance from this impersonal, cosmic force.

Such notions made Fichte a major contributor to Romantic conceptions of nationalism. If all individual egos are subordinate to—and even derived from—the Universal Ego, it follows directly that individual citizens derive their significance from the larger community, rather than the other way around. This encourages the view that the ideal community should be an authoritarian state. Freedom no longer means individual choice; that merely divides and dilutes the nation. Real Romantic freedom means that we realize and fulfil our essence and purpose by merging into the great mass of our biological or national group and sharing in its historic achievements. A nation must express itself through a powerful, unified state—something the German nation had not possessed for centuries.

More particularly, Fichte argued that the Germans themselves were the primordial creative race among the Europeans, the *Urvolk* who had remained true to their *Ursprache*, their original language. The other Europeans, by and large, had long ago surrendered to the ancient Romans and learned to speak a sort of pidgin Latin which mutated into French, Italian, Spanish, and the other Romance languages. Being effectively a chosen race, the Germans were duty-bound to develop a strong state of their own—and, moreover, to stake their claim to supremacy in the competition of the nations. Fichte preached this gospel of communal totalitarianism and German nationalism in his *Addresses to the German Nation.* Significantly, these appeared in 1807–08, in the aftermath of Napoleon's conquest.

Schelling, Fichte's successor, continued in the same line of thought. His *Philosophy of Nature* took an organic view of the universe which was flavored by the recent scientific discoveries in magnetism and electricity. Schelling argued that natural processes reflect the interaction of opposing forces, the positive and negative poles of a magnet being one prime example. These forces of polarized energy, in turn, arise from an ultimate common source: the *Weltseele* or world-soul. As the immanent source of all processes—and, thus, of all things—the world-soul animates the physical universe in a manner somewhat reminiscent of Neoplatonism. Knowledge of the world-soul is accessible through a kind of "intellectual intuition" which perceives the infinite as it is contained within finite things.

Similar themes appear in the theology of Schleiermacher. He was an ordained cleric with a background in Moravian pietism, a movement which emphasized an emotional approach to religious devotion (and which brought about the famous conversion of John Wesley, the English founder of Methodism). Schleiermacher attempted to rescue Christianity from the attacks of the Enlightenment by defining religion in Romantic terms. The core of religion, he taught, is neither doctrine nor ethics but feeling—the profound emotional experience of the finite creature who perceives the infinite and encounters the Creator. Schleiermacher sought to lift Christian religious experience beyond the reach of rational critique; one of the first things he said in his great work on Christian doctrine was that he did not intend to "prove the propositions of the Christian Faith to be consonant with reason."[8] This meant, in effect, that he had to divorce religious experience from traditional theological and moral teaching.

Piety or true spirituality he defined as a kind of feeling, which Schleiermacher distinguished from both knowledge and action. He was very much a Romantic Christian, writing of matters like the in-dwelling of the Holy Spirit in terms which could easily be adapted to a doctrine of immanence and intuition: "He ... within whom revela-tions of his own never rise ... who does not sense now and then that a divine spirit urges him on, that he speaks and acts on holy inspira-tion—that man has no religion."[9] In a Kantian vein, he maintained that moral knowledge arises organically from within the individual; this may mean that certain exceptional people cannot and should not be judged by ordinary, external standards.

Hegel, perhaps the most towering figure in all of nineteenth-century philosophy, rejected any notion of transcendence and pointed to the dynamism of history as the ultimate source and goal of exist-ence. He argued that historical developments, like natural processes, are also polar or dialectical—driven by the interaction and collision of contrary forces. History's overall direction is guided by the action of the *Weltgeist* (world-spirit) or *Zeitgeist* (spirit of the time). A na-tion—or even an exceptional individual—which comes under the tutelage of the world-spirit becomes a law unto itself, and Hegel stipu-lated that it possesses the right to wage war in its own interests. At one point he saw Napoleon as the embodiment of the world-spirit. After Napoleon's fall, Hegel was convinced that the Zeitgeist had passed to the German nation.

In these and other cases, we see the philosophical characteristics of Romanticism: the emphasis on feeling and intuition as the route to the highest truth; a rejection of both the traditional understand-ings of the transcendence of God and the materialism of the En-lightenment, in favor of the immanent folk-soul or world-spirit; and the peculiarly Romantic combination of a narcissistic focus on the self and one's own inner experience along with an emphasis on natu-ral and biological groups as the entities which define and circum-scribe the individual. Many of these, as we saw, appear in the Goddess movement as well.

Of particular interest for our inquiry is Friedrich Karl von Savigny. An historian of law rather than an actual philosopher, Savigny shared the Romantic notion of the nation-state as a single organism with an instinctive drive of its own, a folk-soul. Accordingly, he objected to the idea that laws can or should be codified rationally to apply on a widespread or even universal basis—the Enlightenment notion which Napoleon was, after a fashion, attempting to impose on his European conquests. Savigny argued that law, properly speaking, should be rooted in the organic experience and history of each specific group; the laws of one group (e.g., the Napoleonic French) had no relevance to the life of another (the Germans). There was no natural or transcendent law which applied to all peoples at once.

For Savigny, the true source of valid law was the shared consciousness of the *Volk*. Because of the chaotic political history of the German people, and particularly the massive disruption caused by the Napoleonic conquest and the wars of liberation, the true consciousness of the German people had to be rediscovered in the collective memory of peasant folklore. It was Savigny who sent two of his students, the brothers Grimm, on their epic mission of collecting German folksongs and tales for precisely this reason.[10] It was also Savigny, in later years, who became the teacher and lifelong mentor of Johann Jakob Bachofen, the matriarchy theorist who will occupy much of our time in Part IV.

THE AUTHORS

Dramatic as the accomplishments of the Enlightenment were, it can be argued that Romanticism had an even broader impact on European culture as a whole. While both trends affected philosophy, religion, and politics, Romanticism's appeal to emotion and experience made it particularly attractive to the artistic temperament. Painting, music, architecture, and almost all other art forms were irrevocably changed by the forces unleashed by Romanticism. For our purposes, literature serves well to reveal those forces as they begin their long journey towards the Goddess.

Some typically Romantic themes appear as early as the work of Friedrich Klopstock (1724–1803). Klopstock was an innovative poet who sought to break free of the rigid formalism which characterized

German poetry in his youth. He agreed with Herder that poetry
needed to reinvigorate itself by drawing on traditional Germanic
mythology and folklore, and some of his works display a strong sense
of cultural nationalism. His writing was sometimes reproduced and
circulated privately, from hand to hand; small groups of his fans coalesced into a loose-knit movement which has been described as a
"Klopstock cult." He seems to have accepted the role of patriarch
and prophet, setting a strict moral tone for the exalted role of the
poet.[11]

The relevance of Romantic-era German literature to our quest
for the Goddess can be highlighted by centering our discussion around
the contributions of Germany's greatest literary figure, Johann
Wolfgang von Goethe (1749–1832).[12] In his early life, Goethe was
exposed to a variety of influences. Though he was christened in a
Protestant church, Christianity seems to have had comparatively little
impact on the content of his thought and work. On the other hand,
his maternal grandfather—Johann Wolfgang Textor, Chief Magis-
trate of Frankfurt—is alleged to have had revelatory dreams on a
fairly regular basis, and the young Goethe's penmanship lessons appear to have been accompanied by an introduction to the works of
Cornelius Agrippa, the Renaissance occult philosopher. Sometime
before he left for the University of Leipzig at the age of 16, he had
also encountered the Neoplatonic philosophy of Plotinus and
Klopstock's masterwork, "The Messiah."

After his return to Frankfurt from Leipzig in 1768, Goethe fell ill
and was treated successfully with a healing salt by Dr. J.-F. Metz.
Metz was a member of a pietist group which gathered around a distant relative of the Goethes, Fräulein Susanne Katherine von
Klettenberg; Goethe, his mother and his sister became involved themselves. This circle blended the simple religiosity and moral purity of
the Moravian Church with a strong interest in Hermetic and alchemical studies. Here, if not before, Goethe studied the occult medical
theories of Paracelsus and the arcane symbolism of the Rosicrucian
manifestos; he even participated in alchemical experiments. The
group also plunged enthusiastically into the recently-published visionary reports of Emanuel Swedenborg.[13]

Moving on to Strasbourg, Goethe met and came under the influence of Herder. Herder directed Goethe's attention to the Bible, Homer, Shakespeare, and indigenous European folklore, through which the *Volksgeist* was supposedly revealing itself. With this stimulation, Goethe produced his first published works and gained immediate fame. His drama about Götz von Berlichingen transformed this historical sixteenth-century robber knight into a Germanic hero who sacrificed all to the cause of freedom; the tale was set in a mysterious world of castles, dungeons, and nocturnal meetings. His story *The Sorrows of Young Werther*, based on the suicide of a lovelorn young man of Goethe's acquaintance, prompted a sensational response with its direct appeal to emotion and sentimentality. The Werther costume of blue tailcoat and yellow waistcoat became a fashion statement—although not as extreme as the wave of actual suicides which followed the book.

These and several other works appeared in the 1770s and made Goethe a central figure in *Sturm und Drang,* the "Storm and Stress" movement in German literature. The name was taken from the title of a play by another member, Maximilian von Klinger; its opening lines read, "Hurrah for the tumult and uproar, when the senses reel like a vane in the storm!"[14] Storm and Stress was, in effect, a revolt against the Enlightenment and the direct precursor of actual Romanticism. Its emotionalism was utterly unbridled, whereas the Romantics of later years were capable of an almost analytic examination of their perceptions and intuitions.

Of all the emotions, love held pride of place. Werther died for love, and the Storm and Stress writers pursued the many ramifications of love in their literary efforts. This, of course, led to many new thoughts about the object of man's love—woman. The most radical of the group was Wilhelm Heinse (1749–1803). His novel *Ardinghello* condemned monogamous marriage as a fatal affront to the heart; he portrayed in its place a utopian republic in which strong and independent women would choose sexual partners as they saw fit and would raise children in love with no concern for paternity. The novel's high point was an orgy of group sex staged by the central characters, German artists living in Rome.[15]

Goethe, meanwhile, abandoned the Storm and Stress movement early on. In 1775 he accepted a government position in Weimar, which became his home for the rest of his life. Among the other trappings of the job, Goethe was led to join the Weimar lodge of Freemasons, for whom he later wrote songs and even a play.

The true Romantic movement almost exploded onto the scene in 1796 and 1797. Along with major philosophical works by Fichte and Schelling, these two years saw the publication of distinctively Romantic literature from Ludwig Tieck, Wilhelm and Friedrich Schlegel, and Wilhelm Wackenroder. The latter year also saw the death of fifteen-year-old Sophia von Kühn. Tragic as such an early demise would have been in any case, this event had far-reaching consequences. Sophia was betrothed to Friedrich von Hardenberg, the major Romantic poet better known by his pen-name Novalis (1772–1801). Hardenberg was shattered by the loss of his beloved, and his bereavement lent a powerful tone of mystical melancholy to his writing. The works of Novalis show clearly the influence of Schelling, Fichte, and Schleiermacher, as well as Goethe and others; moreover, he drew on the Moravian pietism of his youth, Neoplatonism (which Goethe also encountered in the same circles), and the recent fad for Mesmerism.

The result was a worldview in which human subjectivity held pride of place. Novalis powerfully influenced his fellow Romantics, holding aloft the impossible dream of an ecstatic encounter with the Infinite—in full, ironic awareness that it was indeed largely impossible. This ultimate experience was, however, accessible in finite form through poetry. Its symbolic form and emotive power made poetry the natural choice for his attempt to capture and express the visionary experience—although Novalis pursued his quest in other ways as well, including the actual practice of magic.[16] He coined the term "magic idealism" to convey his worldview, which he saw as an advance beyond Kant and Fichte. Defying both religious orthodoxy and Enlightenment rationalism, magic idealism entailed "the act of romanticizing," by which he meant elevating the "lower self" into a "higher self" through inward sensibility and nonsensory knowledge.[17]

The endless longing for the Infinite had another finite form—

human love. Whatever the realities of Novalis's relationship with his adolescent fiancée were during her brief life, she evidently became in death his lodestone. He visited her grave repeatedly after her passing, and recorded in his diary the ups and downs of his grieving and the allure of a *Liebestod,* or love-death, which would reunite him with his beloved. This mood was heightened by Friedrich Schlegel's thoughtful gift: a copy of Shakespeare's "Romeo and Juliet." Within three months, however, Novalis was substituting a new, personal religion for his death wish.

His writing career lasted only three years, until his own death at 29 from tuberculosis. They were productive years, however, and Novalis left a significant body of completed work as well as elaborate plans for more. Several recurrent themes remind us of the Goddess movement. His views on the relationship between poetic inspiration and knowledge of the infinite draw close to intuitive immanence, and his pronounced interest in the return of a supposed Golden Age—which, in *The Novices of Sais*, he associates with ancient Egypt—recalls the neopagan paradigm. Most striking in the context of our inquiry is his virtual deification of the deceased Sophia, which is so strongly reminiscent of Dante's devotion to Beatrice, and the resulting prominence of female imagery in Novalis's mystical and spiritual writings.

In *Novices*, for instance, the ultimate revelation takes place in the temple of Isis, where the image of the Veiled Virgin represents the "mother of all things" and the ultimate source of spiritual exaltation. *The Tale of Eros and Fable* is an allegorical narrative about the coming of the New Age: a mythical Sophia, described as the "woman like a goddess," must be reunited in love with her consort Arcturus over the opposition of the Scribe, the symbol of rationalism and arid scholarship; in the end, Sophia is declared "eternal priestess of the heart" as she conducts a sort of eucharistic ceremony through which she proclaims that "the Mother is among us."

In *Hymns to the Night,* a series of poetic reflections on the real Sophia's death, she is elevated as the earthly, feminine counterpart to the cosmic, masculine Christ. Night itself is "maternal wisdom, whose daughter is Love"; it is the abode of "the eternal Mother . . . the

'World's Queen.'"[18]   Novalis uses the deaths of Christ and of Sophia to portray death itself as simply the gateway to another, better world. His *Devotional Songs* are poems of Christian piety, largely orthodox in expression; given Novalis's Protestant background, however, it is noteworthy that the final two songs are addressed to the Virgin Mary, pleading to become her child. As Hiebel has put it, "The *Hymns* are inspired by Sophia and guide the poet to Christ. The *Songs* transfigure the earthly image of Sophia into that of the heavenly queen of the world, by the light of Christ."[19]   In the brief career of Novalis, we have a striking example of the way in which a Romantic sensibility could seize upon a feminine symbol as the repository of emotional sustenance and hope for a New Age. This is not the last time we shall encounter the virtual deification of an actual, deceased woman at the hands of her bereaved lover.

The Romantic emphasis on emotion and love ensured that Novalis was not alone in his preoccupation with the female. The most highly developed arguments on the subject came from Schleiermacher and Friedrich Schlegel. Both insisted that the only "true" marriages were those rooted in an everlasting love between the participants; no other nuptial arrangements could be considered binding. Such true marriages required the legal emancipation and full education of women, so that they could take their place as free individuals and loving partners to men.[20]   At some points, these arguments echo the equity feminism of earlier Enlightenment writers. The distinctively Romantic emphasis, however, comes out in Schlegel's controversial *Lucinde* (1799). This novel's central theme was that love is an end in itself, not merely a means to procreation and social order. In keeping with the Romantic belief in the distinctiveness of biological groups, Schlegel claimed that women are by nature more loving (and therefore more truly religious) than men. Love, subjectivity, and a natural poetry of the soul—supremely Romantic values in themselves—are seen as the inherent, automatic property of women as such. "Women stand less in need of the poetry of poets because their innermost being is poetry."[21]   Here we come much closer to gender feminism, a view of women's emancipation rooted in the idealization of what is supposed to be distinctively female.

The early Romantics were well aware of Goethe's reputation and generally thought highly of him. Novalis referred to him as "the liturgist of the new physics," and a good deal of Romantic writing consciously imitated the novels and lyric poems of Goethe. This high esteem was not fully reciprocated, however. In 1793, Germany's other great dramatist, Friedrich von Schiller (1759–1805), arrived in Weimar. These two literary giants joined forces to promote their rival program for the arts, "Classicism." Drawing on the examples of ancient Greek and Roman literature, they upheld a vision of formal perfection, clarity, and harmony which was far removed from the rampaging emotions of the Romantics—and even further from Goethe's and Schiller's own roots in the Storm and Stress.

The author of *Werther*, however, had another major contribution to offer to the Romantic era. Since his Storm and Stress days, he had been working sporadically on his own dramatic version of the Faust legend. Different parts of it were published at different times, beginning in 1790, but the full text of Part II did not appear until a few months after his death in 1832. *Faust*, therefore, can be considered the lifework of Germany's greatest literary figure; it holds a preeminent place in the history of German culture which no single text does in English. In several specific ways, it illumines our path towards the Goddess.

The traditional Faust legend was well-known and popular in Europe. In the conventional versions, the learned man sells his soul to the demon Mephistopheles in return for magical knowledge and power, and eventually suffers damnation as a result. Goethe not only elaborated on the basic story; he changed its entire dynamic and, with his great gifts of imagination and poetic power, made it into a compelling vision of the meaning of life even as he challenged some of the most fundamental principles of Western civilization. In Goethe's version, Faust does not make a pact to sell his soul to the devil. Instead, Faust and Mephistopheles make a bet: Mephisto will lead Faust out of his dusty study and arid intellectual pursuits into the hurly-burly of real life, and fulfil all his desires; Faust will forfeit his soul only if he ceases his "quest of intense experience"[22] and tries to hold on to a particular moment or circumstance. Faust pursues his quest in defiance of all moral limits, destroying innocent lives along the way. Contrary to the usual versions, however, Faust is saved at the end of the play, but without repentance, and indeed saved in a sense by his sin—his salvation is won and mediated by the spirit of Gretchen, his first love, whose death he caused at the end of Part 1.[23]

Part of what Goethe offers in his version of *Faust* is a poetic vision of living as essentially active and dynamic. Faust himself is a hero, not an object lesson. He turns his back on study, contemplation, abstraction, and any sense of the transcendent; he plunges into activity and experience, and is still planning to go on when he dies at 100 years of age. Goethe emphasizes in the text that man cannot act without erring, without sinning (line 317).[24] To refrain from action is, by implication at least, even worse—it is to choose a kind of sterility, even a kind of death, over fruitful life.

All this suggests the sort of spiritual immanence which was so popular in the Romantic period. In the play, Goethe subverts and ridicules both Christianity and the rationalism of the Enlightenment. In their place he evokes such entities as the *Erdgeist* or earth-spirit. This is not simply another label for the world-soul of the philosophers, for the term earth-spirit in German carried the same sort of connotation that "worldliness" does in English. Faust's interest in life and Nature is not in the abstract or the ideal, but in the real, everyday experiences of temporal pleasure and pain. On the other hand, commentators generally agree that Goethe's vision of the earth-spirit owes a considerable debt to Swedenborg.[25]

With both the Church and the Enlightenment serving primarily as objects of parody, Goethe obviously drew on other resources to probe the meaning of life. By transforming Faust into a hero and Mephistopheles into something of a trickster, Goethe voided the legend of its traditional moral content; his play's essential amorality has been recognized from the outset.[26] Further, commentators have long noted signs of Goethe's neopaganism in the play, from his use of Greco-Roman mythological motifs to the traces of Neoplatonism, Paracelsus, and Swedenborg at various points in the text.

What makes *Faust* especially germane to our inquiry is not, however, the general indications of neopaganism and spiritual immanence in the play; it is Goethe's use of gender symbolism. Two striking instances from the 1832 text of Part II stand out. First, when Faust wants to perform a wonder which finally outstrips even Mephisto's abilities, the demon sends him off to "the Mothers." These are nameless goddesses who dwell beyond time and space, and empower Faust to overcome both temporality and death by bringing Homer's characters Paris and Helen back to life ("Dark Gallery," lines 6173–6306). Second, we have the play's portentous closing lines, uttered as Faust's soul is borne up to heaven by the *Mater Gloriosa*, the "Glorious Mother," and the spirits of four forgiven female sinners: "The Eternal Feminine draws us on high." These episodes have preoccupied students of the play ever since Part II was published, and even before—while he was still alive, Goethe refused to explain "the Mothers" to his disciple Johann Peter Eckermann, and simply repeated Faust's words from line 6217: "The Mothers! Mothers! It sounds so strangely weird!"[27]

Goethe himself said that he based his Mothers on Plutarch's *Life of Marcellus*, chapter 20. Plutarch reported there that the Sicilian town of Engyon had been founded by Cretans and was a cult center for a group of goddesses known as the Mothers. In lines 6286 to 6290 of *Faust*, Mephisto gives as much of an explanation as we get in the drama:

> *Formation, transformation,*
> *Eternal mind's eternal recreation.*
> *Girt round by images of all things that be,*
> *They do not see you, forms alone they see.*

In the context of the play as a whole, this links the Mothers to the process of creation, the cycle of birth, death, and rebirth, which is for Goethe where the meaning of life is to be found.[28] The creative process of transformation is one of the major themes in the play as a whole, the locus of spiritual immanence. The anonymity of these goddesses may have several purposes, but one of them is surely to highlight maternity itself as a symbol of this process.[29]

The "Eternal Feminine" of the final lines of the play clearly cannot be divorced from the Mothers; indeed, the ultimate saving figure is specifically identified as the Glorious Mother. Here, as many other times in the play, Goethe manipulated Christian symbolism to communicate an essentially neopagan message.[30] In this case, the use of such a profoundly Roman Catholic image as the Assumption of the Blessed Virgin by a playwright who had long since turned away from his Protestant background has occasioned much comment; the echoes of Dante's Beatrice have been noted here as well. Within the context of the non-Christian tone of the play as a whole, and particularly the absence of God himself in the concluding scene, the heavenly women who escort Faust to his reward leave a powerful impression of the feminine as the source of salvation.

As Hans Eichner has shown, Goethe in his later writings used gender symbolism in several ways. On the one hand, Goethe joined with the Romantics in upholding human love as a mirror or microcosm of divine love; woman, as the object of man's love, was therefore invested with loving and love-worthy qualities. The result was a literary idealization of women in which femininity became a metaphor of love itself.[31] In addition, however, the major female characters in Goethe's later writing share the quality of passive and even sterile purity, which Goethe tended to contrast with masculine activity— the activity which inevitably incurs error and guilt. The resolution of this paradox seems to be that both purity and activity are necessary, even though they seem contradictory; the feminine ideal of purity inspires the masculine drive to act and achieve. Goethe plays this out through a series of male and female characters who symbolize these qualities quite consistently.[32]

The Eternal Feminine, then, is both the embodiment of love, the highest value in the Romantic scheme of things, and the source of inspiration for the active life required of man. As such, it is essential to the creative process, for which birth and rebirth are the most obvious metaphors. Goethe may not have believed in the Mothers as actual goddesses, but he gave powerful expression to the Romantic idealization of woman. His most enduring expression of the theme occurs in *Faust*, an enormously influential drama which provides a setting rife with occult overtones, Romantic notions of immanence and intuitive perception, and neopaganism. The drama exhibits so many points of similarity with Goddess spirituality that we need not be surprised when it crops up again in the course of this narrative.

The same is true of German Romanticism in general. J. J. Bachofen, whom we shall meet in Chapter 11, has been called "the last of the Romantics," and he will pass on to the Goddess movement some of what we have seen in this chapter. Now, however, we must follow the progress of Romanticism into France, where it will produce even more pertinent information for our inquiry into the origin of the Goddess.

8

Utopian Feminism in France

> *Woman is a religion.*
>
> Jules Michelet

THE SITUATION IN FRANCE was quite different from the state of affairs in Germany. During the 1600s and 1700s, France was the most populous and powerful state in continental Europe. The unification of the French nation had already been achieved centuries ago, and the Bourbon dynasty had been in place since 1598. As we saw in the Introduction, Paris could have been considered the capital city of the Enlightenment. The liberal and radical ideas which emerged there, as the "Ancien Regime" became increasingly fragile and decadent, articulated the widespread discontent which eventually exploded in the French Revolution of 1789. But by most assessments, the revolution was deemed a failure. By 1815 it was clear that its promises of freedom and general prosperity remained unfulfilled. Liberty, equality, and fraternity had not triumphed after all; they were in retreat and disarray.

By this time France itself had changed irrevocably, however, and the Bourbon restoration was not to last. King Charles x aspired to the absolute powers of his forebears, but he lacked the competence to achieve his goal. In the midsummer of 1830, he made a clumsy grab for complete control which simply provoked a popular uprising and ended his reign. The new "July Monarchy" featured Charles's distant cousin, the former Duke of Orleans, reigning as King Louis-Philippe. He was presented to the public as a "citizen king," ruling by constitutional mandate rather than divine right. The situation of the middle classes improved significantly under Louis-Philippe, but the lower classes and the radicals saw little real change, and felt that the chance for a genuine revolution had been squandered.[1]

Freedom of speech and of the press were restored, and provided ample opportunity for writers to express and propagate a deep sense of determination for revolutionary change. This situation brought Paris to the fore yet again. Now, the French capital became the Western world's leading center of radical political thought and utopian speculation. The July Monarchy period (1830–48) witnessed an amazing explosion of ideas and schemes, ranging from elaborate industrialization plans to speculative utopianism, and the pace accelerated as the reign went on.

Another revolution became almost inevitable, and it eventually materialized in 1848. Louis-Philippe was overthrown in February and the Second Republic was proclaimed. The radicals' hopes for a total transformation of society, however, were thwarted again. The new government, still relatively insecure, reacted violently to a further uprising by Parisian workers. The result was the bloodshed of the so-called "slave war" in June. Later in the year came a presidential election; it was won easily by Louis-Napoleon Bonaparte, the former emperor's nephew, largely on the strength of his name. When parliament refused to let him run for a second term in 1852, he staged a coup and established the Second Empire, now calling himself Napoleon III.[2] His regime lasted until the military humiliation inflicted on France by Bismarck's Prussia in 1871.

This is, in brief, the chaotic course of events which unfolded in France over the course of a century. The hopes and dreams of three revolutions and the glories of Napoleonic supremacy alternated with bloodshed, internal repression, and defeat in foreign wars. What could be further removed from the tidy rationalism of the Enlightenment philosophers and their ideal of steady progress?

Here too, Romanticism took root as a reaction to the perceived failures of the Enlightenment. Even though Romanticism did not originate in France, the French nation was somewhat more vulnerable to certain Romantic excesses because of its peculiar history during this period. The erratic and unpredictable course of events in France made a mockery of rational planning in the eyes of many. Further, the passions aroused by the revolutions festered when the uprisings were suppressed, leading to increasingly grandiose schemes and radical plans for a new golden age. Several influential forms of New Age–style utopianism emerged and spread from Paris, including—most important for our purposes—a distinct strain of political/ religious orientation which is best described as "female messianism." This phenomenon added a radical political element to the literary idealization of women which we found in German Romanticism.

BEYOND THE ENLIGHTENMENT

Female messianism is hardly the first idea that comes to mind in connection with the Enlightenment philosophers of France. The status of women did not concern most of them; many kept mistresses, just like the aristocrats whom they criticized so strongly over other issues. As one writer has noted, "the French had a liberal attitude toward sex but not toward woman."[3]

A minority of them did advocate the legal emancipation of women. The Marquis de Condorcet (1743–94), for instance, argued that the so-called natural inferiority of women was not natural at all, but was imposed on them by society. Women's development was stunted by poor education and restrictive laws surrounding marriage and inheritance. To remedy this situation, he called for full educational, legal, and political equality for women, at a point in history when many men did not yet enjoy such rights.[4] His emphasis seems to have been practical and compassionate, certainly not radical by modern standards. While his other dreams of endless progress seem overly grandiose now, messianism is far too strong a term to apply to his views on women.

When we turn to writers who could be considered forerunners of

Romanticism, the phrase "female messianism" seems even less appropriate. The Swiss-born Jean-Jacques Rousseau (1712–78) was one of these, often at odds with his fellow philosophers of the French Enlightenment. While he agreed that there was a serious conflict between the structural inequalities of eighteenth-century European society and the true nature of human beings, he objected to the rationalistic and materialistic assumptions which guided his colleagues' quest for solutions.

Rousseau blamed civilization itself for corrupting the innate goodness of man, and he became famous for his notion of the "noble savage," the unspoiled and untainted natural human being. By coincidence, his speculations on this subject seemed to be confirmed when Tahiti was discovered in the 1760s. Reports from the French captain Bougainville and the Englishmen Wallis and Cook titillated Europe with the not entirely accurate picture of a whole way of life made up of languorous contentment, simple pleasures, and guiltless, free love.[5] Rousseau did not actually advocate a return to primitive living conditions; instead, he wanted to free his contemporaries from corrupting external influences so that their natural goodness could emerge and become fruitful. Rousseau located this natural, immanent goodness not in the mind, but in the feelings and sentiments—particularly the conscience, which he described as a "divine instinct, immortal voice from heaven . . . making man like God!"[6]

Rousseau's view of women was among the most conservative components of his thought. It came to expression, for instance, in his *Letter to M. d'Alembert on the Theatre* (1758). In this published missive, Rousseau condemned the theatre as an extreme example of civilized artificiality in which the spectators sit unnaturally still, forget themselves, and regard the play as a separate reality of its own. Rousseau went on to argue that the theatre reversed proper sex roles by giving prominence to women as actresses and by focusing so much attention on what we now call romantic love. "Since love represents the 'reign of women,' plays devoted to this theme simply help to extend the influence of the female sex; they make 'women and girls the tutors of the public' and give them 'the same power over the audience as they have over their lovers.'"[7]

His influential work *Emile* (1762) presented his scheme for an ideal education. The boy character Emile is to be raised in the country to avoid the moral contaminations of urban life and to establish his affinities with nature. There, his inborn potential for goodness can be actualized; the study of the humanities and sciences leads to the development of classic virtues like courage and temperance. In the fifth book of *Emile*, in contrast, the girl Sophie receives a very different education. She is assumed to be naturally emotional where Emile is rational, and she therefore "dabbles in music, art, fiction, and poetry, all the while refining her homemaking skills" to make her "an understanding, responsive wife and a caring, loving mother." Her fulfillment is defined entirely in terms of her role towards the men and children in her life and towards society in general.[8]

Rousseau clearly held that the innate goodness of human beings, their immanent divine affinities, took different forms in the male and the female. Like several of his other ideas, this one helped to stimulate later notions which he would scarcely have recognized. The concept that specific virtues inhere in the female because she is female, and that these especially must be liberated from the artificial restrictions imposed by society, may sound like Rousseau, but it was not his intended meaning. It did, however, become fundamental to nineteenth-century female messianism and, more broadly, to gender feminism as a whole. Rousseau himself did not consider female virtues special and superior to their male counterparts.

Neither did the so-called "Rousseau of the gutter" (*Rousseau du ruisseau*), Nicolas Edmé Restif de la Bretonne (1734–1806).[9] A child of the lower classes, Restif produced an amazing number of books. Many of them were read primarily for their pornographic details. In semi-autobiographical fashion, Restif explored most of the possibilities of human eroticism, objecting only to the extreme cruelty of his contemporary, the Marquis de Sade. One example is Restif's tale of a young wife who confides in her father that her husband has been beating her, only to discover that her story has stimulated uncontrollable arousal in her own parent.[10]

The more philosophical passages of Restif's books display organic thinking in the extreme. He claimed that stars and planets are alive, and produce plants and animals by a form of celestial copulation; he said that the universe is full of spirits who reincarnate through the stages of rock, plant, animal, and extraterrestrial; he held a pantheistic conception of God and asserted that comets are the result of God's need to urinate ("Dieu amène la comète aussi souvent qu'il a besoin de pisser"). He was also a defender of the charlatan alchemist Cagliostro and composed a sort of communist manifesto.[11]

Organicism seems to be the key to Restif's thought. He insisted that nothing exists except matter, but that matter itself is alive. More explicitly theological than Mesmer, he claimed that God is "a pure vital fluid ... present in all things."[12] The passions, particularly love, are therefore the energy of life itself; sex is an exercise in the sacred. Restif envisioned and wrote about a utopia dedicated to the satisfaction of human desires. Even so, he thought that his utopia could endure only if the satisfaction of the passions was strictly regulated through such means as segregation of the sexes, arranged marriages, and severe punishment for crimes like adultery.

Restif took a rigid view towards women, probably on the grounds that he believed them to be radically different, biologically and organically, from men. His view of the family—and, by extension, the state—was strictly patriarchal. Most people who lived before the 1830s (when scientific investigations finally revealed the existence of the human ovum) assumed that a child developed entirely from semen so long as it found its way into the hospitable environment of a woman's womb. Restif turned this biological guess into an absolute value judgment: "Women do not have the principle of life. It is annexed to the male and is his glorious prerogative." Accordingly, the general function of woman (apart from the specific task of bearing children) was simply to please man.[13]

Neither Condorcet nor Rousseau nor Restif founded a significant movement dedicated to his thought. The first two certainly expressed ideas which were destined to have a long life, although this was not really the case with Restif.[14] On the other hand, we must note several of their crucial contributions: Condorcet's defense of the natural rights of women; Rousseau's emphasis on immanence, the supreme importance of feelings, and the purity of the primitive;

and Restif's defense of the passions and his extreme organicism. All of these find echoes in the idealization of woman which takes place in the early nineteenth century.

Foundations of Gender Feminism

Charles Fourier

Charles Fourier (1772–1837) began and ended his life unhappily. Plagued by religious fears in his youth, he lost his sizeable inheritance and almost his life during the turmoil of the French Revolution. He went on to support himself as a travelling salesman and ended up a lonely, embittered bachelor, but he is known to history as one of the first great utopian visionaries of nineteenth-century France.[15]

Beginning with his programmatic work *The Theory of the Four Movements* (1808), Fourier spelled out a comprehensive view of history, according to which human civilization passes through no fewer than thirty-two distinct, inevitable stages. It is not a steady upward progression—the high point, an eight-thousand-year period of Cosmic Harmony, comes in the middle of the scheme. This is followed by a decline which mirrors the earlier rise, and history ends essentially where it began. Fourier claimed that history started with an apparently pleasant but simple state of affairs he called "Edenism," which resembled, more than anything else, the imaginary Tahiti known to his contemporaries. Then the invention of marriage caused a decline into Savagery, followed by the increasing authoritarianism and violence of Patriarchate and, lowest of all, Barbarism. The rise from Barbarism begins with Civilization, particularly its invention of the arts, sciences, and industry; this was the stage to which Fourier assigned the Europe of his day.

Progress upwards would be steady until the sixteenth age, which sees the full establishment of Harmony. Fourier was much ridiculed for his claims about the future course of human and natural evolution. He insisted, for instance, that human beings would evolve the *archibras*, a long tail with a powerful hand on the end, useful for everything from swimming and working to playing musical instruments. He also claimed that the Northern Lights would solidify into a sort of crown around the earth, reflecting sunlight to moderate the world's climate; this crown would, in addition, emit "boreal citric acid" and turn all the oceans into lemonade.

Fourier's underlying cosmology was rooted in ideas discussed in Chapter 5. As Jonathan Beecher summarized it, his theory "rested on two premises: (1) the universe was a unified system, a web of hidden correspondences or hieroglyphs, and (2) man was at the center of the system."[16] Together, the doctrine of correspondence and the notion of man as microcosm made possible the whole range of analogies and speculations through which Fourier developed his astonishing prescriptions and prophecies. Considerable speculation has gone into the origins of his ideas—unorthodox Freemasonry, Swedenborg, Schelling, Restif, and de Sade have all been suggested as significant influences on Fourier. It is indicative that he first published his theories under the auspices of Pierre Ballanche, a leading mesmerist of Lyons; beyond question, major aspects of his theories are almost indistinguishable from the views of the mesmerist Bergasse. As Darnton comments, however, "Bergasse's *Considérations sur le magnétisme animal* would have been one of the books on Fourier's bonfire; for Fourier imagined burning all books but his own. He denied indebtedness to any author."[17]

At any rate, the key to Fourier's system would have been familiar to Restif: "passionate attraction." In keeping with his general inclination towards organicism and his fondness for analogy, Fourier correlated natural forces like gravity and magnetism with human drives and desires. The result was his detailed list of twelve passions which comprise the energy of life and nature. His blueprint for utopian communal living, the "phalange," was designed to hold 180 people; this number, he claimed, would permit appropriate balance between monogamous and promiscuous inhabitants. The community would guarantee an acceptable minimum of sexual satisfaction to all its members, thus relieving them of the need to seduce or rape. All sexual minorities were to be included; Fourier himself admitted to a voyeuristic interest in lesbianism.[18]

This is the man who has been credited with coining the actual term "feminism."[19] Although he did not always pursue the thought consistently, he did claim that raising the status of women was the key to all other constructive development. The original fall from Edenism into Savagery was caused by the imposition of monogamous marriage in place of free love, a restriction which affected women most; the rise from Barbarism to Civilization, similarly, came with the abolition of the harem and the consequent granting of some minimal rights to females. "Social progress and changes of historical period take place in proportion to the advance of women toward liberty . . . The extension of the privileges of women is the fundamental cause of all social progress."[20]

These words made Fourier the hero of some nineteenth-century women's-rights activists. He shared the common Romantic belief that women were by nature more emotional and loving than men.[21] In his quest for balance and harmony, however, Fourier stopped short of idealizing womankind and calling for a utopian matriarchy; these particular notions would come from others. On the other hand, his system presumed a close link between general sexual freedom and the liberation of women in particular, a combination we find frequently in Goddess books.

Fourierism did become a distinct movement for a time. He had a small circle of committed disciples; when a schism threatened during the last year of his life, he attempted to mediate, and then conferred authority upon Victor Considérant as his official successor. Fourier was in very poor health at the time—he was known to be drinking heavily, even as he complained that the bakers and vintners of Paris were trying to poison him. He refused medical help and was found dead by his cleaning lady on October 10, 1837.[22]

Considérant and the other Fourierists played down the extremes in Fourier's thought. Some devoted themselves to reformist politics and were caught up in the repression which followed the 1848 revolution; others established short-lived phalanges, mostly by emigrating to America. Some almost deified Fourier—Beecher's book about him reproduces an illustration of heaven in which Jesus extends his right and left hands to Socrates and Fourier respectively, with figures like

Moses, Homer, Plato, and Newton in the background. Many outsiders reviled his memory, however. Nathaniel Hawthorne's wife Sophia attributed his "monstrous system" to the fact that he grew up during the French Revolution, when "the people worshipped a naked woman as the Goddess of Reason."[23]

Saint-Simonism

Fourier had competitors as well as disciples and critics. One of the most influential of these was Claude Henri de Rouvroy, the Count of Saint-Simon (1760–1825).[24] He led a colorful life, blending the style of an aristocrat with money-making schemes, military service, conspiracies, and visions of a socialist utopia. Although he knew little science himself, Saint-Simon tried to articulate a model for human society with a scientific basis (in this sense, he is an early "social scientist"). Basically, he argued that human societies must be understood as organisms and studied in a fashion similar to biology. Societies evolve like species; the optimal goal is a social system ruled by elite scientists who oversee a rational division of labor and produce a harmonious, productive industrial society in which all human needs are fully met.

As an organism, human society needs an animating principle, a "soul." Saint-Simon focused on religious issues late in his life, designing what he called New Christianity. Actually, this amounted to little more than the Golden Rule, which he presented as the ethical expression of the organic unity of all members of society. Beyond that, the church of New Christianity would have the role of easing the transition into the technological utopia, caring for the poor and preventing class violence.

Like Fourier, Saint-Simon attracted a group of disciples who carried on after his death. For our purposes, the later Saint-Simonians are more important than their master; it was they who developed an actual religious cult based on Saint-Simon's ideas, and who linked it to a specific understanding of the nature and status of women.[25] Immediately upon his death, Saint-Simon was proclaimed the savior of the world, the successor to Moses and Jesus. Members of his group went on evangelistic tours, proclaiming a happy gospel of the full and complete liberation of human capacities, all on the authority of Saint-Simon's allegedly definitive revelation. Two leaders were recognized as "Fathers" of the movement: Amand Bazard, a logical and principled believer, and Prosper Enfantin (1796–1864), who blended striking physical attractiveness with an even more impressive degree of personal charisma, usually expressed in a Romantically poetic and loving fashion.

The movement experienced a crisis in 1830. The July revolution caught them by surprise, and the leadership was unable to capitalize on the situation in any way at all. Then Enfantin and Bazard fell out over the status of women. Like Condorcet and Fourier before them, the Saint-Simonians had been calling for the emancipation of women along with improvements in the situation of the working classes. Again like Fourier, the movement was looking to the day when human desires would no longer be pent up by the demands of a supposedly archaic religion and social system; the Saint-Simonians referred to this as "the resurrection of the flesh." Enfantin drew a conclusion similar to Fourier's: those who feel a need for sexual variety deserve as much freedom and fulfillment as those who are inclined to monogamy. If the lines of paternity become confused as a result, this can only enhance the status of women as mothers.

Bazard replied that promiscuity would only debase women and the whole movement, but by 1831 he had lost the power struggle in the group and Enfantin emerged supreme. He led the core membership into a monastic retreat to prepare for the evangelization of the world. This isolation under his total personal authority is vaguely reminiscent of some so-called "cults" of recent decades, but the retreat was open to the public. Enfantin calmly accepted the role of prophet and divine incarnation; as one follower testified, "Tu es . . . l'*Homme-Dieu*" (You are the *Man-God*).

Enfantin's version of Saint-Simonism called for women's liberation in more Romantic terms than Fourier used. Women were seen as the ultimate exponents of love, and only their full liberation would allow the complete triumph of love in the world at large. Such ideas were publicized through the widely circulated sermon of January 1,

1832, preached by Enfantin's follower Abel Transon (who later converted to Fourierism). He denounced Christian morality for its emphasis on sexual exclusivity in marriage and announced, "I solemnly proclaim free, free to give their love and their bodies, all women who have been betrayed or sold, bought or taken . . . Jesus brought women a first degree of emancipation . . . We will do something a little bit greater . . . we have come to *achieve* the emancipation of women."[26]

Enfantin went even further than this. The Father, it turned out, was waiting for the Mother. If love were the key to the new age, and women were the exemplars of love, it was almost inevitable that Enfantin would arrive at his doctrine of the female Messiah, his missing partner and superior. As he put it himself, "De cette femme *Messie*, je sens que je suis le *Precurseur*, . . . mes actes . . . découlent tous de ma foi dans les femmes" (Of this woman *Messiah*, I feel that I am the *Precursor*, my deeds all flow from my faith in women). He kept the Mother's empty chair beside him and refused to rule on various theoretical and practical questions until she arrived to speak.

The great Saint-Simonian experiment came to an early and dramatic end. Life in the monastery was gaudy rather than ascetic, and with the titillation of Enfantin's well-publicized teachings as a drawing card, the community itself became both a public spectacle and a scandal. In August 1832, Enfantin and his colleagues were brought to trial and convicted of outraging public morality and were sentenced to a year's imprisonment. Enfantin said farewell by giving up his role as Father and directing his disciples to search for the Mother.

Search they did. Emile Barrault reorganized the group as the Companions of the Woman, dedicated to following "l'inspiration des *femmes* et de la *mère*" (the inspiration of *women* and of the *mother*). This fluidity between the notion of a single female Messiah and the messianic quality of women in general was typical. The group took out newspaper advertisements asking the Mother to reveal herself and wrote letters to prominent women who seemed likely candidates. When two young girls had a vision of the Mother appearing in Constantinople, Barrault led an expedition to the Near East, declaring that May 1833 would be the time of the final revelation. When she failed to appear, one of Barrault's companions claimed that she was in India; Barrault rejected this as a heresy, and the little group dissolved in bickering.

This marked the end of the movement as such. Enfantin was released from prison in August 1833, but he now devoted himself to Saint-Simon's original interest in the development of industry. He spent some years in the management of a railway company in southern France and played a largely unsung role in promoting the Suez Canal project. Some of his followers went on to distinguished careers in business or politics, still bearing traces of his ideal of universal love. More importantly, Enfantin's Saint-Simonism left its distinctive mark on a surprising list of famous people who never actually participated in it: J. L. Talmon names "Carlyle and Mazzini, Heine and de Vigny, George Sand and Michelet, Berlioz and Liszt, and of course Marx and Engels."[27]

Ganneau, Flora Tristan, Alphonse Constant

A similar but less successful cult was established in Paris during the later 1830s by an artist named Ganneau.[28] He founded a movement called "Evadism" (combining "Eve" and "Adam") and took for himself the title "Mapah" (from "mater" and "pater"). Garbed in a gray felt hat, a smock, and clogs, he preached eloquently of love, human fraternity, and sexual equality and wrote condescending letters to the Pope. He was known to Alexander Dumas, and another writer has described him thus:

> In an appalling garret there was a bearded man of majestic demeanor, who invariably wore over his clothes the tattered cloak of a woman, and had in consequence rather the air of a destitute dervish. He was surrounded by several men, bearded and ecstatic like himself, and in addition to these there was a woman with motionless features, who seemed like an entranced somnambulist. The prophet's manner was abrupt and yet sympathetic; he had hallucinated eyes and an infectious quality of eloquence. He spoke with emphasis, warmed to his subject quickly, chafed and fumed till a white froth gathered at his lips . . . he told us one day confidentially that he was Louis XVII

returned to earth for a work of regeneration, while the woman who shared his life was Marie Antoinette of France.[29]

Apparently he was still preaching of all-conquering love in 1849.[30]

There was a more serious claimant to the role of female Messiah than Ganneau's mistress, however. Flora Tristan (1805–44) is best remembered today as a pioneer socialist and feminist. While she never achieved the general fame of her contemporary, the feminist novelist Aurore Dudevant ("George Sand," 1804–76), she made a distinctive contribution to the tradition we are tracing here; she had strikingly grandiose ideas at different points during her short life.[31] Born to a French woman and a Peruvian nobleman, Tristan was happily preparing to be married when the discovery that she was actually illegitimate led to the breaking of the engagement. She went on to marry a printer who turned violently abusive, causing her to run away from him. She took along her infant daughter, who would eventually become the mother of the artist Paul Gauguin.

Once free of domestic entanglements, Tristan led a wildly active life in the 1830s. She joined the Saint-Simonians and took part in the search for the Mother; she introduced herself to Fourier and corresponded with him; she traveled both to England and to Peru, where she met local revolutionaries and petitioned unsuccessfully for financial support from her father's family; and, after several other adventures, she wrote a highly successful autobiography, *Peregrinations of a Pariah*, which was published in 1838. Its success was only enhanced when her jealous husband, who came off poorly in the book, shot her down from behind in the street. She recovered and went on to win a sensational court case against him—she was granted a legal separation, and he was sent to prison.

For the next few years, Tristan was a Parisian celebrity. She toured the literary salons and had her portrait appear in magazines. Drawing on her Fourierist and Saint-Simonian background as well as her personal experience, she became a well-known campaigner for the rights of women and the working class. To Tristan, the highest value was love—universal, asexual love. It appears that she had no further intimate relationships with men; she had one close female disciple,

Eléonore Blanc, and confided in one letter that she had long wanted to make another woman love her passionately.[32]

In 1839, seven years after the appearance of Part II of Goethe's *Faust*, Tristan published a novel of her own entitled *Méphis*. Here, the title is the nickname of the hero, Mephistopheles, a romantically mysterious proletarian male feminist. In long dialogues with the heroine, Maréquita, he recounts tales of his earlier life. At one point, he describes a pair of pictures he had painted: one showed a priest blessing the sword of a warrior, thus linking Christianity, masculinity, and violence; the other featured "la femme *guide de l'humanité*," the loving female savior who would guide the human race into an age of universal peace, all by the gentle force of passionate attraction. Later in the novel, it becomes apparent that Méphis and Maréquita will conceive the female messiah themselves. Commentators on the novel have observed that the hero and heroine represent two sides of the author's own personality.[33] Thus, on one level, all the speeches represent her dialogues with herself. If this is true, it carries the suggestion that on another level she is both father and mother of the female messiah. This literary evidence seems to provide the stepping-stone between the Saint-Simonians' search for the Mother and Tristan's assumption of the role on her own behalf.

Tristan went on to publish her *London Journal* in 1840; it mixes Anglophobia with concern for the status of women across the Channel. Then she became even more active in campaigning for women's and workers' rights. She called for a Workers' Union which, in the style of Fourier and Enfantin, was to establish communal "palaces" in which the lower classes and both sexes could develop fulfilling lives. Her fame was increasing; she and George Sand were the two women whom Karl Marx was told he must meet when he moved to Paris. In 1844 she began a tour of France to promote her ideas, but she fell ill and died in Bordeaux, in the home of Saint-Simonian friends.

In her letters from this period, it is clear that she assumed the messianic role for herself; she even claimed that her sufferings exceeded those of Christ and the apostles a hundredfold. "The Jewish people were dead in abasement, and Jesus raised them up," she wrote. "The Christian people are dead today in abasement, and Flora Tristan, the first strong woman, will raise them."[34] The workers never adopted her scheme, but they did erect a memorial to her during the 1848 revolution.

Flora Tristan had neither success nor successor in the political realm, but her ideas had repercussions in other ways. One of her closest collaborators in her final years was Alphonse Louis Constant (1810–75).[35] Constant had begun training for the priesthood, but his first mentor was an abbot with a keen interest in Mesmerism, prophecy, and occult speculations; he was soon removed from his post for his unorthodoxy. After moving on to another seminary, Constant developed a strong affection for one of his female catechism students and decided against a life of celibacy. He abandoned his training without being ordained to the priesthood, but he was commonly known afterwards as "Abbé" Constant and always retained a personal sense of loyalty to the Catholic Church.

Constant moved on to the heady atmosphere of July Monarchy Paris. He supported himself through his artistic talents and immersed himself in the radical politics of the time. His own ideas were still strongly tinted with mystical notions from his time in the seminary. One of his colleagues was an acquaintance from his school days, the writer Alphonse Esquiros. Esquiros published a novel entitled *The Magician* in 1838; it is said to have featured "a whole harem of female zombies, a brass robot which preached incessantly of the virtues of chastity and an hermaphrodite which carried on a correspondence with the moon!"[36] On one of their excursions, Esquiros took Constant to visit the Mapah, whom he described as "the most eloquent, most radiant and magnificent fool in the visible order of things"; it is Constant's account of this visit which I quoted above.

In 1840 Constant completed a book of his own called *The Bible of Liberty*. Among other things, it suggested that when a poor man falls into despair and contemplates suicide, he should at least take a rich man to the grave with him. Thanks to this incitement to murder, the book was seized at the publisher's, and Constant was jailed through the winter of 1841–42 (as was Esquiros for his communist tract *The Gospel of the People*; Constant later blamed both books on the influence of the Mapah). Evidently, it was during his time in prison that he first discovered the writings of Swedenborg.

By this time he had already met Flora Tristan, probably on the literary salon circuit in 1839 (he was also personally acquainted with the authors Alexander Dumas, Honoré de Balzac, Charles Baudelaire, and Victor Hugo). He drew one of Tristan's magazine portraits, and they were sufficiently close that she went to the trouble of making things more comfortable for him in prison. While he was incarcerated, he later claimed, he had a mystical vision of the end of the world, complete with natural catastrophes and social disintegration; from amidst the death and destruction came a small voice saying, "Brothers, set woman free so that the family may be reborn through love, and so that we may all become one family under the loving guidance of the mother!"[37] His next two books, *The Assumption of Woman* (1841) and *Mother of God* (1844), are fully in the female-messiah style.

In *The Assumption of Woman*, the echoes of Flora Tristan are ringing. The book mixes excerpts from the biblical Song of Solomon and from the writings of some mystical saints with Constant's own commentary. He combines a lament over woman's current social status as a "pariah" with a rhapsody to the saving power of woman's love. Constant, still single himself, joins in the Romantic polemic against marriage as "the most cynical of many forms of prostitution." Love is, however, the very power of God's own creation, and when Christ died he left us in the care of his Mother (John 19:27 as allegorized by Constant). The Virgin Mary thus becomes a symbol of the love of woman which redeems man. "Woman is a mysterious being who bridges heaven and earth and who brings to the wretched dreams of benevolent spirit and consoling angels," Constant proclaimed; she is "the whole of God's grace and of the beauty of the world."[38]

The Mother of God recounts Constant's prison vision. His apocalypse concludes with the defeat of Satan—instead of being vanquished by Christ in battle (Rev. 19–20), the great serpent is reduced to gibbering impotence by the mere presence of Mary, and expires at a touch of her "delicate foot." A star floats out of his open mouth and a heavenly voice announces, "Evil, on dying, has given birth to light. Satan is dead and Lucifer is delivered. Night has given birth to the morning star, and the star, forerunner of dawn, will henceforth shine like a diadem on the forehead of woman." The love of woman reconciles all polarities, even good and evil.

The book goes on to describe Constant's conception of a matriarchal utopia. In the vision, he is guided through the new world order by a young girl. He feels the organic union of the ideal community: "Their souls became part of my soul and their thoughts were as my own . . . we were like members of a single body which have no separate lives of their own." Utopia is, inevitably, governed by maternal love. The wicked are treated as being morally sick, and are reclaimed and redeemed by the love of women, to whom all medical care is entrusted; nurses replace jailers. Education, "the first and greatest task of mental and physical hygiene," is fully under the control of women, since "only women understand the workings of a child's heart." The essential content of education is the unity of God (Satan now being nonexistent), his immanent presence in all human beings, and the resulting organic unity of the human group.[39]

These books by Constant are often ignored in general histories of July Monarchy France. He rarely rates more than a footnote in conventional accounts; when he actually appears in the narrative of one specialist, it is only to be dismissed as "either a charlatan or mentally unbalanced."[40] Constant was, however, on familiar terms with a number of famous and significant people, and some of the ideas expressed in his books appear again later in the hands of better-known writers. Constant's matriarchal apocalypse goes beyond even Enfantin in some respects, and it anticipates some of the themes we shall encounter below in the works of such famous Parisian authors as Auguste Comte and Jules Michelet. The question of Constant's wider influence in the Paris of the 1840s is an interesting one, considering his undoubted later accomplishments, but we will not dwell on the matter here.

When Tristan left on her ill-fated speaking tour, she entrusted to Constant the notes she had made towards her next book. After she died, he edited them and produced her posthumous work, *The Emancipation of Woman, or the Testament of the Pariah* (1845), with Fourier's famous lines about women and social progress as the epigraph. Constant's French biographer judged the book to be Tristan's in content, but Constant's in form and style. The whole relationship between Tristan and Constant is often passed over by the feminists and socialists who write about her, some of whom completely ignore the existence of *The Emancipation of Woman*; it is, for whatever reason, Constant's biographers who usually provide the details on these matters.[41]

Constant remained active in utopian political circles. He produced several more books and even served another short prison term for preaching class war in his book *The Voice of Famine* (1846). He supported himself through his artistic endeavors, including a commission to provide the illustrations for Dumas' *The Count of Monte Cristo*. He participated in the agitation leading up to the 1848 revolution and stood as a candidate in the ensuing election. The voters rejected him, however, and thus brought an end to his political activities. Following this rebuke, Constant undertook a major change of career, and we shall return to him in Chapter 9.

UTOPIANS AND RADICALS

During the last half of the July Monarchy, Paris was the Western world's leading center of radical thought. An economic depression in 1837 had caused widespread impoverishment, and by 1840 there were strikes and demonstrations in the streets of the capital. Calls for a total reorganization of society poured from the publishers, many of them in the idealistic vein which has been aptly named "social romanticism."[42] In 1840 alone, Pierre Leroux, an ex-Saint-Simonian and friend of George Sand, issued his landmark *On Humanity*; radical socialist Louis Blanc published his *Organization of Labor*; Pierre Joseph Proudhon's *What is Property?* popularized the notion that private property is theft; and Etienne Cabet's utopian *Voyage to Icaria* introduced the term "communism" into popular discourse. Esquiros's *Gospel*, Constant's *Bible*, and other such diatribes added to the furor.

It is particularly interesting to note that Karl Marx and Friedrich Engels established their partnership in precisely this environment. Like so many others, they had come to Paris by 1844 because they saw it as the fountainhead of progressive thought.[43] They issued their first collaborative effort, *The Holy Family*, the next year. Despite its title, this document was mostly an advocacy of philosophical materialism in the German tradition, promoting the ideas of Ludwig

Feuerbach against the idealism of Hegel. When addressing women's rights, Marx essentially watered down Fourier—he saw the rising status of women as an indicator of social progress, but not as its cause.[44] At this stage, however, two other names are of paramount importance for our inquiry: Auguste Comte and Jules Michelet.

Auguste Comte

Comte (1798–1857) is a major figure in Western intellectual history for at least two reasons.[45] In "positivism," he created a thoroughly scientific and rational approach to the problem of knowledge, arguing that both theology and speculative philosophy belonged to outmoded stages of human development. Further, in "sociology" (a term he apparently coined), he pioneered some of the basic techniques of social science, claiming that human society could be observed and analyzed like any natural object or process. The goal of what he called "social physics" was not simply to observe, but to design a better society just as an engineer might design a better automobile.

This is the image of Comte known to most educated people today, if they know him at all. Comte himself had a difficult career, however. Despite an amazing memory, he abandoned his education without completing a degree and subsisted for much of his life by teaching courses independently and drawing financial support from friends. He began with a highly significant paid position: he was secretary to, and collaborator with, none other than the Count of Saint-Simon. Their partnership collapsed several years later, after they quarreled over which of them should be considered the true author of one of their joint efforts. Comte also had a stormy marriage to a former prostitute, one Caroline Massin. She nursed him through a prolonged bout of emotional disturbance after he had been discharged "uncured" by a doctor, and she provided indispensable support while he wrote his best-known work, the *Course in Positive Philosophy*. She finally left him in 1842, days after the last installment appeared. The book itself passed almost unnoticed until two supporters of Comte, Emile Littré in France and John Stuart Mill in England, publicized his ideas.

Comte is relevant to our investigation because of the last part of his career, the part which is generally taken less seriously than his early work on positivism. In October 1845, he met and fell deeply in love with Clothilde de Vaux. She was unhappily married to a wastrel, but it seems that her affair with Comte was never consummated; she died of tuberculosis after an intense emotional relationship of only six months. Once again, a dead woman became the repository of a man's ideals and highest aspirations. Consciously imitating Dante's love for Beatrice, if not also Novalis's adoration of Sophia von Kühn, Comte devoted himself to developing a Religion of Humanity in which love itself would rule all, under the benign auspices of a deified Mme. de Vaux herself. Comte designed vestments, rituals, and a sacred calendar in close imitation of the Catholicism he had rejected in his youth; he lived a monastic style of life as High Priest of his new religion and served before her red chair as before an altar. He also undertook close spiritual supervision of the disciples he attracted, punishing disobedience and independent thinking with excommunication. Eventually he presented himself as the personification of the "Great Being" and called upon various rulers and religions of the world to submit to him.

Like other heirs of Saint-Simon, Comte looked forward to a New Age in which industry would flourish to enhance the material well-being of humanity, and in which the workers themselves would enjoy both their labor and the fruits of it. Again, he saw utopia in hierarchical terms, asserting that rulership would belong to an elite group of priest/scientists. And, Comte shared in the idealization of womankind characteristic of his fellows. Comte's ideal woman was of a decidedly Romantic type. He emphasized that even when boys and girls are educated together, they will inevitably develop different sex-related aptitudes as they mature; to minimize the difference between the sexes was simply contrary to nature. Woman, as such, is the incarnation of love and feeling in this world; man is ennobled and purified by worshipping and serving such a radiant being. "The direction, then, of progress in the social condition of woman is this: to render her life more and more domestic."[46] By participating in public life, women would erode those qualities which made them uniquely valuable and indispensable; only domesticity would give free rein to their moral superiority over men.

In Comte's own life, this was not to be. He was nursed through his final days by a young female disciple, Sophie Bliaux. Once he died, however, his wife Caroline reappeared to claim her share of the household assets and to defend her reputation against the insults Comte had enshrined in his will. Littré supported her, while the more recent followers of the Religion of Humanity tried to minimize her claims as Comte himself had wished. As his biographer Standley notes, "it was already apparent that the philosophy designed to bring unity to all mankind had done little to create harmony even within this small group."[47]

Jules Michelet

Although Comte is probably better remembered today, his contemporary Jules Michelet (1798–1874) was much more influential in his own time.[48] There are several interesting parallels in the lives of these two men who were born seven months apart, most of all in their relationships with women. Each contracted an unhappy first marriage; each fell deeply in love with a married woman who died prematurely, and who became the focus of his idealization of womankind; and each ended his days in the fond company of a much younger woman.

Michelet's origins were in the working classes. His father was a printer who served time in debtors' prison and was then put out of business when Napoleon reduced the number of printers who were allowed to operate. His mother, nine years older than his father, appears to have been the dominant presence in the family until her death when Michelet was seventeen. Two years later, he became involved with a woman six years older than himself, Pauline Rousseau. He married her in 1824, in time to legitimize the birth of their daughter Adèle (a son, Charles, followed in 1829). Michelet trained in history and philosophy, and worked his way up from tutoring positions until he was appointed to a professorship in the prestigious Collège de France in 1838. He had already published several books, including the first three volumes of his monumental *History of France*. Very much in the Romantic temper, it defended the ideals of the French Revolution by portraying the masses, the entire people, as the corporate "hero" of the story.

At this stage, Michelet's general philosophy rejected both traditional Christianity and the materialism and rationalism of the Enlightenment. His goal was the liberation of human free will, defying not only the authority of the church and the state, but even the "fatalism" which he attributed to the laws of nature and necessity. Like many of his contemporaries, he was accustomed to the metaphorical equation of man with culture and woman with nature. When depicting the ravages of disease and natural disaster, he typically described nature as a *marâtre*, a wicked stepmother.

Michelet's life underwent a dramatic change in the middle years of the July Monarchy. In 1839, after many unhappy years, his wife Pauline "died of drink, tuberculosis, and neglect."[49] The guilt-ridden Michelet soon found solace. The next year, he met the mother of one of his closest students, Alfred Dumesnil. Mme. Françoise-Adèle Dumesnil had brought Alfred to Paris, leaving her much older husband behind in the family home in Rouen. By all accounts, especially his own, Michelet found in her the soul-mate he had never had before. In response, the woman/nature theme in his writing was transformed into a source of strength and life. Regarding Mme. Dumesnil as the ideal mother and nurturing companion, he generalized his intense feelings about her to nature and womankind as a whole. He discovered and celebrated what Arthur Mitzman describes as "an essentially matriarchal and naturalist core in the religion of Jesus" and lectured on "the maternity of Providence," describing God as "a mother who had to nurse the world drop by drop for the development of liberty."[50] Appearing as it does between Enfantin's quest for the Mother and Comte's Religion of Humanity, this could be considered one of our first real glimpses of the Goddess.

In June 1841, Mme. Dumesnil moved into Michelet's house. She was terminally ill, and Michelet offered his own and Adèle's services to care for her (Adèle later married Alfred Dumesnil). Under such circumstances the emotional intensity of the relationship could only increase, and Michelet's idealization of womankind in the image of Mme. Dumesnil is apparent in the hagiography of Joan of Arc which he wrote during this period. The lady died in his home on the last day of May, 1842. Her passing had at least two noticeable effects on Michelet's work.

First, it heightened even further his idealization of the female. In tones oddly reminiscent of Constant, Michelet upheld woman as the mediatrix of love, intuition, and fecundity. Reversing his earlier stand, he now regarded nature as the source of freedom, and civilization—the machine—as its enemy. Against the rising tide of the industrial revolution, Michelet upheld "woman as the source of pantheist aestheticism for the overspecialized male."[51] Second, Michelet declared war on the church. He was deeply grieved that in her last days, Mme. Dumesnil preferred to confide in her priest rather than in him. His rage eventually found an outlet in his 1845 book *Priest, Woman and Family*. Here he argued that the confessor, being privy to women's innermost thoughts, is able to manipulate their minds to serve the church rather than their families' best interests. Women's distinctive gift of love is thus perverted and made useless. Michelet's public lectures against the Jesuits, who happened to be campaigning for church control over education at the time, were sensationally controversial.

Maternal symbolism was blended with Romantic nationalism in *The People* (1846), a work in which Michelet's writing is said to have "escaped factual limitations" in its exploration of themes close to his heart.[52] Michelet argued that traditional class structure divided the French against themselves, and he sought to overcome it by preaching the organic unity of the nation. Fraternity, one of the great unfulfilled goals of the revolution, was to be achieved through a kind of "pantheistic, matriarchal view of nature and society."[53] Then the French nation could play its true role as the beacon of humanity. "When France remembers what she is and must be—the salvation of mankind—she will gather her children around her and teach them France as faith and as religion . . . And this is not fanaticism."[54]

Michelet's books and lectures became increasingly radical as the 1840s progressed; his classroom was a lively center of revolutionary rhetoric, with both students and police flocking to hear him. Eventually, on January 6, 1848, the government acted—Michelet's course was suspended. Expecting such an intervention, Michelet had his lectures circulated in print. This was probably the peak of his public influence. Michelet's enraged supporters were among the ringleaders of the February 1848 revolution, and his reinstatement in March prompted a public celebration of victory. Surprisingly, however, Michelet was not chosen to participate in the provisional government which resulted from the revolt he had helped to foment. He refused to run in the resulting election; he wanted to create a new religion for the new republic, since this is where he thought the original revolution had most seriously failed. The class strife of June left him completely disillusioned, and he avoided politics ever after.

Several significant events in his life followed. First, he met and married a frail young woman named Athénaïs Mialaret. She came to exercise a profound influence on him and caused a lasting rift between Michelet and his children; she has also been blamed by some historians for the strange directions he took in his writing after their marriage. Second, Michelet lost his professorial position in 1852 after refusing an oath of loyalty to Napoleon III. Third, he spent most of a year in 1853–54 travelling in Italy. In the course of the journey, he went to Acqui to recuperate in the mud baths of a spa. This apparently triggered an ecstatic experience of rebirth in the "maternal embrace of the earth," from which he emerged "shining with a gleam of youth . . . Nature . . . reopened her arms and awaited me."[55]

This new Michelet, no longer a professor, resolved to write for the people rather than the academics. His deeper appreciation of Mother Nature led to books like *The Insect* (1857). Religious concerns are very much in evidence here. The transformation of an insect through the stages of egg, larva, pupa, and adult allows Michelet to argue for human immortality, which was of great concern to him after his son by Athénaïs died in infancy. The communities of ants and bees serve as models of the ideal society, in which the "service" of the lower classes is willing and creative rather than compulsory. Michelet draws attention to the fact that these communities are matriarchies; it is a queen who is nourished and guarded, mostly by female warriors. "It is their pride that when necessary they know how to create their God," he wrote.[56]

New controversy greeted the publication of *Love* (1858) and *Woman* (1859). By now, Michelet's organic philosophy had been reinforced and elaborated through his life with Athénaïs. Her sickliness apparently included vaginismus, which kept their sex life to a minimum. Michelet's biological curiosity led him to make meticulous observations of her physiology, and he claimed to know her menstrual cycles as well as if he had lived in her intestines. Combined with his continued adulation of Mme. Dumesnil, his own motherly care for this semi-invalid left its mark in his works.

More blatantly than many other nineteenth-century writers, Michelet combined a rhapsodic idealization of women with a denigration of their practical abilities in these two books. As he had done since the 1840s, he associated the virtues of love, sympathy and nurture with women as a sex. Now, following the scientific discovery of human ovulation, he tried to argue that these moral characteristics were physiologically located in the womb. Since only these virtues could create the organically unified nation he had sought all his life, he now depended on women to work out the salvation of France. Hence his triumphant proclamation: "Woman is a religion."[57]

What did he mean by this? He was still certain that the sexes are defined and governed by their biology. Michelet's fascination with menstruation led him to believe that women are "wounded" one week out of four, and that two other weeks in the month are affected to some extent as well. Accordingly, women must be protected if they are to survive, and most certainly they must not enter the workforce alongside men. This would not only de-feminize them but endanger them. Whereas the work of men is to create and be productive, the true calling of women is marriage and motherhood. Their gift is not productivity but harmonization, the establishment in the home of a contented equilibrium which would then permeate the public sphere, reconcile classes and regions, and make of France itself a great maternal family. When this happens, France can play its own true role as savior of the world.[58]

Michelet asserted that a woman's life must be a life of self-sacrifice. A real woman cannot exist without a husband; she must be married. Not only that, but her relationship with her children must be one of endless giving—he even celebrated the notion of a young mother gladly and eagerly nursing her infant to the point of her own death.[59] Women may have a messianic role to play in the family, the nation, and the world, but they seem not to derive much benefit from it themselves. Even in his own time, some women objected to Michelet's characterization of them, their physiological characteristics, and their role in the world at large. Modern feminists are even less sympathetic to his ideal of self-abnegation as the special calling of the female.[60] How ironic it is, then, that Michelet was the man who first proposed that witchcraft was a primordial nature religion which survived the centuries as a refuge for women and the poor—those who were oppressed by hierarchical, patriarchal Christendom. Michelet, as we shall see, was to make Wicca possible.

European culture was irrevocably transformed by the middle of the nineteenth century. In the preceding 150 years, the post-Reformation world of Western Christian civilization had been battered by the attacks of the Enlightenment philosophers and their activist interpreters on the matters of traditional religious belief and secular authority. The Enlightenment's rationalistic philosophy largely failed, however, to replace those structures with a satisfying and comforting worldview or a widely acceptable system of governance. Romanticism then moved into the void with its narcissism and tribalism, as well as its appeal to both intense subjective experience and a willing submission to the group constituted by one's own kind. A necessary or at least inevitable reaction to the one-dimensional character of materialistic rationalism, Romanticism's invocation of unbridled feeling and its concomitant rejection of moral and logical limits led it on towards excesses of its own.

Along with all this came the idealization of women as the biological group in which the prime Romantic values were to be found in pristine fullness. Beneath the ritual trappings, this is the core of Goddess spirituality. To see how Michelet's dictum "woman is a religion" becomes an actual reality, we must follow our line of investigation to one specific element in the immediate aftermath of Romanticism: the occult revival of the late nineteenth century.

PART III

THE MODERN ESOTERIC TRADITION

9

The European Occult Revival

I am writing Isis; *not writing, rather copying out and drawing that which She personally shows to me.*

Helena Petrovna Blavatsky

THE 1848 REVOLUTION IN FRANCE stimulated similar uprisings in other parts of Europe, notably in Germany, Austria, and Italy. In all these cases the radicals were defeated; despite some changes in form and appearance, political power remained for the most part with those who had held it all along. As Talmon argues, this series of events was a turning point in modern European history. The failures of 1848 marked a decisive defeat for social romanticism in its revolutionary guise—the idea that oppressed nations and classes could unite against aristocratic and despotic governments and create a utopian society in which the needs of all would be fully and equally supplied. Now, loyalty to nation was more frequently pitted against loyalty to class, and nationalism became wedded to the possession and exercise of power. It is interesting to note that the political unification of Germany and of Italy—which finally did come about in the latter half of the nineteenth century—was achieved from the top down, by powerful individuals like Bismarck and Cavour, and not by popular uprisings.[1]

This development in power politics profited from the popularity of some Romantic themes, especially the idea of the nation as a unified organism with its own destiny to fulfill. The matters which concern us here, however, follow a different path. The truly radical and utopian impulse of the social romantics, when it was denied access to power, sometimes turned in upon itself. The flights of imagination which used to reach out into the world, designing workers' palaces and turning oceans into lemonade, were now redirected into a quest to lift the individual out of the humdrum and sordid world which surrounded him. The Romanticism of the early nineteenth century was mother to the occult revival of the 1850s and beyond.

The latter half of the century witnessed two particular trends which led directly towards the Goddess movement. One was the revival and renewal of the Western esoteric tradition, and the other was the new influence of the East. The primary agent of the latter was Theosophy; to explore the former, we must return to the interrupted career of Alphonse Louis Constant, the radical utopian mystic, political activist, and messianic feminist.

ELIPHAS LÉVI AND THE ESOTERIC TRADITION

Abbé Constant's New Life

As we saw in the preceding chapter, Constant's progress during the latter half of the July Monarchy was hardly a sparkling success.[2] He moved in the circles of radical political activists and was acquainted with some of the major literary figures of the time. He was often in financial difficulty, however, and served two terms in prison. In 1848 he was active on the fringes of the revolution, but he finished as a defeated candidate in the post-revolutionary election. His friend Esquiros unexpectedly won and thus became respectable; the two long-time colleagues, having less and less in common, soon parted ways. Constant then penned his *Testament of Liberty*. This was his farewell to politics, and it included extracts from many of his previous writings, including *Assumption of Woman* and *Mother of God*. This new book, like the others, looked forward to a New Age of love and socialism under woman and the Holy Spirit.

Constant's private life went through some upheaval too. After his first prison term in 1842, he had established a close friendship with the headmistress of a girls' school, who is known to posterity only as Mlle. Eugénie C. Often the couple were accompanied by one of Eugénie's senior students, seventeen-year-old Noémi Cadiot, on their Sunday afternoon promenades. At some point in the winter of 1845–46, Constant and Eugénie became lovers, and she conceived a child. Noémi, however, was thoroughly infatuated with Constant; when she finished school that spring, she arrived unannounced on his doorstep and moved in with him. Her furious father demanded a wedding, and Constant obliged on July 13, 1846. Then, on September 29, his son by Eugénie was born. Eugénie refused to see Constant again and never allowed him to meet his son. The latter did attend Constant's funeral in 1875—the first time he had ever seen his father.

Constant and Noémi had a daughter, Marie, in 1847. From that point, however, problems intervened. The young Noémi became active among the radical political writers along with her husband, using the pseudonym Claude Vignon. She grew especially close to the Marquis de Montferrier and eventually left Constant for Montferrier in 1853. While Constant was away in London the following year, she went back to his house and emptied it—in Thomas Williams's words, "taking with her not only his past but his furniture as well."[3] Their marriage was finally annulled in 1865, on the grounds that "Abbé" Constant had violated his vows to the Church by marrying in the first place (Noémi went on to wed one Maurice Rouvier, who later served as a cabinet minister in the Gambetta government of 1881–82). Meanwhile, little Marie Constant had died at the age of seven, in 1854. The end of the July Monarchy and the establishment of the Second Empire thus coincided with the conclusion of an entire phase in Alphonse Constant's life.

Constant lived alone for the rest of his days. He may, at this point, have called to mind his old bishop's response to reading *The Mother of God*: "If you knew women better, you would not adore Woman so unreservedly."[4] If so, it made little difference; Constant included large excerpts from his early matriarchal works in the books which were yet to come.

The Occult Philosophy of Eliphas Lévi

Even before 1848, Constant's eclectic reading list had included Hermetic and Kabbalistic literature, Paracelsus, Cornelius Agrippa, and Swedenborg. He had been surrounded by Fourierists, Saint-Simonians, and the self-anointed Flora Tristan, not to mention the Mapah. In 1852, while Louis-Napoleon's coup confirmed the final defeat of the revolutionary ideals to which he had given his life so far, Constant met the mentor and catalyst who launched him on his new and lasting vocation.

This was a Pole who went by the name Hoené Wronski (1778–1853). An eccentric of many talents, Wronski had done pioneering mathematical and astronomical research at the Institute of Marseilles during the Napoleonic years, conversing with the leading experts in these fields; then he offended his professional colleagues once too often and was expelled from the Institute. He lived in poverty for the rest of his life, producing manuscripts and publishing them whenever he could accumulate the necessary funds.

Wronski also designed and built mystical mechanisms of various sorts, including perpetual motion machines; as Constant wryly noted, none of them ever worked "because the copper and steel, not understanding any algebra, failed to conform to the evidence of his original designs."[5] His grandest effort was the *prognomètre*, a prediction machine composed of globes, wheels, and little doors covered with mathematical equations and zodiacal symbols. Its purpose was to "determine the equations of all past, present and future events, such that it would determine the value of every possible unknown."[6] This striking expression of faith in the power of science must have been an impressive sight, but it never actually worked either. Years after Wronski's death, Constant spotted it in a second-hand dealer's shop and, overcome by nostalgia, bought it for one hundred francs.

Wronski's importance to Constant lay not in his engineering abilities but in his prodigious intellect. In his book *Messianism* (1847), Wronski proclaimed the coming of a New Age in which religion, philosophy, and science would all be reconciled through the revelation of the true purpose of existence, both personal and national. All history would be explained, and all suffering would cease. In his *Secret Letter to His Highness Prince Louis-Napoleon* (1851), he called on Napoleon III to complete the work of his illustrious namesake by founding a new empire based on the revelation. What especially appealed to Constant, apparently, was the basic idea that the synthesis of all knowledge under a new revelation of the supreme truth would eventually lead to the establishment of a utopian society. With his interests in both utopianism and occultism already well entrenched, Constant responded to Wronski's stimulation by creating his own synthesis of religion, magic, and social engineering. This synthesis was founded on a fresh approach to the neopagan principle of correspondence.

Constant first published his new conceptions in *The Dogma and Ritual of High Magic*, which appeared in installments between 1854 and 1856. Here his change of persona appears—he issued the book under the Hebrew equivalents of his two given names, Alphonse Louis, and thus became Eliphas Lévi. In *Dogma and Ritual*, as in his later writings, Lévi presented the Kabbalah as the key to all mysteries and all knowledge. The true teachings of every religion are merely reflections of the eternal Kabbalistic principles, and religious and social strife arise when people deviate from the Kabbalistic verities. Kabbalism is the foundation of the entire system of correspondences and reconciles all differences of opinion—especially in the realm of religion.

Lévi made at least one vital advance in the doctrine of correspondence. The surviving evidence indicates that he was the very first occult thinker to work out a systematic correlation between the twenty-two paths on the Kabbalistic Tree of Life and the twenty-two Major Arcana of the Tarot, thus harmonizing two important but distinct streams of occult thought. Although others have since tinkered with the specifics, the precise linking of the Kabbalah with the Tarot is one of his lasting contributions to the esoteric tradition.

Lévi sought to reconcile magic with science as well. Typically, he sought to present magical occurrences as essentially natural events, involving a dimension of nature which was simply too subtle to be studied by materialistic science. To explain how magic works, he popularized the notion of the "astral light." Like Mesmer's animal magnetism, astral light is all around us all the time as both a "terrestrial fluid" and "the mother of all forms." Thoughts and mental images can shape it and leave impressions on it; people who see ghosts or talk to spirits may be merely perceiving impressions left in the astral light. The light can also be harnessed, directed, and channeled in tangible ways to produce specific physical and mental effects.

The purpose of learning ritual magic, according to Lévi, is to acquire the ability to manipulate the astral light at will. The rituals and their trappings activate the imagination, which to Lévi "is in effect the soul's eye; . . . thereby we behold the reflections of the invisible world; . . . we heal diseases, modify the seasons, warn off death from the living and raise the dead to life, because it is the imagination which exalts the will and gives it power over the Universal Agent," the astral light.[7] Astral light is a polarized force, and magical operations aim at reconciling its positive and negative, male and female energies in various ways.

As he minimized the supernatural aspect of the magical tradition (A. E. Waite referred to him as an occultist for whom there is no occult), Lévi brought to prominence the psychological dimension of occultism. Instead of evoking spirits, Lévi characterized magical operations as ways of activating, empowering, and directing the will. "Would you reign over yourselves and others? Learn how to will. How can one learn to will? This is the first arcanum of magical initiation."[8]

Other characteristics of Lévi's approach are evident in his 1861 production *The Mysteries of the Qabalah*. This is an allegorical commentary on the Old Testament book of Ezekiel and the New Testament Revelation, accompanied by no fewer than ninety-one of Lévi's own symbolic illustrations. His purpose here was to demonstrate that Kabbalism and its related magical methodologies reveal a single message behind both scriptural books, thus reconciling Judaism and Christianity into a single whole.

Correspondence is the key to Lévi's interpretation of all scripture. In this case, he argued that both the new Temple of Ezekiel

40–46 and the new Jerusalem of Revelation 21 represent the same higher idea: "the embodiment of absolute and universal truth . . . the key to all sciences and religion, the hieroglyphic synthesis of all the conquests of the human species."[9] Lévi claimed that the many sets of seven in the Book of Revelation—letters to seven churches, seven angels, seven stars, seven bowls of wrath, etc.—all refer to seven ages of church history. The sixth began with the Renaissance and the seventh, which corresponds to the Sabbath day and the day of salvation, will come when Christianity itself is reborn through "the manifestation of the lofty truths of the Qabalah."[10]

The Kabbalah is the key to all. The church has long since forgotten this, its true message, but fortunately the Templars and Freemasons preserved it. Lévi, in fact, joined a Masonic lodge in 1861 specifically to remind the initiates of the supposed Kabbalistic meaning of their own rites and symbols, but his ideas were poorly received and he quit some years later.[11] His continued attachment to the Catholic Church is fully in evidence, but it was a Catholicism defined by the Kabbalah which had a hold on Lévi's loyalty.

Eliphas Lévi maintained Alphonse Constant's commitment to the idealization of woman even at this stage of his career, although perhaps with a touch less fervor. In discussing the apparition of the woman in Revelation 12, Lévi remarked that she represents religion or the church as eternal wisdom, high above all change—she is clothed with the sun, symbol of constant light, and has the changeable moon at her feet. "Woman is the mother of God in humanity. She is the queen mother of the world."[12] The day of salvation is also the reconciliation of the sexes, for then "the savior is no longer a solitary crucified man, he is a young triumphant husband . . . Happy, cries the angel, those who are invited to this celestial marriage."[13] Thus wrote the aging, abandoned spouse of Noémi Cadiot.

The remainder of Lévi's career was relatively uneventful. He lived in a succession of Parisian apartments, travelling only twice to England and once to Germany. He wrote prodigiously, often padding new books with passages from old ones; it is noteworthy that his masterwork, *Dogma and Ritual*, contains long extracts from *Assumption of Woman* and *Mother of God*, which he clearly had not renounced.

He took on paying disciples and sent lessons through the mail, a practice for which the phrase "correspondence course" seems more than usually appropriate. Normally, however, he avoided actually performing the rituals he wrote about, often pleading that he could not afford the proper materials and implements.

The most notable exception to this rule was his attempt to invoke the spirit of Apollonius of Tyana, a first-century AD Greek philosopher and miracle-worker. This occurred during his 1854 visit to England, at the request of a lady who was willing and able to fund the entire episode. In *Dogma and Ritual*, Lévi described the cloak-and-dagger manner in which the lady contacted him and the extensive preparations required. At last, on July 24, he stood before an altar in a small room, fully costumed and surrounded by smoking incense; he wanted Apollonius to answer two questions, one from the lady and one from himself.

> The white smoke rose slowly over the marble altar. I felt as though the earth were quaking; my ears were buzzing and my heart pounding . . . I distinctly saw, in front of the altar, a man's face, larger than normal . . . Closing my eyes, I called Apollonius three times; when I opened them again I saw a man before me, wholly covered by a kind of shroud, which seemed more gray than white . . . I began to feel so faint that I took two steps in order to sit down . . . I had vague dreams, which I did not clearly remember afterwards . . . The phantom had not spoken to me, but I seemed to hold in my mind the answer to the questions that I had wished to ask.[14]

Typically, Lévi did not insist that the real Apollonius had really appeared. He acknowledged that his many props and preparations were highly stimulating to the imagination, but affirmed "that I did see and touch, that I saw clearly and distinctly, in a waking state, and that this suffices to cause me to believe in the efficacy of magical operations."[15] The strain was such that he recommended against it as a regular exercise.

Several eyewitness accounts of Lévi survive. The Scottish occultist Kenneth Mackenzie, who paid him a visit in 1861, described him as "a short burly man, with a rubicund complexion, very small but piercing eyes twinkling with good humor, his face broad, his lips small and well compressed together, nostrils dilating. The lower part of his face was covered with a thick black beard and mustache . . ."[16] Louise Hutchinson, one of his English students, wrote that he was "the only man I have known who had attained true inner peace. His good humor was unalterable; his gaiety and liveliness knew no end."[17]

The Spreading Influence of Eliphas Lévi

The quietness of Lévi's life almost obscures his true importance to the Western esoteric tradition, but no figure was more central to the nineteenth-century occult revival. His great goal was to reconcile magic, science, and all religions into a single coherent philosophy. While maintaining his façade as a reasonably orthodox Catholic, he harmonized the great religions of the world by conforming them all to the Kabbalah. Drawing on the blend of mysticism and popular science which dated back at least to Mesmer, he provided a justification for magical study and practice which seemed intellectually respectable and removed occultism from its traditional association with conspirators and charlatans. By emphasizing the role of the individual will and imagination instead of actual spirits and demons, Lévi positioned the esoteric tradition to take advantage of the Western fascination with psychology which followed so soon after him.

Modern high magic owes an enormous debt to Eliphas Lévi. Over and above such concrete accomplishments as the Kabbalah-Tarot correspondences, Lévi adapted the Western occult tradition to the post-Enlightenment world. As Francis King put it, "The major importance of Levi, however, lies . . . in the fact that he was responsible for the surfacing, in an admittedly romanticized form, of the whole underground magical tradition."[18] Through his personal contacts, and even more through his books and written lessons, his ideas percolated through the networks of disappointed utopians and serious magicians, helping to stimulate and shape the accelerating occult revival. His ideas recommended themselves to committed occultists; these are to be distinguished from the nineteenth-century brand of stage mediums like D. D. Home who, around the same time, had begun to materialize money for themselves out of the pockets of enthusiastic and gullible audiences.

Lévi's ideas played a direct role in stimulating the revival of the Rosicrucian tradition in France. Stanislaus de Guaita (1861–97), a would-be poet, devoted his life to the occult after being introduced to Lévi's work. In 1888 he founded the Qabalistic Order of the Rosy Cross, which was said to be headed by six known individuals and six unseen superiors. Along with de Guaita, the former category included two significant individuals.[19] One was Joséphin Péladan (1858–1918), a novelist and former bank clerk who developed the habit of giving himself ancient Near Eastern titles like "Sar Merodack" and dressing in monks' robes or centuries-old fashions. He soon broke with de Guaita and established his own Order of the Catholic Rosy Cross, the Temple, and the Grail. Péladan may have had some conception of distinct magical paths for men and women; he apparently wrote a manual called *Comment on devient fée* ("How to become a fairy") for females, and another, *Comment on devient mage* ("How to become a magician"), for males.[20] Péladan made effective use of his group to promote his interest in the arts. His Rosicrucian Salons featured art exhibits by the likes of Gustave Moreau; it also staged dramatic presentations which included supposedly long-lost plays by the ancient Greek dramatist Aeschylus, which Péladan claimed to have rediscovered. He was also a vigorous promoter of the music of Richard Wagner and helped to launch the career of composer Erik Satie (who, after writing music for Péladan's rituals, left to found his own Metropolitan Church of Art of Jesus the Conductor).

Another of de Guaita's recruits was Gérard Encausse (1865–1916), a medical doctor who practiced occultism under the pen-name Papus. Inspired partly by Lévi, Papus wrote detailed studies of the Kabbalah and the Tarot as well as holistic medicine and hypnotism. He traced the sacred wisdom back to Egypt by way of the Freemasons, Rosicrucians, and Gnostics; interestingly, one of his smaller efforts was a booklet explaining the occult background of Goethe's *Faust*, complete with discussions of pentacles and the astral plane.[21]

Lévi's influence spread abroad as well. One of his favored stu-

dents in his later years was Mary Gebhard, a German of Irish extrac-
tion who actually took Lévi into her own home during the Franco-
Prussian War and who remained active in German occult circles for
many years. As we shall see below, she was among those who helped
establish Theosophy in Germany and thus bridged the Western and
Eastern sides of the occult revival.

Even more important was Lévi's contribution to the Rosicrucian
tradition in England. Lévi visited England in 1854 and became
friendly with Sir Edward Bulwer-Lytton (later Lord Lytton, 1803–
73); in fact, the anonymous lady who asked him to evoke Apollonius
on this occasion was a friend of a friend of Lytton. In 1861, Lévi
returned and stayed a second time in Lytton's home. Lytton was
already a famous author by the time he met Lévi. He was a novelist,
a writer of Romantic potboilers which are considered almost unread-
able today. His most famous book, a nineteenth-century best-seller,
was *The Last Days of Pompeii*. His most famous single line, however,
is the opening sentence from *Paul Clifford*: "It was a dark and stormy
night." Long favored by teachers of literature as a prime example of
how not to write, these seven words have inspired the annual Bulwer-
Lytton Prize, awarded by the English Department at San Jose State
University for the worst new sentence of the year, as well as countless
panels of the "Peanuts" comic strip. Lytton knew his market, however, and was reasonably successful and popular in his time.

Lévi benefited from the fact that Lytton also had an abiding interest in magic and the occult. Several of his novels and short stories
deal with such themes. Moreover, it was some real-life friends and
acquaintances of Lytton who brought about the establishment of
modern Rosicrucianism in England. Even more significantly, this
specific group then gave rise to the Hermetic Order of the Golden
Dawn, the single most important magical organization of the past
hundred years, which in turn launched Aleister Crowley upon a largely
unsuspecting world. We shall explore these developments in the next
chapter, but Lytton's sponsorship of Lévi and his ideas among these
influential people is a critically important link in the chain.

Finally, we must credit Lévi with putting into practice at least
one of his dearest principles. He did not simply idealize women in

the abstract, assigning the female sex a key role in his magical philosophy and utopian speculations; he also accepted female students like Mary Gebhard and Louise Hutchinson and taught them his magic. If Lévi is the one most responsible for bringing the esoteric tradition into the light of day, he is also responsible for opening that tradition, quite deliberately, to women.

Significant as Lévi was, there was one person who could rival him for importance in the nineteenth-century occult revival. As it happens, it was a woman—one of the most amazing women of modern times.

THEOSOPHY

The Life and Times of "HPB"

On or about July 5, 1873, a rather bizarre figure disembarked from the French ship St. Laurent to take up residence in New York City. Obese, with short, frizzy hair and a penchant for outlandish clothes and behavior (she smoked incessantly and swore like a sailor when the mood took her, which was often), she was armed with a mastery of occult lore, an array of magical tricks, and a pair of striking, hypnotic eyes. It was Madame Helena Petrovna Blavatsky (1831–91) or, as she liked to be known, "HPB." She told tales of her world travels, and of being initiated into hidden mysteries by priests and adepts in Egypt and Tibet. Indeed, she told so many stories that it would be difficult to fit them all into a single lifespan. Historians trying to piece the details together still disagree on a number of matters, but the general outline seems to be well established, and even without her many embellishments it is a riveting story.[22]

She was born in Russia, the eldest daughter of an unhappy marriage between an earthy cavalry officer and the refined, well-educated granddaughter of a prince. She saw little of her father, Peter von Hahn, since her mother soon gave up following him around on his military postings. To support herself, HPB's mother (also named Helena) turned her passion for literature into a productive career of novel-writing. Her first book was "a thinly disguised saga of her marital traumas and the hazards of being female."[23]   Soon she was being hailed as Russia's George Sand, its foremost feminist novelist, but tuberculosis cut short both her career and her life; she died in 1842 at the age of 28. Little Helena was just weeks short of her eleventh birthday.

The future Madame Blavatsky, with her two siblings, did most of her growing up in the home of her mother's parents. Grandfather Andrey Fadeyev was a civil servant in the Czarist government and held important posts in newly Russified parts of the Caucasus and Central Asia. In this cosmopolitan setting, HPB apparently reveled in the exotic and fascinating mix of cultures; while her grandfather held administrative jurisdiction over an Asiatic tribe known as the Kalmucks, she got to know them, mastered their techniques of daredevil horsemanship, and admired their colorful variant of Tibetan Buddhism.

Her grandmother, the Princess Helena Dolgokurovna, had married the commoner Fadeyev against her family's advice, but the marriage had proven very successful. The princess herself was a brilliant woman. She spoke five languages and pursued interests in art and archaeology, but her specialty was botany; she carried on correspondence with European scientists and even had a fossil named after her. The princess had also inherited the extensive library accumulated by her father, Prince Pavel (Paul) Dolgokurov. His abiding interests appear to have been alchemy and magic, and HPB reportedly devoured his copies of Paracelsus, Cornelius Agrippa, and other occult classics during her early teens. The prince had been a member of Strict Observance Freemasonry, which had spread to Russia from its home in Germany. As we have seen, this particular rite emphasized the alleged Templar roots of Masonry as well as the importance of the unknown superiors or "Secret Chiefs" who were said to be the true guides of the movement. There were even stories that Prince Paul had met Saint-Germain and Cagliostro in person.[24]

All this took place in pre-revolutionary, pre-industrial Russia. "Holy Mother Russia" was described by some as the most religious nation on earth. The rich heritage of mysticism in the Russian Orthodox Church was surrounded by the folklore and superstitions of dozens of distinct ethnic and tribal groups and millions of uneducated serfs. The result was a world full of angels, miracle-working saints, spirits, and ghosts.

HPB was a high-strung and unmanageable child. She inherited the intelligence and headstrong determination of her mother and grandmother to a degree that drove even them to distraction. Besides the ability to read extensively and quickly, and to remember what she had read, she soon displayed her most formidable talent—persuading other people to believe her. She convinced her playmates that she could see spirits and enjoyed the company of invisible beings. At one point she had the family believing that she was channeling letters from a deceased woman named Tekla Lebendorff. This charade lasted until Mrs. Lebendorff's real-life nephew paid a visit, and laughingly told them that his Aunt Tekla was still alive and that the letters were false.[25]

Through her teens, HPB displayed a strong aversion to men, marriage, and the social life that was expected of well-born young ladies. She does seem to have developed an infatuation for one prince whose family had a history of occult interests, but this relationship was quickly terminated by her family. Probably desperate to get her safely married off, they introduced her to Nikifor Blavatsky, a balding 38-year-old bureaucrat. In one moment of thoughtless spite she accepted his proposal of marriage, and then found that none of her antics could drive him off or deflect her grandparents' determination to proceed with the wedding. Meade describes the entire family escorting Helena to church on her wedding day, "less for the sake of appearances than for security reasons."[26] The marriage was a disaster, since HPB had no intention of allowing it to be anything else, and she fled back home after three months.

Her despairing relatives then sent her off to her long-estranged father, under the escort of four servants, but she escaped their surveillance and ran away again. She landed in Constantinople, a solitary eighteen-year-old woman with no means of support. This is the point at which HPB claimed to have begun her world travels in search of occult wisdom. Reports from those who knew her, while better substantiated, are somewhat less exotic. They told of her travelling

Europe and the Mediterranean as a paid lady's companion; riding horseback in circuses; conducting several affairs; and even bearing a son, Yuri, who suffered from some sort of congenital defect and did not live beyond the age of six. A significant portion of HPB's time was certainly spent in Egypt, learning from and working with mystical teachers and practicing magicians.

Mouthpiece of the Masters

Part of what drew HPB to the United States was her discovery that Spiritualism was still very much in vogue there and offered her a chance to make her mark. As a distinct movement, Spiritualism had appeared quite suddenly in the U.S. a quarter of a century earlier, when some little sisters by the name of Fox started "communicating" with an entity who made rapping noises in their house. This entity revealed itself as the spirit of a man who had been murdered in the house years before, and soon there were séances and mediums all around the country putting the living in touch with the dead. Even famous names like Abraham Lincoln, James Fenimore Cooper, and Horace Greeley turn up as participants in Spiritualistic activities; thousands were fascinated with this "scientific" proof of life after death, and the movement suffered only a minor setback when one of the Fox sisters admitted that she had made the original "raps" by cracking her toe knuckle.

Usually, Spiritualism purported to offer communication between the living and the recent dead, the relatives and friends who were so sorely missed that news of their survival beyond the grave was a comfort in and of itself. Other Spiritualist phenomena, like table-tipping and the materialization of objects out of thin air, were also presented as objective proofs of the reality of the spiritual realm. Here is another instance of the sometimes reciprocal ongoing relationship between rationalism and Romanticism: the craving for objective, "scientific" proof of the reality of spirits.

There were some who went further. Andrew Jackson Davis (1826–1910) had begun as a rural mesmerist healer but, like Edgar Cayce after him, he branched out into writing long "revelations" while in an altered state of consciousness. Davis claimed to have met the spirit of Swedenborg during a somnambulistic trance. His most famous channeled book, *The Principles of Nature* (1847), prophesied about things like cars, express trains, and prefabricated buildings; it also mentioned nine planets (even though Pluto would not be discovered until 1930) and described the forms of life characteristic of Mars, Jupiter, and Saturn. The book taught that every human being has a true "soul mate," who, as it happens, is usually someone other than one's spouse; Davis's own supposed soul mate was married to one of his friends. Davis's philosophy seems to have been largely a mixture of Mesmer, Swedenborg, and Fourier. He insisted that his book was dictated to him by the spirits, however, and rejected all accusations of plagiarism on the grounds that he was not literate enough to do the work involved in copying.[27]

HPB became a close friend of Davis during her early days in America, and she created something of a sensation on the séance circuit herself. She specialized in physical manifestations, seeming to produce sounds and even objects out of thin air. Eventually she made an even more dramatic claim. After serving as a mouthpiece for "John King," a popular spirit who had been frequenting séances for two decades already, she announced in 1875 that she was in the service of the Brotherhood of Luxor, a group of Egyptian adepts or Masters who had chosen her to reveal the ultimate truth to the world at large. This body, like the Rosicrucian Secret Chiefs, was a version of what is now commonly called the Great White Brotherhood: a group of people who have surpassed the rest of us in spiritual evolution and are working behind the scenes to help us along.

To study and promote HPB's revelations from the Brotherhood, the Theosophical Society was established by a small group of her core followers which included Henry Steel Olcott (1832–1907) and William Q. Judge (1851–96). Olcott was named president. He was a lawyer, journalist, and Civil War veteran who had recently left his wife and children for a string of mistresses, and he was more than ready for a cause to which he could devote the rest of his life. Olcott served as HPB's platonic partner, her organizer, and the butt of her temper and ridicule for years. They shared an apartment in New

York, and HPB kept Olcott entertained and obedient. He took over the preparation of meals after she tried to cook an egg by setting it directly onto the coals in the fireplace; on the other hand, he insisted that she had once produced a bunch of delicious grapes out of thin air in mid-winter, just because he expressed a yearning for them. One of the Masters supposedly paid him a visit in the apartment late one night, leaving his turban behind as proof; Olcott kept the turban for years as a tangible sign of the Masters' reality. He remained as president of the Society until his death. Judge, on the other hand, was an unsettled young lawyer whose commitment fluctuated during the early years; he did not abandon his wife for Theosophy until 1884.

The Society's purpose was to combat both Christianity and materialistic scientism in the name of occult wisdom. Its three guiding principles were to form the nucleus of a universal brotherhood, to promote the study of comparative religion and science, and to investigate the hidden laws of nature and the powers of humanity. To publicize these principles, HPB produced her first major book, *Isis Unveiled* (1877). In the preface, she described it as "a plea for the recognition of the Hermetic philosophy, the anciently universal Wisdom-Religion, as the only possible key to the Absolute in science and theology."[28] It traced the secret wisdom of the ages back through the Rosicrucians, the Freemasons, and the Templars to ancient Egypt and even beyond, to India. Gradually, HPB's Masters were becoming Eastern sages—Mahatmas.

Soon the Mahatmas summoned her to India. Leaving Judge in charge of American Theosophy, HPB and the faithful Olcott set out for Bombay in 1878. They managed to recruit support from prominent Anglo-Indians like A. P. Sinnett of *The Pioneer* newspaper, while at the same time "going native" and attracting Indians and Ceylonese to a renewed study and appreciation of their own heritage. The Society established its permanent headquarters in Adyar, Madras, in 1882. This housed Blavatsky, Olcott, and several other full-time members and officers of the Society. It also served as the setting for many of HPB's famous phenomena. Letters from the Mahatmas, particularly a pair known as Koot Hoomi and Master Morya, would suddenly fall through the air onto the intended recipient or appear inside the locked "shrine" or cabinet which sat in the Occult Room. Sinnett later had his collection published as *The Mahatma Letters.*[29] HPB also performed feats like magically producing articles which guests had lost, and some of her colleagues even experienced sightings of the Mahatmas themselves.

Disaster struck after HPB left to visit Europe in 1884. Alexis and Emma Coulomb, her hired housekeepers in Adyar, were apparently afflicted by guilty consciences and empty bank accounts; they decided to reveal Blavatsky's secrets to the public. Emma, it turned out, had been HPB's major accomplice in staging most of the Adyar phenomena. She told the world about the slots in the ceiling through which Mahatma letters could be dropped onto unsuspecting guests, and about the life-sized effigy called Christoforo which, in suitably dim light, could impersonate various Masters. Mme. Coulomb even had a collection of written instructions from HPB, which she turned over to some of Blavatsky's most hated enemies: Christian missionaries in India.

HPB never returned to her beloved India, and her close relationship with Olcott did not survive this revelation of her tricks. Judge came to see her in Paris, and she sent him on to Adyar while she went to stay with one of her German disciples, Mary Gebhard—the former student of Eliphas Lévi. While she was there, Judge and another German Theosophist, Dr. Franz Hartmann, decided to investigate the shrine in Adyar. They were shown it by the local Theosophist Ananda Charloo. When he pulled it out from the wall and thumped on it to show how solid it was, the telltale secret panel in the back popped open. Judge and Hartmann promptly took the shrine away and destroyed it.[30]

To make matters worse, the Society for Psychical Research (SPR) in London had already been investigating the claims of Theosophy and now sent Richard Hodgson to India to complete the inquiry. He met with both the Adyar Theosophists and the Coulombs, who "materialized" their own Mahatma letter just to show him how it was done. His final report concluded that there were no Mahatmas at all; that HPB wrote the Mahatma letters herself; and that not one of her many phenomena could safely be considered genuine.[31] The SPR committee added its own assessment: "we think that she has achieved a title to permanent remembrance as one of the most accomplished, ingenious, and interesting imposters in history."[32]

Few public figures have survived the exposure of their trickeries on this scale. It is a measure of HPB's extraordinary charismatic qualities that even after this public humiliation, she went on to accomplish two major feats which would ensure the survival of the Theosophical Society. The first was the writing of her monumental book *The Secret Doctrine* (1888). More systematic than *Isis Unveiled*, it expounds a view of the universe drawn from both the Indian religious tradition and Western occultism. For readers open to persuasion, *The Secret Doctrine* is stunning in its breadth of scope and its apparent mastery of the intricacies of science, magic, religion, and history; we shall consider its message shortly.

HPB's second crucial achievement was the recruitment of her eventual successor, Annie Besant (1847–1933). Born Annie Wood, she grew up passionately religious and married a Church of England priest. In the memorable words of one of her friends, "She could not be the bride of Heaven, and therefore became the bride of Mr. Frank Besant. He was hardly an adequate substitute."[33] Despite the arrival of a daughter and then a son, the marriage was in trouble almost from the beginning, and Annie left after six years. She also abandoned the Christian religion, plagued by doubts about its dogmas and her inability to reconcile the existence of a loving God with the suffering she saw around her. She became a crusading atheist and socialist, joining Charles Bradlaugh in campaigns where her natural gift of oratory proved to be sensational. Equally sensational was Besant's and Bradlaugh's 1877 conviction of distributing obscene materials, namely a detailed pamphlet on birth control.

Besant experienced a series of personal disappointments over the next decade. Because of her conviction on a morality charge, she lost custody of her daughter Mabel (her son Digby had remained with his father). Her relationship with Bradlaugh went well beyond professional matters, until those who knew them were sure they were in love—a love which was probably reflected in print when Annie wrote an impassioned account of Auguste Comte's devotion to Clothilde de Vaux. Both Besant and Bradlaugh were married, however, and the relationship remained intense but platonic.[34]

It remained so, at least, until Besant encountered Dr. Edward Aveling in 1879. Aveling was informed and articulate, and seemed to share much of Besant's political agenda; according to George Bernard Shaw, however, "as a borrower of money and a swindler and seducer of women his record was unimpeachable."[35] Besant became utterly devoted to him, and this relationship probably was physically consummated. Nonetheless, Aveling soon betrayed Besant for Karl Marx's daughter Eleanor. This was probably just as well for Besant in the long run, since Aveling's behavior tormented "Tussy" Marx until she prevailed on him to commit joint suicide; at the last minute he slipped away and let her go to the grave alone.[36] Besant, meanwhile, rebounded from Aveling's rejection into a brief liaison with Shaw which also proved unsatisfying.

Despite her hectic pace of writing and public speaking, Besant evidently still felt that her spiritual needs were going unmet. Then, in 1888, she was given the assignment of writing a review of the newly published *Secret Doctrine*. As she read it, everything fell into place in her mind, and she made a pilgrimage to HPB in London. Already knowing Besant's reputation and doubtless realizing what an asset she would be for Theosophy, Blavatsky took the calculated gamble of insisting that Annie read the Hodgson Report before committing herself. According to the widely circulated story, Besant read the report, joined anyway, and returned to HPB's presence; when asked for her response to the exposé, she replied, "My answer is, will you accept me as your pupil, and give me the honor of proclaiming you my teacher in the face of the world?"[37]

HPB quickly groomed Besant for the succession, even creating a new Esoteric Section of the Theosophical Society for her to lead. By the time Blavatsky died, Besant's competent hands were ready to steer Theosophy successfully into the new century.

The Teachings and the Teachers

The Secret Doctrine has remained the definitive expression of Theosophical teachings, eclipsing *Isis Unveiled* and smaller efforts like *The Mahatma Letters*. Theosophist Ernest Wood, in the preface to his 1956 effort *A "Secret Doctrine" Digest*, referred to it as "unquestionably the greatest source book in the world" for students of the occult.[38] Even allowing for Wood's confessional loyalty to HPB, the fact remains that Blavatsky's work has had enormous repercussions, both in the esoteric tradition and in the world at large. What, then, does it actually say?

Blavatsky asserted that the teachings of this book represent the essence of eternal wisdom, which was the source of all the world's religions; these now stand revealed as deviations from, and distortions of, Theosophy. *The Secret Doctrine* itself is presented as Blavatsky's translation of the otherwise-unknown *Stanzas of Dzyan*, which she claims to be the oldest book in the world, along with her extended commentary on it. The first volume of the *Doctrine* is titled "Cosmogenesis" and brings all of her knowledge of Western occultism and Eastern philosophy to bear in an attack on modern science. The second half, "Anthropogenesis," elaborates her mystical version of the evolution of humanity: "The aim of this work may be thus stated: to show that Nature is not 'a fortuitous concurrence of atoms,' and to assign to man his rightful place in the scheme of the Universe; to rescue from degradation the archaic truths which are the basis of all religions; and to uncover, to some extent, the fundamental unity from which they all sprang; finally, to show that the occult side of Nature has never been approached by the Science of modern civilization."[39]

Some of the vital underpinnings are clearly derived from Hindu and Buddhist teachings—at least, as Blavatsky understood them. HPB proclaimed that ultimate reality is a single divine essence, "Fohat," and that there is no personal God as distinct from the temporal world. "The fundamental Law . . . is the One homogeneous divine *Substance-Principle . . . Its impersonality is the fundamental conception* of the system."[40] Individual souls are "monads," sparks of divinity trapped in physical bodies and tied to the cycle of reincarnation by their karma until they acquire enough spiritual knowledge to set themselves free from birth and death. As a whole, the universe "is worked and *guided* from *within outwards*. As above so it is below, as in heaven so on earth; and man—the microcosm and miniature copy of the macrocosm—is the living witness to this Universal Law and to the mode of its action . . . The whole Kosmos is guided, controlled, and animated by almost endless series of Hierarchies of sentient Beings . . ."[41] Here, the basic heritage of Western occultism is distinctly flavored with a dash of Swedenborg.

According to *The Secret Doctrine*, a universe passes through a series of seven cycles in the course of its existence. Each cycle is represented by a symbol from *The Stanzas of Dzyan*: the first by an empty circle representing unity, the second by a dot within the circle representing differentiation, and so on. More importantly, each cycle has its own "root race," the form of sentient life appropriate to it. The first race was created on earth by extraterrestrials, the "Lords of the Moon." These original humans were projected like astral bodies from the moon gods; they inhabited an unidentified region called the "Imperishable Sacred Land" and, being bodiless spirits, reproduced simply by deciding that they wished to do so.

In the second cycle, the second root race evolved downwards from the first, becoming "psychic" rather than spiritual. They were the Hyperboreans, who lived in a continent located where Northern Asia and the polar cap are now, although it was warmer then. The third race was native to Lemuria, a now-sunken continent in the Indian Ocean. Descending from a psychic to an intellectual mode of existence, the third race also developed physical means of reproduction. The earlier generations were androgynous and simply secreted their offspring; HPB refers to them as the "sweat-born." As downward evolution took its course, people mutated into distinct sexes for reproductive purposes. The fourth race reached the bottom of the evolutionary descent, acquiring full physical bodies. These were the inhabitants of Atlantis, and HPB gave full credit to stories of the legendary continent.

We now inhabit the fifth cycle, the first to begin the ascent back to the heights of spirituality. Blavatsky had comparatively little to say about the future races; the sixth was to emerge in America and the seventh would witness our final return to cosmic unity and the dissolution of the universe. Using traditional Hindu chronology, she asserted that the seven cycles unfold over a period of 311.04 trillion human years.[42]

Now, a mere one hundred and ten years later, it is her words on the races of the past and present which arrest the average reader. When HPB used the word "race," she meant exactly that. It seems that when one cycle gives way to another, the old land—Lemuria, Atlantis, or whatever—is destroyed along with most of its root race. The survivors then do one of two things: some evolve into the next root race; the rest continue to propagate as declining representatives of an obsolete age until they gradually die out from a sort of racial senility. "Their extinction," she wrote, "is hence a Karmic necessity."[43] Karma does its own work, however; HPB never drops a hint of actual racial conflict.

In the original context, she inscribed those particular words about real people, identifying those racial groups which she described as degenerate remnants of the third root race—the Australian aborigines and the Hottentots. The same is presumed to be true, even if the process is not so far advanced, of the fourth-race leftovers: the East Asians, Polynesians, and American natives. Wood concurred, pointing out that "no amount of culture nor generations of training amid civilization, could raise such human specimens as the Bushmen, the Veddhas of Ceylon and some African tribes to the same intellectual level" as the present fifth race; "the 'sacred spark' is missing in them and it is they who are the only *inferior* races on the globe, now happily—owing to the wise adjustment of Nature which ever works in that direction—fast dying out."[44]

The fifth race, to whom the present cycle in world history belongs, is identified by HPB as the Aryan race. Here she capitalized on some recent research by European scholars who were still in the early stages of studying Asian civilizations on a systematic, first-hand basis. One of their great discoveries was the Indo-European family of languages. They found that many languages of the Indian subcontinent were not only related to each other, but shared words and grammatical structures with Persian, Greek, Latin, and many of the modern European languages. For instance, they could trace the Sanskrit word *matar* as it became the Latin *mater*, the Spanish *madre*, the French *mère*, the German *Mutter*, and the English "mother." For this group of languages and the peoples who spoke them, nineteenth-century scholars adopted the Sanskrit term by which the first Indo-Europeans of India referred to themselves: *arya* ("noble"). According to *The Stanzas of Dzyan*, as described to us by HPB, the symbol of the fifth race, the Aryans, is the swastika.[45]

For loyal Theosophists and New Agers in general, the key question about *The Secret Doctrine*, as of all Blavatsky's writing, is its source. Massive and overwhelming it certainly is; but is it true? Where did HPB get it all? No one disputes the fact that she read widely and remembered prodigious amounts of it. Both *Isis Unveiled* and *The Secret Doctrine* contain numerous references to other books, although the lengthy indexes in modern editions were added after her death.[46] Equally indisputable is the fact that large sections of her books which purport to be her own words are in fact duplications of passages in other, earlier books to which she had access. From the very first appearance of *Isis*, charges of plagiarism have swirled around HPB's writing (for our purposes, it is interesting to note that her favorite sources included Paracelsus, Mesmer, Swedenborg, Lévi, and Lytton). It has been argued that there is almost nothing original in her books at all, apart from the overall conception of the scheme into which these hundreds of acknowledged and unacknowledged quotations have been fit.[47] As Jay G. Williams put it, "her writings are like a tornado which sucks up from world culture all sorts of ideas and images and whirls them into one indistinguishable, but powerful, mass."[48]

But HPB did not claim to be an anthologist, even on a record-breaking scale; she claimed to be the mouthpiece of the Mahatmas, who were inspiring and guiding her books as they were produced. She wrote to her sister Vera, "I am writing *Isis*; not writing, rather copying out and drawing that which She personally shows to me . . . someone enters me. It is not I who talk and write: it is something within me . . ."[49] While working on *The Secret Doctrine*, she wrote to Sinnett that she had no resource books at all—proof positive that the Mahatmas were supplying her information directly. She was supported by the testimony of her companion, the Countess Wachtmeister, even though the Countess had actually packed HPB's library for the move to London and mailed out orders for other materials Blavatsky needed.[50]

The issue of the Mahatmas is one of the major controversies about Theosophy as a whole, given HPB's record as an exceptionally accomplished fraud in other areas. Her public pronouncements affirmed the reality of the Masters and asserted that her teachings and writings derive all their validity from the Mahatmas' involvement in them. Theosophists today certainly do believe in the Mahatmas and therefore insist that HPB was in genuine contact with a group of real entities. Officially, the Masters are not extraterrestrials, but merely human beings who have advanced further in spiritual evolution than the rest of us. They live in Tibet or Central Asia in actual buildings and have real bodies, although their paranormal powers permit them to do things which most of us cannot.

Outsiders have explained the Masters in several different ways, generally as a conscious fraud on HPB's part or, occasionally, as evidence of multiple-personality disorder. There are even some sympathetic commentators who do not commit themselves to the objective reality of the Mahatmas. K. Paul Johnson has argued that behind each Master or Mahatma was a real person whose identity, for political or personal reasons, HPB needed to hide; he suggests that the Mahatma myth got beyond her well-intentioned control and assumed a dogmatic status she never intended for it. Stephan Hoeller replied with the suggestion that the Mahatmas may be authentic Jungian archetypes, realities located in the psyche rather than the Himalayan mountains.[51]

After the Hodgson Report and the exposure of the literary piracy by which HPB produced her books, it is testimony to her impact on the Western world that people are still discussing the matter more than a century after her death. In actual fact, Theosophy has given rise to several schismatic groups and numerous imitators, all claiming direct contact with the Masters. We shall conclude this chapter by taking a look at a few of its major contemporary representatives.

The Legacy of Theosophy

HPB had originally promised William Judge that he would succeed her, even though Olcott was president of the Theosophical Society. Annie Besant's dramatic entry into the movement changed everything, however; Blavatsky spent her last days in Annie's house and it was perfectly clear where she now intended her mantle to fall.[52] Apparently HPB had not taught Mrs. Besant everything she had taught Mme. Coulomb, however. Upon her death, Judge went through her desk and found the distinctive crayons and paper with which Mahatma letters were always written. Soon Besant was finding letters from the Mahatmas telling her that Judge was to take over the direction of the group. She happily proclaimed to the world that the Masters were still engaged in active correspondence, proving that the late HPB had not simply invented them. Besant was, of course, forced to retract when she realized that the new letters were part of Judge's attempt to assert his own control over the movement.

HPB had often alienated supporters; even the likes of Sinnett, who received so many messages from the Brotherhood, eventually quit in a huff. What happened now was different. Members had to decide whether the Mahatmas were really supporting Judge or Besant in the power struggle. On the whole, the Americans sided with Judge and withdrew to form their own society. The Besant-Olcott team remained in charge of European and Indian Theosophy.

Besant eventually moved to India and became president of the society when Olcott died. Under her leadership, Theosophists made some significant contributions to the modernization of Indian society. They started schools and hospitals, and worked to improve the conditions in which many women and children had to live. They also encouraged the movement for India's independence from Great Britain—both Mohandas Gandhi and Jawaharlal Nehru had significant contact with the Society, and Besant's dedicated work on behalf of the cause was recognized when she was elected to a term as president of the Indian National Congress, the umbrella organization of the independence movement.

Another of Besant's accomplishments was the establishment of Co-Masonry in England. Freemasonry was traditionally a male preserve, but some French Masons had broken ranks with the mainstream of the movement by initiating a woman in 1882. By the next year they had organized their own Rite. Francesca Arundale, a prominent London Theosophist, was the first Englishwoman to receive initiation. She brought it to Besant's attention, and Annie soon took office as Very Illustrious Most Puissant Grand Commander of the British Jurisdiction, with the result that English Co-Masonry took on the role of a "Theosophical subsidiary."[53]

Controversy continued to beset Theosophy, however. Besant appears to have been a true believer in the Mahatmas, and the quarrel with Judge did nothing to change her mind. She was not a visionary of HPB's caliber, however, and often depended on others to receive and pass on the spiritual communications. The poor judgment she displayed in her attraction to Aveling and then to Shaw did not, unfortunately, desert her now. At great cost to her credibility, she insisted on keeping Charles Webster Leadbeater as her deputy through much of her tenure as president of the Society; he claimed to be in touch with the Mahatmas and channeled many of the books which appeared under their joint authorship. Repeatedly, however, there were charges of sexual indiscretions with young boys. He was accused of teaching them to masturbate as a means of relief; later, it emerged that he was probably instructing them in magical masturbation rituals akin to the sex magic discussed in the next chapter.[54]

The greatest fiasco of all began in 1909 when Leadbeater persuaded Besant that he had discovered a young Indian boy, Jiddu Krishnamurti, who would be the new World Teacher—a sort of New Age messiah figure. Leadbeater assumed responsibility for Krishnamurti's upbringing and groomed him for years to assume this august role. In 1929, however, Krishnamurti suddenly and publicly renounced his role and broke with Theosophy altogether; he later claimed he had never finished reading a single one of their books.[55] He went on to a successful career as an independent guru, but Besant never quite recovered from the traumatic disruption of her plans and died in 1933. Leadbeater presided at her cremation.

Interestingly, one minor aspect of the campaign to promote Krishnamurti as the World Teacher was a short-lived movement on behalf of the World Mother, in whose name the Coming Age would be designated the Age of Motherhood. This potential Goddess movement never quite got off the ground, even though Besant identified a young female Indian Theosophist, Rukmini Devi, who had supposedly been chosen by the Mahatmas for this mission. *The World Mother* magazine folded after one issue in 1928 and the annual World Mother Day was celebrated only once, despite the fact that Leadbeater supposedly managed to channel an interview with the Mother herself.[56]

The official Theosophical Society has carried on in much quieter fashion since Besant's death, but its legacy permeates the New Age movement. The widespread acceptance of the Indian notions of karma and reincarnation, as well as the more arcane teachings about messages from the hidden masters of the Great White Brotherhood or the coming of the World Teacher, can all be traced to Theosophy.

Several other occult movements arose directly from the original Theosophical Society. Judge's American version was passed on to Katherine Tingley (1847–1929), a Besant-like figure who came from a background in social work and tried to build a utopian Theosophical community at Point Loma, California. She involved the group in war relief during the Spanish-American War and brought a group of Cuban orphans to the United States, in a precursor to the Vietnam baby-lift. She was succeeded by Godfrey de Purucker; he dissolved the Point Loma commune, but the organization continues to be very active in publishing.[57]

Theosophy was established in Germany primarily through the work of Franz Hartmann (1838–1912). A medical doctor, he worked in the United States for eighteen years and became involved in Spiritualism and then Theosophy. His visit to Adyar, where he helped Judge demolish HPB's shrine, came during his roundabout voyage home to Germany. Once he had returned, he founded a sort of Theosophical monastery, wrote books on subjects like Paracelsus and Rosicrucianism, published translations of the works of Theosophical leaders, and established a Theosophical journal which featured a swastika on the cover.[58] In 1902, the German Theosophical Society came under the leadership of Rudolf Steiner (1861–1925). Conflict developed over the orientalism of the Besant-Olcott group and their Mahatmas, and many of the Germans broke away. Steiner led the group for ten years, but in 1912 he left to establish his own, more Christianized occult movement called Anthroposophy, in which the notion of a personified female Sophia plays a significant part. He also developed a distinctive philosophy of education which led to the establishment of "Waldorf Schools" around the world.[59]

Theosophy became a well-established contributor to the esoteric tradition in German-speaking Europe, as can be seen in its influence on two notable Austrian occultists, Guido von List (1848–1919) and Adolf Josef Lanz (better known as Jörg Lanz von Liebenfels, 1874–1954).[60] List has been named as the first popular writer to combine occultism with pan-Germanism, the movement to unite all ethnic Germans—including Austrians—into a greater German state. Early in his life, List developed a technique of astral travel which gave him visions of a glorious ancient Teutonic civilization; he set down his findings in a series of books which gave mystical interpretations to the legends of the Edda and the runic alphabet, and blamed Christianity for the suppression of Germanic culture. After he encountered Theosophy, he elaborated this into a fully racist version of the neopagan paradigm. The ancient Aryans, he claimed, had worshipped the immanent god Wotan; they had been ruled by a hierarchy of initiated adepts known as the Armanists, who in turn were guided by unseen higher beings. Armanist culture retained its spiritual power as long as the Aryans remained racially pure, but the coming of Christianity destroyed nearly all of it. The secret heritage was kept alive by the Templars, Rosicrucians, and Freemasons; List presented himself as the last of the lineage.

List's works acquired a devoted audience in Austria and Germany. In 1905 a List Society was formed to study and propagate his revelations; it included both pan-Germans and occultists, and Franz Hartmann was one of the notable members. They were attracted in part by Lists's vision of an Aryan New Age which would come about through the arrival of a messianic figure he called the *Starke von Oben,* the "Strong One from on High." He eventually predicted that the

Strong One would appear after the tribulations of the Great War—to be precise, in 1932.

Lanz spent his early adulthood as a Cistercian monk with a deep love of the medieval military orders. He left the Cistercians in 1899 for reasons which remain unclear, but soon embarked on a new career in racist occultism; this brought him into contact with the List Society and Theosophy, as well as other such groups. In a book called *Theozoology*, he blended Theosophy and traditional occultism with racism and social Darwinism. This resulted in his doctrine that the earth was originally populated by two root races: the Asings, glorious blond beings with splendid physiques and psychic powers, whose exploits gave rise to the myths of the Germanic gods; and the apes. The course of history was determined by the struggle between the Asings, who created all the arts of civilization, and the apes, whose only interest is in chaos and destruction. According to Lanz, the fatal weakness of the Asings was the fact that their women found the apes sexually irresistible. The fall from ancient glory was caused by the crossbreeding of these two separate species and the loss of the purity of Asing blood. The different races in the world today are characterized by the varying ratios of Asing blood to ape blood in their lineage. The Teutonic Aryans supposedly have the smallest admixture of ape blood, but Slavs and Jews are almost pure ape according to Lanz's scheme. His program to restore the ancient glory of the Aryans included eugenics, strict controls over women to ensure that their alleged susceptibility to ape-men did not subvert the plan, and the enslavement, deportation, and perhaps even destruction of the enemy races.

In addition to his book, Lanz published a tabloid magazine called *Ostara* to propagate his views. It described the endless struggle between the two races and promoted his proposed solutions. Lanz even worked out a set of skull measurements by which an expert could supposedly identify the racial components of any individual. Other writers for *Ostara* included Theosophists and members of the List Society. In 1907 Lanz founded the Order of the New Templars, an occult brotherhood which practiced high magic in old, renovated castles and worked for the restoration of pure Aryan blood.

List and Lanz, beyond doubt, represent the occult racism through which the notion of the Aryan race and its swastika became familiar themes in German nationalist circles. Moreover, the channels through which these themes became central elements of the Third Reich are now well documented. As a young man, Adolf Hitler was a regular reader of *Ostara*. The National Socialists began as the German Workers' Party; this organization was set up and sponsored by the Thule Society, the Munich branch of an occult order which in turn had been founded by members of the List Society. Although it would divert us from our immediate task to pursue the matter here, the fact remains that Nazism was fundamentally a neopagan ideology; its most distinctive and abhorrent ideas, particularly its ascription of ultimate significance to the biological characteristics of race, are clearly identifiable products of the esoteric tradition.

In the English-speaking world, most extensions of Theosophy have maintained their religious/occult focus. Several have been led by women; these include Alice Bailey's Arcane School and Elizabeth Clare Prophet's Church Universal and Triumphant, both of which claimed continuing contact with ascended Masters. A sustained search on the Internet today reveals, however, that the blending of occultism with "Aryan" racism is still to be found among white supremacist and so-called neo-Nazi groups. In such circles, it remains disturbingly evident that there is an affinity between the belief in divine immanence and the ascription of ultimate value to the biological, organic distinctions between peoples.

Sex, Gender, and Modern Magic

Woman is the magician born of Nature.

Moina Bergson Mathers

IN THE ENGLISH-SPEAKING WORLD, to which we now turn, Romanticism never fully manifested the revolutionary potential which it displayed on the European continent. While there are many reasons for this, one explanation is that Great Britain had experienced more successes than failures during the eighteenth century and had less reason than other nations to seek a radical, let alone violent, change of direction. With the full absorption of Scotland into the United Kingdom in 1707, the British used their powerful navy and advanced industries to establish their worldwide Empire. Despite some setbacks like the loss of the American colonies, British foreign policy usually proceeded triumphantly, first driving France out of Canada and India, and then organizing the defeat of Napoleon and the end of his revolutionary schemes. At home, the political structure was flexible enough to permit the gradual reform of the social abuses which accompanied industrialization; although Marx thought that England, as the first real capitalist society, was ripe for the first socialist revolution, it never materialized.[1]

Romanticism remained largely a movement within culture and

the arts. The great English Romantic poets, like Lord Byron and Percy Bysshe Shelley, could express the raging alienation of a tormented soul with the best of the Continentals; indeed, Byron was a significant influence on some of his European colleagues, including Goethe. These two brilliant writers died young, however, and with the later works of Wordsworth and Coleridge, the revolutionary edge was gradually blunted and Romantic literature developed instead an overtone of sentimentalism.[2]

When Romantic nationalism raised its head in the British Isles, it was usually the cultural nationalism of the Celtic minorities. The glories of Scotland's past were brought to the notice of all Europe with the publication of the rediscovered works of the legendary character Ossian. Unfortunately, these soon turned out to be appealing forgeries from the hand of James Macpherson (1736–96), but Goethe and Byron were among those who derived inspiration from the songs attributed to Ossian. Sir Walter Scott romanticized the Scottish heritage in several of his early works, particularly his novel *Rob Roy* (1817), just as he did for the Knights Templar in *Ivanhoe* (1820). Romanticism thus stimulated a genuine interest among such peoples as the Scots in their own heritage and folklore, and a good deal of traditional culture was recorded, preserved and revived as a result. On another level, the practical outcome was not a Scottish national revolution but the tartan-and-kilt tourist industry.

A similar story can be told of Wales, where the flamboyant Iolo Morgannwg (actually Edward Williams, 1747–1826) exceeded Macpherson in his imaginary recreations of ancient Celtic culture. Drawing on some authentic materials, Williams essentially fabricated an entire system of philosophy and ritual which he attributed to the Druids. He "reestablished" the Order of Bards and won them a central role in the national cultural festivals, the *Eisteddfodau*. He also produced a personal reworking of the thirteenth-century *Song of Taliesin*, blending into it some materials he composed himself. This work was often mistaken for the real thing, and it was incorporated into the most famous of Welsh epics, Lady Charlotte Guest's 1849 publication of *The Mabinogion*.[3] The Welsh national anthem and the flag in its present form also date from the nineteenth century, not the distant days of actual Welsh independence.

The impact of Romanticism on British religion was muted as well. Here there was no furious reaction against the Enlightenment, which the Anglican establishment had managed to harness in a generally satisfactory way. Before Romanticism ever reared its head, the emotional dimension of religion received its due from the Methodist revival movements of the Wesley brothers and their colleagues. Romantic interest in the Middle Ages certainly helped to prepare the way for the Oxford Movement, the Anglo-Catholic revival of the mid-nineteenth century, but again this was a matter which was largely contained within the church. The British occult revival, then, occurred in a setting quite different from the radical utopian politics of July Monarchy Paris or the frustrated nationalism of the divided German population. It did occur, however, and British occultists were indispensable to the rise of the Goddess movement.

THE OCCULT REVIVAL IN ENGLAND

At the opening of the nineteenth century, while Novalis was writing of Magic Idealism and the Swedenborgians and Mesmerists were experiencing their visions, an Englishman named Francis Barrett was attempting to evoke demons. Almost nothing is known of Barrett himself, save for his 1801 book *The Magus, or Celestial Intelligencer: Being a Complete System of Occult Philosophy.* The book covers such conventional esoteric topics as the powers of plants and minerals, numerology, alchemy, and Kabbalism. His dull prose pales beside his artwork, however; the book is best remembered for his hideous portraits of various demons, which he claimed to have drawn on the basis of personal observation. The subject matter of Barrett's book brought him into line with the Rosicrucian tradition as it was then understood. He seems to have wanted to start a small group for the practice of magic, but it is not clear whether he managed to do so in actual fact.[4]

The first certain sign of increased English interest in the occult appears, like English Romanticism itself, in literature. Marie Roberts's recent study *Gothic Immortals* traces the development of what she calls "the Rosicrucian novel" in early nineteenth century fiction. The common denominator of most of these novels is the quest for physical immortality through unholy means—the use of magical "science" to revoke the Fall of Man and gain control over the forces of life and death. The Rosicrucian adepts who embark on this quest appear, accordingly, as either villains or tragic heroes.[5]

Several of these stories emerged from the members of a single family: William Godwin (1756–1836), who was briefly the husband of Mary Wollstonecraft; their daughter Mary (1797–1851); and Mary's husband, Percy Bysshe Shelley (1792–1822). Godwin was a man of the Enlightenment whom Roberts describes as "a political reformer and anarchist philosopher."[6] Like many of his scientific generation, he was interested in the question of whether the human lifespan could be extended, perhaps even indefinitely. This, it seems (along with a chronic need for funds), led him to pen the novel *St. Leon* (1799) about the fortunes—mostly unpleasant—of an adept who had achieved immortality.

In chronological order, Shelley came next with his early novel *St. Irvyne: The Rosicrucian* (1810) which appears to imitate *St. Leon* in form; it also displays Shelley's passionate enthusiasm for Goethe's *Faust*.[7] Mary Shelley's *Frankenstein* (1818) is the most famous of the genre, although the Rosicrucian role of the immortal adept is divided here between the occult scientist and his monstrous creation. "Frankenstein," notes Roberts, was also the name of the castle inhabited by an alleged eighteenth-century Rosicrucian necromancer named Johann Konrad Dippel, who seems to be the model for Dr. Victor Frankenstein.[8]

Mary Shelley returned to the theme in "The Mortal Immortal" (1833), the tale of a pupil of Cornelius Agrippa who drinks the elixir of life by mistake and then must face the tedium of an endless worldly existence. Outside Godwin's extended family, the list of Rosicrucian novels included the Rev. Charles Maturin's *Melmoth the Wanderer* (1820), another cautionary tale of the endless despair that comes with the magical, and therefore illegitimate, acquisition of endless life in this world.[9] In 1834, Godwin adopted a different tone and issued *Lives of the Necromancers*, his attempt to debunk the reputations of Agrippa, Dee, and other supposed adepts. Still the Enlightenment rationalist, he warned that occult phenomena are "products of auto-suggestion and superstitious fears."[10]

Such warnings fell on many deaf ears, it seems. By this time, Edward Bulwer-Lytton was already establishing his career as a popular novelist who would make great use of the Rosicrucian theme. He published his first such story, "The Tale of Kosem Kesamim: The Magician," in 1832; it deals with an adept who fails in his quest for physical immortality but discovers the better alternative of eternal life in heaven.[11]

Zicci (1838) was a short published piece in a similar vein which Lytton went on to use as the basis for his major occult work *Zanoni* (1842); he had the narrator report that both stories were based on coded manuscripts he obtained in a secondhand bookshop from some-one who might have been an actual Rosicrucian.[12] The plot of *Zanoni* deals with two sages: Mejnour possesses the elixir and lives forever on earth, but Zanoni abandons that quest for the higher goal of love, and gains true immortality by sacrificing his life on the guillotine for the heroine Viola. The fact that the hero is an occult adept who perishes at the hands of "enlightened" French revolutionaries says much about where Lytton's sympathies lay.

In Lytton's *A Strange Story* (1862), a materialistic scientist even-tually comes to believe in the immortality of the human soul after surviving a dangerous encounter with a villainous Rosicrucian. The conflict between reason and spirituality appears here again, and Rob-erts suggests that "the rationalization of the occult is central to the novel's narrative purpose." In that respect, it is interesting to note that this novel was written after Lytton had become acquainted with Eliphas Lévi, who even appears as a character in the book.[13] Lévi, as we have seen, popularized the esoteric tradition partly by minimiz-ing its supernatural overtones, preferring to describe the astral light and its magical manifestations as another dimension of nature itself.

From these indications of Lytton's lifelong interest in the occult, what do we learn about the state of esoterica in England? Was he a practicing magician or a member of an occult order? The evidence is surprisingly mixed. In a letter to a friend, he wrote, "I do believe in the substance of what used to be called Magic, that is, I believe that there are persons of a peculiar temperament who can effect very extraordinary things not accounted for satisfactorily by any existent philosophy."[14]   Lytton also lurked somewhere in the background of Eliphas Lévi's famous invocation of Apollonius of Tyana, as we saw previously. There is, however, no firm proof that Lytton belonged to an organized group or, for that matter, that there was such a group available to him any earlier than the 1860s. His grandson, who wrote his biography, asserts that Lytton was Grand Patron of the "Society of Rosicrucians." He has no hard data to offer, but he points to the absence of actual evidence as constituting reliable proof in itself—Lytton, allegedly, was scrupulously observing the requirements of secrecy which came with his position.[15]   In one of the Mahatma Letters, Koot Hoomi supposedly told A. P. Sinnett that Lytton had led a short-lived club for a dozen practicing magicians.[16]   In his own correspondence, Lytton dropped hints of his inside knowledge of Rosicrucianism, but the veracity of these comments is open to doubt.[17]

On the other hand, there is no question but that Lytton's thought and work was influenced by some of his Romantic predecessors whom we have already considered. As Roberts argues, one of the recurring themes in Lytton's work is the clash between the ideal and the actual, between imagination and reason; his goal is a higher perspective which reconciles the two. Roberts points out that this whole endeavor owes a great deal to Lytton's knowledge of the philosophy of Hegel—who himself employed the symbolism of rose and cross to express precisely the same theme.[18]   Moreover, Lytton's great Rosicrucian novel *Zanoni* shows considerable influence from the work of Novalis and his philosophy of Magic Idealism, according to which the true poet, like a magician, actually shapes reality through his word. "The Romantic artist is in tune with the Rosicrucian idealist . . . The distinctions between the macrocosm and the microcosm collapse into one another . . . This is the point at which the artist-magician declares himself a god in the solipsistic exercise of his own creative powers."[19]

These themes from the German Romantics, transplanted in part through Lytton's fiction, took root and grew among those who regarded *Zanoni* as a faithful and authentic portrait of the Rosicrucian tradition and attempted to put it into practice—a group which included not only the English Rosicrucian revivalists but Madame Blavatsky herself. The first such group of which we can speak with any confidence was established in the mid-1860s. According to Ellic Howe's classic study, the Societas Rosicruciana in Anglia ("Rosicrucian Society in England," abbreviated as Soc. Ros. or SRIA) was founded in 1867 by Robert Wentworth Little, a London Freemason. It functioned as an occult study group superimposed on Masonry; only Master Masons were allowed to join, and then they could proceed up the nine grades of initiation which are familiar from the Golden and Rosy Cross of eighteenth-century Germany.[20]

Howe suggests that Little acquired much of his material from Kenneth Mackenzie (1833–86), a wide-ranging occultist and Tarot specialist who had paid a personal visit to Eliphas Lévi in 1861. Mackenzie knew German and claimed to have been initiated into a German Rosicrucian group, although there is no surviving evidence of any such group at this time. McIntosh, however, cites an anonymous source who told him that Little's group branched off from a previously existing Masonic Rosicrucian organization in Scotland.[21]

The early members of the group, besides being Master Masons, shared a strong interest in Spiritualism and psychic phenomena (as did thousands of their contemporaries). Their understanding of Rosicrucianism was shaped largely by the Golden and Rosy Cross structure of nine ranks, Lévi's theories of occultism, and Lytton's novel Zanoni. In fact, Lytton was named honorary grand patron of the SRIA without being asked, simply because Zanoni seemed like such a good portrait of Rosicrucianism that he himself was presumed to be a real expert. When he learned about it, however, he insisted that his name be removed.[22]

Little died in 1878 and was succeeded as Supreme Magus by Dr. W. R. Woodman (1828-91), a medical doctor with a strong predilection for the Kabbalah. Newer members who shared his interests included Dr. William Wynn Westcott (1848-1925), a coroner, and Samuel Liddell Mathers (1854-1918). Mathers was a character who defies concise description, but his knowledge of obscure occult texts was combined with a genius for designing rituals which had a powerful psychological impact on the participants. This new generation of members gradually shifted the focus of the S RI A from Spiritualism to the traditions of high magic.

Woodman, Westcott, and Mathers would soon become the founding members of the Hermetic Order of the Golden Dawn (commonly abbreviated as the G D), an incomparably important contributor to the development of modern magic. One of the many striking features we shall observe in the Golden Dawn is the fact that these Masonic Rosicrucians, all males, sought from the very beginning to recruit female members to join them in their endeavors. As Mary K. Greer notes of the G D, "for the first time men and women worked together as equals in magical ceremonies . . ."[23] While Greer has filled a void by providing a detailed multiple biography of the four most important female members of the G D, there remains the prior question—what prepared these men for the apparently unprecedented decision to accept women as full and active magical partners, and actually to seek them out?

Sex Magic and Female Magicians

Women have been surprisingly few in our account of esoteric movements so far. Theosophy has its recent tradition of female leadership, but even with that, HPB could hardly be called a feminist. She often dressed as a man and mouthed many of the misogynist clichés of her time, and her Mahatmas were male one and all. Annie Besant's career as a crusader for women's rights was more eclipsed than enhanced when she joined the Theosophical Society. The most notable magicians and occultists we have discussed up to now have been men, and most of the organizations have been restricted to the male sex. Within the larger purview of our inquiry, we have had one active woman, Flora Tristan, to set against the feminine phantoms of Sophia von Kühn, *Faust's* Gretchen and the Mothers, the Saint-Simonians' absentee Mother, Mme. Dumesnil, Mme. de Vaux, and the idealized woman of Constant/Lévi. All of the latter had their greatest impact, and some their actual origin, in the minds and imaginations of men.

Inevitably, there were a few exceptions. Some Masonic histories include the story of the Hon. Elizabeth Aldworth (née St. Leger) who was caught spying on a Masonic initiation in 1712 and, presumably to bring her under the vow of secrecy, was promptly initiated herself. While the evidence concerning this case seems credible enough (the date places it earlier than the Grand Lodge regulations which formally excluded women), it bears a striking resemblance to some twentieth-century stories of initiation into witchcraft which are almost certainly fraudulent, as we shall see in Chapter 14.

A. E. Waite has described a document dated September 12, 1794, recording the initiation of Dr. Sigismund Bacstrom into the otherwise-unknown Societas Rosae Crucis on the island of Mauritius at the hands of "a certain Comte de Chazal." The document stipulates that the Order did indeed admit qualified women, listing as examples the mythical Semiramis, Miriam the sister of Moses, the wife of the Kabbalistic alchemist Nicolas Flamel (d. 1417), and Leona Constantia, Abbess of Clermont, who is supposed to have been initiated in 1736.[24] In assessing the truthfulness of this account, it is worth noting that Bacstrom also reported several successful experiments in producing gold under the alchemical guidance of the ninety-six-year-old Comte.

In 1850, Mary Anne Atwood published a well-informed alchemical manual entitled *A Suggestive Inquiry into Hermetic Mystery*; her father, Thomas South, was known to be interested in such esoteric lore. As we saw in the last chapter, Co-Masonry started in France in 1882, but the lodge which first initiated Maria Deraismes was disfellowshipped by the others and had to develop its own rite. Co-Masonry was not established in England until the turn of the century, under the auspices of Theosophy. This record hardly seems sufficient to account for such a pronounced change in procedure on the part of Victorian Freemasons as we discover in the Golden Dawn. What made the times ripe for co-educational magic? There appear to be at least two answers to this question—one general, and the other personal.

First, the latter half of the nineteenth century witnessed a new development in the esoteric tradition itself: the rise of sex magic. While sexual motifs had been common in the alchemical literature especially, this was usually a case of marriage and intercourse being employed as symbols of something else, namely the "Great Work" of making the philosophers' stone in a grand synthesis of all the polarities. New to the nineteenth century (but earlier than Freud) was the increasingly widespread acceptance of the idea that alchemy and other occult disciplines were actually symbolic of sex, and not the other way around.[25]

The discovery of Tantrism helps to account for this. Tantra is a set of Hindu and Buddhist disciplines, ancient by Western standards, in which mystical enlightenment is sought through—yet again—the reconciliation of all opposites.[26] "Left-handed" Tantra involves actual participation in "the five forbidden things" as a means of breaking down dualities and achieving ultimate cosmic consciousness. The fifth forbidden thing is ritual sex, and there is an entire body of Tantric literature and art elaborating on this theme. According to Cavendish, Western occultists were introduced to Tantra in 1865 by Edward Sellon, "a minor pornographer and industrious lecher who wrote *Annotations Upon the Sacred Writings of the Hindus.*"[27]

At around the same time, the American Pascal Beverly Randolph (1825-75) hit upon the idea of sex magic by himself. He was the illegitimate mulatto son of Edmund Randolph (who was Attorney General and Secretary of State under George Washington and a onetime Governor of Virginia) and a mother whom he described as "a beautiful *sang-melée* of . . . Madagascan, French, Spanish, Indian and Oriental . . ."[28] P. B. Randolph never knew his father, and his mother died during his childhood; he was essentially self-educated and went to sea at the age of twelve. After familiarizing himself with Spiritualism and Mesmerism, he set up his own medical practice dispensing homemade potions. Following further travels in Europe and Asia, he claimed to have received Rosicrucian initiation and began spreading his own form of the Order, called the Brotherhood of Eulis, in the United States.

"Eulis" is what he called his system of sex magic, which essentially prescribed ritual intercourse as a way for male and female to exchange and combine their psychic energies. Thanks to the sexual imagery in the religious art of ancient Egypt and India, he claimed, "the believers would involuntarily realize those truths in their sexual couplings . . . utilizing the creative energy of all the couples, the Hierophants could people the astral sphere with divinities and demiurges . . . The astral collective of people, therefore, creates power."[29] Randolph provided general rules on the conduct of sex magic ("Formulate your desire in advance and don't forget that desire at the moment of coition") and delineated the occult properties of various positions for intercourse. Randolph's magic, in theory at least, absolutely requires male and female partners.[30]

He is supposed to have established the Brotherhood of Eulis in 1870, but there is little surviving evidence as to whether it actually operated as described. It lasted only a few years, until his headquarters was destroyed in the Great Boston Fire; many misfortunes then followed him, ranging from an alleged long-distance "occult war" with HPB to a nasty encounter with armed robbers. Randolph ended his life in Toledo, where he married and had a son before committing suicide in 1875.

Randolph claimed friends in high places, including Abraham Lincoln, who is said to have appointed him principal of a school for liberated slaves in Louisiana after the Civil War. He also said that he had once participated in a magical working with Eliphas Lévi and Napoleon III; Lévi's reservations towards both practical magic and Louis-Napoleon himself make this story doubly doubtful.[31] On the other hand, Randolph freely admitted that his version of Rosicrucianism was entirely his own invention: "I studied Rosicrucianism, found it suggestive and loved its mysticism. So I called myself *The Rosicrucian*, and gave my thought to the world as Rosicrucian thought . . . Very nearly *all* that I have given as Rosicrucianism originated in my own soul . . ."[32]

Randolph and Tantra together paved the way for Hargrave Jennings's *The Rosicrucians: Their Rites and Mysteries* (1870). Howe refers to this book as "nonsense from start to finish"; Cavendish describes it as "a comic muddle of fake antiquarianism, romantic Druidry, the Grail legends, gnosticism, the Cabala, the mysteries of Mithras and lunatic philology"; McIntosh, somewhat more gently, calls it "an extremely muddled work which brings in a lot of irrelevant information."[33] The book which elicits all these jibes is essentially about sex in occultism. Jennings would have been a marvelous resource for Freud; in his eyes every bump was a phallic symbol and every dent a vulva, above all the female Rose and male Cross. In the late nineteenth century this book had its enthusiasts, however, apparently including Lytton and Kenneth Mackenzie.[34] Their support brought the new theories of sex magic within the purview of the SRIA and into the immediate environment of the Golden Dawn.

The second, more personal factor which bears on the inclusion of women in the GD is the role of Anna Kingsford (1846-88).[35] An independently wealthy woman, she was plagued by asthma all through her short life. She was, however, prodigiously talented and lent her efforts to several causes. One, naturally, was the status of women and the right to vote; others included mystical Christianity, Spiritualism, and the anti-vivisection movement. Kingsford was so determined to fight vivisection that she left her clergyman husband to study medicine in Paris (the English medical schools were still closed to women). There she met Edward Maitland, her step-uncle, a Spiritualist writer who had been on the 1849 gold rush to California. Kingsford herself had been having visions, perhaps arising from her use of ether to combat her asthma; at any rate, she and Maitland established a platonic partnership which lasted for the rest of her life. They shared trance-visions and even developed a tag-team method of channeling books: working in separate rooms, one would take over where the other had left off, supposedly without comparing notes. They also shared the Romantic notion that "intuition or imagination was the source of wisdom, and it was a feminine function."[36]

Back in London, Kingsford's combination of striking beauty and stirring oratory attracted great attention for her causes. In 1882 she was recruited to take charge of the London chapter of the Theosophical Society, which A. P. Sinnett seemed to be mismanaging, but her dubious attitude towards the Mahatmas soon made her relationship with HPB unworkable. Kingsford and Maitland then went on to found their own Hermetic Society in 1885, which both Westcott and Mathers joined prior to their Golden Dawn days. In this context, there can be little doubt that the vivid example of the Kingsford-Maitland spiritual partnership, surrounded by the Tantric-Randolph-

Jennings emphasis on sex and gender in magic, made a co-educational magical order seem both obvious and necessary. Mathers, in fact, was to contract a platonic magical marriage of his own, but the order came first.

THE HERMETIC ORDER OF THE GOLDEN DAWN

Westcott was the driving force behind the establishment of the Golden Dawn.[37] Although, as Howe pointed out, his daytime work as a coroner involved the meticulous examination of physical and factual evidence, he obviously indulged in fantasy and the occult on a grand scale during his leisure time. He was a Master Mason and a Rosicrucian, succeeding Woodman as Supreme Magus of the SRIA in 1891. Through the SRIA he was acquainted with Kenneth Mackenzie, who had known Lytton well and had met Lévi, helping to popularize the French magus's ideas in England; both Lytton and Mackenzie, as we saw, had kind words to say about Jennings's Rosicrucian book as well. Westcott is reported to have taken two years' retreat in the late 1870s to study alchemy, Kabbalah, and Hermetic philosophy. Evidently, none of his other activities fully satisfied his desire for "a school for Cabbalistic and occult instruction,"[38] and thus arose his plan for yet another order.

As Howe described in detail, Westcott came into possession of a document which has become known as the "Cypher Manuscript"; at some point there was a suggestion that it had been found, *Zanoni*-style, in a secondhand bookshop. Once decoded (it was written in a well-known substitute alphabet which was easily accessible in the nearby British Museum library), it was found to contain partial instructions for the performance of five ceremonial initiations. At the very beginning, the manuscript mentions the "Fratres and Sorores [of this Temple of the] Golden Dawn."[39] Thus, both the name and the sexual inclusiveness of the new order were based on this manuscript.

While Howe could not determine the actual origin of the Cypher Manuscript, it does appear to date from the 1870s or 1880s, although old paper and brown ink were used deliberately to give it the appearance of great age. Greer supports the theory that the manuscript was Mackenzie's handiwork; on the other hand, some of Westcott's correspondence suggests that the Reverend A. F. A. Woodford, an active Freemason and acquaintance of both Mackenzie and Westcott, had obtained it from a French contact who, in turn, linked it back to Eliphas Lévi.[40] Mackenzie died in 1886 and Woodford in 1887, so either way, Westcott was free to do with it as he wished. Howe fully demonstrates the fictitious character of Westcott's next steps—he essentially invented a pedigree and a source of authority for the Golden Dawn.

Westcott claimed that he found with the manuscript another piece of paper which identified a certain Fräulein Anna Sprengel as a German adept of the Golden Dawn. He even had her address, care of Herr J. Enger at the Hotel Marquardt in Stuttgart. He exchanged a series of letters with her, and she conferred upon him the authority to establish a branch of the GD in England. She even awarded him, by mail, initiation into the fifth and then the seventh grades of the order.

Howe's extensive investigations into the details of this story had only one positive result: he was able to document the existence of the Hotel Marquardt. He found no corroboration whatsoever of a Fräulein Sprengel or a Herr Enger staying there or residing nearby, and no sign of an order called the Golden Dawn (*goldene Dämmerung*) anywhere in Germany. On the other hand, Howe turned up ample evidence that the letters from Anna Sprengel were faked, written by an English-speaker with a poor command of German. Probably Westcott composed them in English, had an English friend translate them into German and mail them back to him, and then had another acquaintance retranslate them into English—all to create the impression that the Golden Dawn was a longstanding and authentic part of the esoteric tradition in Europe.

Some commentators have remarked that Westcott's invention of Anna Sprengel is not very different from the role of the Secret Chiefs in Rosicrucianism or from HPB's Mahatmas. The new departure which pertains to our inquiry, however, is that the imaginary Fräulein Sprengel, holder of no less than seventh-grade rank in the German

Golden Dawn, was a woman—quite possibly the first female Secret Chief to appear in the Western tradition.

Westcott turned the Cypher Manuscript over to Mathers, who elaborated it into full-blown rituals designed for actual performance. In fact, there is a letter from Westcott to Mathers proposing that they jointly head up a new organization based on Woodford's manuscript; it is dated October 4, 1887, a full seven weeks before Westcott supposedly received his letter of permission from Fräulein Sprengel. As Howe notes, this may indicate that Westcott had not invented her yet; it also suggests that Mathers was party to the whole scheme from day one.[41]

When he became involved with the Golden Dawn, Mathers was already eccentric to say the least. He seems never to have held a real job; his two consuming passions were the military and the occult, although he pursued boxing and fencing on the side. He spent much of his life in libraries reading and translating arcane texts, and making an impression on those around him. Waite described his own experience of seeing Mathers staggering around the British Museum Reading Room with huge loads of books, and confronting people with such profound announcements as, "I have clothed myself with hieroglyphics as with a garment."[42]

Born in 1854, Mathers was initiated into Masonry in 1877 and into the SRIA in 1882. Especially keen on Celtic mythology and all things Scottish, he claimed descent from Rob Roy's Clan MacGregor and insisted that he held the title "Comte de Glenstrae," named for the MacGregors' ancestral home; eventually, he was known to all as "MacGregor" Mathers. Besides Mackenzie, Westcott and the other Rosicrucians, Mathers met Anna Kingsford while she was still a Theosophist. Kingsford introduced him to HPB who attempted to recruit him to Theosophy as well, but he declined owing to his lack of interest in the mysteries of the East. He was already working on his adaptation of an old Kabbalistic text which he would eventually publish in 1887 as *The Kabbalah Unveiled*; he evidently shared his work in progress with HPB, and much of what she says about Kabbalism in *The Secret Doctrine* shows his influence.

Mathers did join Kingsford's Hermetic Society in 1885 and gave talks there on the Kabbalah during the following summer. His wife later wrote that he was attracted to Kingsford's organization because he shared her "ideals of esoteric Christianity and the advancement of woman."[43]   There are suggestions that he was behind one of Kingsford's less appealing projects, trying to kill vivisectionists by magical means. Apparently two of her targets did in fact die soon after she cursed them, but her attempt to eliminate Louis Pasteur failed.[44]

The well-read Mathers was the obvious choice when Westcott needed to have the Cypher Manuscript transformed into something practical. His vast knowledge of esoteric lore and his proficiency in designing impressive rituals enabled the Golden Dawn to commence operation in the spring of 1888. Woodman, Westcott, and Mathers were awarded fifth-degree rank automatically by Fräulein Sprengel, but their first new initiate was a woman.

The basic history of the Golden Dawn and its structure has been recounted many times, so we shall skim it quickly in order to focus on our particular question. Mathers designed a system based on the nine grades of the Golden and Rosy Cross by way of the SRIA, and added two more: Neophyte for the beginner, sporting the rank of zero, and a tenth rank called Ipsissimus at the top of the hierarchy. At least part of the reason for having ten initiatory grades was to permit a full system of correspondences between the ranks and the ten sephiroth of the Tree of Life.

The Hermetic Order of the Golden Dawn was actually the Outer Order, the public face of the movement; it consisted of the first four grades and emphasized theoretical study of the esoteric tradition. There were oral and written examinations to be passed before one could be initiated into a higher level. The Inner Order was known properly as the Ordo Rosae Rubeae et Aureae Crucis (Order of the Ruby Rose and Golden Cross), or RR&AC for short. Consisting of grades five through seven, the three "Adeptus" grades, it involved actual magical practice—most often the consecration of talismans and other implements, as well as exercises in soul travel to other places, other times, and other dimensions. Initiation into the Inner Order, at the fifth rank, took the candidate through one of Mathers's most impressive ceremonies: a reenactment of the discovery and opening of Christian Rosenkreutz's tomb. The top three ranks made up the Third Order and were reserved for the Secret Chiefs, with whom Mathers was soon claiming direct contact.

What was the point of it all? Greer provides an evocative description:

> The Order of the Golden Dawn was a Hermetic Society whose members studied the principles of occult science and the magic of Hermes . . . The students' goal was to unite the Will with the highest Self. Will (with a capital W) was the consciously focused intention of one's highest, divine, or God-like Self . . . First they would examine and purify themselves using tools of astrology and divination, and then they would become one with their own divinity. The Golden Dawn provided both the knowledge and the medium through which they could transmute their vital life forces into the higher currents of life in order to commune with planetary spirits, angels, and gods. This involved a union of soul, mind, and body—necessitating correction of imbalances, combining of opposites, reclaiming what was lost, and surrender to dissolution and chaos. It required destruction and re-creation of the soul. . . .[45]

Considering the frequency with which Golden Dawn materials have been published since the Order's heyday, not to mention the many continuing magical groups which have descended from it directly or indirectly, it is surprising to discover that some central questions about the group remain unanswered. The role of sex magic in the GD is one of the most contentious of these questions. We do know that the group was heir to a considerable amount of sexual imagery in traditional occult lore, and that it was closely linked to people like Mackenzie and Lytton who encouraged the spread of Jennings's sexual interpretation of Rosicrucianism. On the other hand, those involved in the GD workings almost always denied that sex was involved at all. Certainly, there were many male-female magical partnerships in the group; moreover, Greer quotes a 1921 letter from Mrs. Mathers to Paul Foster Case, an initiate of the Thoth Hermes Temple in New York, advising him that instruction in sex theory should be withheld until a person reaches "quite the higher Grades."[46] None-theless Mathers, the man who designed the GD rituals, never con-summated his own worldly marriage with his mystic partner; this fact alone renders it very unlikely that physical sexual activity played any part in the Golden Dawn.

John Michael Greer and Carl Hood have offered a plausible specu-lation on the matter. They suggest that the GD teachings did indeed employ sexual imagery as one expression of the traditional occult emphasis on the unification of polarity; Mathers's own *Kabbalah Unveiled* includes the statement that "hence that which is not both Male and Female together is called half a body." Since we do know for a fact that some Golden Dawn rituals involved so-called astral travel, it seems reasonable to suppose that upper-level GD magic may have included sex magic of a completely nonphysical kind.[47]

Be that as it may, the extent to which modern magical groups remain indebted to the Golden Dawn amply illustrates the accom-plishments of Mathers and his colleagues. There seems to be little reason to doubt that his system of indoctrination and ritual initia-tion made a powerful impact on many of the individuals who partici-pated in it.[48] This combination of a comprehensive and coherent occult philosophy with effective rituals and the actual practice of high magic allowed the Golden Dawn to flourish within certain limits. Between 1888 and 1896, five temples were established and more than three hundred initiations took place; in that period, 119 of the ini-tiates were women.[49]

More striking than the statistic is the caliber of the people in-volved, since many of them were comparatively prominent in fields like literature, drama, and medicine. It was, as much as anything, the clash of so many powerful egos within such a small group that led it to dissolve into bickering rival fragments in 1901. By that time, Mathers had made loyalty to himself the key to all advancement in the Order; when he decided to eliminate Westcott's influence, he in-formed the other members that the Sprengel correspondence had indeed been forged—evidently not realizing the extent to which this death blow to the GD's credibility implicated him as well.[50]

Today, the best known of the initiates is the Irish poet W. B.

Yeats. He had already steeped himself in Irish folklore and had participated in Hermetic studies and Theosophy when he joined the Golden Dawn in 1890. He stayed on through all the coming troubles and remained a leading member of one of the groups which carried on the Golden Dawn tradition, the Stella Matutina. In 1893, while he was still in the GD's Outer Order, he wrote to a fellow Irish nationalist: "Now as to Magic. It is surely absurd to hold me 'weak' or otherwise because I chose to persist in a study which I decided deliberately four or five years ago to make, next to my poetry, the most important pursuit of my life. . . . If I had not made magic my constant study I could not have written a single word of my Blake book, nor would *The Countess Kathleen* have ever come to exist. The mystical life is the centre of all that I do and all that I think and all that I write."[51]

More pertinent to us here, however, is the involvement of women. The Golden Dawn was particularly notable for the importance of its female members. First in seniority was Mina Bergson (1865–1928), the product of a musical European Jewish family and sister of the philosopher Henri Bergson. Henri apparently never participated in actual magic, but his philosophy was notable for its emphasis on the superiority of intuition over reason and the immanentist notion of the *élan vital* or "life urge."[52] Mina, on the other hand, seemingly found her destiny upon meeting Mathers in the British Museum when she was an art student. As Greer comments, "Since meeting Anna Kingsford and Edward Maitland, Mathers had been searching for a partner in his magical endeavors. Mina Bergson—artistic, psychically sensitive, beautiful, from a family rooted in the Kabbalah, drawn to the ancient religious symbols housed in the museum, a Taurus to his Capricorn, ripe for his training—was perfect."[53]

Mina assisted Mathers in his work by means of her gift for channeling and recruited her friend Annie Horniman to the Order as well. It was Bergson who underwent the first formal initiation into the Golden Dawn, on March 1, 1888. Two years later, she changed her given name to a more Celtic "Moina" and contracted her platonic marriage with Mathers himself. She worked with him for the rest of his life, helping to run the Golden Dawn and also sharing with him in the "reestablishment" of the Rites of Isis after they moved to Paris in 1892. Much of the arcane knowledge generated in both movements was, in effect, channeled through her. After Mathers's death in 1918, she headed the main faction of the Golden Dawn and participated in other occult organizations until her own death ten years later. Her last days were marked by several feuds, and she was accused of putting the defense of her late husband's reputation ahead of the quest for truth.[54]

Annie Horniman (1860–1937) came from a rich family; her Quaker grandfather made his fortune by inventing the tea bag.[55] Rebelling against the religious and social restrictions placed on her, she insisted on enrolling in art school, where she met and befriended Mina Bergson. Bergson was a much better artist than Horniman, whose life's work actually lay in the theater. She was passionately devoted to drama, made frequent pilgrimages to the annual Wagner festival at Bayreuth, and helped to introduce the plays of Ibsen to the English public. She was an early initiate into the GD and was the first to be ritually admitted to the Inner Order, on December 7, 1891.

Horniman's wealth was of great benefit to the Order. Because of her friendship with Mina, she supported Mathers for years, first hiring him to work in her father's private museum and then sending him frequent gifts of money in London and in Paris. The rebellious temperament which had led Horniman to defy her Quaker family by involving herself in art and theater probably played a role in motivating her to join the GD; it did not desert her afterwards, however, and she fought ongoing battles with Mathers and other members. Mathers expelled her for insubordination in 1896, but she was readmitted in 1900, just in time for the final breakup. She tried to take over the fragmenting Order, claiming contact with a Secret Chief called the Purple Adept, but failed and quit again.

She maintained contact with other members during her exiles, however, and assisted several of them financially. She helped Yeats stage several of his plays and eventually built the Abbey Theatre in Dublin for him. Then, "as proprietor of the Gaiety Theatre [in Manchester], she pioneered the modern British repertory movement."[56] Her contributions to the theater won her the Companion of Honour in 1932. She and Mina also reportedly joined the Quest Society in the 1920s; this was an esoteric study group established and run by the prominent Theosophist G. R. S. Mead.[57]

Florence Farr (1860–1917), a noted actress at the time, was initiated in 1890 (the same year in which she began an affair with George Bernard Shaw, who had long since left Annie Besant behind). She moved quickly up the ranks, and when the Matherses moved to Paris in 1892, she became the effective head of the Order in England—although this did prompt complaints about "petticoat government" from Westcott and others. Her theatrical abilities, along with those of Horniman, contributed greatly to the staging of the initiations, solstice and equinox rituals, and other ceremonies. Farr maintained her involvement in the dramatic life, acting in and producing several plays by Yeats. She also started a special group within the GD which concentrated on Egyptian magic. Following the breakup of the Golden Dawn in 1901, she joined the Theosophical Society and published a number of books on occultism. Finally, in 1912, she left England to become principal of the first girls' college in Ceylon, which was being established by the Hindu guru Sir Ponnambalam Ramanathan; already in 1902, her "spirit guides" had told her that the Christ force was working through him.[58] She died there of breast cancer in 1917.

Maud Gonne (1866–1953), a leading crusader for Irish independence, was initiated in 1891 after being introduced to the GD by Yeats, whose long, passionate love for her was to remain physically unrequited (as late as 1917 he proposed to both Maud and then her daughter Iseult, and was rejected by each of them). Gonne quit the Order in 1894, fearing that its strong Masonic overtones made it pro-British (even though Mathers himself was a well-known Jacobite, a supporter of the long-departed Stuart dynasty). Still, she occasionally joined Yeats either physically or on the "astral plane" for magical workings; they even carried on a so-called spiritual marriage by way of soul travel. At one point they tried to create a distinctively Irish mystery religion, but Gonne's activism made her restless with mystical matters which diverted her energy from politics.

Even after the breakup, the GD tradition continued to attract women of leadership caliber. One of the contemporary organizations in the Golden Dawn lineage is the Society of the Inner Light, founded by Dion Fortune (1891–1946).[59] Her real name was Violet Mary Firth; her pen name was adapted from her Golden Dawn motto, *Deo Non Fortuna* ("by God, not by chance"). Fortune was an occult novelist as well as a practicing ritual magician, and several of her stories feature Celtic goddesses. One of her particular goals was to establish a purely Western mystery tradition, purified of the Oriental elements introduced by Theosophy. She joined Moina Mathers's Alpha and Omega Lodge after World War I; the two feuded, however, and engaged in psychic and magical battles with each other in which cats were strangely prominent. Fortune accused Mrs. Mathers of inflicting a plague of cats on her house by occult means; and, after fighting an out-of-body battle with Moina over access to the astral pathways, Dion reported finding cat scratches all over her back.[60] Fortune's own group continued afterwards to follow many of the Golden Dawn traditions. The magical records of her disciples Christine Hartley and Charles Seymour, which have been published in recent years, contain extensive descriptions of their trance visits to Atlantis and other times and places.[61]

The sudden prominence of women in both Theosophy and the Golden Dawn has been noted on occasion, but probably needs more sustained investigation. Commonly, it is suggested that the new occult orders offered women paths to spiritual progress and leadership roles which, at this time, were available to them in few other areas. This argument from opportunity may account for some particular cases, but it is clearly inadequate as a general explanation. Women like Phoebe Palmer in the American holiness movement and Catherine Booth in the Salvation Army had already assumed positions of public spiritual leadership in a highly visible fashion while remaining essentially within the bounds of orthodox Christianity. The esoteric tradition, particularly in its Masonic Rosicrucian form, was far more "patriarchal" than the church—prior to the GD, it had not allowed women to join at all. Suddenly, however, when Westcott and his friends wanted female partners for their magic, the women came.

There was, without doubt, a positive attraction in the esoteric tradition for some women. In an interview with Frederic Lees, Moina Bergson Mathers articulated it this way:

> How can we hope that the world will become purer and less material when one excludes from the Divine, which is the highest ideal, that part of its nature which represents at one and the same time the faculty of receiving and that of giving—that is to say, love itself and its highest form—love the symbol of universal sympathy? That is where the magical power of woman is found. She finds her force in her alliance with the sympathetic energies of Nature. And what is Nature if it is not an assemblage of thought clothed with matter and ideas which seek to materialize themselves? . . . Have you ever realized that there does not exist a single flame without a special intelligence which animates it, or a single grain of sand to which an idea is not attached, the idea which formed it? It is these intelligent ideas which are the elementals, or spirits of Nature. Woman is the magician born of Nature by reason of her great natural sensibility, and of her instructive sympathy with such subtle energies as these intelligent inhabitants of the air, the earth, fire, and water.[62]

Here in the Golden Dawn, the first significant magical order to admit women alongside men, we find the key elements of traditional esotericism, from Neoplatonic spirituality and divine immanence to ceremonial magic, all thoroughly blended with the Romantic idealization of women as spiritually pure channels of love, intuitively connected to nature. The GD and its successors and imitators were not just "any port in a storm" to their serious female members; they were more like functioning temples of womanhood, where men—even some powerful and respected Victorian men—had surrendered their spiritual autonomy.

All that is missing is the Goddess herself. Between her and the GD, however, stands the Great Beast.

ALEISTER CROWLEY

Modern sex magic is commonly associated with the infamous Aleister Crowley (1875–1947). He was born Edward Alexander Crowley, to a father who owed his wealth to his brewery and a mother who was committed to the strict evangelical sect known as the Plymouth Brethren. He was raised in a series of English boarding schools where, by his own account, he was most strongly affected by the use of caning as a means of discipline and by an undercurrent of homosexual activity in the all-male environment. He developed a rebellious temperament which led his Bible-reading mother to call him "The Beast 666," and he spent the rest of his life living up to that billing.[63]

He entered Cambridge to study Classics but spent most of his time writing poetry, playing chess, and mountaineering. He later claimed he could have become a Grand Master at chess but was put off the whole idea at his first major tournament when he saw what dusty old men the other Masters were. He was an accomplished climber, but ruined his standing with other mountaineers during a 1905 expedition to Kanchenjunga, the third-highest mountain in the world. Crowley was leader of the expedition, but he alienated his colleagues and porters to the point that many were deserting him. When one group fell into a crevasse on their way back down the mountain, Crowley refused to help them; instead, he hurried back to civilization and emptied the expedition's bank account.[64] As for poetry, he marveled that little Warwickshire had produced England's two greatest poets—himself of course, but Shakespeare as well.[65]

The other interests developed by Crowley during his university days were sex and magic. He was extremely active sexually and the trouble caused by his homosexual liaisons contributed to his departure from Cambridge without a degree. Crowley's rebelliousness was all-embracing, but his parents' Christianity held first rank on his list of enemies; consequently, he began to seek out ways of contacting the devil. He apparently encountered some books by members of the Golden Dawn—Waite's *Book of Black Magic and of Pacts* and Mathers's *Kabbalah Unveiled*—before being introduced to the Order itself.

His career in the GD was brief and destructive. He was initiated into the Outer Order in November 1898 and ascended the ranks quickly, but he antagonized most of the other members of the London temple. Yeats scathingly remarked that Crowley did not belong in the GD since it was a mystical society, not a moral reformatory; Crowley charged in return that Yeats was simply jealous of his incomparably superior poetic talent.[66] When the London group started squabbling with Mathers in 1900, Crowley sided with the Chief and tried to take over control of the London temple. He failed, then put Mathers to a test of his own, and broke with him as well. By 1901 Crowley was on his own, and the Golden Dawn was on the verge of collapse.

Crowley travelled extensively during the rest of his life. He went to Egypt in 1904 with his new bride, Rose Kelly (sister of Gerald Kelly, a GD member who went on to serve as president of the Royal Academy and received a knighthood). There, with Rose serving as medium, he was contacted by his spiritual alter-ego, "Aiwass." The result was the channeled *Book of the Law*, Crowley's seminal work. He later visited America and spent a few years in Sicily, running a magical commune called the Abbey of Thelema. He eventually died, a hopeless drug addict, in a boarding house in Hastings, England. Along the way, he went through a lengthy series of partners from both sexes; it seemed there was always a "Scarlet Woman" to ride the Beast (Revelation 17:1-6), but some of his most important rituals were performed with male partner/pupils like Victor Neuburg.

His course was set, however, from the time of his visit to Egypt— the rest of his life was given over to magic, with sex magic as a prominent component. He started an order of his own, known as the Argentium Astrum or "Silver Star." He was also invited to become the English head of the Ordo Templi Orientis ("Order of the Eastern Temple," or OTO). This was a German occult group which included Dr. Franz Hartmann, the Theosophist and List Society member who had helped to demolish HPB's shrine in Adyar. Crowley shared two things with the OTO—an interest in Tantric sex magic and a feud with MacGregor Mathers—so they made common cause. Crowley helped the OTO redesign the teachings and rituals of their upper ranks. By the time he was finished, the seventh-grade instruction was devoted to the theory of sex magic; the eighth dealt with practical autoeroticism; the ninth was for heterosexual ritual activity; and the tenth, apparently Crowley's own innovative contribution, centered on homosexual ceremonies. Crowley remained English head of the OTO until his death, and several chapters of the Order are still active.

Crowley courted publicity and controversy through both his writings and his public actions; he reveled in the press descriptions of him as "the wickedest man in the world." In 1916 he raised himself to the ninth rank, Magus, by performing a self-initiation ritual in which he baptized a frog, named it Jesus Christ, and crucified it; in 1921 he elevated himself to Ipsissimus, virtual Godhood.[67] One public ceremony at the Abbey of Thelema was intended to culminate in the blood sacrifice of a male goat while it was coming to sexual climax with Crowley's current Scarlet Woman, Leah Hirsig. The goat failed to play its full part, but it was sacrificed anyway. Episodes like this, along with reports of drug use, Crowley's obscene writings, and the accidental death of his disciple Raoul Loveday led Mussolini to expel the Beast from Italy in 1923.[68]

The core of Crowley's teachings was the importance of the will. Probably his most famous aphorism is his version of Rabelais' slogan: "'Do what thou wilt' shall be the whole of the Law."[69] He sometimes spoke of the "true will" in an almost mystical sense, to distinguish it from momentary whims; it is rather like a personal destiny which must be discovered within the self. He regarded ceremonial magic as a series of techniques in which one finds one's true will and gains the power to exert it on one's environment. Magic itself he defined as "the art of causing change in conformity to will." (He preferred to spell it "magick," to distinguish high magic from the carnival tricksters and to give it a better numerological correspondence; numerology was also the reason he invented the name "Aleister"). By his definition, every intentional act is a magical act; the disciplines of ritual magic simply make it more effective.[70]

Crowley regarded sex as one of the purest and most powerful expressions of will, indeed a "sacrament of the will," to be cultivated and employed in as many forms as possible. In orgasm, he said, we experience the unification of soul and body. He argued that children should be familiar with the sight of sexual activity, and sometimes expressed a degree of tolerance towards rape.[71]   He did, nevertheless, champion his own view of the liberation of women. One of his other slogans, "Every man and woman is a star," meant that each individual has an equal right to pursue his or her own course through the universe without obstruction from others. He also said, "Collision is the only crime in the cosmos," and his list of human rights includes the right to kill anyone who interferes in one's pursuit of one's true will. Consequently, he was opposed to any restrictions which would inhibit women from the total freedom he also advocated for men. Monogamy was particularly to be avoided, as it was so contrary to the free exercise of sexuality; Crowley claimed that men actually create a "false consciousness" in women to make their dependence seem voluntary. He therefore called himself "the fiercest of feminists," arguing that women needed complete freedom from the control of men.[72]

At the same time, Crowley often expressed negative views about women themselves. He defended the all-male character of Masonry, asserted flatly that women have no serious mental or moral potential, and commented that his youthful sexual needs should have been met as casually as milk was delivered to the door.[73]   To be fair, he expected liberated women to behave as he did, suggesting that they would pick up and discard lovers just as they would newspapers. Crowley was often deliberately outrageous, and it is sometimes difficult to know when he actually meant what he was saying. It is true, however, that several of the women who worked and lived most closely with him ended their lives in mental hospitals, including both of his legal wives, and the fact that he placed homosexual magic at a higher level than heterosexual rituals may confirm an element of misogyny in his thinking.

He developed his own version of a New Age philosophy based on an ancient Egyptian trinity. He proclaimed that the previous ages of Mother Isis (matriarchy, which prevailed until 500 BC) and Father Osiris (patriarchy, running from 500 BC to 1904 and the *Book of the*

Law) were being succeeded by the age of Horus, the free and con-
quering Child. This third age would be characterized by freedom of
the will, with a new religion which he called Crowleyanity. Crowley
recognized that his magical system was not for everyone; in fact, he
gloried in its elitism. On the other hand, he saw a role for a more
popular and accessible version of his teachings. In a 1915 letter he
wrote, "The time is just ripe for a natural religion. People like rites
and ceremonies, and they are tired of hypothetical gods. Insist on
the real benefits of the Sun, the Mother-force, the Father-force and
so on. . . . In short, be the founder of a new and greater Pagan cult."[74]
His friend did not take the advice, but others did. Modern Wicca,
mother to the Goddess movement, is precisely that sort of natural,
neopagan religion, and some of Crowley's own teachings are fundamental to it.

One of Crowley's major contributions to the esoteric tradition as
a whole was to make it less esoteric. Partly because of his own all-
consuming need for attention, he performed and published on a large
scale. In the course of it, he revealed matters which were usually
placed under vows of secrecy, including details of many of the Golden
Dawn rituals. His own quest for publicity served to increase general
awareness of high magic. In addition, the connection between female liberation and general sexual freedom lived on through the occult tradition and gained immeasurably in popular recognition
through the titillating high profile maintained by Crowley in his books
and his well-publicized antics. This theme can be traced back at
least to Fourier and Enfantin, and it reappears in most of today's
Goddess literature. Along with Crowley's emphasis on absolute personal freedom, his insistence that sexual experience of any kind can
constitute a sacrament of the will is part of his legacy to the twentieth century.

His influence is still significant. One recent study comments,
"The fact remains that if you're interested in magic as a spiritual discipline, you must deal with Crowley . . . Today the truth of Crowley
lies in what you can make of him for yourself. As a myth, he is
numinous with initiatory energy, of a dangerous and therefore powerful type."[75] The OTO carries on, the Beatles put Crowley's face into

the crowd on the cover of their *Sergeant Pepper* album, and investigations of Satanic cults often allude to lurid passages from the Great Beast somewhere along the way.

Crowley played a personal role in the story of the Goddess as well. Wicca might be somewhat different today had not its founder, Gerald Gardner, made Crowley's acquaintance. Gardner will be our focus in Chapter 14.

PART IV

MATRIARCHY AND WITCHCRAFT

Bachofen's Theory of Matriarchy

To man's superior physical strength woman opposes the
mighty influence of her religious consecration; she
counters violence with peace, enmity with conciliation,
hate with love.

Johann Jakob Bachofen

ALEISTER CROWLEY'S CALL for a popular new pagan religion was to bear fruit in the New Age Movement—particularly in its most highly organized form, modern witchcraft, and Wicca's more mainstream spin-off, Goddess spirituality. Nevertheless, the Goddess movement would not be what it is (indeed, it might not exist at all) but for the trends set in motion by two particular books. As we saw earlier, the Goddess spirituality of the past twenty-five years is a blend of two earlier phenomena: Wicca, with its roots in the occult tradition; and the theme of ancient utopian matriarchies, which appeared in certain circles of radical feminism. Two books, written in different places and different languages but appearing within a year of each other, set these phenomena in motion.

The train of events leading to Wicca began with one of the last great works of Jules Michelet, *La Sorcière* (*The Witch*, 1862). This appears to be the very first significant publication to argue that the witchcraft of the Renaissance and Reformation periods, the great age of witch-hunting, had been an independent and valid religion. We shall take up *La Sorcière* and its successors in Chapter 13.

In 1861, the year before Michelet's book appeared, Johann Jakob Bachofen published *Das Mutterrecht*. The title is usually translated as *Mother-Right*; *Mother-Law* or *Mother-Justice* are equally possible renderings of the German and they should perhaps be kept in mind, since Bachofen trained as a lawyer and specialized in the history of law. At any rate, this is the book which first proposed that all human societies passed through a stage of female rule before patriarchy was imposed on them, and that those woman-centered cultures bore the distinct marks of the feminine in their religion and social organization.

Mutterrecht is long, detailed, complicated, and poorly organized; even some German scholars report that they find it turgid and difficult to read.[1] It is noteworthy, therefore, that its impact on the Goddess movement stems from the publication of selected excerpts—not the entire text—in an English translation for the Bollingen Series in 1967. The circumstances behind this translation are interesting in themselves, but that story must wait for the next chapter. Although the word "matriarchy" (literally, "mother-headship") appears regularly in this English translation, Bachofen did not use its German equivalent, which in fact may not have been coined yet. In addition to *Mutterrecht,* he used *Gynaikokratie* (literally "rule by women"), which different translators sometimes render as "gynocracy" or "gynecocracy."[2]

When Elizabeth Gould Davis's *The First Sex* appeared in 1971, it was liberally sprinkled with quotations from the Bollingen Bachofen, including the very first words of Davis's prologue. This was the book which inaugurated the modern, radical feminist celebration of the ancient matriarchies. Following Davis's lead, Bachofen is cited approvingly by Merlin Stone, Riane Eisler, Elinor Gadon, Monica Sjöö, and Margot Adler as well.[3] Our major interest in *Das Mutterrecht* is the contribution it made to the rise of the Goddess movement and the use made of it in that context, which is not necessarily what Bachofen himself intended for it. First, however, we must come to grips with the book on its own terms.

BACHOFEN'S THEORY OF MATRIARCHY

In *Mutterrecht*, Bachofen presented a scheme of the history of social evolution which he believed to be valid for all cultures of the world.[4] Essentially, he argued that there were three stages through which any real civilization necessarily developed. The first stage was a pre-civilized state of nature. There were no stable social structures in truly primitive times; human beings would have made short-term alliances with each other for specific purposes, and no more. Bachofen singled out sexual relationships as the critical factor in social organization. In this early stage, he claimed, people would have coupled as and when they saw fit, without consideration of marriage or family. They probably had no idea that intercourse led to pregnancy, and the concept of fatherhood would have been unknown. Children would simply arrive and would become the shared responsibility of the group. Bachofen gave this stage the symbolic title "tellurian," or earthly; the unstructured sexual life he named "hetairism," from the Greek word for a courtesan. Aphrodite, the Greek goddess of love, was the representative deity of hetairism.

Bachofen believed that women would have become dissatisfied with hetairism. On the one hand, they were constantly subject to the sexual urges and demands of the men. Men dominated women at this stage through "purely physical tyranny."[5] On the other hand, women were primarily responsible for the children they bore and nursed, so they would have wanted more stability and reliability in everything from food supplies to social arrangements. Bachofen was convinced that mothers with their newborns were the first human beings who learned to love, and that gradually their love would be extended equally to everyone they knew. Driven by such needs and inclinations, the women took charge and established gynecocratic cultures.[6] Of necessity, women used force to impose the new system on men; these female warriors were the original Amazons, responding in kind to the abuse they experienced from males.[7] Once the second stage was firmly established, asserted Bachofen, women ruled differently—primarily through their special religious qualities: "At all times woman has exerted a great influence on men and on the education and culture of nations through her inclination toward the supernatural and divine, the irrational and miraculous . . . Herein lies the magic power of the feminine figure, which disarms the wildest passions and parts battle lines, which makes woman the sacrosanct prophetess and judge, and in all things gives her will the prestige of supreme law."[8] Thus it is that so many virtues and values were given female names and personified as goddesses.

Bachofen held that the establishment of gynecocracy was a significant and necessary step forward in the development of civilization. Crucial to this step was the establishment of exclusive marriage as the norm in family life. "Matriarchy subsists within and not outside of matrimony."[9] Hetairism had worked to the benefit of men because they could impose themselves on women through their sheer physical strength. In the female cultures, however, "woman counters man's abuse of his superior strength by the dignity of her enthroned motherhood"; accordingly, "matriarchy is necessary to the education of mankind and particularly of men."[10] What men learned was the practice of such virtues as chastity, bravery, and chivalry.[11]

Symbolically, Bachofen designated this second stage as "lunar" rather than telluric; the female cultures were associated with the left hand, the night, and the rhythms of nature. In Greece, the earth goddess Demeter and her daughter Kore exemplified the stable virtues of the gynecocracy, so different from the uninhibited Aphrodite. It was not to last, however. Bachofen was convinced that "the progress from material existence [represented by the physical mother-child bond] to a higher spiritual life [exemplified by the abstract, legal father-child relationship]" was the unalterable direction of human development.[12] He asserted that the spread of the cult of Dionysus was a crucial element in the fall of the gynecocracies. In contrast to the strict morality associated with Demeter, this orgiastic, phallic god was a throwback to hetairism and was met at first with Amazonian resistance. His virility, however, apparently put the men of the matriarchies to shame, and women flocked into his cult. This served to unravel the fabric of the female civilization and permitted the rise of patriarchy.[13]

Thus began the third, "solar" stage, represented by the god Apollo. Bachofen highlighted the ancient Greek play *Oresteia*, by Aeschylus, as a parable of the transition. In the play, Orestes is put on trial for murdering his mother; this was an act of revenge, commanded by Apollo, because she had brought about the death of Orestes's father. Orestes is acquitted at the end when Apollo and the goddess Athena together announce that the father is the true parent of the child and merits supreme loyalty. This drama, according to Bachofen, is an echo of the actual process by which patriarchy first supplanted matriarchy.[14] The final and lasting victory was not secured in Greece, however; it was the Roman Empire which made the new system permanent.[15]

Bachofen saw patriarchy as a further advance in the development of civilization—it represented "the highest calling, the sublimation of earthly existence to the purity of the divine father principle."[16] The symbolic values of patriarchy are the reverse of the system it replaced: the right hand, the day, and the sun.

> The phallic sun, forever fluctuating between rising and setting, coming into being and passing away, is transformed [under patriarchy] into the immutable source of light. It enters the realm of solar being, leaving behind it all idea of fecundation, all yearning for mixture with feminine matter. . . . Apollo frees himself entirely from any bond with woman. His paternity is motherless and spiritual, as in adoption, hence immortal, immune to the night of death which forever confronts Dionysus because he is phallic.[17]

> Triumphant paternity partakes of the heavenly light, while childbearing motherhood is bound up with the earth that bears all things; the establishment of paternal right is universally represented as an act of the uranian solar hero, while the defense of mother right is the first duty of the chthonian mother goddesses . . . For him [the patriarchal Greek] the source of immortality is no longer the childbearing woman but the male-creative principle, which he endows with the divinity that the earlier world imputed only to the mother.[18]

Patriarchy, to put it briefly, represented a further progression because it fostered the higher quest for immaterial, abstract, and spiritual values instead of merely physical goals; in Bachofen's eyes, the
immortality of the soul was perhaps the single most important discovery and belief in human history.[19] The change from materialism
to spirituality, however, was inevitably accompanied by a fall in the
status of women: "The progress of civilization is not favorable to
woman. She is at her best in the so-called barbaric periods; later
epochs destroy her hegemony, curtail her physical beauty, reduce her
from the lofty position she enjoyed ... the more primordial the people,
the more the feminine nature principle will dominate religious life
and the higher woman's social position will be."[20]

Expressed in this way, Bachofen's position was almost the exact
opposite of Fourier's. Bachofen's celebration of patriarchy does not
always seem to be wholehearted, however; in the same passage, he
referred to the "foppishness" of the men in the advanced civilizations, including his own, where women have lost their status. He
also pointed out what was presumably lost with the gynecocracies:
"Yet the love that arises from motherhood is not only more intense,
but also more universal. ... Whereas the paternal principle is inher-
ently restrictive, the maternal principle is universal. ... The idea of
motherhood produces a sense of universal fraternity among all men,
which dies with the development of paternity."[21] There seems to be
more than a touch of nostalgia when he says, "The matriarchal age,
with its figures, deeds, upheavals, is beyond the poetry of cultivated
but enfeebled times."[22] The patriarchal cultures destroyed the
achievements of the female civilizations and virtually erased them
from memory.

After presenting these ideas in a lengthy introduction, Bachofen
proceeded to demonstrate them by examining a series of ancient cultures. The Bollingen abridgement includes some of his comments
on Lycia, Athens, Lemnos, Egypt, India, and Lesbos. Entirely missing from the translation are his sections on other peoples of the
Aegean area: Crete, Orchomenos, and the Minyans, the Elians, the
Locrians, and Mantinea. His two final sections included the
Pythagoreans, a philosophical movement rather than a distinct cul-

ture, and the Cantabreans of the Pyrenees. As Georgoudi comments, "in this fresco real countries such as Lycia, Crete, and Egypt appeared alongside peoples such as the Pelasgians and the Minyans, whose historical reality has been contested, as well as frankly mythical tribes such as the Pheacians and Teleboans."[23]

BACHOFEN'S METHODS

Georgoudi's remark raises the question of Bachofen's methodology: what did he accept as reliable evidence, and what did he do with it?

Carrying out his research in the 1850s, Bachofen had access to two general types of evidence. First, he made a study of as many archaeological remains as he could. He lived in Basel, Switzerland, and journeyed to various museums and to Italy itself to study Roman remains at first hand. This sort of work was central to his first book, *An Essay on Ancient Mortuary Symbolism* (1859).[24] The original edition of *Mutterrecht* also included several illustrations of ancient Italian art, which Bachofen linked mostly to the mysteries of Dionysus.[25]

His main body of evidence, however, had to be literary. As a trained specialist in Roman law, Bachofen was extremely well-read in ancient literature, ranging from Homer in the eighth century BC onwards well into the Christian era. He quoted these sources frequently, often in the original Greek or Latin without translation. On the other hand, his quotations and acknowledgements of scholars from his own time are fairly sparse.[26] He introduced *Mutterrecht* by saying that his topic was something which had been noticed by few and fully explored by none; it was "virgin territory."[27] Apparently he felt his work was sufficiently original that relatively few of his predecessors warranted citation in it.

While he was fully conversant with the writings of ancient historians and philosophers, the most striking feature of Bachofen's methodology to the modern reader is his approach to myth. He took the stance that myths are usually older than actual historical records, and that they contain a core of historical fact which can be recovered and used to supply the information which we lack from other sources: "The mythical tradition is seen to be an authentic, independent record of the primordial age, a record in which invention plays no part. . . . It is a manifestation of primordial thinking, an immediate historical revelation, and consequently a highly reliable historical source. . . . Since the beginning of all development lies in myth, myth must form the starting point for any serious investigation of ancient history."[28] Some myths do contain relatively obvious historical connections. Bachofen preferred those which did not: "in this case the myth is no longer an elaboration on a single isolated incident but the expression of a great and universal manifestation of the times—thought, expressed, and handed down in the form of a single real event."[29]

It is not always easy to discover what historical facts might be contained in stories which commonly feature deities of various grades, not to mention centaurs and other such mysterious beings. Although he did correlate some of his mythological information with the available historical records in *Mutterrecht*, Bachofen had already discovered another way: "There are two roads to knowledge—the longer, slower, more arduous road of rational combination and the shorter path of the imagination, traversed with the force and swiftness of electricity. Aroused by direct contact with the ancient remains, the imagination grasps the truth at one stroke, without intermediary links. The knowledge acquired in this second way is infinitely more living and colorful than the products of the understanding."[30]

Bachofen, it seems, developed his preference for instantaneous intuitive insight over rational analysis during his earlier study of tomb art. This preference is fully at work in *Mutterrecht*, visible in the way he quickly sketches out an entire cultural ethos like hetairism or gynecocracy from relatively minor details in the plot lines of myths. Particularly interesting in terms of our inquiry is the small set of correspondences which inform his cultural types: mother and father correlate respectively to the left and right hands, the earth and the heavens, the moon and the sun, night and day, matter and spirit, and even the numbers five and seven.[31]

Another striking component of Bachofen's theory is his commitment to organic and evolutionary thinking. His overall approach is to treat nations and cultures like individual organisms which grow and develop through predictable and necessary stages, noting that atrophy, arrested development, and regression may take place in some cases. His belief that all cultures develop in a uniform pattern from hetairism through gynecocracy to patriarchy is as sure as his confidence that infancy and childhood always precede adulthood.

Finally, we may note one extension of this principle of uniform evolution—Bachofen's technique of minimizing the differences between the ancient cultures in order to harmonize them into his scheme. After he argued that the parallels he found between historical records and myths prove that the myths should be taken seriously as history, he went on to say, "the parallels cannot always be taken from one and the same people."[32] He was so certain that gynecocracies arise always for the same reasons, and always with the same characteristics, that he felt free to collect and combine the evidence from different times and places into a unified whole. Thus, for example, Greek myths and literature like Sophocles's *Oedipus at Colonus* play a dominant role in guiding Bachofen's interpretation of ancient Egypt.

Several of these observations—particularly Bachofen's organicism and his preference for intuitive approaches to knowledge—evoke elements of Romanticism and its aftermath. Some commentators, in fact, have described Bachofen almost as a Romantic born too late, an exponent of views which were in some cases over half a century old and widely discarded.[33] To watch Bachofen at work, we shall examine the case which he himself thought was strongest and most persuasive—ancient Lycia.

THE LYCIAN GYNECOCRACY

Like any scholar, Bachofen was working in an intellectual context shaped by some established views which he favored and others which he hoped to correct or, at least, undermine. For Bachofen, the loyal heir of Romanticism, the adversary was rationalistic, positivistic scholarship. In the study of ancient literature, for example, such scholarship tended to emphasize the meticulous collection of detailed evidence for the purposes of analysis—distinguishing and separating books and parts of books according to place and time of composition and developing historical theories on the basis of the results.

One typical product of this sort of nineteenth-century "higher criticism" in scholarship was the Graf-Wellhausen explanation of the Pentateuch. The first five books of the Bible were traditionally believed to have been written by Moses himself. After locating several passages in those books which seem to reflect a time later than the life of Moses, the Graf-Wellhausen exponents dissected the text according to the various differences of style and vocabulary they found in different parts of it. They concluded that the Pentateuch had been made up from four different bodies of literature (nicknamed the J E D P theory) which had not been edited together into one continuous story until the fifth century B C, approximately seven hundred years after Moses himself. This conclusion, of course, cast considerable doubt on the factual accuracy of the biblical narratives.

Bachofen apparently considered this type of scholarship to be nitpicking of the worst order, since it drowned the spiritual significance of a text in a flood of technical details. One of his particular antagonists was Theodor Mommsen, arguably the dominant classical scholar of the nineteenth century, who brought this dissecting spirit into Bachofen's own intellectual preserve: Roman law.[34] Bachofen's commitment to an immediate intuitive grasp of the inner meaning of texts and artifacts was, at least in part, his reaction against the count-measure-and-calculate mentality which so offended him.

We can see his preferred approach quite clearly in his discussion of ancient Lycia, a small state located on the southwest coast of what is now Turkey. He presented this as his strongest case and used it as his first example in *Mutterrecht*. Here he could work with a few historical reports as well as myths. Herodotus (the great Greek historian, fifth century B C) and Nicolaus of Damascus (a Greek writer living in Rome, first century B C) had written that the Lycians passed on their names and inheritance through the female line rather than the male. Heraclides Ponticus (a Greek philosopher, fourth century B C) stated flatly that the Lycians had been ruled by women since the beginnings of their history. To press beyond these bare statements to the character and ambience of gynecocracy, however, Bachofen turned to myth. The myths most ready to hand were two stories about Bellerophon which appear in the writings of Plutarch (first century

A D; Plutarch attributes the first narrative to Nymphis of Heraclea, third century B C). Bellerophon himself had been mentioned as early as Homer's *Iliad* (eighth century B C), where he established himself as king of Lycia by defeating the Amazons, but Bachofen does not focus on this earlier version of the story.[35]

Both of Plutarch's narratives show Bellerophon being offended by the Lycians and inducing the sea-god Poseidon to devastate their lands; but in both cases, Bellerophon relented at the behest of the Lycian women. In the first story, it is said that the Xanthians (citizens of one Lycian city) adopted a matrilinear system of names to commemorate the women's success. In the second tale Bellerophon overpowered two enemies of Lycia, an invader named Amisodarus as well as the Amazons. He was not given a satisfactory reward, however, and so Bellerophon convinced Poseidon to send a flood in revenge. The Lycian men could not persuade Bellerophon to make peace, but "when the women, gathering up their garments, came toward him, he retreated out of modesty, and at the same time, as it is related, the waters went back with him."[36]

Bachofen put his intuition and his correspondences to work on these two myths. The water, sent by Poseidon at Bellerophon's request, is "the male fecundating power," whereas "woman is equated with the earth." The struggle between sea and land is, then, an instance of the conflict between patriarchy and matriarchy. Even though Bellerophon defeated the Amazons, whom Bachofen dismissed as "this extreme offshoot of mother right," it is the proper women who win the decisive victory. Bellerophon "bows to the sign of feminine fertility," presumably the exposed anatomy of the Lycian women. This act of submission, according to Bachofen, makes Bellerophon "the virtual founder of Lycian matriarchy."[37] This is an unexpected role indeed for the king described by Homer. There is much more, but this is enough to illustrate Bachofen's approach to a specific case. Few other historians were persuaded by his methods and arguments, as will become evident. Here we shall simply note what some of the recognized difficulties are.

With respect to the historical records concerning Lycia, the first problem is the fact that Herodotus and Nicolaus were not talking about gynecocracy at all. The subject of rulership never surfaces in the passages cited by Bachofen; they address only the matter of names and lineage. Even if we accept that the Lycians had a matrilineal inheritance system, this in no way guarantees that they were ruled by women. The Egyptians, as we saw in Chapter 3, had a system of matrilineal patriarchy over extended periods of time. Bachofen apparently assumed that female predominance in one area of life would extend automatically to all others. Although he cannot be faulted for this, Bachofen was also unaware of Lycian inscriptions which have been discovered in the meantime and which include some patrilineal elements after all.[38] It is nevertheless significant that none of the most crucial evidence about Lycian gynecocracy came from Lycia itself—a problem which recurs with some of the other nations he discussed as well.

As for Heraclides' report, Bachofen failed to provide the full quotation. This Greek writer, who did in fact say that the Lycians were ruled by their women, also said that they had no written laws at all and lived by piracy and robbery. If he was telling the truth, the Lycian matriarchy was singularly lacking in some of the virtues which Bachofen ascribed to the gynecocracies. More likely, however, Heraclides was indulging in some polemic and trying to make the Lycians look as foreign and unappealing as possible to his readers. As Wesel has pointed out, the status of Greek women in Heraclides' time was so low that most other cultures would have looked matriarchal by comparison.[39] But this is the sort of critical assessment of an ancient text, focusing on the personal agenda of the author in his own historical context, which Bachofen repudiated heart and soul.

Turning to the Bellerophon stories, the most immediate critical question is that of the date of the respective records. Bachofen felt that he could understand the ancient Lycians better through the myths recorded in Plutarch than through Homer's tale, although the latter is approximately eight centuries older and that much closer to the times it purports to describe. Asserting that invention plays no part in myth, Bachofen was free to pick and choose which version of which myth suited him, regardless of the historical and literary context in which it is found. He was also free to combine them as he saw fit. He could equate matrilinearity in other sources with matriarchy in Heraclides, add the women's peaceful but successful assertion of their will against Bellerophon from Plutarch, link them all with the woman/ earth correspondence which is not mentioned in any of those texts, and arrive at an ancient utopian gynecocracy with little more ado.

The other major difficulty is that Bachofen's reliance on his own intuition provides no objective standards by which to judge his assertions. He is rightly credited with encouraging the world of scholarship to take mythology more seriously, to see it as an expression of a cultural worldview rather than just a collection of stories which were invented to compensate for primitive ignorance about how the world really works. On the other hand, when he elevated his discussion from stories of an interrupted flood to an elaborate clash of gender-based value systems, he did so with an unquestioning ease which few scholars can accept in the absence of reliable and supportive facts. Bachofen did claim to be engaged in objective scholarship: "The material alone is my preceptor. It must first be assembled, then observed and analyzed. Only in this way can one hope to disclose a law that is inherent in the matter itself and not in our subjective spirit."[40] By sacrificing critical details like facts and dates on the altar of his personal gift of imagination, however, Bachofen left his entire theory in the realm of the subjective.

Joseph Campbell opened his introduction to the Bollingen Bachofen with the words, "It is fitting that the works of Johann Jacob [*sic*] Bachofen (1815-1887) should have been rediscovered for our century, not by historians or anthropologists, but by a circle of creative artists, psychologists, and literary men."[41] Intended as praise, these words also reveal Bachofen's almost complete failure to win over the experts in his own field. *Mutterrecht* was not well received by the scholars of Bachofen's time, and its long-term impact was to lie in other sectors of modern society instead. At this point, knowing what Bachofen said and how he justified it, we must try to ascertain why he said it—what forces shaped and motivated the man who wrote of woman's rule.

BACHOFEN'S LIFE AND THOUGHT

Bachofen was Swiss by birth and lived almost all of his life in his home city of Basel.[42] He was the eldest son of a well-established family, financially secure through their silk business, and a lifelong Protestant churchgoer. He was reportedly devoted to his mother— so much so that he lived in his parents' house until after her death in 1856, and did not himself marry until nine years later, when he was fifty years old.[43] This, we may note in passing, was after the publication of *Mutterrecht*.

Rather than enter the family business, Bachofen went to the University of Berlin to study law between 1835 and 1837. His teacher, who became his lifelong mentor, was Friedrich Karl von Savigny. As we saw in Chapter 7, Savigny was part of the great generation of Romantic-era scholarship in Germany. One of Savigny's deepest convictions was the necessary connection between national codes of law and the organic distinctiveness of the nations themselves. He objected to the French policy of imposing the Napoleonic Code on the various different peoples they had conquered, and he inspired the Grimms to collect folktales in order to assist in the recovery of the Germanic national consciousness. Being Swiss, Bachofen seems to have remained relatively free of the German nationalism which some of Savigny's views entailed, but this organic philosophy of culture appears clearly in *Mutterrecht*.

There were several other factors which would likely come to the attention of a university student in Berlin at this time. Savigny himself had been a colleague of Fichte and Schleiermacher; Schelling was still alive, and Bachofen was also influenced by less famous Romantic scholars like Boeckh and Creuzer.[44] Hegel had died in 1831, but his philosophy was to dominate much of the nineteenth century; when Bachofen writes that "human culture advances only through the clash of opposites," more than one commentator detects the influence of Hegel's dialectical view of history.[45]

Two other features of intellectual life in Berlin at this time are worthy of note. First, the death of the already legendary Goethe and the sensational subsequent publication of the second part of *Faust*—featuring the Mothers and the Eternal Feminine—had occurred in 1832, just three years prior to Bachofen's arrival. Second, in the very year that Bachofen took up residence in Berlin, the government had taken controversial repressive action against the "Young Germany" movement. This group, of which the poet Heinrich Heine remains the most famous, brought the wrath of the authorities down upon itself partly because it was discussing and propagating the theories of Enfantin's Saint-Simonism.[46] In his brief autobiographical sketch (written for Savigny at his request), Bachofen mentioned almost none of this; by all accounts he was a most unlikely candidate for the Saint-Simonians in particular. On his own testimony, he was already consumed by his interest in antiquity, almost to the exclusion of the studies required for his examinations.[47] Nevertheless, his ongoing friendship with Savigny confirms the influence of Romanticism on some of his ideas and procedures.

Bachofen moved on to spend the year 1839–40 at the School of Law in Paris. Again, the general context is interesting to note. Fourier and Enfantin were both recent memories; Michelet and George Sand were already well known; this was the peak year of Flora Tristan's celebrity status and the beginning of the flood of utopian socialist literature. This time, Bachofen did give some indication that he was aware of events around him; he reported meeting the Italian professor of law Count Pellegrino Rossi, whom he described as pandering to student opinion by pretending to support "trial by jury, the constitutional charter, freedom of the press, Polish independence, and similar catchwords of the revolutionary journalism of the time."[48] This final dismissive phrase suggests that Bachofen disapproved of both the Count's cynical public pose and the actual political positions which are detailed in the list.

After further studies in England, Bachofen returned to his parents' home in Basel and domiciled there. In 1841 he took up a position as Professor of Roman Law at the University of Basel; he was made a judge in 1842 and a member of the town council in 1844. In that same year, however, a newspaper campaign suggested that he had gained his professorship through family connections rather than by merit, and he resigned. The following year he left the town council as well. From 1845 to 1866 he held a position on an appeals court and lived on his family's wealth and his earnings as a private teacher.[49] *Mutterrecht*, as we saw, was preceded by his study of mortuary symbolism; it was followed in 1870 by *The Myth of Tanaquil*, in which he attempted to uncover the entire ethos of the Roman West through his intuitive extrapolations from a single tale.

He made occasional trips to Greece, Spain, and especially Italy to pursue his interest in Roman relics. He was in Rome itself during the 1848 revolution there, and his comments are informative with respect to his own attitudes: "But the peace of mind I should have required was soon shattered by the wild passions that had chosen Rome as their arena at this time. Rossi fell on the second day after my arrival. The storming of the Quirinal, the flight of the Pope, the Constituent Assembly, the proclamation of the Republic, followed in swift succession . . . finally, on my journey homeward, I beheld the breakdown of all order. Since then the storm has subsided. Once again Italy has become for me the land of antiquity and of tranquil studies."[50] Everything so far indicates the accuracy of Wesel's thumbnail sketch of Bachofen: "ein Patrizier, fromm, konservativ und reich" (a patrician, pious, conservative and rich).[51] How did such a man become, even if unintentionally, a founding father of the Goddess movement? This he certainly is; no less an authority than Margot Adler wrote, "the modern revival of Goddess spirituality is hard to trace (in writing) much further back than the ideas of J. J. Bachofen."[52]

The ideas to which she refers are easy to identify within our frame of reference. We have already seen that the key tenets of Goddess spirituality include the neopagan paradigm, the priority of intuitive knowledge, and a utopian view of woman-centered communities which harks back to the Romantic idealization of women. All three of these ideas are expressed in Bachofen's work. Already in his first major book, *Mortuary Symbolism*, Bachofen announced his own agenda while defining the discipline in which he wished to work:

Other spheres of archaeology may captivate our understanding, the contemplation of tombs wins our hearts; it not only enriches our knowledge but provides food for our spiritual needs. Wherever possible I have taken this aspect into account and attempted to intimate those sublime ideas which the ancients conceived in the presence of death and which cannot be expressed in language but only in symbols. Herein I have primarily acceded to a need inherent in my own nature, but perhaps I have also come closer to realizing the supreme aim of archaeology than is possible through an approach limited to the form and surface of things. And this aim, I believe, consists in communicating the sublimely beautiful ideas of the past to an age that is very much in need of regeneration.[53]

This is, in effect, Bachofen's espousal of the neopagan paradigm. His view of the upward evolution of human culture did not lead him to conclude that his own civilization was the best and highest of all so far; his love of antiquity prevented such a stance. His descriptions of the gynecocracies, as we have just seen, often carry an approving and even nostalgic tone. As Joseph Campbell commented, "Both Bachofen's critics and his admirers have frequently remarked his tolerance of both the pagan-Oriental and the Christian-Occidental—archaic matriarchal and progressive patriarchal—strains in our compound modern heritage."[54]

On the second point, we have already seen his intuitive approach to archaeology at work. With regard to the influence of the Romantics, when Bachofen sings the praises of the gynecocracies, he does so in terms fully consistent with the idealization of the female so prevalent in that movement. Woman-created, woman-ruled cultures would naturally, he asserted, reflect the distinctive nature of women themselves. The matriarchal women Bachofen discovered through his intuitive archaeology reigned over happy, virtuous, and cohesive societies: "The idea of motherhood produces a sense of universal fraternity among all men, which dies with the development of patriarchy. . . . Matriarchal states were particularly famed for their freedom from intestine strife and conflict."[55]

How could this have been? How, indeed, could women maintain their control over the physically stronger males?: "To man's superior physical strength woman opposes the mighty influence of her religious consecration; she counters violence with peace, enmity with conciliation, hate with love; and thus she guides the wild, lawless existence of the earliest period towards a milder, friendlier culture, in whose center she sits enthroned as the embodiment of the higher principle, as the manifestation of the divine commandment."[56] Bachofen was firmly convinced that religious beliefs were the core of all cultural value systems.[57] He was equally sure of the characteristics a womanly religion would necessarily display, and sounded surprisingly like Michelet and even Constant when he expressed it: "Mystery is the true essence of every religion, and wherever woman dominates religion or life, she will cultivate the mysterious. Mystery is rooted in her very nature, with its close alliance between the material and the supersensory; mystery springs from her kinship with material nature, whose eternal death creates a need for comforting thoughts . . . disclosing death as the indispensable forerunner of higher rebirth. . . ."[58] All of this seems to bring Bachofen into line with today's Goddess movement, accounting for his larger popularity in the literature of feminist spirituality, reflected in Adler's comment which we just noted. Although he may have been a rich, conservative patrician and even a pious Protestant in everyday life, Bachofen's written legacy embraces the major building blocks of the modern Goddess movement.

These observations raise the possibility that Bachofen himself was much more aware of, and influenced by, the fashionable people and ideas of his student days than he acknowledged in print. As we noted earlier, he was much more liberal in quoting ancient sources than contemporary writers, convinced as he was of his own originality. Moreover, the English abridgement of his work eliminates the latter quotations altogether. Based on that alone, we would have to content ourselves with the circumstantial evidence we saw above, noting the individuals, ideas and events which were prominent during his student days in Berlin and Paris. Did Bachofen really remain entirely unaffected by Romantic neopaganism and utopian feminism as a young man, only to give voice to the same ideas independently in his middle age?

There is, in fact, more to the story than this. If we go back to the full, original text of *Mutterrecht*, we find that Bachofen was very much aware of these ongoing ideological trends as he wrote. The true climax of his book occurs, not quite at the end of it, but in the final lines of his chapter on Pythagoreanism and other systems, which was not included in the Bollingen abridgement at all: "From this I draw the rewarding conviction that the inquiry which is now reaching its end will not be fruitless for generally furthering the comprehension of antiquity and also the deeper knowledge of the course of development of the modern world, for which French writers (Michelet, *Woman*, p. 240 ff.; Girardin, *Equality of Children in the Eyes of the Mother*, p. 7 ff.) are recommending the return to the Isis-principle and to the natural reality of mother-law as the sole remedy."[59]

What did he mean by Michelet's "Isis-principle"? In Chapter 10 of Book II in *Woman*, dealing with ancient Egypt, the famous French Romantic sang it out: "Woman rules. . . . The great god is a mother . . . . Loving Africa, out of its deep desire, called forth the most touching object of the religions of the world. . . . Which? The living reality, a good and fertile woman."[60]

Bachofen said that he did archaeology in the hope of contributing to the improvement of the modern world. Clearly, his conscious purpose in writing *Mutterrecht* was not just disinterested antiquarianism, but was closely linked to his awareness of what Michelet and other French radicals were proposing. Given Bachofen's general reluctance to cite contemporary sources, we are probably justified in assuming that Michelet and the others informed a greater portion of Bachofen's work than this one concluding passage, but without acknowledgement.

As one example, we may consider Bachofen's discussion of bees. This occurs in the Lycian chapter in *Mutterrecht*; less than a third of the passage appears in the Bollingen condensation.[61] Naturally, Bachofen treats the beehive as an exemplary case of gynecocracy in nature. Indeed, in the full text he emphasizes the bees' *"zauberähnliche Anhänglichkeit"* (magic-like affection or attachment) to the mother/queen, in contrast to the negligence and hostility they display towards the various father/drones who may even be driven out or killed once their procreative role has been fulfilled. The sources to which Bachofen alludes in this passage are with one exception classical authors, including Virgil, Aristotle, and Heraclides.

These ancient writers did discuss the communal life of bees, but the crucial factor for Bachofen was the specifically matriarchal character of the hive. This was not known until the seventeenth century, when the Dutch scientist Jan Swammerdam discovered that the rulers of the hives also laid the eggs, and therefore must be queen bees rather than kings. Bachofen may possibly have worked out the matriarchal implications of the beehive for himself, but we cannot ignore the fact that Michelet had recently said most, if not all, of the same things in *The Insect* (1857). He had one entire chapter entitled "The Bees of Virgil" and gave as much emphasis as Bachofen to the superfluous status and sad end of the male drone. Michelet also described a group of black ants who were enslaved by red ants, but who ended up in effective control of the life patterns of the anthill. He suggested that they experienced "the pride of governing the strong, and of mastering the masters."[62] This theme of the subtle control— almost consensual—of the weak over the strong is typical of both Michelet's and Bachofen's views on how female predominance works.

(The only non-classical source named by Bachofen in this passage is a study of bees in mythology; it told him, for instance, of a folk custom in India where a bride's genitals are anointed with honey before the wedding. Such stories enabled him to establish another correspondence: milk and honey with motherhood, and wine with the masculine Dionysus.)

It seems beyond doubt, then, that a crucial part of Bachofen's purpose in writing *Mutterrecht* was to respond to the work of the French utopian feminists. What actually was his response? What "fruit" did he hope to see his book bear? The answer appears in the passage leading up to his citation of Michelet: "Wherever we look, the same truth confronts us: no people whose religious perception is rooted in matter has succeeded in achieving the victory of pure spiritual paternity and securing it lastingly for humanity. On the destruction, not on the development and gradual purification of materialism, rests the spirituality of the totally fatherly God."[63] To Bachofen, that is, matriarchy had its place and its glory as a step up from hetairism on the way to patriarchy. Its time has gone, however, and the further progress of the human race depends on the total and utter triumph of father-law over mother-law. Michelet and Girardin, he wanted to tell his readers, were wrong; they were pointing back and downwards, instead of ahead and upwards.

Any doubts we may have about Bachofen's views on this question are laid to rest by *The Myth of Tanaquil*. His neopaganism was not matriarchal. Those "sublimely beautiful ideas of the past" which he wished to communicate to his own needy age were not primarily those of the gynecocracies, but those of patriarchal Rome. *Tanaquil*, in his hands, is the story of Rome's victorious struggle to establish and spread occidental patriarchalism against the resistant and threatening matriarchalism and "base sensualism" of the orient. This was no matter for gentle, motherly persuasion. Bachofen saw no possible compromise between matriarchy and patriarchy: "The destruction of the Asiatic element was prerequisite first to the existence, then to the power of Rome, and usually to both at once. Hence the unparalleled fury with which everything that could not be assimilated to the new idea was swept from the face of the earth. . . ."[64] Only thus could humanity's advancement to a higher stage of cultural development be assured:

> What reduced the cultures of the Orient to the base sensualism manifested in the deification of the harlot? Beyond a doubt it was the attitude that places man at the mercy of natural forces. And what enabled Rome to transcend this stage and endowed it with the superiority that makes its colossal work of destruction seem justified? Surely it was the spiritual liberation following the ascendancy of historical consciousness over the natural idea . . . here again it is clear that our Western life truly begins with Rome. Roman is the idea through which European mankind prepared to set its own imprint on the entire globe, namely, the idea that no material law but only the free activity of the spirit determines the destinies of peoples.[65]

With this hymn to the freedom of the spirit over all physical necessities, Bachofen showed that he was still, in the twilight of his life, a Romantic at heart. But this student of Savigny was clearly a Romantic of a German more than a French type, drawing on the past as a model for the present instead of envisioning a radical New Age such as none had seen before. Bachofen's role in today's Goddess movement would probably amaze and distress him. He might, in fact, feel an affinity for those fathers of his hetairic age who knew not their own children and could not envision their own role in creating them.

The modern appropriation of Bachofen's work in Goddess literature is diametrically opposed to his own intentions in writing *Mutterrecht*. It is, in fact, not *Mutterrecht* itself but the Bollingen abridgement which is the crucial document for Goddess spirituality. Bachofen's contributions to the Goddess movement, indispensable though they are, have been indirect rather than direct; it will take another chapter to unravel that part of our story.

12

Spreading the Theory of Matriarchy

The world-historical defeat of the female sex.

Friedrich Engels

OVER A CENTURY PASSED between the publication of *Das Mut-terrecht* in 1861 and the rise of Goddess spirituality as a distinct movement. As we have already seen, the appearance of the Bollingen abridged translation in 1967 had a decisive impact on Elizabeth Gould Davis and all who followed her. The fact that someone found it worthwhile to translate Bachofen after all that time is interesting in itself—doubly interesting in view of the fact that George Boas opened his preface to the Bollingen volume by noting that Bachofen's theory is now "almost universally discredited."[1] In this chapter, we must survey what had become of the Bachofen legacy in the intervening hundred years, and who kept sufficient interest in it alive that it would merit the effort of translation.

There are several paradoxes associated with Bachofen. One, of course, is the Goddess movement's adoption of this wealthy patriarch as one of its sources of inspiration. Another is the fact that Bachofen's theory was so thoroughly rejected in the fields for which it was intended—ancient history and anthropology—while it was preserved and nurtured in such a variety of other settings, including radical politics, literature, and psychology. This chapter cannot provide an exhaustive investigation of all these areas, but we shall acquaint ourselves sufficiently with each of them in order to understand their contribution to today's Goddess spirituality.

HISTORY, ANTHROPOLOGY, AND MATRIARCHY

On the whole, Bachofen's theory has never been well accepted among his fellow scholars of antiquity.[2] Many of the reasons for this amount to unfortunate timing—Bachofen was born both too late and too early. He was too late in the sense that he was a quintessential Romantic working a half-century after the highpoint of that cultural trend. In particular, his forthright espousal of a primarily intuitive method for studying ancient myths and artifacts set him at odds with the mainstream scholarship of his own time, which was deeply imbued with the scientific and positivistic ethos. To most other scholars, Bachofen's personal insights were pure speculation, largely unsupported by the hard data which a theory like his requires if it is to be entertained seriously. It is, perhaps, useful to recall that Bachofen had relinquished his academic post after only three years and worked largely alone after that, receiving less of the stimulation and correction which comes from discussing one's developing ideas with professional colleagues.

He was also born too soon. His three major books on antiquity were published between 1857 and 1870. This means that they appeared just before the study of ancient times was changed forever by two new fields of scholarship: scientific archaeology and anthropological fieldwork. In terms of archaeology, we must recall that Bachofen's explanations of the inner dynamics of pre-Greek and non-Greek cultures had been based almost entirely on Greek literature. Shortly after his books came into circulation, our knowledge of those cultures suddenly expanded beyond all expectation with the discovery and excavation of Troy, Knossos, and other ancient sites. Thanks to this new array of actual physical remains from the early civilizations, Bachofen's whole approach suffered almost instant obsolescence. At around the same time, improvements in transportation and the expansion of European hegemony throughout most of the world gave Western scholars the opportunity to disperse across the globe. They came face-to-face with living cultures of all sorts, including many which they labeled "primitive." Again, a flood of new information swamped Bachofen's theory.

The root problem was actually a fairly straightforward one. Bachofen had claimed that patriarchy arose first with the Greeks, and that the cultures which immediately preceded them had been gynecocracies; further, he had asserted that primitive, pre-civilized life would follow the pattern of hetairism. But the Mediterranean archaeologists found no matriarchies, and the travelling anthropologists sent back no reports of either gynecocracy or hetairism, despite the many varieties in sex roles they encountered. With all this new information available, writers like Edward Westermarck thoroughly discredited Bachofen's theory.[3]

Scholars are rarely unanimous on anything, however, and there were some who continued to give Bachofen currency. During his own lifetime, his work was warmly received by the American ethnologist Lewis Henry Morgan. Morgan had already published a major study of the Iroquois, in which he noted some authoritative roles which pertained to the women of the tribes. Upon discovering *Das Mutterrecht*, he used it extensively in his 1877 book *Ancient Society*. He took over the three-stage scheme of cultural development, using the terms "savagery," "barbarism," and "civilization."[4] Morgan's book was quite influential at the time; in the words of one recent commentator, it "became the foundation for all subsequent research on the history of early human societies, despite its many factual and interpretive errors."[5]

Bachofen's work also found a place in the English-speaking world of scholarship through a small but influential group of Cambridge academics. Several British scholars had been more open to the theory of matriarchy than Westermarck, but those with the most lasting importance were Sir James Frazer (1854–1941) and Jane Ellen Harrison (1850–1928). Although he never traveled outside Europe, Frazer was a dedicated reader and collector of myths and folklore from around the world, as well as a prolific writer. His most famous work, *The*

Golden Bough, is reminiscent of Bachofen in some respects; it begins with an evocative description of an ancient Italian custom, and then branches out with the help of all the data he can amass until he has articulated a comprehensive theory of the history of religion around the world.

Frazer's thesis, however, was quite unlike Bachofen's. He proposed that all the religions of the human race had originated as fertility cults. He was especially interested in ritual death and sacrifice, and argued that behind many religious customs lies a widespread original practice centered on the shedding of blood to renew the life of the earth. In particular, he claimed that primitive cultures regularly sacrificed their chief or king while he was still strong and virile, in order to transfer his strength to the earth and to avoid the problems of aging, feeble leadership. Frazer popularized the notion that Christianity, with its dying and rising god-king, is simply a distorted version of the original and universal fertility cult.

In John B. Vickery's phrase, *The Golden Bough* was part of the "dissolvent literature" which paved the way from the Victorian era's rising tide of religious doubt towards the skepticism and relativism which characterizes much of the twentieth century.[6] Frazer's theory of the origin of religion also leaves little room for a matriarchal period dominated by female values. In the first edition of *The Golden Bough*, published in 1890, Frazer made no mention at all of such ideas. He included only one reference to Bachofen: a citation from *Tanaquil* to support a relatively small detail in his argument.[7]

In 1903, Harrison published her landmark work *Prolegomena to the Study of Greek Religion*.[8] Her guiding principle was her belief that ritual was the foundation of religion and mythology, not the other way around, and that this reflected "the primacy of emotion" in human life.[9] In this book she did espouse the theory that pre-Hellenic culture in Greece was matriarchal until the invading Indo-European Hellenes imposed patriarchy by force. Because of her focus on ritual as the key to everything else, she argued that the frequency of cults dedicated to goddesses in ancient times was a reflection of the high social status of women. She also maintained that the goddesses were originally one, and that their fragmentation into different female deities was a result of the patriarchal conquest. At various points in the book Harrison expressed a strong preference for matriarchy, suggesting that it maintained the living emotional link to nature which was severed by patriarchy; she also pointed to monogamous marriage as one of the means by which patriarchal control was established.[10]

Harrison acknowledged the influence of Bachofen in one footnote, referring to *Mutterrecht* as "a book which, spite of the wildness of its theories, remains of value as the fullest existing collection of ancient facts."[11] Renate Schlesier has suggested that Bachofen's notion of hetairism may be the "wild" theory which Harrison found repellent, although his final call for a complete, uncompromising triumph of patriarchy may have been equally offensive to her.[12] Conceding that the term matriarchal was "awkward," Harrison expressed a preference for a more recent (1896) article by E. B. Tylor, which she described as the "clearest and most scientific statement of the facts."[13] Inevitably *Prolegomena*, a book by a female historian which not only supports the theory of matriarchy but condemns the rise of patriarchy, has been a popular source in the Goddess movement.

Goddess books rarely include the information that Harrison later changed her views on this subject. One of the factors prompting the change may have been the publication of the massive and definitive third edition of Frazer's *Golden Bough*, the encyclopedia-sized version which appeared in installments between 1907 and 1915. Issues germane to the matriarchy theory, which were entirely omitted from the first edition, now received sustained attention from Frazer. He referred to "the [sexual] license of an earlier age" in a way which evokes Bachofen's hetairism and provided extensive discussions of agricultural goddesses whom he had largely ignored in the first edition.[14] Frazer also noted many instances of matrilineality, inheritance through the female line.[15] Like Westermarck, however, he insisted that neither the worship of goddesses nor the custom of matrilineality prove that there was actual female rule; in fact, he virtually dismissed the entire possibility of a society in which men did not hold power.[16] Both *Mutterrecht* and *Tanaquil* now appeared in Frazer's bibliography. He still found the latter useful for interpreting the royal lineage of the ancient Roman kings, but after paying trib-ute to "the learned Swiss scholar, J. J. Bachofen," he admitted in a disarming footnote, "To be frank, I have not had the patience to read through his long dissertation."[17]

By the time Harrison published *Themis* in 1912, she too recog-nized the distinction between matrilineality and matriarchy. Her emphasis shifted from the mother-daughter pair of Demeter and Kore to the mother and son, Semele and Dionysos.[18] The significance of this she explained as follows: "It may seem strange that woman, al-ways the weaker, should be thus dominant and central [in a relief from the Capitoline altar]. But it must always be observed that this primitive form of society is matri*linear* not matri*archal*. Woman is the social center not the dominant force. . . . In primitive matrilinear societies woman is the great social force or rather central focus, not as woman, or at least not as sex, but as mother, the mother of tribes-men to be."[19] This shift in emphasis from general womanhood to specific motherhood puts Harrison's updated view at odds with today's Goddess writers. Even worse, perhaps, Harrison now placed a male god at the head of the pre-patriarchal order: "Kronos the king repre-sents the old matrilinear days. . . ."[20] When the transition to patriar-chy occurred, she suggested, Kronos the king-god was replaced by Zeus the father-god. By the time she published *Epilegomena to the Study of Greek Religion* in 1921, Harrison appeared to have dispensed with matriarchy altogether. She now described social evolution from "the old family group with the dominant sire" through totemic and tribal stages to the emergence of the individual.[21]

Her earlier espousal of the matriarchy theory has naturally meant that Harrison is invoked frequently in Goddess literature. As with Bachofen, we may wonder whether she herself would have approved. In her case, the continued celebration of *Prolegomena* is at least accu-rate in its assessment of the views she expressed there; the fact that she later abandoned those views is usually just ignored. Elizabeth Gould Davis did not ignore Harrison's later views, however; she effec-tively censored them. Rather than bypass *Themis*, she distorted it with selective quotations. I offer five examples:

The matrilinear stage had long been buried and forgotten. . . .
(Harrison, *Themis*, 498)

Their gynocratic past "had been buried and forgotten," writes
Jane Harrison. . . . (Davis, *First Sex*, 65)

The man doing woman's work has all the inherent futility and
something of the ugly dissonance of the man masquerading in
woman's clothes. . . . (Harrison, *Themis*, 495)

Jane Ellen Harrison's remark about the incongruity of the male
adopting the role of mother can be expanded to include the "inherent futility and ugly dissonance" of the father-god taking
over the role and functions of the mother-goddess. . . . (Davis,
First Sex, 115)

Inspired by what Jane Harrison calls "patriarchal malice," the
cruel myth of Eve's guilt has succeeded in its purpose. . . . (Davis,
First Sex, 144, citing *Themis*, 500)

In the third passage, there is no quotation from Harrison; neither
Eve nor the phrase "patriarchal malice" occurs on or near page 500 of
Themis, which deals with quite different matters. At best, the Goddess literature treats Harrison as it does Mellaart, clinging to her
earlier opinions and ignoring her later revisions; at worst, Davis loots
Harrison's work for useful items and, failing that, invents whatever
she cannot find.

The Cambridge anthropologist William H. R. Rivers (1864-1922)
is also worthy of note. He was trained in medicine and psychology
as well, and he did important field work in the Torres Straits, south
India, and the south Pacific.[22] In the earlier part of his career, he
subscribed to the general notion of cultural evolution as it was familiar to Bachofen and Morgan, and he followed Morgan's lead in reconstructing the history of kinship systems through a close study of
the terminology used by particular peoples. In his extensive report
on Melanesia, for example, he described a social structure for which
he borrowed Frazer's term "gerontocracy": rule by old men. Mixed
with this essentially patriarchal structure, however, were terms and

customs which indicated that a mother's relatives played a significant role in the life of a child. Rivers speculated that these features
of Melanesian society were relics, like linguistic fossils, from an earlier matrilinear system for which he also used the Bachofenian term
mother-right.[23]

Rivers himself, like most anthropologists of the early twentieth
century, gradually abandoned the theory of uniform cultural evolution in favor of diffusion, the theory that significant cultural change
normally occurs through direct contact between different cultural
groups.[24] Kinship and related gender issues, however, were clearly
among his central interests—interests which he would stimulate in
Robert Graves.

BACHOFEN AND RADICALISM

Bachofen, as we saw, was anything but a political radical. Though
his contribution to radical thought was relatively minor as well as
totally unintentional, it plays a necessary part in our broader inquiry,
since the Goddess movement as a whole has such close affinities to
radicalism today.

Marx and Engels were of German origin but established their
partnership in July Monarchy Paris in 1844. Thus, they were at least
aware of many of the individuals and ideas we surveyed in Chapters
7 and 8, and Marx softened a passage from Fourier for use in their
first joint effort, *The Holy Family*. The true foundation document of
Marxist feminism is Engels's *The Origin of the Family, Private Property, and the State* (1884). Engels relied heavily on Morgan's *Ancient
Society*, and through it he adopted at least parts of Bachofen's theory.
He postulated a stage of total promiscuity which was followed first
by a matrilineal and matriarchal phase (which included monogamy)
and then by patriarchy. As an economics-minded materialist, Engels
argued that the transition from matriarchy to patriarchy occurred
when the center of production moved out of the household, where
woman held sway, to the field and pasture. In his famous phrase, this
was "the world-historical defeat of the female sex."[25]

Other Marxists followed suit to some degree, although the idea of ancient matriarchies was never a major concern for this future-oriented ideology. August Bebel, for instance, argued on the basis of Bachofen's theory that the institution of slavery began when men forcibly usurped power over women.[26] Later, Robert Briffault elaborated on the ideas of Bachofen, Morgan, and Engels in his massive work *The Mothers* (1927). One theme that survives here is the idealization of women. Briffault argued that matriarchal authority was not based on violent force as is patriarchy, but would have arisen spontaneously when men recognized women's practical and magical expertise. As a result, female preeminence would have been accepted voluntarily by the males, since female power is much more pleasant to experience than male power. This has ensured Briffault a degree of recognition in the Goddess movement.[27]

The radical fringe of nineteenth-century feminism appropriated Bachofen's work as well. This is evident particularly in the work of Matilda Joslyn Gage (1826–98), an American suffragist who became so extreme that she eventually parted ways with better-known figures like Elizabeth Cady Stanton. In her last major book, *Woman, Church, and State*, Gage founded her argument on Bachofen's matriarchy-patriarchy sequence and celebrated the glories of the ancient, pagan matriarchates, citing Morgan as well. She also claimed that pagan societies of the present, such as Hindu India, continue to exhibit matriarchal values (she did not mention traditions such as *sati*, widow-burning, which had been outlawed by the British rulers of India). Gage's main point, however, was that Christianity was the specific source of women's sufferings. The Christian religion, according to her, pioneered and promoted a whole range of horrors: she held the Church responsible for the practice of polygamy, prostitution, and public nude baptisms for women. She is also the one who first claimed (on the basis of unidentified historical records) that no fewer than nine million women perished in the witch hunts, which thus constituted a literal war against women.

Gage's assertions were so far-fetched that her book soon went out of print. It was revived by a feminist publishing house in 1972, and became an immediate favorite of Mary Daly and other radicals.[28] The nine million figure, in particular, has become a dogma in feminist spirituality; I myself was accused of "Holocaust Denial" for questioning it in print.[29]   One wonders how the genteel patriarch of Basel would have felt, had he lived to see his work used in this fashion.

BACHOFEN AND LITERATURE

As we have seen, Joseph Campbell attributed the twentieth-century revival of interest in Bachofen to "a circle of creative artists, psychologists, and literary men: a young group around the poet Stefan George, in Munich, in the twenties."[30]   Campbell erred in his chronology; he was referring to the Cosmic Circle, a neo-Romantic group which was active between 1897 and 1903. The Circle included Ludwig Klages, who has been described as a "philosopher of the irrational," and Alfred Schuler, who "practiced a kind of magic" to reawaken the lost energies of the Roman Empire.[31]   As Richard Noll has reported, "In 1899 Klages introduced Bachofen's *Mutterrecht* to the group, which collectively began an intense period of study to understand the implications of Bachofen's research. Soon the Cosmic Circle conducted elaborate ceremonial invocations and rites of worship to the Great Mother Earth (*Erdmutter*) and glorified in theory and practice Bachofen's initial stage of hetairism (*das Hetärentum*). The cult promoted open opposition to Judeo-Christian culture and the bourgeoisie."[32]

This group did include the noted nationalist poet Stefan George (1868–1933); after 1903 he went on to establish his own circle, "complete with recitals of prophetic poetry, ceremonial talismans and gowns, the wearing of bishops' miters, etc."[33]   Klages, Schuler, and George were all prominent in the pre-Nazi *völkisch* (nationalist-racist) subculture and serve to illustrate the strong neopagan element which was present there. George parted company with the other two as they became more explicitly anti-Semitic. He himself was taken as an inspiration by some Nazis and their sympathizers despite his own distaste for the movement. Josef Goebbels, an aspiring author in his student days, attempted unsuccessfully to join the George circle; Claus von Stauffenberg, the army officer who would almost assassinate Adolf Hitler in 1944, succeeded.[34]

The theory of matriarchy was not ignored in the English literary tradition either; here, its most influential and vociferous proponent was Robert Graves (1895–1985). Graves evidently had a somewhat sheltered upbringing, and he was shattered by his experiences in the trenches of World War I. He received psychiatric treatment from none other than W. H. R. Rivers, who had left anthropology behind to work as a neurologist. Alastair Reid, a longtime personal acquaintance of Graves, attributed his initial "interest in matriarchal societies and woman rule" to his ongoing discussions with Rivers. In his personal life, Graves's long affair with the dominating American writer Laura Riding is the other factor which reinforced his matriarchalism, according to Reid.[35]

On a more literary and intellectual level, it seems that Graves did not read Bachofen directly, but he was thoroughly steeped in Frazer's *Golden Bough* and conversant with Harrison's work.[36] Graves seized upon the notion of ancient, goddess-worshipping matriarchies with a vengeance. Beginning with three books written in the mid-1940s (*King Jesus*; *Hercules, My Shipmate*; and especially *The White Goddess*), he elaborated the matriarchy theory in something very close to the form it assumes in the contemporary Goddess movement. Graves painted a rosy picture of life in the ancient Mediterranean world under the Triple Goddess (maiden, mother, and crone) who, he claimed, was the sole original deity. Under her tutelage, women held sway in society and human beings lived in immediate, emotional contact with the life-force of nature; this contact was the essential inspiration of true poetry. The rise of patriarchy, which fragmented the Goddess into dozens of distinct but limited female deities and then replaced her with a God, also subordinated women to men and devalued poetic insight in the name of analytical logic and reason.[37]

One of Graves's most striking contributions was his forceful presentation of the rise of patriarchy as an unmitigated catastrophe which reversed the proper order of things. First Olympian Apollo, then Judeo-Christian monotheism, and then analytic reason had taken turns at suppressing the feminine dimension of existence; the result is the whole range of modern ills from poverty of the inner life to repressive social institutions and the industrial corruption of the earth.

In Graves's version of the neopagan paradigm—for this is what it is—poets rather than Templars and Freemasons were the secret custodians of matriarchal values during the reign of the patriarchs. His prophecy and hope was for the "Return of the Goddess" (the title of one of his poems), an apocalyptic event which would lead to the destruction of the present order and its replacement by a renewed Goddess-worshipping, earth-preserving matriarchy.[38]

Graves was a creative writer above all else, and his fiction and poetry have generally been regarded in that light. *The White Goddess* is a different sort of book. Graves claimed in his 1960 postscript to have written the bulk of it in less than a month, driven by a sudden inspiration which interrupted his work in progress on Welsh poetry. Moreover, it reads in part like a genuine attempt to argue for the historical reality of matriarchy in ancient times, and many readers naturally take it as such. Professional historians do not, since Graves's methods and source materials do not stand up to the scrutiny of specialists. To note one problem, Graves relied on Lady Charlotte Guest's collection of Welsh legends, *The Mabinogion*. As we have already seen, Lady Charlotte included some of the Iolo Morgannwg creations in her influential work, thus handing them on to writers like Graves; the latter, as Hutton puts it, therefore "built a fantasy on a forgery."[39]

Most expert interpreters of Graves consider *The White Goddess* to be an extended metaphor, and claim that the real subject at issue is not the actual history of Western civilization but Graves's wrestling with his own muse; the major themes of the book are the themes of most of his work—life, death, and love.[40] On the other hand, his poetic worship and prose defense of the Goddess often sound real enough, and Reid claims that by the late 1950s, at least, "He had grown deeply serious about the Goddess . . . Robert did believe, insistently so, and. . . . the belief sustained and justified him."[41]

Graves is another pivotal figure in our story. More than a few participants in Wicca and Goddess spirituality say that reading *The White Goddess* was a factor in stimulating their interest. He was very much an individual, however, and disavowed any personal participation in occult activities or organizations. His knowledge of witchcraft seems to be derived entirely from the readily available books of

Margaret Murray and Gerald Gardner (which we shall examine in the next two chapters), enlivened by his own penchant for creative etymologies.[42] It is the witches' knowledge of Graves, not his knowledge of them, which would turn his personal muse into the figurehead of a dynamic cultural movement.

Nevertheless, Elizabeth Gould Davis did not need to alter her quotations from Graves as she did those from Harrison; in fact, Graves himself is quoted on the back cover of the Penguin edition of *The First Sex* in the following words: "The present intolerable world situation . . . cannot even begin to ease until the basic argument of Elizabeth Gould Davis's *The First Sex* is accepted by all schools and universities."

BACHOFEN, JUNG, AND THE OCCULT

Bachofen and the Roots of Psychotherapy

The idea that Bachofen's theory might have made a significant contribution to twentieth-century psychology and psychoanalysis seems, on the face of it, at least as unlikely as his adoption by witches, Marxists, and radical feminists. Once again, he himself would probably be more than surprised to discover what has become of his work. Already in 1970, Henri Ellenberger was able to demonstrate that "the influence of Bachofen's ideas . . . on dynamic psychiatry has been immense," and illustrated his point with reference to all three of the great founders of psychoanalytic theories—Sigmund Freud, Alfred Adler, and Carl Jung.[43]

This insight is vastly more significant now than when Ellenberger wrote it. In recent years, "revisionist" studies of Freud and Jung have appeared, filling in many gaps in their life stories from newly discovered letters and other records from them and people who knew them. These studies have demonstrated repeatedly that large portions of the theories of Freud and Jung were not discovered in the course of clinical work with patients after all. Instead, they were based on existing literature which the two men had read, reinforced through self-analysis. Some of the crucial components of these theories were developed at least partly in response to issues in Freud's and Jung's personal lives, before being generalized into principles which were supposed to apply to everyone.[44] That being the case, the question of Bachofen's place in the background of psychoanalysis is of more than casual interest.

We cannot pursue that issue in its entirety here. In terms of our quest for the sources of the Goddess movement, the importance of Freud and Adler is entirely eclipsed by that of Carl Gustav Jung (1875-1961). The popularity of Jung and some of his disciples in Goddess literature was noted in Chapter 2: Gimbutas made extensive use of Jungian theory to interpret objects and decorative patterns on "Old European" artifacts as Goddess symbolism; Gadon hailed Jung as the man who "discovered that the Goddess was a potent force in the unconscious"; and Shinoda Bolen and Goldenberg were trained in Jungian analysis. In the rest of this chapter, we must explore the connections between Jung and the Goddess more fully. This involves not only the influence of Bachofen but Jung's general psychological theories and his broader interest in the occult.

The Doctrines of Jungianism

Jungian psychology is guided by the idea that there is a "collective unconscious," a level of consciousness which is deeper than our individual, everyday awareness. The collective unconscious has different levels of its own, which correspond to social groups which increase in breadth as one goes deeper, from family to nation to race to species. It is also the home of "archetypes," sets of symbolic correspondences (sun/light/enlightenment/fire/libido) which we can access directly through the mind. Such access is achieved through "active imagination," a sort of deliberate visionary experience which, for most people, should be learned only under the direct guidance of a trained Jungian analyst. The goal of Jungian therapy is "individuation": through active imagination, we are led to recognize that our personalities include a whole series of polar opposites like rationality and irrationality, the "animal" and the "spiritual," masculinity and femininity, etc.; by exploring them all and bringing them into harmony, we achieve "self-actualization."[45]

Jung's extensive knowledge of the esoteric tradition as well as ancient and non-Western religions made an important contribution to his theories. He claimed to discover, in the fantasies of his patients, images which matched specific symbols and concepts from those traditions, even though the patients had no direct knowledge of them. Jung argued that when the same image occurs, say, in a Hindu scripture, an alchemical allegory, and a modern psychotic hallucination, then the Eastern sage, the alchemist and the psychotic must all have perceived the same thing when in their altered states of consciousness—the archetype.

Two quotations from Jung will suffice to make his general approach clear:

> The point of view I have adopted is that of modern empirical psychology and the scientific method. . . . The idea of immortality is a psychic phenomenon that is disseminated over the whole earth. Every "idea" is, from the psychological point of view, a phenomenon, just as is "philosophy" or "theology." For modern psychology, ideas are *entities*, like animals and plants. The scientific method consists in the description of nature. All mythological ideas are *essentially real,* and far older than any philosophy. . . . In so far as such ideas are universal, they are symptoms or characteristics or normal exponents of psychic life, which are *naturally* present and need no proof of their "truth." The only question we can profitably discuss is whether they are universal or not.[46]

> . . . ghost stories, warning visions, and other strange happenings are constantly being reported . . . despite the disapproving silence of the "enlightened," it has not remained hidden from the wider public that for some time now there has been a serious science which goes by the name of "parapsychology". . . .
>
> [Anelia Jaffé] understands the art of leaving the story just as it is, with all the trimmings that are so offensive to the rationalist. In this way the *twilight atmosphere* that is so essential to the story is preserved. An integral component of any nocturnal, numinous experience is the dimming of consciousness, the feeling that one is in the grip of something greater than oneself, the impossibility of exercising criticism, and the paralysis of the will

. . . . That, indeed, is the uncomprehended purpose of the experience—to make us feel the overpowering presence of a mystery.[47]

Jung himself claimed that one particular case revealed this crucial insight to him. He reported having had a patient who saw an upright tail or tube on the sun; the patient has been nicknamed "The Solar Phallus Man" as a result. Jung reported that some time after he treated this individual in 1906, he read two new books on Mithraism, published in 1907 and 1910 respectively, which revealed that this ancient rival to Christianity had also possessed a symbol with the phallus-sun association. (The 1907 book, incidentally, was by G. R. S. Mead, the prominent Theosophist.) Since the sun does not really have either a tail or a phallus, and the patient had the vision before the books were even available to read, Jung argued that the phallic sun image must be an archetype in the collective unconscious to which both his patient and the ancients had access.[48]

The earth/Mother/Goddess is, as we might expect, another such archetype. Jung's follower Erich Neumann devoted a whole book to this one topic; as Gadon puts it, "From the Jungian perspective, the Goddess is an archetypal image at work within the human psyche that finds outward expression in the ritual, mythology, and art of early humans as well as in the dreams, fantasies, and creative works of our own time."[49]

Jung in Historical Context

Who was Carl Jung? He was, like Bachofen, a German-speaking Swiss native of Basel; in fact, as a boy, he knew the elderly matriarchy theorist by sight.[50] He trained in medicine, developing a particular interest in the mind and mental illness, and then went to work at the prestigious Burghölzli mental clinic in Zurich. While there, he learned about the new theories of Sigmund Freud and became Freud's supporter and disciple. John Kerr argues that, contrary to psychoanalytic tradition, it was actually Jung who put Freud on the map by lending to his theories the powerful reputation of the Burghölzli.[51]

Jung was, from 1905 to 1913, one of Freud's leading pupils and champions. Freud was the elder man and the pioneer; he evidently saw Jung, the Swiss Protestant, as the chosen son and crown prince who would establish psychoanalysis in the wider world beyond its original circle of Viennese Jews.

The split between Freud and Jung, when it came, was intense and painful; they were virtual enemies ever afterwards. This has been attributed to a number of different factors, including their differences of opinion over issues of sexuality, religion, and the occult as well as the conflicting temperaments of two intelligent, innovative and charismatic personalities. Freud maintained a lifelong curiosity about occult phenomena, but he was essentially a materialist whose most famous statement on religion was entitled *The Future of an Illusion*.[52] Jung insisted on the overwhelming significance of religious and spiritual elements in psychology. Jung took several years to recover from his break with Freud, and Kerr reports that the trauma brought him near to insanity.[53] Essentially, he cured himself by plunging into the development of his distinctive ideas, experiencing active imagination himself; then, beginning in 1919, he offered these therapeutic discoveries to the world. To understand the nature of Jung's contribution to the Goddess movement, we must come to grips with the manner in which his ideas were developed and shaped.

First we must consider his early environment. Jung's family believed that his paternal grandfather, who was a Grand Master of Swiss Freemasonry in his day, had also been an illegitimate son of the legendary Goethe.[54] Jung himself was strongly affected by his reading (at his mother's encouragement) of *Faust*. He wrote later that it "poured into my soul like a miraculous balm," and "gave me an increased feeling of inner security and a sense of belonging to the human community." This stood in contrast to his view of Christianity; his own father was a Protestant pastor, but Jung regarded Christian theology as "fancy drivel . . . a specimen of uncommon stupidity whose sole aim was to obscure the truth."[55] Frau Jung's family, on the other hand, had a history of involvement in occult activities. Her father seems to have been a spiritualist and visionary who, throughout his long second marriage, reserved a special chair for weekly visits from the spirit of his deceased first wife. When Jung went to medical school, he based his dissertation on his experiences at séances performed by his own cousin, Hélène Preiswerk.[56]

In Jung's time, German Switzerland and southern Germany seem to have become the headquarters of a neo-Romantic counterculture; Noll compares it to the California of the 1960s. Contemporary influences during Jung's childhood included the philosophy of Friedrich Nietzsche, who equated spiritual liberation with the rejection of all civilized restraint on behavior, and Richard Wagner, whose dramatizations of Germanic mythology had taken on heavily neopagan overtones. As Noll puts it, Wagner "envisioned the operatic spectacles of his later decades as great Teutonic mystery-plays, and he sought to unite the soul of the German peoples through his music and Germanic mythological themes." From 1876 onwards, Wagner's opera house in the town of Bayreuth served as the center of a "mystery cult with mystical overtones" as well as the headquarters of a world-wide network of Wagnerites. His devotees included everyone from German nationalists and racists to Theosophists and Annie Horniman.[57] Bachofen's theory had a definite presence in this geographical and cultural context, as the example of the Cosmic Circle shows.

The Development of Jung's Theories

At various points in his life, Jung steeped himself in the literature of alchemy, Hermeticism, the ancient mystery religions, and eventually the Asian and native American religious traditions. In the foreword to a collection of Jung's writings dealing with occultism, William McGuire began with the observation that "the occult was in the forefront of Jung's interest from the very beginning of his career, and before."[58] His family background makes this more than evident. Even during his undergraduate days at the University of Basel, he brought an extensive knowledge of Swedenborg, Mesmer, and other such writers to bear in the discussions of the Zofingia student association.[59]

These interests seem to have received extra encouragement from Jung's contact with Otto Gross in 1908. Gross was a fellow Freudian at this point, brilliant and charismatic. He was also a sort of Nietzschian, an anarchist who believed that the erotic impulse was so fundamental to human nature that it must not suffer restriction in any way. This principle guided his idiosyncratic interpretation of Bachofen—he demanded a return to gynecocracy at the same time as he pursued, with considerable success, the lifestyle of hetairism. He left a wake of seductions and broken marriages behind him as he went. He was also addicted to morphine and cocaine, and this was the reason he was admitted into Jung's care, on Freud's recommendation, at the Burghölzli.[60]

Noll believes that Gross stimulated Jung's interest in Bachofen; whether or not this is true, it is certain that Jung knew Bachofen's work, since his personal copy of *Mutterrecht* still survives. Both Ellenberger and Noll suggest that Bachofen's story of patriarchy overthrowing matriarchy influenced Jung's belief that every man has a repressed feminine side to his personality, the "anima." (Kerr, on the other hand, argues that the anima theory came later, as a product of Jung's own brush with insanity and his broken relationship with Sabina Spielrein.[61])

The patient Gross affected the therapist Jung more than the other way around. Jung wrote excitedly to Freud about the endless discussions they had. The impact on Jung was profound—he abandoned his middle-class, Protestant commitment to monogamy and accepted his polygamous impulses as normal and natural. Freed of any sense of guilt, he began the extra-marital affair with Spielrein, who had come to him as a patient and then became pupil, lover, and colleague (her fascinating and tragic life is a major subject of Kerr's book). Such relationships would continue for almost the rest of Jung's life, his devoted and long-suffering wife Emma notwithstanding; he wrote to Freud that "the prerequisite for a good marriage . . . is the license to be unfaithful."[62]

Jung's effect on Gross was not nearly so profound—he simply escaped over the hospital fence and went off to find another fix.

The next major episode in Jung's life was the 1912–13 break with Freud. As mentioned, he was deeply traumatized by this development, but eventually recovered by putting himself through the therapeutic process of active imagination which he later refined into the basis of his approach to psychotherapy. In *Memories, Dreams, Reflections* he described this process of inducing visions in himself and told of encountering other beings as a result. They had names like Salome, Elijah, Philemon, and Ka. "Philemon represented a force which was not in myself. . . . At times he seemed quite real to me, quite real. . . . I went walking up and down the garden with him . . . And the fact was that he conveyed to me many an illuminating idea . . . . Later, Philemon became relativized by the emergence of yet another figure, whom I called Ka. . . . In time I was able to integrate both figures through the study of alchemy." The real lesson in all this, according to Jungianism, is that we can learn things from deep within ourselves which the conscious mind does not know.[63]

The most important vision of all, however, is not described in any of Jung's books; it has become known from notes taken at one of his 1925 seminars, which have been published only in the last decade.[64] Jung "descends" to meet Salome and Elijah. Salome tells him that he is Christ and asks him to heal her blindness; when he refuses, a snake coils around him until he finds himself held in the posture of crucifixion. His head is transformed into the face of a lion, so that he comes to resemble a well-known sculpture of Mithras. Jung himself told his seminar that this was an experience of deification, and admitted that "one gets a peculiar feeling from being put through such an initiation."[65] He evidently considered himself individuated, healed, and self-actualized once he discovered his own divinity.

Reassessing Carl Jung

Keeping in mind what we have seen in the preceding chapters, the similarity between Jung's own description of his experiences in active imagination and the high-magical soul travel practiced by Kabbalists, Theosophists, and Golden Dawn magicians seems quite striking. Similar techniques were being employed between 1890 and 1914 by occultists of the Alpine German communities, including Guido von List. Jung's early and constant interest in the occult gives us ample reason to suspect that his visionary techniques were, at least in part, adapted from the established practices of the esoteric tradition. The fact that deification was both the goal of magical practice and the outcome of Jung's experience reinforces this observation.

It also leads to a fundamental question. Did Jung really study the fantasies and visions of his patients, then discover their correlations to the symbols of various religious and magical traditions, and then arrive at his hypothesis of the collective unconscious and the archetypes? Or, did he take his basic ideas directly from the esoteric tradition and his studies in comparative religions, and interpret himself and his patients accordingly? If the latter is closer to the truth, this would change our understanding of the whole nature of Jungianism—from a scientific discipline which discovered objective correlations between ancient myths and the fantasies of modern individuals, to a psychological application of the magical tradition itself. The collective unconscious, for example, may be merely the Romantic, neopagan folk-soul in scientific garb; the archetypes may be the psychologized apparitions of Eliphas Lévi and his many heirs.

This is what Noll argues in *The Jung Cult*, and he offers what may be a crucial piece of evidence: the possibility that Jung falsified his account of his linchpin case, the Solar Phallus Man. As we saw, the whole Jungian theory is founded on the claim that the solar phallus vision was a spontaneous production on the part of the patient, which only later was discovered to match newly-published information on Mithraist imagery. The Solar Phallus Man was actually the patient of Jung's assistant, Dr. Johann Jakob Honegger Jr.[66] Honegger did not begin practicing until 1909 and he committed suicide in 1911, leaving Jung free to claim the case in later years. This would mean, however, that the solar phallus vision must have occurred after the books on Mithraism were published, not before. Consequently, the patient could have read the books before having the vision, and Honegger and Jung could have read them before interpreting it. Not only that, but the sun/phallus correlation was already accessible in two older, well-known books: first, a survey of mythology by Friedrich Creuzer, published back in the Romantic days of 1810-12, which Jung himself is said to have "devoured with passionate interest"; and, second, none other than Bachofen's *Mutterrecht*.[67]

Noll's assertion is a controversial one, striking as it does at the very foundation of Jung's credibility and even his moral stature. If the sequence of events was as Noll suggests, the solar phallus vision was perfectly explicable in terms of the patient's probable everyday knowledge; there was no need at all to postulate an archetype or a collective unconscious, unless the "need" was Jung's own. The debate goes on.[68]

Jung's Legacy

Jung's importance to our question does not arise from his influence on psychology and psychiatry, which has been limited; Freud, Adler, and others have generally had more to do with the way those professions have developed. It is not part of our purpose here to assess the value of Jungian psychology as therapy. Like Bachofen himself, however, Jung has had an extraordinary impact in fields other than his own professed specialty.

Most important to us here is Jung's influence on the study of religion and mythology. As we saw, Jung's basic theory holds that the same archetypes are available to all members of the race or species; this is why, he said, so many symbols from religions around the world resemble each other. The widespread tendency to identify the sun as male (or a god) and the moon as female (or a goddess) is one such example. Bachofen and others had already made this precise point, and it is a crucial one when Goddess writers attempt to interpret the artistic remains of preliterate civilizations. It is much easier to argue that wavy lines painted on a pot represent water, and therefore fertility, and therefore the bounty of nature, and therefore the Goddess, if one knows Jungianism than if one does not.

Jung's influence was spread through several institutional channels. The C. G. Jung Institute trains and certifies practitioners of Jungian analysis. Also, during his lifetime, some wealthy American disciples of Jung established the Bollingen Foundation, named after his rural home in Switzerland. Bollingen sponsored scholars and writers whose views on various subjects were harmonious with Jung's, and the Foundation devoted itself to their publications. It produced the collected works of Jung in English translation, naturally enough, but major scholars of comparative religion like Heinrich Zimmer and Mircea Eliade also worked and published through Bollingen. This connection helped them to make their reputations in the English-speaking world of scholarship. It was Zimmer's idea, in fact, that Bollingen should produce an English translation of the abridged German edition of Bachofen's work. Zimmer apparently saw Jung as Bachofen's heir in the quest to "decipher mythology as the everlasting romance of the soul"; Jung approved the project personally, recalling his childhood experiences of seeing Bachofen in person on the streets of Basel.[69]

The most famous of all these Bollingen figures is Joseph Campbell. He began by editing Zimmer's work for publication after the latter's premature death, but he went on to achieve fame with his own, essentially Jungian interpretations of world mythology. In this book, we have encountered him through his introductions to the Bollingen Bachofen itself and to Gimbutas's *Language of the Goddess*, where he cites Bachofen again. His influential books and his popular public television series with Bill Moyers all make the point that mythology arises from common human perceptions and that most myths, therefore, mean basically the same thing. The biblical religions exist apart from this, however, because their emphasis on a transcendent creator rules out the neopagan/Jungian notion of the god within. Campbell told his own biographers, "Clearly Christianity is opposed fundamentally and intrinsically to everything that I am working and living for."[70]

Jung shared some of this antipathy towards traditional Christianity, as his negative attitude towards his pastor father makes clear—not to mention his youthful vision of God's excrement falling on Basel's cathedral.[71] Christian symbols which could be reduced to archetypes were acceptable and useful, but nothing that implied an exclusive source of authority outside the human soul could fit within the Jungian framework.

This hostility has not been fully reciprocated by mainstream religious institutions. Jung is taken seriously in seminaries and is frequently quoted from the pulpit. When the Anglican Bishop of

Vancouver, Michael Ingham, called for the church to institute the sacramental blessing of same-sex relationships in a widely-distributed sermon in September 1996, Jung was among his most frequently cited authorities. Jung lent himself to such a role because he, unlike Freud, at least thought that religion (as he defined it) was valuable and important. As the revisionist literature on Jung becomes better known, this situation may change. Already, the Board of Directors of Anglican Renewal Ministries of Canada has dropped the popular personality test, the Myers-Briggs Type Indicator (MBTI), from its leadership training program because of the neopagan elements in Jung's personality theory, on which the MBTI is entirely based.[72] This is one of the most popular personality tests available today; its frequent use by personnel and human resources administrators in both government and corporate circles may be the most influential channel through which Jungian ideas propagate themselves in contemporary society.

Most relevant to our inquiry is Jung's status in the world of contemporary occultism. Jung, perhaps more than anyone else in the twentieth century, has made large portions of the esoteric tradition intellectually respectable by restating them in contemporary semiscientific terminology. People who would never dream of summoning demons can be quite comfortable discussing archetypes; "individuation" and "self-actualization" sound technical and even trendy, whereas "self-deification," if it is not simply baffling, may evoke memories of Crowley.

In New Age circles, Jung's ideas are ubiquitous. It is not only the Goddess movement, but also modern Gnostics and Hermeticists who have come to regard Jung as essentially one of their own.[73] They may be right, up to a point. If Noll is correct in his reconstruction of Jungianism, then some of its central elements amount to another twentieth-century expression of the esoteric tradition. The idea that Jungian psychology can be used to substantiate the Goddess myth by guiding the interpretation of artifacts, for example, falls to the ground if both movements drew their sustenance from essentially the same sources in nineteenth-century occultism. In that case, the commonalities between Jungianism and New Age religions are anything but surprising; branches on the same tree tend to bear the same fruit.

We have now traced the most significant paths taken by Bachofen's matriarchy theory during the century between its original publication and its appearance, in condensed form, in the English translation which has had such a profound effect on the Goddess movement. Most of the major features of Goddess spirituality have made their presence known in the course of this survey. What remains lacking in the complete picture is an institutional structure which could undergird a movement of this type; for that, we must return from Bachofen to Jules Michelet and follow the rise of modern witchcraft.

13

Michelet's Reinvention of Witchcraft

> *Nature makes them Sorceresses.*
>
> Jules Michelet

BACHOFEN'S 1861 MUTTERRECHT shares its importance as a cornerstone of Goddess spirituality with Michelet's 1862 *La Sorcière*. Although Goddess writers commonly cite Bachofen, he would probably be disturbed by what they have done with his theory. Michelet might well be pleased to see the modern fruits of his efforts, since it took less than a century before something like the sort of witchcraft he described was actually being practiced. To understand Michelet's accomplishment properly, we should refresh our memories as to the context in which he was writing. He had left his university post as a protest against the establishment of the Second Empire in 1852 and turned his hand to evangelizing his views of the French Revolution and France's destiny to the common people. *The Insect, Love,* and *Woman* had been three of his most recent efforts when he turned his attention to the topic of witchcraft. Michelet's innovations will show up more clearly if we recall the state of question on this subject before he wrote.

PERCEPTIONS OF WITCHCRAFT

In the wake of the Enlightenment, it was generally assumed—on

rationalistic grounds—that witches did not actually exist. Historians ever since have been confronted with the task of explaining why
the witch hunts of Renaissance and Reformation times had occurred.
There is now an enormous literature on the witch hunts themselves.
Our real requirement at this point is to do for Michelet approximately what we did for Bachofen: to clarify his concept of witchcraft, and trace it from him to the twentieth-century Wiccans who
gave us the Goddess. Assessing the relationship between Michelet's
portrait of witchcraft and the actual targets of the witch-hunters is a
problem of a different order; although we cannot ignore it entirely, it
need not detain us for long.

The first point to be remembered is that witches were not especially feared or hunted through most of European history. The *Canon
"Episcopi"* of AD 906, for example, did fulminate against "wicked
women who, turning back to Satan and seduced by the illusions and
phantoms of the demons, believe and openly avow that in the hours
of the night they ride on certain animals, together with Diana, the
goddess of the pagans, with a numberless multitude of women. . . ."
Other, roughly contemporary sources describe similar practices, introducing the biblical name Herodias or the Germanic Holda with
or instead of Diana. The thrust of the Canon, however, is clear—
women who do these things are acting on a delusion and should stop
doing so. The text goes on to say that the error in all this is to "think
that there exists some divine power other than the one God." In
short, the greatest danger was that one might actually believe in these
false things.[1]

To justify hunting witches, one had to insist that they were real
and dangerous, not that they were deluded participants in imaginary
activities. Witchcraft was not declared a sinister reality, a heresy
worthy of hunting, until the decree of Pope John XXII in 1318 (two
years after the Inquisition destroyed the Knights Templar); the notorious efforts to discover, try, and execute witches on a significant
scale took place between Pope Innocent VIII 's call to arms in his Bull
Summis Desiderantes (1484) and the quickly discredited outbreak in
Salem, Massachusetts, in 1692.[2] As the Enlightenment dawned, belief in witches dwindled away with many other notions involving the

supernatural. According to recent studies, the complete death toll for the witch-hunting period in Britain, Europe, and North America probably falls between forty thousand and one hundred thousand.[3] With such a wide range in estimates, it is virtually impossible to determine how large a proportion out of the total number of deaths from anti-heresy crusades and religious wars the "witches" comprised during this violent period.

There are now two widespread scholarly views on the witch hunts: the so-called "rationalist" view, which holds that there was no such thing as witchcraft and the Inquisition invented it so as not to run short of heretics to hunt; and the "romantic" view that there really was something there, although it was not what the hunters thought or said it was—namely, an organized cult of Satan-worshippers with supernatural powers.[4] At this juncture we shall consider one classic expression of each view.

One of the more influential examples of the "romantic" view is Elliot Rose's *A Razor for a Goat* (1962). Rose discounts the supernatural elements which permeate the records of the witch trials and focuses on the question of organized witchcraft (as opposed to herbal medicine and the charms and spells of common folklore). Recognizing that virtually all of the recorded confessions by witches were made under threatened or actual torture, Rose professes to disregard about ninety percent of their details, but not all. Essentially, he argues that the circumstances were ripe for an alternative religion in the thirteenth century, and the witch hunts began as a crackdown against just such an alternative. His suggestion is that the witch cult originated with the "goliards," a large class of wandering scholars who had trained for the priesthood but never received ordination because there were too few available parishes. Knowing Latin and the rudiments of ritual, goliards could have set themselves up as purveyors of blessings and exorcisms, and formed alliances with village and rural people—mostly women, in all probability—who possessed a repertoire of traditional potions, spells, and ceremonies. The goliards had their own renegade fraternal order, the *Ordo Vagorum*, which would have functioned as the unifying network of the cult until it was broken by the witch hunters.[5]

Norman Cohn is among the best-known representatives of the "rational" approach. His book *Europe's Inner Demons* (1975) is only partly about witchcraft. His overall purpose is to trace the history of the stereotypical conspiracy theory of pre-modern times. His basic argument is that there was a standard definition of a sinister, conspiratorial organization working to undermine society at large; this definition was operating at least as early as the Roman persecution of Christians, and has simply changed hands and altered appropriate details as it has pursued its course over the centuries. The early Christians, the heretical Cathari and Albigensians, the Knights Templar, and the so-called witches were all tarred in turn with the same brush, as can be seen in the fact that the accusations against them all were so similar. In Christian times, the central elements in the stereotype included repudiating Christ, worshipping the devil, murdering and eating babies, and holding orgiastic celebrations full of promiscuity and incest.

Cohn argues that these charges became part of a standard list of crimes which told heresy hunters what to ask when interrogating accused individuals; with the use of torture, confessions which matched this list could be assured. There is ample evidence that the Cathari and the Knights Templar actually existed, although the validity of these charges against them is extremely dubious. In the case of an alleged witch cult, there is no reliable evidence—that is, evidence which is not tainted by the threat of torture, or by the self-interest of the witch hunters—to demonstrate that it ever existed at all.[6]

More recent discussions have tended to move away from this basic question of whether there was or was not a real witch cult. As Diane Purkiss illustrates, the history of the witch hunts has become a forum for discussions of feminist methodology, focusing on such issues as what the accused witches and witch-hunters thought they were doing, and what historians think they are doing when they study these particular events. In such contexts, the gender issue receives more attention than either Rose or Cohn gave it. While some writers see witch-hunting as the patriarchal war against women which Gage described, Purkiss points out that most accusations of witchcraft were actually made by women, not by men; their accusations tended to emphasize matters of health, food, children, and cleanliness.[7] This may suggest that "witchcraft" was the form that heresy-hunting took when it impinged on the domestic, female sphere of life.

For our purposes, there is no need to choose among these theories. None of these views includes the suggestion that anything like an organized movement of witches carried on between the seventeenth and nineteenth centuries; even Rose indicates that the witch hunts would have been successful in exterminating any organization that might have existed. There appears to be no direct continuity from the actual hunted witches to the books of Michelet and his followers, except in a purely literary sense.

There were, however, other people writing about witches in the nineteenth century. Along with the "Rosicrucian novels" which we noted in Chapter 9, the Romantic era stimulated a new and positive literary image for the witch. Rather than a malevolent hag, Shelley and others portrayed the witch as "a figure of beauty explicitly linked with a lost pre-industrial past of intuition and imagination . . . such figures represent the goal of the poetic quest for wild beauty and for poetic mastery of it."[8]

Another view entirely was advanced by Karl-Ernst Järcke in 1828. Järcke was a professor of law at the University of Berlin, and thus a colleague of Savigny, the mentor to the Grimms and Bachofen. Järcke edited an old record of a witchcraft trial for publication and included with it an explanation of his own as to what he thought was actually happening at the time. Writing in the aftermath of the French Revolution and the Napoleonic wars, he was well aware of the fear of occult conspiracies which arose in connection with the Golden and Rosy Cross, the Illuminati, and various French groups. A devout Roman Catholic, Järcke argued that the Church had not gone witch-hunting in error; rather, witchcraft too had been a conspiratorial movement in which ancient rites had been preserved and which was working for the downfall of Christendom. In other words, behind the popular image of witchcraft was a more down-to-earth reality, an actual and potentially dangerous (neo)pagan organization. It appears that Järcke was the very first to suggest that witchcraft had been neither a supernatural Satanic force nor a practical fiction to keep the witch hunters in business, but an actual remnant of Europe's original pagan religion. Franz Josef Mone followed in 1839 with the suggestion that witchcraft had always been a secretive cult which was despised even by the better class of ancient pagans.[9]

Jules Michelet agreed that witchcraft was a survival from pagan times; but, unlike Järcke and Mone, he sided with the witches against the church.

MICHELET'S *La Sorcière*

Even more than most of Michelet's works, *La Sorcière* was a passionately written history full of his lessons for the present and future. As one commentator has noted, "For Michelet history was not a compilation but a cure."[10] In a concluding note to *La Sorcière* Michelet himself said, "The object of my book was purely to give, not a history of Sorcery, but a simple and impressive formula of the Sorceress's way of life . . ."[11] It incorporated some material from his previous histories, and he claimed to have been working with the records concerning witchcraft for thirty years by the time he completed this book.[12] On the other hand, Cohn points out, Michelet wrote the whole book in just two months; he comments that "the aging romantic radical had neither time nor desire for detailed research."[13] Michelet's well-established political views dominate his material so totally that professional historians have generally dismissed his thesis. His passionate eloquence, however, has made the book into one of his greatest achievements, if continuous popular readership is any indication of greatness. It was translated into English in 1939 under the somewhat misleading title *Satanism and Witchcraft*; I shall continue to use the French title, which reminds us of Michelet's own emphasis on the individual female witch.

Michelet's basic agenda, as we have seen, blended messianic French nationalism with the Romantic idealization of women and the poor and a bitter hostility towards the church. With that information in hand, the basic content and tone of *La Sorcière* are quite predictable—witchcraft was, in Cohn's words, "a justified, if hopeless, protest by medieval serfs against the social order that was crushing them," and was essentially a cult of nature and fertility.[14] The book is divided into two parts. In the first, Michelet gives his description of the origins of witchcraft and its development up to the medieval period; in the second, he covers its degeneration and destruction in the course of the witch hunts.

In his introduction, before he has produced any evidence whatsoever, Michelet makes two striking pronouncements: first, that women are natural witches; and second, that witchcraft was humanity's original religion, arising from women's place in primitive societies. The passage needs to be quoted in full to catch Michelet's tone and vision:

> "Nature makes them Sorceresses,"—the genius peculiar to woman and her temperament. She is born a creature of Enchantment. In virtue of regularly recurring periods of exaltation, she is a Sibyl; in virtue of love, a Magician. By the fineness of her intuitions, the cunning of her wiles—often fantastic, often beneficent—she is a Witch, and casts spells, at least and lowest lulls pain to sleep and softens the blow of calamity.
>
> All primitive peoples start alike; this we see again and again in the accounts given by travelers. Man hunts and fights. Woman contrives and dreams; she is the mother of fancy, of the gods. She possesses glimpses of the *second sight,* and has wings to soar into the infinitude of longing and imagination. The better to count the seasons, she scans the sky. But earth has her heart as well. Her eyes stoop to the amorous flowers; a flower herself in her young beauty, she learns to know them as playfellows and intimates. A woman, she asks them to heal the men she loves.
>
> Pathetic in their simplicity these first beginnings of Religion and Science! Later on, each province will be separated, we shall see mankind specialize—as medicine-man, astrologer or prophet, necromancer, priest, physician. But in these earliest days woman is all in all, and plays every part.[15]

In Michelet's telling, the earliest religion was one which focused on the joys of nature, fertility, and healing. These were woman's essential prerogative; even when all else is lost, he says, "Woman is the one thing left in the world most replete with nature."[16] It was Christianity and its secular ally, feudalism, which destroyed this beautiful harmony. The Church and its faith were opposed to joy, nature, and reason; thanks to its doctrine of original sin, the Christian religion supposedly decreed that women were unworthy of protection, leaving nobles and their retainers free to indulge in recreational rape and abuse.[17]

Through most of Part I of his book, Michelet tells the story of a hypothetical peasant woman who is subjected to a whole range of horrors: being deflowered by her feudal lord on her wedding night; trying to support her husband through the risks and gambles of peasant life, subject always to the lord's whims; giving in to the temptation to work magic on her husband's behalf, and seeing their subsequent prosperity alienate them from the other peasants; and being publicly stripped and beaten by the lord's henchmen because the lady of the manor was jealous of her beauty. Even her husband does not protect her, and she flees to the caves and hills, where she becomes a full-blown witch for lack of any other option. As Michelet states unequivocally, "The Sorceress is the Church's crime."[18] Michelet describes in colorful terms how the woman gave herself to Satan. Satan, he says, is the witches' god simply because the Christian God sided with the Church, the aristocracy, and the men; what alternative did poor women have? He also asserts, however, that women kept the worship of the old pagan gods alive. They preserved the ancient wisdom which the Church repudiated, especially in their realm of healing. Michelet trumpets the old claim of Paracelsus that he learned far more medicine from gypsies and healing women than from the universities of his time.[19]

According to Michelet, witchcraft was not simply a pursuit of solitary women; it was the continuing remnant of ancient pagan religion which was celebrated communally among the peasants. In his description of the witches' "sabbaths," oppressed peasants gathered under the leadership of the sorceress to celebrate the old gods and the old joys; she symbolically mated with a wooden image of Satan and, after the feasting and drinking, she offered her body as an altar for offerings to the devil and his demons. "The crowd, united in one and the same giddy madness, felt itself drawn into a single personality as well by the subtle influence of the feminine element as by a vague, undefinable emotion of fraternity. . . . What was the boon they craved? That we, their far-away descendants, might win enfranchisement."[20] As Cohn remarks, "none of this figures in any contemporary account of the witches' sabbat."[21]

The second part of Michelet's book describes not only the terrors of the witch hunts but the degeneration of the witch cult itself. The emphasis turned from healing and fertility to debauchery and wickedness. Why? Because men took over supremacy within the cult from women, setting themselves up as pretentious wizards, and because aristocrats began joining the cult for their own entertainment. Women and peasants, hounded from the outside, were betrayed from within as well and witchcraft itself was doomed.[22]

Michelet strikes a pose of optimism in his epilogue, however. By this point, he has identified Satan as the symbol of this world—nature, reason, and science, everything which opposed Christianity. He repeats that science had begun with women and was the property of the sorceress, and looks forward to a feminine New Age in which woman would be, not a witch, but a benevolent fairy:

> Woman, busied during the later centuries with men's affairs, has in requital lost her own true role,—that of *healing,* and *consoling,* that of the fairy that restores to health and happiness.
>
> This is her true priestesshood,—hers by right divine, no matter what the Church may have said to the contrary.
>
> With her delicate organs, her love of the finest detail, her tender appreciation of life, she is called to be its quick-eyed confidante in every science of observation. With her gentle heart and sweet pity, her instinctive kindness, she is a heaven-sent healer. . . .
>
> She will pursue the sciences, and bring into their domain gentleness and humanity, like a smile on Nature's face.
>
> Anti-Nature pales in death; and the day is not far off when her final setting will mark a dawn of blessed augury to mankind.[23]

There is, he insisted, no possible compromise between "Satan," the symbol of worldly joy and knowledge, and a church which depended for its very existence on guilt, grief, and ignorance.

La Sorcière is of critical importance in at least two ways. It was, as we noted, the first influential book which could be said to take a stand in favor of witchcraft, extinct though Michelet knew it to be, rather than against it. He agreed with Järcke and Mone that there really had been an organized witch cult which preserved pagan beliefs and practices from pre-Christian times. When Christianity came to rule Europe, the old paganism had to be practiced in secret, and this is what witchcraft actually was—the somewhat pathetic remains of an older, once-vibrant religion.

Second, Michelet's continuing Romantic idealization of women permeates everything he has to say about witchcraft. It was, of course, a longstanding convention that witchcraft was peculiarly a women's heresy. Even so, gender lines were not firm. According to surviving records of actual witch trials, men were also accused of witchcraft, and most descriptions of covens—if they can be believed at all— indicate that men led them. It seems likely that a majority of witch trials were based on accusations made by women, not by men. The notion of a goddess scarcely even appears; the constant factor is the devil, or horned god, depending on one's perspective.[24] Michelet, however, was not inhibited by this evidence. To him, witchcraft was quintessentially a women's religion; his reconstruction of the cult fits his well-established feminine ideal to the last detail. Having already looked favorably upon the notion of matriarchy in his book *The Insect*, he now projected it backwards to the origins of religion and science, and forward to the New Age which he thought he could see dawning. This is what makes it so striking that *Mutterrecht* and *La Sorcière* were published only a year apart. In Michelet's case, however, what he said in *La Sorcière* was only an extension of what he had been saying for most of the preceding decade, at least.

Michelet's witchcraft is a priestess-led, woman-centered nature religion, older than Christianity, opposed to it, persecuted and destroyed by it, and morally superior to it. *La Sorcière*, however, is not so much an encouragement to witchcraft as a condemnation of the church; it does not seem at all likely that Michelet had ever met a witch, or ever expected to do so. It was one thing to portray the witch cult as an understandable, though doomed, protest against patriarchal, ecclesiastical, and aristocratic injustice; it was quite another thing to say that it still existed. The role of making this announcement to the world would fall not to Michelet, but to an American.

CHARLES LELAND'S *Aradia*

Leland's Life and Careers

As with Bachofen's matriarchy theory, it took some time for Michelet's image of witchcraft to find a home in the English-speaking world, where the Goddess movement would eventually arise. This step was taken by Charles Godfrey Leland (1824–1903). Leland led a varied and fascinating life and made his mark in several different fields.[25] He was born in Philadelphia to an Episcopalian family who became Unitarians; he himself rejected Christian orthodoxy in his teens.[26] He was raised on the lore of the American Revolution and was entertained by his mother and the family servants with stories of witches and ghosts; he also became acquainted with some of the local native people and heard their stories. Two of his strongest motivations in later life were the quest for freedom and the love of mystery.

During his years in school and as an undergraduate at Princeton, Leland sampled a wide range of ideas. One of his teachers was Bronson Alcott, the famous Transcendentalist. Transcendentalism was, in some ways, as close as America came to a genuine Romantic movement. Leland reported that Alcott believed in teaching by "sympathetic intellectual communion"; "he encouraged me to read everything and to learn almost nothing."[27] Leland's reading during these years included some names now familiar to us: the Hermetic literature, Neoplatonism, Cornelius Agrippa, Paracelsus, Barrett's *The Magus*, the novels of Lytton, and "God knows how many Rosicrucian writers became familiar to me."[28] Most important of all, according to Leland himself, was Rabelais; reading this libertine French poet (whose motto, "Do what thou wilt," would be appropriated by Crowley as well) was Leland's personal "Damascus experience."[29] According to his niece, Elizabeth Pennell, he left Princeton as "a dreamer to whom the past was more real than the present, and the mysteries of nature and philosophy as important as the practical problems of existence."[30]

He traveled next to Germany, where he studied at both Heidelberg and Munich. Studies apart, he visited old castles and read up on European witchcraft. The highlight of his stay in Germany was probably his visit to Justinus Kerner. Kerner (1786–1862) was a physician and mystical poet with a strong interest in the occult. His greatest burst of fame occurred during the two years (1827–29) he housed and worked with Fredericke Hauffe, the "Seeress of Prevorst." Kerner had been treating her with Mesmerism, and she experienced prolonged trances during which she reported visions of the spiritual world and produced prophecies and supernatural advice. Kerner ran a series of experiments on her, and the whole phenomenon attracted visits from people as famous as Schelling and Schleiermacher.[31] Kerner became famous for his hospitality as well, and Leland was one of his callers some twenty years after the days of the Seeress.

Leland relocated to the Sorbonne in October 1847—a portentous move, since it brought him to Paris in time for the suspension of Michelet and the resulting uprising of 1848. Inspired by the revolutionary rhetoric of Romantic writers like Byron and Dumas, not to mention his own national myth, the visiting American student took his place on the barricades. He sent home a description of the revolt in a vivid letter dated February 29, 1848, which Pennell reproduced in her biography. "One effect which it had in a small way was to make all Paris acquainted, intimate even," he wrote; one cannot help wondering whether he encountered Alphonse Constant among his revolutionary comrades. "It is really delightful to be an American here in Paris at present; they consider us as, in fact, doubly distilled Republicans."[32]

His studies complete, he returned to the United States. He spent some years practicing law and journalism; he was a strong abolitionist and served in the Union army during the Civil War. After the war, he did some prospecting for oil in Tennessee on the strength of a letter of recommendation from none other than Col. Henry Steel Olcott, the future Theosophist. In the course of his travels he was also "initiated" into an Indian tribe with which he spent a period of time.[33] Another of his major preoccupations was schooling; over the years he developed an elaborate philosophy of progressive education. Financial independence came in the late 1860s. First he received a sizeable inheritance; then he published the work that made him famous in literary circles, the "Hans Breitmann Ballads." These were satirical songs, supposedly composed in fractured English by a German immigrant, and they proved immensely popular. Leland never had to work for a living again, and even in England the name of Hans Breitmann assured him entry into the company of artists.

Leland in fact spent ten years in England, from 1869 to 1879, and made the acquaintance of such literary greats as Carlyle, Browning, and Tennyson, as well as Max Müller, the translator of *The Sacred Books of the East*. Best of all, perhaps, he struck up a lasting friendship with one of his childhood idols, Lord Lytton. Leland, like Eliphas Lévi before him, enjoyed Lytton's hospitality and friendship, and remained devoted to him. Leland's niece found that as late as 1893 he was still copying out passages from *Zanoni* and other Lytton novels for his own use. This, evidently, was a passion she did not share: "I admit frankly that I cannot now read the novels, though I did once go through them all, beginning with the *Last Days of Pompeii*, which in my school-days was thought especially adapted to improve the mind and do no harm in the process. But to open any one of them of late years means to be bored to extinction."[34]

In England, Leland fully indulged his interest in folklore. He devoted himself to the study of the Gypsies and absorbed so much of their culture that his friends and relatives called him "the Romany Rye" for the rest of his life. One of his greatest accomplishments was to be accepted into the company of another small subculture, the tinkers; he emerged with the first systematic study of their language, Shelta.[35] He also played a leading role in establishing folklore as a serious academic discipline, and became the very first member of the Folk Lore Society.

Leland spent the last part of his life on matters like this. He also dabbled in Theosophy, establishing personal contact with A. P. Sinnett, his former officer Col. Olcott, and Franz Hartmann; Pennell reproduced a letter in which he referred to scrying in magic mirrors with the latter two men.[36] His role in the development of modern witchcraft came late, with the publication of *Aradia* in 1899. To permit an accurate assessment of this book, however, we must digress briefly to consider another influential effort which preceded it— *Algonquin Legends*.

Leland's Algonquin Legends

In 1884, Leland published his collection of stories from several native tribes in the area of New England and the Maritime Provinces of Canada. He had spent the previous two summers in the region to collect his information. This book has been influential in a number of ways, not only as a resource through which anthropologists and other non-natives might seek to understand the worldview of some of North America's earlier inhabitants, but even as a means by which some of today's "First Nations" attempt to deepen their sense of their own heritage.[37] Our interest here is not in the content of the book but in Leland's methods, insofar as we might learn something to assist us in understanding his witchcraft book.

The opening story in *Algonquin Legends* is the tale of the birth of Kluskap and his evil twin, Malsum the Wolf, and their subsequent mortal struggle. Kluskap and Malsum are in the womb together; Malsum cannot wait to be born and, despite Kluskap's objections, bursts out of his mother's womb, killing her. Each of the twins can be killed by only one thing, but when they agree to let each other know the secret of their mortality, Malsum alone tells the truth—he can be killed by a fern root. Kluskap gives several false answers to the question, and each time Malsum tries to kill him, it is without success. Eventually Kluskap uses the fern root to kill Malsum, whose corpse becomes the Chic-Choc mountain range in the Gaspé. Thomas Parkhill has conducted an intensive investigation into this story and the way Leland acquired it.[38] The results of the study call into question Leland's sources, his methods, and his use of the story.

Parkhill demonstrates that Leland had four sources of information on the Kluskap-Malsum story, none of them first-hand. One was a nineteenth-century tourist guide, M. F. Sweetser's *The Maritime Provinces*, which told a lively story of the conflict between Glooscap and his brother (who was neither a twin nor a wolf). The story is clearly designed for the entertainment of the traveler, and is not attributed to any native source. The second version was in a manuscript from a fellow collector of stories, Simon Rand. It has the twins and the birth story as well as the final conflict, but Rand himself included a note expressing doubt as to its authenticity.

The other two versions came from one of Leland's intermediaries, Edward Jack. In a letter to Leland, he included a one-line reference to Glooscap having to kill his wicked brother, who was then turned into the mountain range. Leland wrote back asking for more details, and Jack eventually passed on a fuller version from "my Indian," Gabe Aquin. This contains the birth story of the twins and their final battle, but identifies Wolf as Glooscap's pet rather than as his wicked brother. Aquin, the source of this fourth version, turns out to have been an exceptionally cosmopolitan Maliseet—he had long been on friendly terms with British army officers in New Brunswick and had done the social rounds in England in 1883, even meeting royalty.

In short, not one of these versions contains the full Kluskap-Malsum story as Leland eventually recorded it, and not one of them comes from an unimpeachable source of pure aboriginal tradition. It is probably relevant to note, in addition, that Leland paid at least one of his correspondents at a rate of one dollar for an eight-page story and complained if they were longer—a policy which might well have had an impact on the number and the length of the stories he received, and therefore on their content as well. Jack also bought his information from Aquin.[39] Confronted with what appear to be insignificant fragments of minor tales, Leland himself worked them up into the sort of "good read" for which he had long been famous.[40] Perhaps more significant in the long run, he put the story into such a position of prominence that it has exerted a strong influence on the interpretation of other, more authentic narratives. Even Joseph

Campbell relied primarily on Leland in his discussion of Abenaki and Micmac mythology.[41]

To the best of my knowledge, no one has done this sort of detective work with *Aradia*, but this insight to Leland's practice of his craft as of 1884 cannot be ignored when we turn to his later study of witches.

Aradia *and Modern Witchcraft*

After the publication of *Algonquin Legends*, Leland left North America again; he spent most of the rest of his life in Florence, Italy. There, he claimed, he met a woman called Maddalena who became his "collector of folk-lore."[42] She was "a young woman who would have been taken for a Gypsy in England, but in whose face, in Italy, I soon learned to know the antique Etruscan, with its strange mysteries, to which was added the indefinable glance of the Witch."[43] Besides seeing it in her eyes, Leland apparently was told that she was a witch by inheritance from her female ancestors. He claimed to have learned from her that witchcraft was "the Old Religion," earlier than Christianity, and that it had its own scripture. After keeping him waiting for years, Maddalena finally gave him a copy which he published as *Aradia*.

Alternating stories and ritual instructions, with Italian text as well as English rendering, *Aradia* tells of the goddess Diana and her beloved brother Lucifer, who is driven from paradise because of his pride in his beauty. Together they have a daughter, Aradia (Herodias). Seeing that the rich on earth have oppressed the poor and driven them into hiding in the woods, Diana sends Aradia to them as a kind of Messiah (Leland uses the term in his Appendix) to teach them witchcraft. Witchcraft, in *Aradia*, combines the celebration of nature's bounties with magical powers for use against the rich:

> And thus it shall be done: all shall sit down to the supper all naked, men and women, and, the feast over, they shall dance, sing, make music, and then love in the darkness, with all the lights extinguished; for it is the Spirit of *Diana* who extinguishes them, and so they will dance and make music in her praise.[44]

And when ye find a peasant who is rich,
Then ye shall teach the witch, your pupil, how
To ruin all his crops with tempests dire,
With lightning and with thunder (terrible),
And with the hail and wind. . . .

And when a priest shall do you injury
By his benedictions, ye shall do to him
Double the harm, and do it in the name
Of me, Diana, Queen of witches all!

And when the priests or the nobility
Shall say to you that you should put your faith
In the Father, Son, and Mary, then reply:
Your God, the Father, and Maria are
Three devils. . . .[45]

In his Appendix, Leland provides a commentary which spells out the implications of this scripture. He articulates a version of the neopagan paradigm, claiming that the poor were worse off under Christendom than they were before or since. He emphasizes the centrality of women and goddesses, arguing that female equality had been the keynote of the esoteric tradition—he names the Neoplatonists, Kabbalists, Gnosticism, "Heretic Christianity," and even the Knights Templar, as well as the Fox sisters.[46] And he insists that *Aradia* itself is very old—even though he claims to have seen only a recent copy.

There are, however, numerous problems with taking *Aradia* at face value. While no one disputes the fact that various folk customs have survived in Europe over many centuries, it is a very different thing to argue that an entirely separate religious tradition has maintained its continuity and integrity through almost two millennia of Christian dominance, generally without detection. The simpler explanation of *Aradia* is that it was created either by Leland or at his behest. He already had, ready to hand, everything he needed to invent his version of witchcraft before he issued this book. Names like Herodias and Lucifer have been common currency in Europe since the Vulgate, and Diana is familiar in this sort of context from the

Canon "Episcopi". As Elliot Rose noted, the general picture of witch-craft which emerges from *Aradia* bears a closer resemblance to the Inquisition's stereotyped heresy than to a survival of pre-Christian paganism. "The whole work reads much more as if one of its authors was consciously seeking to establish that the witch-cult was a cult of this particular nature. . . ."[47]

Most of the content which Leland ascribed to witchcraft, and the way he interpreted it as a protest movement among women and the poor, can be found in Michelet—who, let us remember, was at his most prominent when Leland was studying in Paris, and whom the American actually cites in his Appendix.[48] Leland's description of the sabbat, like Michelet's, gives a positive tone to the traditional written descriptions of witch ceremonies—gluttony and debauchery become celebrations of nature and fertility. Much of *Aradia* reflects the themes which concerned Leland throughout his life: folklore as a living link with the purity of human life in the days before civilization, and revolutionary social justice. *Aradia* makes so much more sense as a Leland production than as a Leland discovery that some historians of witchcraft, like Cohn, do not even trouble to refute it. Now that we have Parkhill's discoveries about how Leland went about generating his folklore material, it is difficult to believe that his story of witchcraft is any more reliable as a factual report than his story of Kluskap.

MARGARET MURRAY's *Witch-Cult*

While *Aradia* is often celebrated by Wiccans and ignored by histori-ans, the witchcraft theory of Margaret Murray (1863–1963) has suffered quite a different fate—often given only token acknowledgement by modern witches, it has been thoroughly and repeatedly demolished by scholars. Murray was an historian and anthropologist; like Jane Harrison, she was strongly influenced by Frazer and *The Golden Bough*. She did excavations in Egypt and wrote a respectable book on that subject, but she gained what fame she has from a series of books on European witchcraft.

The first, *The Witch-Cult in Western Europe* (1921), was a detailed examination of the records of European witch trials, complete with long quotations in the original languages and archaic spelling. Murray proposed to take all the testimony from the trials seriously except for the supernatural elements. Then she attempted to provide straight-forward rationalistic explanations—for instance, when witches reported that the Devil felt cold when he had intercourse with them, Murray proposed that an artificial phallus was used during the ceremonies.[49] From her study of this material, she asserted that witchcraft was the original religion of Europe, the legacy of an early dwarf race which gave rise to later folk tales of fairies. Even in the 1600s it was still a highly organized religious rival to Christianity. It centered on worship of a pre-Christian horned god (the "devil" who attended the meetings was supposedly a man wearing stag or elk horns) for whom she used the Latin names Janus or Dianus. This "Dianic cult" operated in small covens and held regular "sabbats" for worship and "esbats" for business meetings.

The content of Murray's witchcraft was shaped by Frazer rather than by Michelet and Leland, neither of whom appear in *Witch-Cult's* bibliography. She presented witchcraft as a nature religion focused on fertility; this theme was expressed through both sex magic and blood sacrifice. Murray emphasized that sacrifice was essential to the cult, with animals being slaughtered at the esbats and children on special occasions. Following Frazer, she argued that the god/chief was sacrificed every seven to nine years to restore the fertility of the earth; according to her, the deaths of famous individuals like King William Rufus of England and Joan of Arc were among these sacrifices.[50]

Murray made no suggestion that witchcraft was in any way a women's religion. She emphasized that the chief deity of the cult was a male god and most often took the form of a man when he appeared in a coven. The covens themselves generally had a male leader; Murray briefly entertained the possibility that the chief woman in a coven represented a Mother Goddess, but commented that this was rare and that if there had ever been a central goddess, she had long since been superseded by the god. Covens could be led by women, but most often the head female was merely substituting for the male.[51]

Both Goddess and High Priestess are almost invisible in Murray's rendition of witchcraft.

In *Witch-Cult*, Murray argued that Europe was Christianized from the top down; the witch-cult survived longest among peasants and the lower classes, although some members of the nobility continued to be involved. She wrote two later books, *The God of the Witches* (1933) and *The Divine King in England* (1954), in which she asserted that witchcraft was also the true but hidden religion of the European ruling classes through most of history, and that most of the kings of England had died scheduled, sacrificial deaths.

Almost nobody now takes the details of this theory seriously, particularly in its later form; trying to find a regular, cyclic pattern in the deaths of the English kings is enough to defeat most attempts. Both Rose and Cohn subjected Murray's theory to close scrutiny and rejected it almost root and branch. Cohn in particular went back to the original sources, the trial records Murray used, and demonstrated that she had made her case look far more persuasive than it is by means of selective quotation. She deleted so many of the supernatural elements in the confessions that what was left looked reasonable enough to bear the weight of her theory; in actual fact, however, this completely distorts the records themselves, where the natural and the supernatural are woven tightly together.[52] Wiccans appreciate Murray's confirmation of Leland's claim that witchcraft is Europe's old, original religion, but they much prefer Michelet's and Leland's descriptions of it.

It is interesting, therefore, that Murray's theory has been subject to more sustained attacks from historians than have the others. Purkiss suggests that the professional clique of male historians was singling out Murray for attack because of her sex as much as her faulty methodology. As Cohn and Rose themselves indicated, however, they targeted Murray because her theory, when they wrote, had achieved a surprising and disconcerting degree of prominence and influence. It had even been enshrined as the official word on witchcraft in successive editions of the *Encyclopedia Britannica*.[53]

Murray's theory requires this level of scrutiny for another reason. The fact is that when witchcraft suddenly appeared in modern times as a functioning religion, it was not in Italy or America, not in France or Germany or Switzerland, but in Murray's homeland of England. The first public witch was a man, an Englishman, in whom the trends and ideas we have been pursuing for the last several chapters finally coalesce into an operational new religion, and who received Murray's personal blessing. His is the last story we must hear, for he brought into being the first popular Goddess religion in Western society.

14

Gardner and the Goddess

The Goddess came right down and I was her mouthpiece.

Christine Hartley

As Ronald Hutton put it, "the public history of Wicca begins with the repeal of the Witchcraft Act of 1736 . . . a heavy-handed piece of Enlightenment rationalism."[1] By the 1730s, the formal witch hunts in Great Britain had already come to an end; it was generally presumed at this point that all reasonable people knew that there was no such thing as witchcraft. This Witchcraft Act replaced the legislation under which the actual hunts had been administered. For the next two centuries it was illegal to present oneself, or to accuse someone else, as a witch. This was essentially a law against lies and false witness. In June 1951, the British Parliament replaced this Witchcraft Act with the Fraudulent Mediums Act, which narrowed the scope of prosecution to those psychic performers who deliberately set out to bilk whatever clientele they could attract. Now, for those who might have wanted to claim to be witches, their greatest risk was ridicule.

It was not long before someone was willing to brave that risk in a larger cause. According to Aidan Kelly, an English newspaper story on July 29, 1951 announced the opening of Cecil H. Williamson's

Folklore Centre of Superstition and Witchcraft on the Isle of Man, with opening ceremonies by the "resident witch," Dr. Gerald B. Gardner.[2] Gardner thus became the first fully public witch of modern times. His leading role in the modern witchcraft revival is debatable only in terms of details; it is certain that there would be no Wicca, as we know it today, without him. All the same, Wicca is not something that sprang from his own head alone. He brought to it a great deal of acquired information and technique, and he found an audience which was prepared for what he had to offer. We need to get acquainted with both of these factors before we can make sense of Gardnerian witchcraft and its offspring.

WITCHCRAFT BEFORE GARDNER

As we saw in the last chapter, modern historians agree that the sort of witchcraft defined by the witch-hunters never existed. They disagree as to whether there was some other movement or social phenomenon which was the specific target of the hunts, or whether the hunts were self-sustaining and generated their victims almost at random. Historians seem to agree again on the point that, whatever was happening during the witch hunts, there is no organized witch cult which continued in existence from those times to the present.

Aidan Kelly has collected reports on several different groups that called themselves witches and seem to have existed in rural America prior to Gardner's career; he presumes that such groups probably existed in England as well.[3] Their basic principles, insofar as these can be articulated, are vastly different from the witchcraft associated with Gardner. On the whole, these groups seem to be expressions of the folk traditions of low magic, such as can be found in almost any culture in the world. This raises the large question of whether or not an anthropological, cross-cultural definition of witchcraft is possible, and what it might be.[4] We need not settle this question here, for the paths which lead us through British and American Wicca to the Goddess are quite specifically those which converged at the feet of Gerald Gardner.

In that connection, however, we must note an interesting development which had been taking place in Dion Fortune's occult order, the Fraternity of the Inner Light. Fortune, whom we met in Chapter 9, had established this group as an "outer court" for Moina Mathers's Alpha and Omega Lodge, her remnant of the Golden Dawn; after they quarreled, Fortune made the Fraternity an independent order. Fortune's teachings stressed a mystical approach to Christianity, in opposition to the orientalism which had been popularized by Theosophy. At the same time, many of her occult novels purported to portray pre-Christian British paganism and emphasized goddesses. In *The Sea Priestess* (1938), for example, she described magical marriage as a sacrament in which "the woman must take her ancient place as priestess . . . the initiator, not the initiated. . . . When the body of a woman is made an altar for the worship of the Goddess who is all beauty and magnetic life . . . then the Goddess enters the temple." Two of her most frequent sayings apparently were: "A religion without a goddess is halfway to atheism"; and, "All the gods are one god and all the goddesses are one goddess and there is one initiator."[5]

Some of her followers were profoundly attracted to her portrait of this supposedly indigenous heritage. Preeminent in the "pagan" section of the Fraternity was a partnership composed of Charles R. F. Seymour and Christine Hartley, whose magical diaries have been published by Alan Richardson. They performed visionary trance travels together, returning with mental images of scenes from their previous lives when, for instance, they supposedly officiated together in the Temple of the Sun on Atlantis.[6]

In various visions they reported encountering the deities of ancient civilizations, including goddesses like Isis. Sometimes they used a general title like "the Great Mother" or simply "the Goddess." On October 8, 1937, Seymour wrote, "The garden [in the vision] was full of scarlet flowers and sweet smelling bushes, and the Goddess said— a dedicated worshipping priestess and priest will always light my altar fires. Will you serve me and bring my joy and life and love to the hearts of men and women?" Part of Hartley's record for October 15 read, "Then at one time the Goddess came right down and I was her mouthpiece and spoke as she dictated, and then I was the priestess giving the responses. It was most strange and very wonderful."[7]

On June 21, 1938, Seymour recorded this thought: "I got the idea of linking the old symbolism of indigenous women's mysteries with the pagan mysteries of England right down to the present day and through the witchcraft period."[8] One week later, Hartley wrote the lines which have especially attracted the attention of Gardnerians and their observers:

> Started when I walked over the threshold of the house and felt witchcraft all around me. Went upstairs extremely desirous of being a witch. When we had settled down I kept getting little pictures of Ishtar worship through the ages, the most constant being one of silhouetted witches in pointed hats and ragged skirts dancing round a fire. . . . She spoke through me . . . she stressed again the necessity for Joy in worship and that she was the goddess of Love of Life as well as of Love in the more conventional sense. She said that people had forgotten her and that her altars were broken down and that she had been transformed into the Virgin Mary which was not the fullness of her worship but only one side of it. . . . I could see Yesod [the ninth sphere on the Tree of Life] misty and cloud-like and at last I got the beginning of the vision as I stood with her just inside a tunnel and saw the fields of Ishtar. . . .[9]

Here are four private texts from 1937 and 1938, more than a year before Gardner would ever claim to have penetrated a coven of witches. Together, they contain almost everything we have been seeking: the Goddess herself, openly worshipped in ages before recorded history, the epitome of natural beauty, joy, and love; her immanence, as she speaks through the priestess; the destruction of her altars and the mutilation of her being by the Christian religion; the call for priestess and priest, in that order, to restore her worship on the earth; all linked with the idea of witchcraft.

Seymour also wrote an essay entitled "The Ancient Nature Worship" in which he claimed, "The witch-hunting of the fourteenth to eighteenth centuries was an effort to stamp out an old religion surviving from pre-Christian days. Its sin was that it celebrated with joy and laughter the great nature festivals." As Kelly comments, "He had obviously been reading Margaret Murray,"[10] and probably Leland too. But Seymour and Hartley were not witches at this point; at most, they were "desirous" of becoming so. They were not making herbal medicine or hexing their neighbours' crops. They were cultured, well-read individuals (Hartley was a book editor who had handled the obstreperous T. E. Lawrence, "Lawrence of Arabia"); even more importantly, they were experienced high magicians of the Golden Dawn lineage with all that it entails. It is this refined expression of the elite esoteric tradition, and not the grassroots, mother-to-daughter tradition of peasant folklore, which typifies the beginnings of Wicca.

GARDNER BEFORE WITCHCRAFT

Gerald Brosseau Gardner (1884–1964) was an asthmatic English child whose Irish nurse, "Com," had a strong penchant for travel.[11] She persuaded his parents that he would be much better off wintering in a warmer climate. As a result, his upbringing was a series of travels and stops through Europe, Africa, and Southern Asia; this ended only when Com finally married a plantation owner in Ceylon in 1900, when Gardner was in his teens. The Bracelin biography of Gardner suggests that the new family's home was not far from the bungalow which was shared briefly by Aleister Crowley and Allan Bennett soon after the turn of the century.[12]

Gardner was essentially self-educated, reading indiscriminately anything he could pick up along the way. In later years he said he held a doctorate from the University of Singapore, but apparently the university did not even exist at the date when he claimed to have received the award.[13] Gardner's working career was divided between the British imperial civil service in Southeast Asia and a rubber plantation in Malaya. Keenly interested in folklore and magic, he acquainted himself with several tribal peoples and published a serious study of the *kris*, the Malayan ceremonial knife. Like many expatriate Englishmen all over the world, he became a Freemason; he also dabbled in Asian philosophy and magic, sunbathing and nudism.

Kelly emphasizes the likelihood that Gardner's upbringing also featured corporal punishment in the form of caning, as was the case for many English males of his time. In his case, Kelly believes that it produced a "sexual addiction": "it was forced upon him, as it was upon most Englishmen of his generation . . . even as adults, they needed to be beaten on their bare buttocks (or at least to fantasize about that) in order to achieve an erection and so be capable of sexual intercourse. It is eminently clear from Gardner's sexual interests and tastes that this had been his experience, and that fantasizing was not sufficient to meet his needs."[14]

Gardner retired to England in 1936 and used his free time to indulge in the activities he enjoyed most.[15] He joined both a nudist club in the nearby New Forest area of southern England and the Folk-Lore Society which had been founded by Leland, serving on its Council in the late 1940s. He attended Spiritualist séances but found them boring, and he kept up his Masonic connections. According to the Bracelin biography, he went for a walk one day in 1938 and stumbled across something called the First Rosicrucian Theatre in England. Although he was less than impressed with the play he saw, he was apparently intrigued by the group performing it and got involved with them. The theater was a project of the Fellowship of Crotona, many of whose members were both Rosicrucians and Co-Masons. One was the current head of English Co-Masonry: Mabel Besant-Scott, daughter and successor of Theosophy's Annie and now a close neighbor of Gardner's.[16] Two of the others were Charles Seymour and Christine Hartley, the disciples of Dion Fortune whom we just met. Yet another was Louis Wilkinson, a longtime friend of Aleister Crowley, who would later conduct Crowley's funeral and then serve as one of his literary executors.

Gardner himself claimed that he noticed a small group of people within the Fellowship of Crotona which seemed distinct from the other members and was centered around "Old Dorothy" Fordham, née Clutterbuck. Investigating further, he found that they were an authentic coven of traditional witches. He realized the rarity of such a find and sought initiation into the coven in order to learn as much as he could about them before witchcraft died out entirely, as it seemed about to do. They initiated him, so he said, in September of 1939.

GARDNERIAN WITCHCRAFT

Aidan Kelly, a Wiccan trained in biblical criticism, applied his skills to Gardner's archive and produced a meticulous account of the changes which took place as the witchcraft "revival" unfolded. It will suffice for our purposes here to summarize his findings.

Gardner asserted that following his initiation into the coven he participated in several magical rites designed to forestall a Nazi invasion of England during the Battle of Britain the following year. His first publication on witchcraft, however, was a novel entitled *High Magic's Aid*, which did not appear until 1949. He said that he had had to wait for Old Dorothy's permission to reveal as much about witchcraft as appeared in that story. Kelly has compared this published text with *Ye Bok of ye Art Magical*, Gardner's early private ritual notebook, to reconstruct the first stages of Wicca.

The major finding in Kelly's investigation is the fact that virtually everything in the earliest stratum of Gardnerian witchcraft can be traced to literary sources which were available to him, and nothing indicates that there was any practicing coven at all before 1939. The basic framework of early Gardnerian witchcraft was taken from Murray's *Witch-Cult in Western Europe*, which provided the terminology of covens, esbats and sabbats along with the horned god. This was developed into a set of rituals using material from several of Crowley's books, MacGregor Mathers's *Greater Key of Solomon*, gleanings from Frazer and Harrison, and the Co-Masonic, Rosicrucian, and Golden Dawn backgrounds of the Crotona members themselves, among whom the first witches were recruited.[17]

The extent of Gardner's relationship with Crowley is a matter of some debate. On two points there is no doubt: the two men met personally more than once, finding considerable common ground, with Crowley initiating Gardner into the fourth degree of the OTO; and, there are extensive verbatim passages from Crowley's works in Gardner's early witchcraft rituals. Witnesses disagree over the actual extent of their friendly collaboration, which seems to have been confined to the last year of Crowley's life. There is a widely circulated story to the effect that Gardner actually hired Crowley to write some of the ceremonies; Valiente suggests that this rumor arose from the fact that Gardner paid Crowley £300 for his OTO initiation, and then used some OTO texts in his ceremonies.[18] It is generally agreed, however, that the central principle of Wiccan ethics (the so-called Wiccan rede, "An ye harm none, do what ye will") is an adaptation of Crowley's maxim, "'Do what thou wilt' shall be the whole of the law."[19]

Ye Bok seems to have served as the rough draft for some passages in *High Magic's Aid* and in Gardner's first *Book of Shadows*. As Doreen Valiente noted, the phrase "book of shadows" was not part of the earliest Wicca—it was completely unknown until the 1949 publication of a magazine article about the practice of shadow divination in India.[20] Gardner most likely took the phrase from there; since then, it has become the conventional title for a Wiccan's magical diary.

The year 1949, as attested by *Ye Bok* and *High Magic's Aid*, was a milestone in the shaping of Gardnerian witchcraft. Several classic Gardnerian ceremonies had appeared by this point: the casting of the circle at the beginning of ceremonies, which is clearly based on Mathers; a pentacle consecration taken from Crowley; and the ceremony of Drawing Down the Moon, invoking the Goddess in the body of the Priestess. In the third of these, the ritual resembles the marriage passage in Fortune's *Sea Priestess*, while the actual ritual text is a blend of Crowley and *Aradia*. The three rituals of initiation have some obvious Masonic elements embellished with borrowings from Crowley, Dion Fortune, and even Rudyard Kipling.[21]

Kelly made two particularly significant points about this stage of Wicca's development. First, his identification of Gardner's literary sources leaves little doubt that Gardner's own witchcraft texts were his personal creation and not something handed on to him from an ancient tradition; paradoxically, then, Wicca is not a revival of an old pagan religion, but a modern paganization of materials which originated either within the Judeo-Christian tradition (the Kabbalah) or in direct reaction to it (Crowley). Second, Gardner had put his personal stamp on the coven—the initiation rituals include nudity and the necessity of scourging or whipping as "purification" and as a preliminary to the "Great Rite," the sex magic of the third degree.

These features were fully in place by the time Gardner published his first "non-fiction" book on his new religion, *Witchcraft Today*. It appeared in 1954, following two significant events: the repeal of the Witchcraft Act, which allowed the public affirmation of witchcraft; and the death of Old Dorothy, which Gardner allegedly took as a release from his vow of silence, and which also removed the person who might have been in the best position to contradict him.

Thus freed to speak to the public, Gardner took the pose of a disinterested investigator describing a little-known religion which was on the verge of extinction. He described himself as an anthropologist, and then wrote of witnessing and being told those things which he himself had in fact been composing over the previous decade.[22] The book appeared with an encouraging foreword from Margaret Murray herself, and it gave currency to several ideas which are prevalent among witches today: the use of the Anglo-Saxon word *wica*, which Gardner erroneously translated as "the Wise"; the definition of magic as psychological or parapsychological, not strictly supernatural; Gage's claim that nine million people perished during the witch hunts; and the benediction "Blessed be."[23] Gardner presented, as a parallel to the Christian story of the crucifixion and resurrection of Jesus, the following myth of the Goddess ("G.").

Now G. had never loved, but she would solve all mysteries, even the mystery of Death, and so she journeyed to the nether lands. The guardians of the portals challenged her. "Strip off thy garments, lay aside thy jewels, for nought may ye bring with you into this our land." So she laid down her garments and her jewels and was bound as are all who enter the realms of Death, the mighty one.

Such was her beauty that Death himself knelt and kissed her feet, saying, "Blessed be thy feet that have brought thee in these ways. Abide with me, but let me place my cold hand on thy heart. And she replied: "I love thee not. Why doest thou cause all things that I love and take delight in to fade and die?" "Lady," replied Death, "'tis age and fate, against which I am helpless. Age causes all things to wither; but when men die at the end of time, I give them rest and peace and strength so that they may return. But you, you are lovely. Return not; abide with me." But she answered: "I love thee not." Then said Death: "As you receive not my hand on your heart, you must receive Death's scourge." "It is fate, better so," she said, and she knelt. Death scourged her and she cried, "I know the pangs of love." And Death said, "Blessed be," and gave her the fivefold kiss, saying: "Thus only may you attain to joy and knowledge."

And he taught her all the mysteries, and they loved and were one; and he taught her all the magics. For there are three great events in the life of man—love, death and resurrection in the new body—and magic controls them all. To fulfil love you must return again at the same time and place as the loved ones, and you must remember and love her or him again. But to be re-born you must die and be ready for a new body; to die you must be born; without love you may not be born, and this is all the magic.[24]

Many of the key elements of Gardnerian witchcraft are reflected in this myth. We may note particularly the centrality of the Goddess as a character; the ritually oriented nudity, binding, and scourging; the belief in reincarnation; and the emphasis on sexual love as the epitome of magic. As a component of witchcraft, this myth was new when it appeared in *Witchcraft Today*; it was soon made the basis of a revised ritual of second-degree initiation. Although the Goddess is prominent in the tale, she and her Priestess were still in some ways secondary to the God and the Priest, who in practice directed the rituals. The Priest acted as ceremonial magician in casting the circle, so that the Priestess could then function as a folk-witch; it was the Priest who, by his power, "drew down the moon" into the Priestess.[25]

These sex roles began to change in the course of the 1950s, when Doreen Valiente was serving as Gardner's High Priestess. Valiente was already active in occult circles when she heard of Gardner in 1953 and sought him out. Informed enough to spot the passages from Crowley in the rituals, and knowing that the Great Beast's name was enough to discourage many potential inquirers, she obtained Gardner's permission to rewrite many of the rituals. Gardner and Valiente also worked together on preparations for his later book, *The Meaning of*

Witchcraft (1959), which was a more thoroughgoing attempt to create a continuous history of Wicca from the Stone Age to the present.[26]

By the mid-1960s, the Goddess was indubitably the supreme deity in Wicca, and ritual authority was vested in the High Priestess. Kelly traces much of the new Goddess theology to Graves's *White Goddess*; he suggests that Valiente used Graves's material to help her replace the passages from Crowley which she was trying to eliminate. Chas Clifton, on the other hand, has argued that Dion Fortune's novels—which predate Graves's Goddess books and were certainly familiar to Gardner's intimates—have been underestimated for their influence on Wicca. Although Valiente acknowledges the many rituals she redesigned and the influence of Fortune's and Graves's ideas within Wicca, she has denied being the one who brought them together. She insists that the Goddess was already central to Gardnerianism when she joined, so this is one detail which remains uncertain.[27]

The crucial fact is that after all our journeys to Malta and Crete, to Goethe's Weimar and Enfantin's Paris, led on by Lévi's ideal Woman and the actual HPB, we have finally found our Western Goddess religion.

Wicca after Gardner

Kelly makes a persuasive case that all organized witchcraft in the English-speaking world merits the title "Gardnerian." Some groups operate in a direct line of initiation from Gardner's original work, the Wiccan equivalent of apostolic succession. Others are more indirect, having broken ranks at some point in the past forty years; still others, perhaps the majority, are self-starting groups which use and adapt Gardnerian concepts and ritual designs which are easily accessible in books. Most of the distinctive features of Gardnerianism are shared to a greater or lesser degree among the visibly practicing groups today, even though they cannot be found in the documented records of witchcraft in any era before Gardner's. Such notions do, almost always, appear in the esoteric and other sources he knew and from which he evidently took them. A list of these features includes the following:

- the password "perfect love and perfect trust"
- casting the circle
- raising "the cone of power"
- binding and scourging
- the preeminence of the Goddess and the High Priestess
- belief in reincarnation
- the phrases "so mote it be" and "blessed be"
- the nine million witch-hunt victims

Gardner's sources, as we have seen, included the Masonic and Rosicrucian practices of his own time; Asian ideas familiar from his years there, and/or mediated through Theosophy; and books like those of Leland, Murray, Mathers, and Crowley. There is nothing, on the other hand, that can be reliably identified as a living tradition of native British witchcraft. As Kelly bluntly expressed it, "If Gardnerians are Witches, then they are the first true Witches in history; if those other people back then were Witches, then Gardnerians are not."[28] Margot Adler said it another way, singling out "the most authentic and hallowed Gardnerian tradition—stealing from any source that didn't run away too fast."[29]

Goddess spirituality, when it can be distinguished from actual witchcraft, is marked by a decreased reliance on the Wiccan infrastructure of covens and initiatory rituals, and a countervailing increase in political consciousness and content. While Wicca itself is a product of wartime and postwar England, Goddess spirituality is very much the child of American second-wave radical feminism; to come full circle in our inquiry, we now need only to bridge that gap.

Gardner welcomed and sought publicity, and by the end of his life there were several British covens made up of initiates he had attracted. Raymond Buckland had read *Witchcraft Today*, as well as Murray's *Witch-Cult*, before contacting Gardner and eventually being initiated in 1964. English by birth, he was resident in Long Island by this time and established the first Gardnerian coven in the United States. After operating the coven and a witchcraft museum for almost a decade, and serving as America's leading spokesman for Gardnerianism, Buckland broke away to form his own "tradition."

Operating under the name Seax-Wica, it employed Germanic-Saxon terminology and symbolism and minimized the hierarchical and secretive aspects of organized witchcraft. Eventually he withdrew from the limelight altogether, but he was pivotal in establishing Wicca in the United States. One high-profile Wiccan brought into the Gardnerian tradition by Buckland is Margot Adler herself, the National Public Radio figure, author of *Drawing Down the Moon*, and granddaughter of psychologist Alfred Adler.

Alex Sanders was an Englishman who had to try more than once to get a Gardnerian initiation. One High Priestess, Patricia Crowther, decided after meeting him that he was unsuitable. Another one apparently did initiate him, but instead of fitting into the Gardnerian movement, Sanders started making a name for himself in the media as the so-called King of the Witches. He claimed to represent a pre-Gardnerian, traditional form of witchcraft. This was his story: as a young boy, he accidentally discovered his grandmother nude, inside a magic circle, performing some occult rite. She quickly initiated him into the witch cult, partly so that he would be bound by the oath of secrecy not to reveal what she had been doing.

His tradition, which became known as Alexandrian witchcraft, was in most respects indistinguishable from Gardnerianism. Sanders proved an embarrassment to many other Wiccans. He recruited his Witch Queen, 18-year-old Maxine Morris, by persuading her to take part in a nude outdoor ritual and secretly ensuring that the tabloid press knew about it. The next day, her picture was on the front pages, and she was irretrievably committed. They married and worked together for eight years before Sanders's flagrant bisexuality helped to destroy their relationship, and no one succeeded him as King when he died.[30] Janet and Stewart Farrar are probably the best known Alexandrians. They have several jointly authored witchcraft books to their credit, including *The Witches' Goddess* (1987), a survey of female archetypes and deities complete with specific rituals for worshipping each of the latter.[31]

A seemingly independent American tradition of witchcraft was established by Victor Anderson. This was his story: as a young boy, he accidentally discovered an old woman nude, inside a magic circle;

she quickly initiated him into the witch cult. Anderson's "Faery Tradition" was developed in conjunction with a younger man known by his Welsh pseudonym, Gwydion Pendderwen. Pendderwen had contact with the Alexandrian tradition, meeting both Sanders and Stewart Farrar during a visit to Britain in the 1970s; as a result, the Faery Tradition rituals contain Alexandrian material (although, given the nature of the relationship between them, this is often hard to distinguish from the Gardnerian version). Pendderwen wrote songs and rituals which have remained widely popular among neopagans, although he died in an automobile collision in 1982.

By this time, the Faery Tradition had already recruited its most successful exponent: Miriam "Starhawk" Simos. She has been a central figure in taking the Goddess beyond the confines of Wicca into the broader stream of contemporary feminism and political activism. She is reportedly active in both mixed covens and female-only groups, as well as teaching in Matthew Fox's Creation Spirituality Institute and giving seminars and workshops across North America and overseas. Her first book, *The Spiral Dance* (1979), concludes with an elaborate table of correspondences illustrating the blend of high and low magic which Gardner set in motion. The moon, for instance, is correlated to woman, cycles, and water; to the letter S and the numbers 3 and 9; to willow trees, bananas, and ginseng; to the angel Gabriel, the goddesses Artemis and Isis, and the kabbalistic sphere Yesod.[32] Starhawk's bibliography includes not only the expected names from Wicca and feminist spirituality, but others now familiar to us: Mathers, Frazer, Harrison's *Prolegomena*, Besant and Leadbeater, Crowley, and Graves.

As we saw in Chapter 2, the teaming of Starhawk and Zsuzsanna Budapest was a significant step in coupling Wiccan Goddess worship with radical feminism. Budapest, a Hungarian refugee in her childhood, claims to have coined the term "feminist spirituality."[33] She started her Susan B. Anthony Coven #1 in 1971 as an expression of the lesbian separatist perspective which goes by the name of the Dianic Tradition (referring to the goddess Diana, not the Dianus of Margaret Murray). The rituals in her *Holy Book of Women's Mysteries* are necessarily innovative and liberally sprinkled with the folklore of her homeland. Nevertheless, Gardnerian influence is still evident in the phrases "So mote it be" and "Blessed be," the casting of the circle and the password "perfect love and perfect trust," the Murrayite esbats and sabbats, and the use of Leland's Aradia story. All of these appear in Gardner's books and rituals. He is not included in Budapest's list of suggested further reading, but the names of Helena Blavatsky, Alice Bailey, Jane Harrison (only for *Prolegomena*), and Robert Graves do appear. Budapest herself told Margot Adler that she was familiar with "Dianic Witchcraft, the English literature" before she started her coven.[34] Kelly's observation that all Wicca is Gardnerian seems to hold true even in the case of Budapest.

WICCA AND THE GODDESS

In Chapter 2, we saw that today's Goddess spirituality is constituted from a combination of modern witchcraft with the renewed interest in the matriarchy theory which accompanied the rise of radical feminism in the late 1960s. This represents a new, though hardly unprecedented, variant in the blending of religion and politics. The fact remains that Gardnerian Wicca was the first modern Western Goddess religion. The appearance of the Goddess in other radical feminist circles, and then in churches and universities, did not occur until after the establishment of modern witchcraft as a viable new religion. The major Goddess books show clear signs of their dependence, not only on Wicca itself, but on the various sources of witchcraft and matriarchal theory which we have been tracing.

We have already seen, for instance, that Davis's *First Sex* was strongly affected by the appearance of the Bollingen Bachofen, since quotations from it head several of her chapters. Briffault, the Jungian Robert Eisler, and Robert Graves also figure prominently, along with occultists like Lewis Spence. The same is true of other major proponents of the Goddess; as time goes on, the pattern of mutual interdependence becomes clearer. Merlin Stone, who documented her sources very precisely, made extensive use of Bachofen, Frazer, Harrison's *Prolegomena*, Murray, Briffault, Graves, and Joseph Campbell. Riane Eisler repeatedly cites Bachofen, Harrison's

Prolegomena, Briffault, Graves, Jungians like Campbell and Neumann, Gimbutas, and Stone herself, as well as matriarchal philosopher Mary Daly. Elinor Gadon, in turn, relies on Bachofen, Harrison's *Prolegomena*, Briffault, Graves, Jung, Neumann, Campbell, Dames, and Gimbutas as well as other established Goddess proponents like Stone, Budapest, Starhawk, Carol Christ, Daly, and Eisler.

They used many other sources as well, of course, and I am not suggesting that any of them failed to read widely in the course of preparing their various books. Nor, for that matter, am I attempting to establish some sort of guilt by association, as though I could discredit the entire Goddess movement by linking it, superficially and artificially, through Gardner to Aleister Crowley and other unsavory characters. The point is that Goddess spirituality as we know it today is a version of the neopagan paradigm, from the ancient utopian matriarchies through the oppressive reign of Christendom, epitomized in the witch hunts with their alleged nine million victims, to the return of the Goddess as queen of a post-Christian and postmodern world; immanentism and intuitive epistemology are among its dominant characteristics. These are the features of Goddess spirituality which characterize it as a religious movement and allow us to locate it within the general history of Western religion, spirituality, and ideology.

The broad scope and wide range of our investigations in this book have been necessary to accomplish that task. This way, I could demonstrate that Goddess spirituality is neither the modern expression of an actual pre-Christian, pre-Jewish, pre-Greek, utopian, female-centered civilization, nor a creative contemporary innovation in religion; it is neither primordial nor pristine. It is, instead, one of the latest adaptations of the Western esoteric tradition as it was filtered through Romanticism—and a very effective and marketable adaptation it has proven to be. Without Bachofen's invention of the matriarchy theory, which appealed to neopagan psychologists and to political and literary radicals, and without Michelet's imaginary version of witchcraft as a religious protest against Christian patriarchy, which appealed to spiritual seekers on the fringes of serious occultism, we would never have heard of the Goddess. There were goddesses aplenty in ancient times, but "the Goddess" as known to twentieth-century feminist neopaganism is a different phenomenon with its own, recent pedigree.

One feature of Aeschylus's *Oresteia* which consistently offends the Goddess writers is the myth which tells that the goddess Athena sprang into existence from the head of her father Zeus, without being born of a mother. Our lengthy investigation leads to the recognition that today's Goddess, the figurehead of radical feminist spirituality, has no mother either. She has not one, but two fathers: the patrician, patriarchal Bachofen, and the passionate, maternal Michelet; Gerald Gardner, for good measure, plays the role of midwife. The Goddess, in short, represents the imaginary feminine ideal of Romantic men.

The modern Goddess religion is another manifestation of the European neopagan counterculture, which has been active and growing since Romantic times; these roots are obscured by the fact that this newest manifestation took place in America, an ocean away from its immediate forebears. Moreover, it is indeed a religion, even when it is taught as history or therapy in modern universities. Partly because of its alliance with and usefulness to a vocal and visible political movement, gender feminism, Goddess spirituality seems well on the way to becoming the most successful of all these neopagan manifestations in the English-speaking world.

Back to the Garden—or the Jungle?

ODDESS SPIRITUALITY is not simply a theory about the origins of civilization; it is also a vehicle for the social agenda of radical gender feminism. Far from being a curiosity of history or academic theory, this is a movement which is propagating its prescription for social and cultural transformation in and through some of the leading institutions of Western society—a stunning achievement for a religion less than half a century old. Clearly, it has not accomplished this in isolation: Goddess spirituality is an extreme expression of a much larger upheaval in the modern social order. Nevertheless, we can recognize beyond serious question that the ideas and values associated explicitly or implicitly with the Goddess are among those which are, in fact, altering profoundly the way we live, love, work, worship, and speak.

This study has been a twofold exercise in history: an investigation of the Goddess movement's false claims to ancient origins, and an exploration of its actual roots in the Western esoteric tradition. It remains now to recall the characteristic and salient features of the Goddess movement as we discovered them, and then to assess the role these principles are playing in the ongoing efforts to achieve a radical transformation of Western civilization.

The Esoteric Tradition
and the "Return" of the Goddess

During the Renaissance, age-old practices of magic and divination were grafted together into a coherent worldview which was dominated by the themes of polarity and correspondence and informed by mystical philosophies like Neoplatonism, Gnosticism, and Hermeticism. The result was a set of alternative traditions which regarded the cosmos as an organism, animated by an immanent spiritual presence which was accessible within the individual soul. One of the most distinctive elements in the esoteric tradition across the centuries has been this tendency to focus on the immanence of the divine or the spiritual, at the expense of transcendence.

This was most evident in the emphasis given to the notion of the human being as the microcosm—the idea that everything outside us is also within us, even God or the gods, so that each of us is subjectively the deity of our own universe. Our own physical nature is one of those many dimensions of reality which are interlinked through the doctrine of correspondence. There are planets, constellations, metals, numbers, and even gods and spirits which correspond to our various bodily organs and energies. While one product of this worldview is the tradition of holistic medicine associated with Paracelsus, another is the more general principle that immanent spirituality is inseparable from our physical being. In a profound sense, it is the very fact that we are alive, our organic biology itself, which is divine.

This belief can be elaborated in ways which emphasize either individualism or communalism. Traditional high magicians like Paracelsus, Cornelius Agrippa, and John Dee usually pursued the quest in solitary fashion or with a single close colleague. In these cases, it is the individual who is the microcosm of the universe, the organic divinity, and not a particular mass of people. When occult organizations first emerged in such forms as Rosicrucianism and unorthodox Freemasonry, they provided instruction and initiation for individuals who sought the path of illumination. Those who committed themselves to this arduous search, however, typically placed themselves under the authority of a hierarchy of seen and unseen superiors whose spiritual accomplishments had supposedly reached an advanced level. Here, part of the allure of the esoteric tradition was and is the satisfaction and excitement of being grafted onto a secretive brotherhood which has mastered the mysteries of existence and reveals them progressively to worthy initiates. These two tendencies towards individualism and communal identity were both reinforced in the nineteenth-century Romantic, neopagan reaction to the Enlightenment.

The Enlightenment had already brought a mood of individualism to the fore in society at large. Much of Enlightenment thought was founded on the rejection of traditional, external authorities in favor of one's own personal judgment in all areas of thought and life. The idea of the social contract envisioned a societal order which was rationally designed according to the wishes of the individuals who created it, and which was founded on their willing consent to participate. At the same time, however, Enlightenment materialism reduced the ultimate significance of human beings by denying the relevance, or even the reality, of their spiritual dimension. Max Weber's phrase "the disenchantment of the world" applies with particular poignancy to this diminution of what it means to be human.[1]

This paradox in Enlightenment-style individualism led to some dramatic responses in the Romantic era. On the one hand, the dignity accorded to the free individual was taken to an extreme; on the other, the intrinsic spirituality and the ultimate significance of human beings was defiantly reaffirmed. Drawing on the heritage of the esoteric tradition, Romantic neopagans sought to re-spiritualize the world at large and the human being in particular. They commonly emphasized the immanence of the divine within the human person, located precisely in his or her nature as a living organism. This led sometimes to a sort of narcissism, a belief that exploring and expressing the self was the same thing as discovering God. Neopaganism offers the highly seductive invitation to assert one's inner divinity by breaking all boundaries and escaping all limits. It tells us that we are not just accidental collections of molecules, or bags of skin full of membranes, organs, blood, and gastric juices; we are not even creatures and servants of a supreme being to whom we owe our selves and our lives. We are, instead, deities in our own personal and subjective worlds. On this point, the attitude of the stereotypical Romantic is at the opposite extreme from the views we might expect of a materialistic modernist.

This attitude was expressed metaphorically by some of the most influential Romantic writers and dramatists. Goethe's transformation of Faust from a villain to a hero was not unique, but merely one of the most striking examples. Faust was already a potent symbol in European culture of the individual who throws off all external restraint in the quest of personal power and experience, but it was Goethe who made Faust succeed and triumph. Further, it was not only Faust whose fictional excesses made him an inspiration for later neopagans. The Knights Templar and the Renaissance witches were eventually canonized as martyrs of the esoteric tradition. This was not because these groups were thought to be innocent of all charges against them. On the contrary, it was because modern neopagans actually believed many of the accusations and twisted them to match their own Romantic, occult religiosity; then they were able to claim that the Templars and witches were their persecuted forebears.

In the occult revival, the quest for personal deification was undertaken in all seriousness. The members of the Golden Dawn sought to experience their own divinity through ritual and trance, while Aleister Crowley acted it out in almost every way he could imagine. Theosophy introduced an array of Eastern concepts, terminology, and techniques to those engaged on this quest. Related phenomena like Jungian psychology show the same tendencies at work, using another different range of vocabulary. In numerous manifestations of the esoteric tradition, the discovery of the deity within the individual soul is presented as the ultimate goal of human endeavor.

On the other hand, the tendency to associate immanent divinity with the community received even stronger emphasis under the influence of Romanticism. If human beings are really nothing more than temporary physical entities whose only destiny is to enjoy what pleasure and security they can before their time expires, then the

Enlightenment notion of a state based on a social contract is all that is really necessary. Such an artificial and mundane definition of the community, however, can feel just as demeaning as individualistic materialism to those who are particularly sensitive. When Enlightenment philosophers disenchanted the world by eliminating spirituality from it, they also dissolved the intangible bonds of community by means of their skepticism towards the traditional institutions of family, church, and state.

Romantics sought to re-enchant the world as a whole by asserting the immanence of the divine, its constant presence in the earth and in human beings; in the same way, they also attempted to restore the sense of community by grounding it in organic nature. From the Germanic folk-soul of Fichte and Savigny to the messianic revolutionary France of Michelet, we observe a sustained effort at defining the national community along the lines of blood, ethnic kinship, and shared corporate history (a history which could be made as glorious and inspirational as any writer or speaker wished). The individual was invited to discover his or her fulfillment and true significance within the context of the group to which he or she belonged by nature and by birth—not merely by choice and whim.

The esoteric tradition had long postulated that divinity inheres in biology. Now the Romantics opened the way to the belief that those things which either unite us or distinguish us organically from each other may be the most important things of all. It was not rational individualism but Romantic nationalism which decreed that all Germans and all Italians should be united in single states, or that Slavs, Hungarians, and Greeks should be free from the alien rule of Austrians and Turks, or that people of Jewish descent did not belong in European states. In this fashion, the Romantic inclination towards personal narcissism was converted into communal tribalism. The history of European nationalism in the past century shows clearly that the refusal of moral limits, the claim to unimpeded self-fulfillment, also carried over from the personal sphere to the political.

The occult revival took this theme just as seriously as it did the idea of personal deification. Ethnic trappings became increasingly prominent in neopagan activities, whether it was the pseudo-Celtic mysticism and Isis-worship of MacGregor and Moina Mathers, the Egyptian and Indian ambience of Theosophy, the Aryan visions of Guido von List and Jörg Lanz von Liebenfels, or Dion Fortune's quest for the British folk-soul. These observations illustrate how easily the notion of divine immanence blends with the neopagan paradigm. The Romantic ideal for society was to restore the human community on the basis of our organic existence, the immanence of divinity in our biological being. To be persuasive, this ideal would have to include an impressive account of how "natural" human groups developed; it must also explain what has gone so wrong that a restoration has become necessary. In partisan hands, this might well mean the idealization of one group's origins and history, and perhaps even the concomitant demonization of another.

These purposes can be accomplished in two steps: first, by appealing to the far-off past of a people to provide their essential identity, suitably embellished to enhance their self-esteem; and, second, by condemning the dominant forces of the times since then, which are usually identified as the Judeo-Christian tradition and the Enlightenment. The esoteric tradition had already founded its worldview on the ancients as it understood them, particularly the Neoplatonists, Gnostics and Hermeticists. The Romantic neopagans and occultists blended this idealized view of the past with their predisposition towards organicism and communal immanentism, and emerged with their various ethnic versions of the neopagan paradigm.

In terms of the history of Western religion, this is the context within which the modern Goddess movement developed. Its central themes and practices, particularly its insistence on divine immanence, organicism, and the interconnectedness of all things are in a direct line of descent from Renaissance high magic through Romanticism and the occult revival. In keeping with earlier versions of the neopagan paradigm, the Judeo-Christian religious tradition, the Indo-European cultures of Greece and Rome, and their modern heirs of the Enlightenment are still cast as the villains who usurped and destroyed the healthy primordial ways. What makes the Goddess movement distinctive within the esoteric tradition is the fact that it applies the principle of divine immanence in our organic existence to the dimension of sex rather than to individuality, race, or ethnicity. The high status of women as a biological group is presented as the crucial societal component of Goddess cultures. Goddess spirituality is, in short, a contemporary expression of the esoteric tradition, shaped by the ways in which this tradition was filtered through Romanticism.

As we saw previously, precursors of equity feminism can be found among Enlightenment thinkers who argued in favor of individual freedom and the removal of all artificial barriers to achievement which had been erected by tradition. This implied that women should be made equal to men as individuals in the eyes of the law, and that they should have access to the same educational and other opportunities as men. The thrust of this approach was and is to regard both men and women as unique individuals, and not primarily as stereotyped members of two distinct sexes.

By way of contrast, the organic element in Romantic thought led to an emphasis on the general biological differences between the sexes, ascribing supreme significance to the femaleness of women and the maleness of men. At the same time, the prized Romantic values of emotion, intuition, affinity with nature, and boundless love coincided with the qualities which traditional stereotypes had already assigned to women. These notions combined in the Romantic idealization of the female. Novalis's Sophia, the various "Mothers" and other female characters of Goethe's *Faust*, Enfantin's female messiah, Michelet's Mme. Dumesnil, Comte's Mme. de Vaux, and Constant's vision of a matriarchal New Age all display this elevation of womankind to the status of a loving and nurturing savior whom men must serve and adore, since they cannot fully emulate her.

Here we see themes typical of gender feminism: it is the quintessentially and characteristically female which needs liberation and which the world itself requires for its welfare, not the personal uniqueness of individual women. Here also lie the roots of the Goddess movement, with its insistence that the ultimate divinity does not transcend gender but is specifically and emphatically female— and that she constitutes our best and perhaps only path to regeneration for precisely that reason.

In the nineteenth century, gender feminism was largely the preserve of men; it was their idealization of women, not the realities of average men's and women's lives, which proceeded to inform and govern the early stages of the occult revival and the invention of modern witchcraft. Constant maintained his matriarchal vision after he became Eliphas Lévi and made high magic accessible to the wider public, including women. Michelet became progressively more insistent that society needed women's allegedly superior love and spirituality as he came at last to write his witchcraft book. Bachofen, contrary to his own intentions, made his imaginary ancient matriarchies so appealing that some of his readers were bound to see them as an improvement over the present. The most important of those readers were, again, male—Morgan and Engels, Klages and George, Gross and Jung. Of the female writers who discussed the matriarchies, Gage was ignored and almost forgotten, while Harrison gradually abandoned the whole idea.

The direct route from the Romantic idealization of women to the Goddess movement ran through the esoteric tradition. It was in the Hermetic Order of the Golden Dawn that women started working magic alongside men—men who believed that specifically female powers and energies were of the utmost significance to their own quest. It was in Spiritualism and Theosophy that women like the Fox sisters, Blavatsky, Besant, and Kingsford became prominent mediums and channelers. These trends coalesced in the groups around Dion Fortune, Mabel Besant-Scott, Christine Hartley and Charles Seymour, and "Old Dorothy" Fordham; they were enriched by the writings of Charles Godfrey Leland, Sir James Frazer, Margaret Murray, and Robert Graves.

The immediate result was Gardnerian witchcraft—Wicca—the first Goddess religion of the modern English-speaking world. Wicca reached America in time to influence second-wave feminism, giving the Goddess access to the liberal and radical forces in North American culture. Nothing about the Goddess myth correlates with what we know of the ancient civilizations which her devotees claim as their foremothers; everything, however, has clearly identifiable roots in the modern subcultures which began with Romanticism and the nineteenth-century occult revival. It is not Crete, Malta, the Balkans,

Lycia, and Greece who bequeathed the Goddess to us, but Constant, Michelet, Bachofen, Leland, and Gardner.

Clearly, the story of the ancient utopian Goddess cultures is a gendered version of the neopagan paradigm. The immanent Goddess is essentially the folk-soul of women, and female sexuality is a special expression of the divine energy. In the Goddess movement, consequently, the neopagan rejection of moral limits is most fully articulated in the realm of sex. We see this in the systematic rejection of monogamy and normative heterosexuality, in the encouragement of wide sexual experience (especially lesbianism and bisexuality), and in the sacramental significance which is assigned to ritual sex and even abortion. Only the absolute priority given to sex and gender is new with the Goddess movement and unique to it; all the underlying themes and principles are well established in the Western occult tradition.

We best understand the significance of the Goddess movement in today's society by recognizing it as a recent derivative of the esoteric tradition, one which is specifically focused on sexuality and gender politics. Contrary to the cliché, the rest is not yet history, for the repercussions of these developments continue to grow and spread around us.

A Grimoire for Gender Politics

Now that we have unmasked the Goddess, we have a clearer perception of the character of Goddess spirituality as an historical construct and a New Age religion. We have still to explore its significance as a force for social change, however. Goddess literature is written not merely to satisfy antiquarian curiosity, but to recruit and encourage people to work for the New Age of gender feminism. The supposed ancient Goddess cultures are presented as models for a new society and as guarantees that the radical feminist agenda is fully practical; we are urged to be confident that this vision of the new society will work today and tomorrow, precisely because it worked gloriously well in the early days. In that spirit of continuity, we should expect Goddess devotees and their gender feminist allies to approach contemporary issues in a way which is consistent with their approach to history and spirituality.

At its most basic level, the writing of history is founded on the search for reliable facts about the past. Most readers of history rely on historians to adhere to the principle of methodological objectivity in the sense that it was recently defined by Henry Ashby Turner, Jr. Methodological objectivity does not pretend that the historian has no opinions, or that the results of his or her work constitute some kind of immutable reality. Instead, "It instructs historians to seek out all available evidence on the subject of inquiry, to respect the integrity of that evidence, altering nothing and omitting nothing relevant from consideration. It requires them to exercise skepticism in evaluating the evidence by subjecting it to multiple tests of authenticity and reliability. It calls upon historians to identify the sources of their evidence so that others may scrutinize their use of it. And it enjoins them not to go beyond the evidence in reconstructing what occurred in the past."[2]

Two of Turner's points are critically important to our question: the assembly of evidence and the task of interpretation. By measuring Goddess books against this standard, we can identify the principles and procedures which are embodied in them and which can, in turn, be employed in current debates about the nature and direction of Western society.

Selecting the Evidence

One phenomenon which emerged in Chapter 3, as we surveyed the alleged ancient Goddess cultures one by one, was the very selective use of evidence on the part of Goddess writers. This is, up to a point, an inevitable predicament for anyone who wishes to argue a case in anything beyond the narrowest possible terms. On large and complex questions, it can be exceedingly difficult to introduce absolutely all the relevant evidence and still maintain a coherent presentation of one's point. Even the order in which one presents the evidence is based on a process of selection. So the issue here is not a yes-or-no question as to whether evidence has been handled selectively; it is a question of the extent of selectivity, its effect on the argument as a whole, and the standards which govern it. Is the final result a clarification or a distortion of the actual facts?

In the Goddess literature, we saw this selectivity operating in several different ways. First, choices were made regarding which archaeological finds from the ancient cultures were reported and described. We were told about the cowrie shells and red ochre in Paleolithic burials, but not about the fact that it was mostly men who have been found buried this way. We were told that Çatal Hüyük houses were all the same size, but not that only four percent of the town had been excavated at all. Consistently, the omitted evidence turned out to be the sort of information which seriously undermined the Goddess's claim in one way or another. To find it, we needed to consult the reports of Mellaart, Trump, and others who had actually worked on the sites under excavation and attempted to give reasonably complete accounts of their finds. This situation highlights the fact that virtually no reputable Old World archaeologists are also Goddess devotees; further, it invites the suspicion that the selection of evidence in Goddess books has been carried out in strict subservience to the needs of the case the writers are trying to argue.

Goddess literature is even more selective, to move on to a second instance, when it addresses its own recent past. Wiccans are often fairly forthright about their debt to Gardner and, in turn, his debts to the various occult movements with which he had personal contact. Some, like Valiente, still insist that there was an authentic witchcraft tradition which Gardner discovered and adapted. Others, like Adler and Kelly, are content to regard Wicca as an entirely new religion; they judge it solely by the aesthetic and emotional experiences which are available through its rituals, rather than on the basis of its claims to an ancient pedigree. Politically oriented Goddess writers are not usually so flexible on this matter. For them, it is vital to insist that matriarchal models of a healthy society really did exist and functioned successfully, so that they can serve as examples for today. Budapest, Gadon, Eisler, and Sjöö are typical of this point of view.

Either way, it is rare for Goddess writers to trace the elements of their ideology back to nineteenth-century Romanticism and occultism. Michelet, Bachofen, and Leland receive some acknowledgement, but not a sustained discussion; the German Romantics, Enfantin, Constant, and the others almost never come into play. When the history of female messianism and the spread of sexual magic are left out of account, it is easier to create the impression that the Goddess must have originated in ancient, pre-patriarchal times.

A third body of evidence which tends to be ignored in Goddess literature comes from the actual living goddess religions in the world today, particularly in Asia. Here there is no need to argue whether such religions exist or not. Goddesses like Durga and Kali are widely popular in India today and have been adored in devotional movements which go back many centuries. In Japan, the preeminent position in the Shinto pantheon is held by Amaterasu, the sun goddess. Surely it would be more effective to promote the Goddess by pointing to the benefits of her contemporary manifestations than by focusing on cultures which disappeared thousands of years ago?

The problem here, it seems, is that these contemporary examples of goddess religion fail to display the utopian values which Western devotees ascribe to their Goddess. The deity of Western Goddess spirituality is supposed to be inextricably linked to high status for women, egalitarian social structures, peace between communities, and harmony with nature—all simply because she is female. Forcing the goddess religions of Asia into this ideological framework is a daunting task. It is also somewhat risky, for in the late twentieth century many Westerners have visited Asia themselves or have Asian friends and colleagues; the Goddess writers cannot monopolize and select the evidence to which the wider public has access.

There are, in fact, many features in Hinduism which seem at first glance to be attractive to Western neopagans. Classic Hindu philosophy has a strong element of immanentism, asserting that the innermost and true Self is identical with the cosmic Absolute. The Indian notions of karma and reincarnation, having been filtered through Theosophy, are common currency in many New Age circles. Indian culture possesses the allure of the oldest living major civilization on the face of the earth, and the subcontinent has in fact produced more female heads of state and government than any other comparable region in this century: India's late Prime Minister Indira Gandhi; Pakistan's former Prime Minister Benazir Bhutto; Sri Lanka's President Chandika Kumaratunga and Prime Minister Sirimavo Bandaranaike; and Bangladesh's two most recent Prime Ministers, Begum Khaleda Zia and Sheikh Hasina Wazed.

Even so, India cannot meet the needs of the Western Goddess movement. The Goddess supposedly stands for equality, but the caste system was woven into Hinduism for centuries and has only begun breaking down in recent times, under the pressure of modernization. The Western Goddess stands for peace, but the central myths involving Durga and Kali are battle stories. In her iconography, Durga holds the ten weapons of the major gods in her ten hands as she goes forth to fight. Kali is dressed in a necklace of skulls and a skirt of severed forearms, with a cleaver in one hand and her tongue lolling out between her fangs. Even her most famous saint, Ramprasad, addressed her as a "mad goddess"; the English word "thug" originated from the name of one sect of her devotees, who used to kidnap travelers for the practice of human sacrifice. The warlike symbolism has profound spiritual significance for these goddesses' devotees, but the real substance of that significance is not easy for Westerners to grasp and adapt.[3]

The general status of women in India does not serve the movement's purposes either. The tradition of *sati*, burning a widowed woman to death on her husband's funeral pyre, was outlawed by India's British rulers, but Mary Daly has ensured in *Gyn/Ecology* that it is not forgotten. There has been a widely reported epidemic of brides being murdered when their dowries run out, as well as the use of abortion for sex-selection; an overwhelming number of aborted fetuses in some clinics are apparently female. It appears from demographic figures that the subcontinent is one of the few places on earth where females can expect to live shorter lives than males. For all the goddesses and female rulers and the rhetoric of "Mother India," Western feminists are not in a position to argue that the subcontinent has become a woman's utopia.[4]

Similar problems would confront any attempt by the Goddess movement to hail Japan as a model. Amaterasu may be preeminent among the *kami,* but her social significance is her role as ancestress of the emperors, who were all male. As for peace and social harmony, medieval Japan was characterized by a caste system of its own and plagued by endemic civil wars; even Buddhist monasteries kept standing armies. More recently, events like the rape of Nanking and the Bataan "death march" took place under Amaterasu's banner. Again, few Western feminists seem to regard the status of women in Japan, at any point in its history, as something to emulate.[5]

My point here is not to criticize the Asian cultures, much less to attempt a cross-cultural ranking of atrocities. It is only to illustrate the fact that, in these real and specific cases, the well-established worship of goddesses has not guaranteed the peace, the equality, and the high status of women which we have been told to expect when a goddess reigns supreme. We have not found a single example, either past or present, where we can say with assurance that this has actually happened.

The Goddess literature fails dismally to meet the standard articulated by Turner for the full reporting of information. It distorts the evidence it presents from ancient European civilizations, sidesteps its own inheritance from nineteenth-century Romantic neopaganism, and ignores the Asian goddesses and their cultures. In each of these cases, the result is clear: solid facts which undermine the claims of the Goddess movement are kept rigorously out of sight, where they cannot harm the speculations and arguments from silence which make up most of the discussions of the Goddess cultures. In this way, the Goddess books conceal the fact that the movement's key doctrine, the correlation between the female deity and the earthly utopia, appears to be completely unsubstantiated.

Interpreting the Evidence

The other salient point in Turner's definition of valid historical writing is the principle that we must remain bound to the actual evidence we possess and cannot legitimately deviate from it in any significant way when we make assertions about past situations and events. In the Goddess literature we have surveyed, selective reporting of evidence is not the only problem. The difficulty is compounded by the manner in which that partial and distorted information which survives the selection process is made to serve as the foundation for grandiose speculations about the entire religious, political, and social culture of each of the ancient civilizations.

Goddess writers routinely expect us to believe that female figurines are always the Goddess of motherhood and fertility, and never representations of actual women, or symbols, or decorations, or toys. We are expected to believe that the size of beds in Çatal Hüyük reflects an entire scheme of societal preeminence, and not just domestic convenience and practicality. We are expected to believe that the round walls of the Maltese temples represent the anatomy of the divine feminine bringing an entire worldview in its wake, instead of being simply an impressive response to the architectural opportunities presented by the island's geological attributes. We are expected to believe all this and much more, not because the ancients left us written texts explaining what they meant, but because the Goddess evangelists demand our assent. In some of these cases, simpler and more mundane explanations were dismissed or ignored; in others, the authors presumed to announce definitive interpretations of relics for which no truly compelling explanation presents itself.

How do the Goddess writers themselves purport to know all these things? As we noted at several junctures, intuitive or even (using Eisler's own term) psychic factors are made to serve in place of actual information. This is the other crucial component in the way the Goddess literature is written, and it seems to arise from the dual nature of Goddess spirituality as a product of the esoteric tradition blended with radical gender feminism. Ultimate occult knowledge is gained through intuition and inner experience. Magical activities of various sorts are employed specifically to stimulate and enhance such experiences; the Romantic idealization of women associated these prized intuitive experiences with the female sex especially. Now, radical feminist writers are arguing an analogous case in defense of intuitive, "female" modes of knowledge.

Epistemology, the branch of philosophy dealing with the nature of truth and how we can know it, has been a subject of ongoing debate among feminist scholars. While their views are no more unanimous than those of any other such group, there does seem to be a general consensus on what constitutes a specifically feminist epistemology. This consensus revolves around an alleged distinction between male and female perceptions of reality. We are told that female consciousness (either stereotypically or naturally) perceives connections and thinks holistically, whereas male or patriarchal consciousness supposedly emphasizes various forms of separation, distinction, and analysis. Spiritual transcendence, for example, is portrayed as a classically male value, alienating the inner self from the body and the world. The results of this alienation are said to be many: fear and guilt over sexuality; willingness to accept and inflict suffering; and failure to preserve the ecological order. Female consciousness is said to be the antithesis of all this, promoting the unity of self and body, an emphasis on joy and pleasure, and an acceptance of human beings' place and responsibility within nature. The two sexes have different epistemological perspectives and, as a result, they live in what might be called parallel worlds.[6]

What does this mean when it comes to the sort of historical inquiries we have witnessed and pursued in this book? It seems to mean that Turner's cautions about extravagant interpretations of historical evidence can be ignored as a matter of course. In the Goddess literature, we have found departures from these principles which are so flagrant as to appear deliberate. They are indeed deliberate—radical feminist epistemology rejects the goal of objectivity in all its forms as a patriarchal alienation of the student from the object of study. Female consciousness is supposed to seek connection, not alienation; synthesis, not analysis. How does it make that connection? It subordinates cognitive rationality to emotion and intuition, which are presented as more holistic and self-involving methods of perception.[7] This may mean, for instance, that the present needs of the writer or the intended audience will shape not only the writer's interpretation of the evidence, but the selection and reporting of the evidence itself.

Not all radical feminist writers are actual Goddess worshippers, but some knowledge of feminist epistemology does allow us to understand what is being done in the Goddess literature. When evi-

dence is twisted or ignored, it is not just a matter of sloppy scholarship; it is a matter of principle, of asserting a supposedly female way
of knowing in the face of traditional, patriarchal scholarship. One
minor example of this occurred during a session at the 1992 annual
meeting of the Canadian Society of Biblical Studies. A feminist
scholar told her audience that it is indeed "ethical" for an historian to
ignore historical evidence in order to construct a narrative which
would prove fruitful in dealing with contemporary political situations, while still presenting it as history. Hermeneutical support for
this position was drawn from Jacques Derrida and Elizabeth Schüssler
Fiorenza, among others.[8] The most extreme Goddess literature, from
Elizabeth Gould Davis to Monica Sjöö, is perfectly "ethical" by this
definition, although not perhaps by any other.

Extreme opinions on these subjects are not limited to the Goddess movement. As John M. Ellis pointed out, radical feminist theory
in general is founded on a specific view of the past: in the interests of
mobilizing support for the advancement of their political agenda,
they castigate all of pre-feminist Western culture as the product of a
patriarchal conspiracy to oppress women.[9] This amounts to little
more than a secular version of the neopagan paradigm expressed in
the Goddess literature, and it typically requires the same distortion
and manipulation of factual evidence to assert itself. Accordingly,
many of today's academic radicals explicitly reject the quest for objective truth; they claim that objectivity is not only impossible to
achieve in pure form, but actually illegitimate in the first place because it expresses a patriarchal, oppressive mentality. They argue that
all human beings see the world in terms of a subjective "perspective"
which is irrevocably shaped by the group to which the individual
belongs: race, sex, or social class. Most scholarship, therefore, is
simply the narcissistic exploration of one's own perspective.[10] While
all this appears radical and avant-garde when it is given a label like
"postmodernism," our investigations in this book turned up the same
kind of ideas among the Romantics. The objections to destructive
analytical reason; the quest for organic connectedness; the priority
accorded to feeling and intuition; the focus on biological and social
groups as distinct entities with their own separate "truths"; and, most

importantly, the special association of these values with the female sex; all these carry strong reminders of that earlier generation of radicals.

Here, in the realm of the quest for knowledge, we find the familiar Romantic narcissism being deployed as a method of argument. The subjective requirements of the writers' arguments dictate the selection and manipulation of evidence; objective standards for proving or disproving their assertions are not simply ignored but repudiated in the name of subjectivity itself. While this may appear to be a relatively abstract issue on paper, its potential for practical application is disturbing. To examine this situation as we bring our inquiry to a close, let us consider two distinct arenas within which the struggle is being pursued: the academy and the abused women's shelter.

GENDER POLITICS IN PRACTICE

Gender Issues on Campus

As we saw in Chapter 1, universities have been hospitable and supportive to the Goddess almost from the beginning of the movement. It is, in addition, especially among academics that the broader plans of gender feminism seem to have been most fully articulated and even implemented. Moreover, universities and colleges train the majority of those individuals who go on to leadership roles in other sectors of society, including government, the caring professions, and the clergy. Repudiating the quest for objective truth and arguing that all teaching is therefore indoctrination, radical professors are increasingly open about using the classroom for recruitment, turning students into political activists.[11] The campus, therefore, is a natural place to look for signs of the radical feminist New Age as it emerges.

What would it mean to translate neopagan feminism from purely religious terms into those appropriate to an educational institution? From what we have seen already, we would expect an emphasis on organicism, on biological distinctions among human beings, to be assigned high priority. In any institution, this would likely demand close attention to the racial and sexual makeup of the workforce and clientele; in an educational institution, it could also mean a redefinition of knowledge and scholarship in terms of those biological boundaries. This, in turn, would foster a communal subjectivism in which the perspectives attributed to specific groups would determine the nature and value of academic activities. Finally, in keeping with the theme of the organic connectedness of all things, we should anticipate efforts to impose these ideas across the board, without limit.

The evidence from Canadian academia, to which I have readiest access, bears out these expectations. We do indeed find that the racial and sexual composition of faculties has become a recurring subject of high controversy. Calls for action to ensure gender balance are made with regularity. Every April, the Canadian Association of University Teachers publishes a "Status of Women Supplement" with its monthly *Bulletin*.[12] The 1993 Supplement was dedicated to "educational equity" and included a list of fifty-four characteristics of a supposedly "woman-friendly" university which had been compiled in 1992 by the Canadian Federation of University Women. This document is clearly founded on the assumption that universities today are woman-hostile places where routine denigration in the classroom, alienation in the curriculum, low pay, prohibitive barriers to hiring and promotion, and endemic harassment and assault constitute the normal female experience on campus.

One of the recommendations stipulated that a woman-friendly institution would set a five-year deadline for gender parity in its departments, with punitive measures for those which failed to meet the target. Interestingly, the argumentation elsewhere in the Supplement did not rely on the simplistic idea that the composition of faculty should duplicate the composition of the general population. Instead, we read that people who differ from each other by sex, race, class, and physical ability actually inhabit "parallel worlds"; different groups perceive the world in terms of specific "perspectives" which, it seems, can never be fully escaped or transcended. Therefore, students need to be taught by someone of their own kind, not merely by someone who already knows those things they wish to learn. Women's "truth," according to gender feminists, is best taught to women by women.

Accompanying this concern over who teaches whom is the debate over what is taught. Efforts to break the so-called "hegemony of dead white males" over knowledge in general and curriculum in particular have been familiar in North America for some time. The lead article of the 1993 Supplement dismissed the achievements of almost the entire Western intellectual heritage in just such terms: "these 'socially constructed ideas' strut about to parade as absolute concepts in academic robes . . . they were framed by a patriarchal power structure that is also white, able-bodied, heterosexual and middle-class." The woman-friendly university is described as one which features "a university-wide policy emphasizing a balance in course content with regard to male and female scholarship, perspectives and concerns"; this is to be carried out by revising the courses in all departments, but especially by expanding Women's Studies programs and compelling all students to take at least one such course. Mary Daly long ago demanded that the Goddess be given parity with the biblical God in university religion programs, and we saw in Chapter 1 how much progress has been made toward this end.

There are potentially serious, practical dangers in all this. The emphasis on subjective perspectives associated with distinctive biological and social groups, over objective truth, means that scholarly investigation and debate has been transformed from a quest for knowledge into a quest for power. When objective truth is discarded as the measure and goal of scholarship, the standard to which all alike must submit, then power is all that remains to settle disagreements. Those who believe that different groups have different "truths" and live in "parallel worlds" cannot, in the end, win or lose a debate through an appeal to objective, verifiable evidence. A particular perspective can triumph only when the people who hold it triumph.[13]

These new initiatives on campus are to be pursued into as many areas of life as possible, including thought and speech as well as behavior. In the proposed woman-friendly university, all faculty without exception would be required to participate in workshops on sexual harassment, violence against women, "subtle" discrimination, and the use of "gender-neutral" language—off campus as well as on. Action on all such matters would be closely monitored "to determine whether awareness level is adequate." "Totalitarian" does not seem too strong a word for this proposal to institute the mandatory inspection of professors' levels of awareness.

Although the Supplement is published by the Canadian Association of University Teachers, its recommendations are certainly not ignored by academic administrators. At the University of Waterloo, for instance, CFUW's portrait of the woman-friendly university formed the basis of the 1993 status of women report by the Advisory Council on Academic Human Resources, which calls for the implementation of numerous measures by the end of the millennium. This report is now available on-line as an official university document.

What does all this mean to academic freedom? By the traditional definition, academic freedom was established to protect individuals from harassment by the institution and the state. The gender feminist agenda seems to require that this hard-won and tenuous freedom is to be sacrificed when necessary in the quest for biological balance on faculties. As it was put in the 1993 Supplement, "Arguments about academic freedom are being used by some people in the university against those who have been underrepresented in the universities. This must not be allowed to occur. CAUT cannot allow it. Provincial associations cannot allow it. Faculty associations cannot allow it. And individual faculty members, wearing all their hats, whether as members of Senates or members of faculty associations, cannot allow it to happen and must work to stop it."

This is not just a new wrinkle on the old idea of academic freedom. Taken at face value, this statement calls for various authorities to prohibit certain arguments in the defense of academic freedom from being made at all. It presents a striking paradox: discussions about academic freedom should be censored.

The next Supplement, in 1994, was devoted in its entirety to this problem of academic freedom. In the lead article, "Academic Freedom *is* the Inclusive University," the authors note that academic freedom was originally intended to protect those scholars who hold and advance unpopular ideas from retaliation by authorities and vested interests. The inclusive university, according to the authors, must do much more than merely ensure that such freedom is secured for every individual member of the university community, regardless of race or sex. Instead, they say, the university environment must be perceived as a system of power relationships. It is dominated by a "masculinist model of discourse ... which seeks to establish/entrench power imbalances without regard for the 'other' in the discourse." Because it focuses on the individual, this so-called masculinist discourse "does not acknowledge power imbalances in relations based on gender, race, sexuality, class, and other dimensions of difference." We are expected to believe that these socio-biological dimensions of difference overwhelm simple relationships based on professional collegiality, or on professors' and students' mutual engagement in the learning experience. Moreover, these power imbalances are said to be preserved and enhanced by "the hegemony of objectivity over subjectivity," which serves to stifle the perceptions and reactions of the "vulnerable" groups—women and minorities.

On one level, the thrust of this particular article is simply to assert that academic freedom is compatible with increasing diversity in the makeup of faculties and student bodies. Indeed, its positive emphasis on welcoming more kinds of people into academia struck some radical feminist commentators as insufficiently militant in the struggle against sexism and racism. For our purposes, it is interesting to note the correlation between the emphasis on biological distinctives and the defense of subjectivity, two quintessentially Romantic neopagan themes. More important, however, is the question of whether these principles are truly compatible with the atmosphere of calm civility which the authors advocate.

The Supplement of 1996 suggests a disturbing answer to this question. The theme that year was "systemic discrimination," or the so-called "chilly climate" for women in universities. Unlike most legal definitions of discrimination, systemic discrimination does not involve actual structures or procedures which, either explicitly or implicitly, impede the progress of certain groups. The chilly climate is a matter of attitudes and informal behavior which cause the member of an officially designated disadvantaged group to feel unwelcome or underestimated. Here the notion of a subjectivity defined by the socio-biological group truly comes into its own.

The subjective nature of the chilly climate makes it difficult to handle in conventional legal fashion. The point at issue is primarily the feelings of the complainant, and only secondarily the specific actions and words of any alleged offender. Accordingly, crusaders against systemic discrimination have sometimes objected to normal procedures of investigation, which require charges to be substantiated by verified evidence. As John Fekete has reported at length, chilly-climate fighters argue that when a complaint of systemic discrimination is made against a professor, it should be accepted at face value, regardless of due process or factual evidence, "'for to dispute it is to invalidate the experiences of the women who made their disclosure. . . . Due process has no place, because it effectively channels discussion away from the real complaint, which is the condition of women.'"[14] Here we see the Goddess writers' cavalier attitude towards factual evidence being applied to present-day episodes in which individuals' reputations and careers are easily put at risk.

The real issue in a case of systemic discrimination, we are told, is the general situation of women as a group—not the established facts of the particular episode which might be under investigation. Any such investigation, it seems, should be used to decrease the power differential between men and women as a whole, instead of concentrating on finding out whether the particular complaint was justified or not. By that standard, the male must always be guilty to one degree or another, simply because he belongs to the officially designated advantaged group. This, perhaps, is the sort of reasoning behind the famous American episode in which a female dean suggested that men might benefit from being falsely accused of rape.[15] It may also have played a role in the recent controversy at Simon Fraser University in British Columbia, where a male swimming coach was fired after being charged with sexual harassment by a female student; subsequent investigation led to his reinstatement after the evidence showed that the charge was false, and that she had actually been harassing him.

Canada is certainly not an isolated case. Many of these reflections have been inspired by developments in the United States, where the gender feminist effort to transform the university continues apace.

Waterloo's status of women report, for instance, upholds the example of Brown University's "Odyssey Two" program in which faculty consult with students to increase gender and racial balance in curriculum and course content. Moreover, the CFUW document on the woman-friendly university parallels the recent proposal "Vision 2000" issued by the New England Council of Land-Grant University Women. Here again are calls for accountable and enforceable measures for numerical gender parity on faculty and in "non-traditional" disciplines for women; extensive revisions to course content and teaching styles to meet the supposedly distinctive needs of females; and an affirmation of the centrality of Women's Studies not only as an academic discipline but as a privileged source of advice and admonishment for the administration and other departments. As Daphne Patai points out, several of the universities addressed in the report have already approved its goals in principle, even though it amounts to "a stunningly imperialistic move to put in place a questionable feminist agenda, thinly disguised as a plea for equal opportunity and fairness."[16]

The typically neopagan principles of organic community, biological distinctives, and subjectivity lead to predictable results when they are put into practice. They form the foundation of a proposed system in which individual rights can be dismissed in the name of the welfare of groups, and such allegedly abstract principles as right and wrong have lost their status. "Remember. Failing that, invent."

The Goddess and the Shelter

"The Goddess is alive, magic is afoot!" The first place I recall seeing this slogan was on a car parked outside a shelter for battered women. Discussions of epistemology and campus politics may seem academic in every sense of the word, but related issues are affecting the everyday lives of thousands of people. Some of the central ideas of this book—the ultimate importance of biological distinctives and the idealization of women—may now have their most dramatic impact in the dysfunctional households and broken homes of modern society.

Here, as on campus, the Goddess is one visible manifestation of the larger presence of radical gender feminism. Women's shelters are, by definition, designed exclusively for women who have suffered at the hands of men. As such, they represent one side of the most antagonistic form of relations between the sexes. In this selective and, one might say, partisan environment, it is only to be expected that some staff and clients might gravitate towards the view that women and men are vastly different by nature and, moreover, that this is a difference in moral quality: women are less violent and oppressive, more loving and nurturing, and simply better than men. Some might argue that this can be helpful in the short term for individual women who are attempting to get over some traumatic experiences and make a fresh start in life. It is another matter entirely, however, when the moral idealization of women becomes a factor in public policy and directs society's efforts to deal with problems of interpersonal and domestic violence.

As a foster parent, I have become acquainted with almost two dozen young people who have come into our home for varying periods of time, and I have shared experiences with many other foster parents and social workers. I know, from this personal exposure, the wide range of the difficulties which afflict the homes and families in modern society. Moreover, I would contend that a substantial experience in providing foster care presents a more comprehensive cross-section of contemporary social problems than one might expect to witness in shelters designed primarily for just one of these problems. This experience has taught me that evil is no respecter of persons. All sorts of people may inflict all sorts of harm on all sorts of other people, if they have the inclination and opportunity to do so. Neglect, physical abuse, and even sexual abuse are perpetrated by both young and old, by both rich and poor, by both male and female. Sadly, the abusers are often passing on the abuse they themselves have experienced; many of them were not effectively exposed to positive and productive ways of living and behaving during their own childhoods. These problems are compounded by the wide prevalence of addiction to an increasing number of substances and activities.

In much of the public debate, however, this complex situation has been narrowed and twisted by the rhetoric of gender feminism into "male violence against women" and even "the war against women."

It is widely asserted and believed that women, as biological females, are essentially nonviolent, innocent victims; violence is framed as a gender issue, a problem not just in individuals but in males as a sex. Radical feminism is virtually defined by this commitment to the intrinsic "goodness of women."[17] This set of assumptions, so reminiscent of the nineteenth-century idealization of women, has had a decisive impact on research into family violence and on the resulting public policy initiatives. The same tendencies we saw in the discussions of ancient Goddess cultures—inflating and even inventing favorable evidence while ignoring and concealing contrary data—are also common in discussions of this critically important issue. Male violence is highlighted and magnified while female violence remains largely invisible.

Reports on the frequency of male violence against women are in fact magnified in several different ways. For instance, there is the common suggestion that women would never lie about something like rape; the crime is so horrible and shaming that no woman would claim to have undergone it unless she really had done so. If a case comes down to a man's word against a woman's, say radical feminists, the woman should always be believed. Actual law enforcement reports, however, indicate that false accusations are made more often concerning sex crimes than in almost any other type of major offense.[18]

Another effective way of inflating the threat to women from men is to define violence against women as broadly as possible. As Fekete pointed out, the notion of the "continuum" of sexual violence has been introduced to replace the normal categories used in discussing crime. According to the gender feminist definition of the violence continuum, male violence against women is not to be understood in the context of other forms of violence, such as male to male, female to female, or female to male. Rather, it is presented as one end of the spectrum of patriarchy. This spectrum is said to extend through various degrees of harassment, the use of generic language, and other forms of insensitivity on the part of men; all of these are thus redefined as different levels of violence against women.

The very high statistical rates of violence against women which appear in some studies were produced by broadening the definition of violence in this fashion. Fekete meticulously investigated one of the most extreme examples of all: the 1993 report by the government-funded Canadian Panel on Violence against Women. This document claimed that no fewer than 98 percent of all Canadian women had experienced "some form of sexual violation." Sexual violation, in this case, meant anything from forcible rape to "unwanted hugs and kisses . . . being followed by . . . verbal propositions, or any suggestive or otherwise unwelcome sexual remarks." In a study like this, casual comments are ultimately indistinguishable from violent assault. As Fekete went on to ask, "Is there anybody whose life has been completely devoid of any uncomfortable sexual language or sexual ambivalence and even the slightest physical friction? It is astonishing that the number is not 100 percent."[19]

This report was widely criticized in the Canadian media when it appeared, but its conclusions remain in active circulation. The student newspaper at my own university featured it in a box under the heading "Women's Reality" as recently as September 23, 1997. Even for people who find the 98 percent claim incredible in itself, the continued publication of reports like this contributes to a general consensus that male violence against women is at epidemic proportions. Even former United States President George Bush spoke out against the so-called war against women.[20] Lost in all this gender rhetoric is the fact that, by a wide margin, most of the victims of serious violence are men. Males usually constitute between two-thirds and three-quarters of murder victims, and are the normal targets of all other forms of violence except sexual assault.[21]

In addition to demonizing men by inflating the figures on male violence almost to the limit of the numerically possible, gender feminist advocates have promoted the idealization of women by sidestepping or rejecting the evidence that, in the domestic context, women are as capable of violence and as likely to employ it as men are. Violence in the public sphere is certainly a male preserve; the vast majority of both the perpetrators and the victims are men. On the other hand, there are studies going back at least ten years which show that in the home women resort to violence approximately as often as men do, that they are more likely to use weapons, and that they do not employ violence merely in self-defense—they attack too. Since men are usually physically stronger than women, they are more likely to do the sort of damage that can lead to a court case, even if they were retaliating to violence initiated by the female. At the same time, men who are injured by their wives are often ashamed to report it and are sometimes disbelieved when they do so.[22]

A significant amount of this information has sometimes been held back, or released in muted fashion. Many of the major research studies have been framed specifically to report on male violence against women, to the exclusion of other forms of violence. Accordingly, the Kentucky Commission on Violence against Women never formally published its own finding that 38 percent of all the assaults reported in its 1978 survey, presumably including street crime as well as domestic violence in the total, were committed by women; the information was uncovered and reported years later.

Similarly, in 1993 Walter DeKeseredy and Katharine Kelly of Carleton University in Ottawa produced a national study on campus date-rape which was designed specifically to produce data on male violence against women (it received wide negative publicity over its claim that 81% of female university students had experienced some form of abuse at the hands of men; the definition of "abuse" was broad enough to include anything from clumsy flirting to violent rape). That same survey generated data on female violence which the authors took years to release; Fekete reports that the two researchers actually fell out over the matter. DeKeseredy apparently justified his reticence by arguing that "the battered husband syndrome is a backlash," even though his study dealt with campus dating and not with violence in the home. In 1997, a full four years after the data on male violence were released, DeKeseredy published the information on females after working on the material with Daniel Saunders and Martin Schwartz, American researchers who were already on record as skeptics towards the issue of violence by women.[23]

As other writers have noted before, such manipulation of the public debate on interpersonal violence is most graphically illustrated in the contrasting reactions to two recent multiple murderers. In 1988, a Chicago woman named Laurie Dann set fire to the Young

Men's Jewish Council, poisoned food at some fraternities, and shot or burned more than half a dozen elementary schoolboys, including her own son. These events, by and large, received only passing attention and were treated as the deplorable actions of a disturbed individual. The episode was not considered to be typical of anything broader, even though every victim of this woman was male, and no public policy initiatives emerged in response to it.

In 1989, a Montreal man named Marc Lépine harangued fourteen female engineering students over his hatred of feminism before murdering them and shooting himself. Almost instantly, this event was transformed beyond the horrible tragedy it was, into a microcosm and symbol of the war against women. The Montreal Massacre is now a fixture in Canadian public discourse, used as a trump card whenever gender feminist allegations about violence are challenged. Millions of dollars in public money were directed to research and remedy the problem of male violence against women, including the surveys mentioned above. The event is still commemorated annually on campuses across the country with marches and vigils by white-ribboned faculty and students.[24]

These incidents seem to illustrate a major difference between the way North Americans regard men who kill women, and how they react to females who kill males. As always, we must be careful not to over-generalize from single episodes. Murder of any kind is much less common in Canada than in the United States, and may have a more traumatic impact on the public for that reason as well. It would do us no good at all to transform the Montreal Massacre from one kind of symbol into another, representing the gender feminists' distortion of the issue of interpersonal violence. That distortion remains a fact, however.

The Romantic idealization of women as intrinsically loving and communally minded, over against the individualistic, self-isolating and violent male, has had such wide currency in the past century that it has become a difficult task to argue a contrary case. While families and relationships continue to crack under the strains which life in the late twentieth century places on them, the task of reconciliation becomes ever more difficult as the new sex stereotypes of the abusive male and victimized female make their way into law and public policy. Explicitly or implicitly, this framing of the issue of violence is rooted in the view that Western societies embody a patriarchal conspiracy against women, a view which comes to its most evocative expression in the neopagan paradigm of the Goddess movement.

So, WHAT OF THE LIBRARIAN, the counselor, the entrepreneur, and the others we left chanting in the woods? In a modern secular society, few of us would seek to interfere with their recreational rituals. The quiet gentleness of their activities in the glade, however, masks a set of ideas and values which lend themselves all too easily to the destruction of the careers, families, and personal lives of a great many people. When an ideology so closely bound to the veneration of biological distinctives becomes entrenched in major institutions and public policy, the opportunity for abuse on a large scale is disturbing indeed.

As a citizen, I cherish the freedom and respect for personal dignity which Western civilization has bequeathed to our day; I believe we must defend them articulately against notions and proposals which might polarize us in biological groups and even tempt the proponents of such groups towards totalitarian means to achieve their ends. As a scholar, I maintain that we must be open to and guided by all the available facts, not only those which suit particular political agendas. As a family man, I am convinced that we will never make our homes happier and our streets safer by trying to build a new social order on a foundation of falsehoods. The Goddess herself is the deification of a lie: the Romantic, neopagan idealization of the female over against the male. Her rise to prominence and significant influence in contemporary society serves as a prime example of how seductive and potent such falsehoods can be.

Notes

Introduction

1. Some selected aspects of the Goddess phenomenon have received critical attention from scholars and journalists. See Jon D. Levenson, "The God of Abraham and the Enemies of 'Eurocentrism,'" *First Things* (October, 1991), 15-21; William Oddie, "The Goddess Squad," *National Review* (November 18, 1991), 44-46; Mary Lefkowitz, "The Twilight of the Goddess," *New Republic* (August 3, 1992), 29-33, and "The New Cults of the Goddess," *American Scholar* (Spring 1993), 261-68; and Philip G. Davis, "The Goddess and the Academy," *Academic Questions* 6:4 (Fall 1993), 49-66, and "Unmasking the Goddess," Anglican Free Press 11:2 (July 15, 1994), 3-6. At the time of writing, I have learned of two book-length examinations of the Goddess movement which I have not yet been able to obtain: Aida Besancon Spencer et al., *The Goddess Revival* (Baker, 1995), and Lotte Motz, *The Faces of the Goddess* (New York: Oxford University Press, 1997).

2. See J. L. Talmon, *The Origins of Totalitarian Democracy* (New York: Frederick Praeger, 1960), pp. 17-37.

3. Frank Manuel, *The Prophets of Paris: Turgot, Condorcet, Saint-Simon, Fourier, and Comte* (New York: Harper & Row, 1962), pp. 303-04.

4. Christina Hoff Sommers, *Who Stole Feminism? How Women Have Betrayed Women* (New York: Simon & Shuster, 1994), p. 22.

5. Paul Johnson, *The Birth of the Modern: World Society 1815-1830* (London: Weidenfeld and Nicolson, 1991), pp. 1-62.

6. Ibid., p. 143.

7. Talmon, *Romanticism and Revolt: Europe 1815-1848* (London: Thames & Hudson, 1967), pp. 136-50; W. M. Simon, "The Historical and Social Background," in *The Romantic Period in Germany: Essays by Members of the London University Institute of Germanic Studies*, ed. Siegbert Prawer (London: Weidenfeld and Nicolson, 1970), p. 19.

1 *The "Return" of the Goddess*

1. There are several useful surveys of modern neopaganism and witchcraft, including Margot Adler, *Drawing Down the Moon: Witches, Druids, Goddess-Worshippers, and Other Pagans in America Today* (1st edition, New York: Viking, 1979; 2nd edition, Boston: Beacon, 1986); Cynthia Eller, *Living in the Lap of the Goddess: The Feminist Spirituality Movement in America* (New York: Crossroad, 1993); and T. M. Luhrmann, *Persuasions of the Witch's Craft: Ritual Magic in Contemporary England* (Cambridge, Massachusetts: Harvard University Press, 1989).

2. *Womanspirit Rising: A Feminist Reader in Religion*, eds. Carol P. Christ and Judith Plaskow (San Francisco: Harper & Row, 1979); *The Politics of Women's Spirituality. Essays on the Rise of Spiritual Power within the Feminist Movement*, ed. Charlene Spretnak (Garden City, NY: Doubleday, 1982).

3. For example, see Sommers, *Who Stole Feminism?*, p. 32.

4. Luhrmann, *Persuasions of the Witch's Craft*, pp. 99-100.

5. Eller, *Living in the Lap of the Goddess*, pp. 18-21, 33-35.

6. The quotations are from Studio D's catalogue, *Beyond the Image* (National Film Board of Canada, 1991), p.3.

7. At the time of writing, this brief critique of seven specific claims made in the film was accessible at www.patriarchy.com/~sheaffer/texts/goddess_rem.html. A similar rebuttal was produced earlier, in print form, by two professors at the University of Alberta: Ruth Gruhn and Helga Vierich, "The Goddess Myth," *The Merge Journal Reprint Series* 6:1 (n.d.).

8. Shirley Ann Ranck, *Cakes for the Queen of Heaven. A Ten-Session Adult Seminar in Feminist Thealogy* (Boston: Section of Religious Education, Unitarian Universalist Association, 1986). On the use of *Cakes* in other American denominations, see Levenson, "God of Abraham," p.21.

9. To the best of my knowledge, the earliest report of *Cakes* being used in the United Church of Canada appeared in the *United Church Observer* 56:10 (April 1992): 26-27.

10. *Voices United: The Hymn and Worship Book of the United Church of Canada* (Etobicoke, Ontario: United Church Publishing House, 1996). "This is God's wondrous world" is Hymn 296; the phrase "Mothering Christ" occurs in verse 2 of Hymn 320.

11. Donna Steichen, *Ungodly Rage. The Hidden Face of Catholic Feminism* (San Francisco: Ignatius, 1991), p. 51.

12. "Collaborative ministry must be faithful to sacramental doctrine," *L'Osservatore Romano Weekly*, July 7, 1993, 10.

13. The Reimagining Conference received widespread media coverage over its more sensational aspects. An extensive, detailed and critical account of the conference is available from the American Family Association, P.O. Drawer 2440, Tupelo,

MS 38801; this includes information on how to obtain audio cassettes of the actual proceedings. For a one-year-later critical retrospective, see James R. Edwards, "Earthquake in the Mainline," *Christianity Today* (November 14, 1994): 38-45. A report on a more recent Re-Imagining conference was published by Rev. Donna F. G. Hailson, "Re-Imagining Revisited," *Touchstone* 10:2 (Spring 1997): 24-29.

14. See Roger Kimball, *Tenured Radicals: How Politics Has Corrupted Our Higher Education* (San Francisco: Harper, 1990).

15. Marianne Ferguson, *Women and Religion* (Englewood Cliffs, NJ: Prentice-Hall, 1995), pp. 207-08.

16. Diane Stein, *The Women's Spirituality Book* (St. Paul: Llewellyn, 1992), p. 151.

17. Charlene E. Wheeler and Peggy L. Chinn, *Peace and Power: A Handbook of Feminist Process*, 3rd ed. (New York: National League for Nursing), pp. xi-xii.

18. See Kathleen Heinrich, "The Greek Goddesses Speak to Nurses," *Nurse Educator* 15:5 (September/October 1990): 20-24.

19. See, for instance, Dorothea Hover-Kramer, Ed.D., R.N., "Energy Fields: Implications for the Science of Human Caring," *Journal of Holistic Nursing* 37:3 (1990): 5-9. For critical assessments of TT and related New Age therapies, see Sharon Fish, "Nursing's New Age," *Spiritual Counterfeits Project Newsletter* 14:3 (1989): 1-8; and "Therapeutic Touch: Healing Science or Psychic Midwife?" *Christian Research Journal* (Summer 1995): 28-38. I am very grateful to Sharon Fish and to Judith Shelly, editor of the *Journal of Christian Nursing*, for providing me with the material on neopaganism in nursing.

20. Jean Shinoda Bolen, *Goddesses in Everywoman: A New Psychology of Women* (San Francisco: Harper & Row, 1984).

21. Heinrich, "Greek Goddesses," 20-24.

22. Valerie Abrahamsen, "The Goddess and Healing: Nursing's Heritage from Antiquity," *Journal of Holistic Nursing*, 15:1 (March 1997): 9-24.

23. Jean Watson, "A Frog, a Rock, a Ritual: Myth, Mystery and Metaphors for an Ecocaring Cosmology in a Universe That Is Turning Over," in *Exploring our Environmental Connections*, eds. Eleanor A. Schuster and Carolyn L. Brown (New York: National League for Nursing Press, 1994), pp. 17-39.

24. "A Response to Energy-based Theories and Therapies," *Nurses Christian Fellowship* (1996), n.45.

2 *The Story of the Goddess*

1. Elizabeth Gould Davis, *The First Sex* (New York: Penguin, 1975), p. 35.

2. Ibid p. 336.

3. Ibid. p. 162. For more on Margaret Murray's work, please see Chapter 13 of the present work.

4. Margot Adler, a Wiccan priestess herself, indicated that most neopagans had abandoned matriarchy theory already when she published the first edition of *Drawing*

Down the Moon, pp. 80-91. Davis's book is singled out for repudiation by some professed feminist scholars, including Judith Ochshorn, *The Female Experience and the Nature of the Divine* (Bloomington: Indiana University Press, 1981): xiv; Elizabeth Dodson Gray, *Patriarchy as a Conceptual Trap* (Wellesley, Mass: Roundtable, 1982); and Tikva Frymer-Kensky, *In the Wake of the Goddesses: Women, Culture, and the Biblical Transformation of Pagan Myth* (New York: Free Press, 1992), p. vii.

    5. Eller, *Living in the Lap*, p. 56.

    6. Merlin Stone, *When God Was a Woman* (San Diego: Harcourt Brace Jovanovich, 1976).

    7. Ibid., pp. 100-125.

    8. Ibid., p. 127.

    9. See the particularly detailed treatment of Hitler's family background in John Toland, *Adolf Hitler* (Garden City, N.Y.: Doubleday, 1976), I: 4-11; Toland also reproduces Hitler's birth certificate and the newspaper announcement of his birth, both of which confirm the obvious fact of his natal surname.

    10. Mary Daly, *The Church and the Second Sex* (New York: Harper & Row, 1968); *Beyond God the Father: Toward a Philosophy of Women's Liberation* (Boston: Beacon, 1973).

    11. Daly, *Gyn/Ecology: The Metaethics of Radical Feminism* (Boston: Beacon, 1978).

    12. Daly, *Pure Lust: Elemental Feminist Philosophy* (Boston: Beacon, 1984).

    13. Zsuzsanna Budapest, *The Holy Book of Women's Mysteries. Feminist Witchcraft, Goddess Rituals, Spellcasting, and Other Womanly Arts...* (Oakland: Wingbow, 1989).

    14. Starhawk, *The Spiral Dance: A Rebirth of the Ancient Religion of the Great Goddess* (San Francisco: Harper, 1979).

    15. Starhawk, *Dreaming the Dark: Magic, Sex and Politics* (Boston: Beacon, 1982).

    16. Adler, *Drawing Down the Moon*, 2nd ed. (Boston: Beacon, 1986).

    17. Riane Eisler, *The Chalice and the Blade: Our History, Our Future* (San Francisco: Harper, 1987).

    18. Eisler, *Sacred Pleasure: Sex, Myth, and the Politics of the Body—New Paths to Power and Love* (San Francisco: HarperCollins, 1996).

    19. Michael Dames, *The Silbury Treasure: The Goddess Rediscovered* (London: Thames & Hudson, 1976); *The Avebury Cycle* (London: Thames & Hudson, 1977).

    20. Elinor Gadon, *The Once and Future Goddess: A Symbol for Our Time* (San Francisco: Harper, 1989).

    21. Hallie Inglehart Austen, *The Heart of the Goddess: Art, Myth, and Meditations of the World's Sacred Feminine* (Berkeley: Wingbow, 1990); Anne Baring and Jules Cashford, *The Myth of the Goddess: Evolution of an Image* (London: Viking Arkana, 1991); Donna Wilshire, *Virgin, Mother, Crone: Myths & Mysteries of the Triple Goddess* (Rochester, Vt.: Inner Traditions, 1994).

    22. Monica Sjöö and Barbara Mor, *The Great Cosmic Mother: Rediscovering the Religion of the Earth* (San Francisco: Harper, 1991); quoted phrases are from pp. 210, 247, 260, 388-89, and 428-29.

23. Naomi Goldenberg, *Changing of the Gods: Feminism and the End of Traditional Religions* (Boston: Beacon, 1979).

24. Jean Shinoda Bolen, *Goddesses in Everywoman. A New Psychology of Women* (San Francisco: Harper & Row, 1984).

25. Marija Gimbutas, *The Language of the Goddess* (San Francisco: Harper San Francisco, 1989); *The Civilization of the Goddess* (San Francisco: Harper, 1991).

3 *A Search for the Ancient Goddess*

1. Gertrude Rachel Levy, *The Gate of Horn: A Study of the Religious Conceptions of the Stone Age, and Their Influence upon European Thought* (London: Faber & Faber, 1948), p. 62.

2. Ronald Hutton, *The Pagan Religions of the Ancient British Isles* (Oxford: Blackwell, 1991), p. 37.

3. Andrew Fleming, "The Myth of the Mother Goddess," *World Archaeology* 1 (1969): 247-261.

4. See, for example, *The Megalithic Monuments of Western Europe: The Latest Evidence presented by Nine Leading Authorities*, ed. Colin Renfrew (London: Thames and Hudson, 1983), where Fleming's findings are confirmed by Ruth Whitehouse for the central Mediterranean region (p. 59), by Donald Trump for Malta (p. 71), and by Michael J. O'Kelly for Ireland (p. 123). See also Hutton, *Pagan Religions*, pp. 38-39.

5. Gadon, *Once and Future Goddess*, p. 9; Eisler, *The Chalice and the Blade*, p. 5.

6. Hutton, *Pagan Religions*, p. 2.

7. Ibid.

8. Ibid., p. 4.

9. Ibid.

10. Ibid., p. 10.

11. Sarunas Milisauskas, *European Prehistory* (New York: Academic Press, 1978), p. 32.

12. Hutton, *Pagan Religions*, pp. 13-14.

13. Ibid., p. 14.

14. Ibid., p. 41.

15. Davis, *First Sex*, p.78. See also Eisler, *Chalice and the Blade*, p.25; Gadon, *Once and Future Goddess*, p.27-28; Sjöö and Mor, *Great Cosmic Mother*, p.89.

16. James Mellaart, *The Neolithic of the Near East* (London: Thames and Hudson, 1975), pp. 98-111.

17. Ian Hodder, "Contextual Archaeology: An Interpretation of Catal Hüyük and a Discussion of the Origins of Agriculture," *London University Institute of Archaeology Bulletin* 24 (1987): 43-56.

18. Eisler, *Chalice and the Blade*, p. 25; Gadon, *Once and Future Goddess*, p. 28.

19. Eisler, *Chalice and the Blade*, p. 25; Gadon, *Once and Future Goddess*, p. 27.

20. Gadon, *Once and Future Goddess*, p. 57.

21. David Trump, "Megalithic Architecture in Malta," in Renfrew, *Megalithic Monuments*, pp. 64-66.

22. Ibid., p. 71.

23. Gadon, *Once and Future Goddess*, p. 58.

24. Renfrew, *Before Civilization. The Radiocarbon Revolution and Prehistoric Europe* (London: Jonathan Cape, 1973), p. 156.

25. Ibid., pp. 159-66.

26. Ibid., pp. 153, 157.

27. Hutton, *Pagan Religions*, p. 42.

28. Ibid., pp. 131-32.

29. Gimbutas, *Civilization*, p. viii.

30. Lefkowitz, "Twilight of the Goddess," pp. 29-33.

31. Brian Hayden, "Old Europe: Sacred Matriarchy or Complementary Opposition?" in *Archaeology and Fertility Cult in the Ancient Mediterranean: Papers Presented at the First International Conference on Archaeology of the Ancient Mediterranean*, ed. Anthony Bonanno (Amsterdam: Grüner, 1986), p. 26.

32. Gimbutas, *The Goddesses and Gods of Old Europe 6500-3500 BC: Myths and Cult Images* (Berkeley: University of California Press, 1982), p. 237.

33. Hutton, *Pagan Religions*, p. 40.

34. Gimbutas, *Language*, p. 321.

35. Hayden, "Old Europe," p. 22.

36. Joseph Campbell, "Foreword," in Gimbutas, *Language*, pp. xiii-xiv.

37. Gimbutas, *Language*, p. xx.

38. General descriptions of the Indus Valley finds are accessible in A. L. Basham, *The Wonder That Was India* (New York: Grove, 1959), pp. 14-24; and Troy W. Organ, *Hinduism: Its Historical Development* (Woodbury, N.Y.: Barron's Educational Series, 1974), pp. 39-47.

39. Paul Younger, *The Indian Religious Tradition* (Varanasi: Bharatiya Vidya Prakashan, 1970), p. 7.

40. Cited in Hutton, *Pagan Religions*, p. 38.

41. Thomas Hopkins, *The Hindu Religious Tradition* (Encino, Calif.: Dickenson, 1971), p. 8.

42. Davis, *First Sex*, p. 177; Eisler, *The Chalice and the Blade*, p. 31; Gadon, *Once and Future Goddess*, p. 87.

43. Jacquetta Hawkes, *Dawn of the Gods* (London: Chatto & Windus, 1968).

44. R. F. Willetts, *Civilization of Ancient Crete* (Berkeley: University of California, 1977), pp. 116, 129.

45. Ibid., pp. 120-24.

46. Ibid., pp. 125-26.

47. Hawkes, *Dawn*, p. 233.

48. Ibid, p. 225.

49. Yannis Sakellarakis and Efi Sapouna-Sakellarakis, "Drama of Death in a Minoan Temple," *National Geographic*, February, 1981, 205-22.

50. Eisler, *Sacred Pleasure*, p. 428n.7.

51. Renfrew, *Before Civilization*, p. 208.

52. Milisauskas, *European Prehistory*, p. 208; Renfrew, *Before Civilization*, p. 209.

53. Hawkes, *Dawn*, pp. 42-43.

54. J. Walter Graham, *The Palaces of Crete*, revised ed. (Princeton: Princeton University Press, 1987); Willetts, *Civilization*, pp. 133-34.

55. Hawkes, *Dawn*, pp. 224-25.

56. Milisauskas, *European Prehistory*, p. 251.

57. See Willetts, *Civilization*, p. 129, and the sources cited there.

58. For the Egyptian-Minoan analogy applied to the question of matriarchy, see Uwe Wesel, *Der Mythos vom Matriarchat: Über Bachofens Mutterrecht und die Stellung von Frauen in frühen Gesellschaften* (Suhrkamp Taschenbuch Wissenschaft, 333; Frankfurt am Main: Suhrkamp, 1980), pp. 47-53.

59. Willetts, *Civilization*, pp. 47-51.

60. Monique Wittig, *Les Guerillères*, as quoted in "Why Women Need the Goddess," *Womanspirit Rising*, p. 277.

4 *The Foundations of "Thealogy"*

1. Sjöö and Mor, *Great Cosmic Mother*, p. 407.

2. Ferguson, *Women and Religion*, pp. 207-08.

3. Eisler, *Chalice*, pp. 12, 27.

4. Adler, *Drawing Down the Moon*, 1st ed., pp. 80-91.

5. Adler, *Drawing Down the Moon*, 2nd ed., pp. 189-97.

6. Ferguson, *Women and Religion*, pp. 25, 209, 242.

7. Eller, *Living in the Lap*, Chapter 7.

8. See, for instance, Gadon, *Once and Future Goddess*, and Sjöö and Mor, *Great Cosmic Mother*.

9. See e.g. Starhawk, *Spiral Dance*, pp. 93-107.

10. Gadon, *Once and Future Goddess*, p. 167.

11. Eller, *Living in the Lap*, pp. 132-35.

12. Daly, *Beyond God the Father*, pp. 16-19. Over against this we might set John Wesley's description of God as "the great Male before whom we are all female."

13. Daly, *Beyond God the Father*, throughout; Starhawk, *Spiral Dance*, p. 9; *Dreaming the Dark*, pp. 1-14; Sjöö and Mor, *Great Cosmic Mother*, pp. 230-31, 418-20; Gadon, *Once and Future Goddess*, p. 181; Eller, *Living in the Lap*, pp. 136-39

14. Z. Budapest, *Holy Book*, p. 112.

15. Eisler, *Chalice*, pp. 105, 112, 121.

16. Budapest, *Holy Book*, pp. 3, 177.

17. Sjöö and Mor, *Great Cosmic Mother*, pp. 225, 428-29.

18. Starhawk, *Dreaming the Dark*, p. 7; Gadon, *Once and Future Goddess*, pp. 233-308.

19. Eller, *Living in the Lap*, pp. 83-129; Luhrmann, *Persuasions*, pp. 175-263.

20. Eller, *Living in the Lap*, pp. 105-09; Luhrmann, *Persuasions*, pp. 180-202.

21. Starhawk, *Dreaming the Dark*, p. 34.

22. These ideas make up the general thrust of Goddess books which focus on sex, including Mary Daly's *Pure Lust*; Starhawk's *Dreaming the Dark*; and Eisler's *Sacred Pleasure*. The view that bisexuality represents a freer and fuller expression of sexuality is also argued in Margot Adler, *Drawing Down the Moon*, 2nd ed., pp. 150-151; Gadon, *Once and Future Goddess*, pp. 304-06; Sjöö and Mor, *Great Cosmic Mother*, p. 18. Budapest includes directions for a lesbian Great Rite in *Holy Book*, pp. 98-197.

23. Becky Gwyn Wilson, "Sacred Prostitution: World's Oldest Religion?" *Gnosis* 37 (Fall 1995): 8-9.

24. Starhawk, *Dreaming the Dark*, p. 142.

25. Joseph F. Fletcher, *Situation Ethics: The New Morality* (Philadelphia: Westminster, 1966).

26. Hugh M. Hefner, "The Playboy Philosophy," *Playboy* 26:1 (January 1979): 81-82.

27. David Sheff, "Playboy Interview: Betty Friedan," *Playboy* 39:9 (September 1992): 52-53.

28. Catharine MacKinnon, *Feminism Unmodified: Discourses on Life and Law* (Cambridge, Mass.: Harvard University Press, 1987), pp. 134-45.

5 *European Magic and Occultism*

1. Bronislaw Malinowski's 1925 essay "Magic, Science and Religion" was reprinted in Malinowski, *Magic, Science and Religion and other essays* (Garden City, N.Y.: Doubleday, 1954), pp. 17-92.

2. See, for instance, Arthur Versluis, "Magic & Religion: Secret Partners?" *Gnosis*, 2 (spring/summer, 1986), 22-25.

3. See Richard Cavendish, *A History of Magic* (London: Weidenfeld & Nicolson, 1977), pp. 46-52.

4. Cavendish, *The Magical Arts: Western Occultism and Occultists* (London: Arkana, 1984), pp. 1-29.

5. Ibid., p. 13.

6. Ibid., pp. 43-80.

7. Ibid., p. 50.

8. Ibid., p. 51.

9. Ibid., p. 52.

10. Ibid., pp. 181-228.

11. Ibid., pp. 187-88.

12. Ibid., pp. 194-96.

13. Ibid., pp. 199-201.

14. Mary K. Greer, *Women of the Golden Dawn: Rebels and Priestesses* (Rochester, Vt.: Park Street Press, 1995).

15. Cavendish, *Magical Arts*, pp. 207-11.

16. Eden Gray, *The Tarot Revealed: A Modern Guide to Reading the Tarot Cards* (New York: Signet, 1969), p. 19.

17. Ibid., pp. 40, 72, 94, 128.

18. Ibid., p. 145.

19. Ibid, pp. 156, 162, 174.

20. Ibid., pp. 210-211.

21. Cavendish, *Magical Arts*, pp. 229-80.

22. Francis King, *The Magical World of Aleister Crowley* (London: Weidenfeld & Nicolson, 1977), p.9.

23. Cavendish, *Magical Arts*, p. 256.

24. Alan Richardson, *Dancers to the Gods* (Wellingborough: Aquarian, 1985), pp. 72-73.

25. Summaries of Neoplatonic ideas which are germane to later Western occultism are available in David Stevenson, *The Origins of Freemasonry: Scotland's Century 1590-1710* (Cambridge: Cambridge University Press, 1988), pp. 77-82; and Kenneth Stein, "The Star-Gods of Neoplatonism," *Gnosis* 38 (Winter 1996): 30-36.

26. Stevenson, *Freemasonry*, p. 79.

27. Stevenson, *Freemasonry*, pp. 82-87; Stephan A. Hoeller, "On the Trail of the Winged God," *Gnosis* 40 (Summer 1996): 20-26; Gary Lachman, "The Renaissance of Hermetic Man," *Gnosis* 40 (Summer, 1996): 28-33.

28. The relevance of ancient Gnosticism to contemporary occultism was the theme of two issues of *Gnosis*: no. 1 (Fall-Winter 1985-86) and no. 23 (Spring 1992).

29. Cavendish, *Magical Arts*, pp. 81-97, 117-21; *Gnosis* 3 (Fall-Winter 1986-87).

30. Gershom Scholem, *Kabbalah* (New York: New American Library, 1974), pp. 144-52.

31. Cavendish, *Magical Arts*, p. 118.

32. Scholem, *Kabbalah*, p. 6.

33. Raphael Patai, *The Hebrew Goddess*, 3rd ed. (Detroit: Wayne State University Press, 1990), pp. 96-111, 155-60, 202-20.

34. Cavendish, *Magical Arts*, pp. 143-80.

35. There are still some actual practitioners of alchemy. See *Gnosis* no. 8 (Summer 1988); Joseph Rowe, "The Quintessence of Alchemy: The *Gnosis* Interview with François Trojani," *Gnosis* 40 (Summer 1996), 34-40.

36. Cavendish, *Magical Arts*, p. 156.

6 *The Western Esoteric Tradition*

1. Cavendish, *History of Magic*, pp. 88-89.

2. Lachman, "Renaissance of Hermetic Man," 31-32.

3. Cavendish, *History of Magic*, pp. 89-90; Christopher McIntosh, *The Rosicrucians: The History and Mythology of an Occult Order*, 2nd edition (Wellingborough: Crucible, 1987), pp. 34-35.

4. McIntosh, *Rosicrucians*, pp. 35-36.

5. Cavendish, *History of Magic*, p. 94.

6. Frederick Copleston, *A History of Philosophy*, 3:2 (Garden City, N.Y.: Image, 1963), pp. 65-71; Cavendish, *History of Magic*, pp. 97-98; Lachman, "Renaissance of Hermetic Man," p.32-33.

7. Cavendish, *History of Magic*, pp. 95-96; Cherry Gilchrist, "Dr. Dee and the Spirits," *Gnosis* 36 (Summer 1995): 33-39.

8. Frances Yates, *The Rosicrucian Enlightenment* (London: Routledge and Kegan Paul, 1972), p. 39.

9. Except where otherwise noted, the information here is taken from Yates, *Rosicrucian Enlightenment*; McIntosh, *Rosicrucians*; and McIntosh, "The Rosicrucian Dream," *Gnosis* 6 (Winter 1988): 14-19.

10. McIntosh, *Rosicrucians*, pp. 63-64; see also Yates, *Rosicrucian Enlightenment*, pp. 31, 144-51.

11. McIntosh, *Rosicrucians*, pp. 44-45, 51.

12. Stevenson, *Freemasonry*, pp. 13-25.

13. See, for example, Richard Smoley, "Masonic Civilization," *Gnosis* 44 (Summer 1997): 12-16.

14. See Desmond Seward, *The Monks of War: The Military Religious Orders*, 2nd ed. (London: Penguin, 1995).

15. A photograph of the carving is reproduced in Richard Smoley, "The Temple and the Scrolls. The *Gnosis* Interview with Christopher Knight," *Gnosis* 44 (Summer 1997): 26.

16. Yates, *Rosicrucian Enlightenment*, pp. 193-205; McIntosh, *Rosicrucians*, p. 82.

17. McIntosh, *Rosicrucians*, pp. 83-84.

18. McIntosh, *Rosicrucians*, p. 84; A. E. Waite, *The Brotherhood of the Rosy Cross* (New York: Barnes & Noble, 1993), pp. 422, 530.

19. McIntosh, *Rosicrucians*, pp. 72-75.

20. Ibid., pp. 88-90.

21. Ibid., pp. 95-100.

22. Ibid., p. 85.

23. James F. Lawrence, "The Swedenborgian Church: An Exoteric Journey of an Esoteric Teaching," *Gnosis* 12 (Summer 1989): 56.

24. Lachman, "Heavens and Hells," *Gnosis* 36 (Summer 1995): 48.

25. Lawrence, "Swedenborgian Church," 57.

26. Lachman, "Heavens and Hells," 48.

27. Unless otherwise noted, this discussion of Mesmer and mesmerism is based on Robert Darnton, *Mesmerism and the End of the Enlightenment in France* (Cambridge, Mass.: Harvard University Press, 1968).

28. Ibid., p. 58.

29. The role of mesmerist and other occult groups in pre-Revolutionary France has been extensively explored in Auguste Viatte, *Les Sources Occultes du Romantisme. Illuminisme—Théosophie 1770-1820*, 2 vols. (Paris: Editions Champion, 1969); see also Darnton, *Mesmerism*, pp. 40-45.

30. Darnton, *Mesmerism*, p. 68.

31. Ibid., p. 67.

32. Ibid., pp. 116-22.

7 Romantic Neopaganism in Germany

1. Talmon, *Romanticism and Revolt*, p. 138.

2. Johnson, *Birth of the Modern*, p. 141.

3. Here (as also in Chapter 8) I shall not attempt to provide a comprehensive description, much less a critical analysis, of the achievements of monumental figures like Kant. My more limited goal is to identify the sources and sponsors of particular themes germane to the Goddess movement, and the chains of transmission though which they reached it. Kant's significance to Romanticism is made clear, for instance, in Talmon, *Romanticism and Revolt*, pp. 152-54.

4. Paul Roubiczek, "Some Aspects of German Philosophy in the Romantic Period," in *Romantic Period*, ed. Prawer, pp. 306-09.

5. Ibid., pp. 306-09. See also Talmon, *Romanticism and Revolt*, pp. 82-84.

6. F. M. Barnard, *Herder's Social and Political Thought: From Enlightenment to Nationalism* (Oxford: Clarendon, 1965). See also L. A. Willoughby, *The Romantic Movement in Germany* (New York: Russell & Russell, 1966), pp. 2-3; Oskar Walzel, *German Romanticism*, trans. Alma Elise Lussky (New York: Capricorn, 1966), pp. 15-21; Talmon, *Romanticism and Revolt*, pp. 96-101.

7. Unless otherwise noted, the sources from which this description of Fichte, Schleiermacher, Hegel, and Schelling is taken are these: *Communism, Fascism, and Democracy: The Theoretical Foundations*, ed. Carl Cohen (New York: Random House, 1972); Johnson, *Birth of the Modern*; Prawer, *Romantic Period in Germany*; Talmon, *Romanticism and Revolt*; Walzel, *German Romanticism*; Willoughby, *Romantic Movement*.

8. Friedrich Schleiermacher, *The Christian Faith*, trans. H. R. MacIntosh and J. S. Stewart (Edinburgh: T. & T. Clark, 1928), p. 3.

9. Schleiermacher, *On Religion—Discourses to the Educated Among Its Contemners*, as cited in Frederick Hiebel, *Novalis: German Poet—European Thinker—Christian Mystic* (New York: AMS Press, 1969), p. 32.

10. Willoughby, *Romantic Movement*, pp. 47, 53; Theodore Ziolkowski, *German Romanticism and its Institutions* (Princeton: Princeton University Press, 1990), pp. 15, 81-86, 95, 293.

11. Richard Friedenthal, *Goethe: His Life and Times* (Cleveland: World Publishing Company, 1965), p. 37.

12. The information on Goethe, unless otherwise noted, is taken from Friedenthal, *Goethe*, and Alice Raphael, *Goethe and the Philosophers' Stone. Symbolical Patterns in "The Parable" and the Second Part of "Faust"* (London: Routledge and Kegan Paul, 1965).

13. Friedenthal, *Goethe*, pp. 67-68; Jane K. Brown, *Goethe's Faust. The German Tragedy* (Ithaca and London: Cornell University Press, 1986), pp. 7-13.

14. Friedenthal, *Goethe*, p. 143.

15. Walzel, *German Romanticism*, p. 78-79.; Friedenthal, *Goethe*, p. 276-77.

16. Walzel, *German Romanticism*, p. 27.

17. Hiebel, *Novalis*, pp. 49-51.

18. Ibid., pp. 68-69.

19. Ibid., p. 86.

20. Walzel, *German Romanticism*, pp. 79-83.

21. Ibid, p. 84.

22. Hans Eichner, "The Eternal Feminine: An Aspect of Goethe's Ethics," in Goethe, *Faust: A Tragedy*, trans. Walter Arndt, ed. Cyrus Hamlin (New York: W. W. Norton, 1976), p. 623.

23. Brown, *Goethe's Faust*, p. 246.

24. Eichner, "Eternal Feminine," 621; Brown, *Goethe's Faust*, pp. 103-104.

25. Brown, *Goethe's Faust*, pp. 48, 248; Friedenthal, *Goethe*, pp. 68, 497.

26. Eichner, "Eternal Feminine," 623; Brown, *Goethe's Faust*, pp. 26, 120.

27. Friedenthal, *Goethe*, p. 493.

28. Harold Jantz, *The Mothers in Faust: The Myth of Time and Creativity* (Baltimore: Johns Hopkins, 1969), pp. 81-84.

29. Jantz, *Mothers*, pp. 44-45, 59-62; Brown, *Goethe's Faust*, p. 235.

30. Friedenthal, *Goethe*, p. 491.

31. Eichner, "Eternal Feminine," 616; see also Jantz, *Mothers*, p. 34; Brown, *Goethe's Faust*, pp. 58, 100, 183.

32. Eichner, "Eternal Feminine," 617-21.

8 *Utopian Feminism in France*

1. Talmon, *Romanticism and Revolt*, p.40; Johnson, *Birth of the Modern*, pp.968-75.

2. Talmon, *Romanticism and Revolt*, pp. 166-74, 188-92.

3. J. Salwyn Schapiro, *Condorcet and the Rise of Liberalism* (New York: Octagon, 1978), p. 188.

4. Schapiro, *Condorcet*, pp. 188-95; Manuel, *Prophets of Paris*, pp. 303-04.

5. See Robert Langdon, *Tahiti: Island of Love* (Sydney: Pacific Publications, 1968), pp. 9-47; David Howarth, *Tahiti: A Paradise Lost* (New York: Penguin, 1983), pp. 9-55.

6. Jean Jacques Rousseau, *Emile* (London: Everyman, 1961), p. 254. See also Ronald Grimsley, *Rousseau and the Religious Quest* (Oxford: Clarendon, 1968), pp.58-68.

7. Grimsley, *Jean-Jacques Rousseau* (New Jersey: Barnes & Noble, 1983), pp. 39-40. I am quoting Grimsley, who has included the phrases from Rousseau's *Letter* in the passage.

8. Grimsley, *Jean-Jacques Rousseau*, pp. 64-65; Rosemarie Tong, *Feminist Thought: A Comprehensive Introduction* (Boulder: Westview, 1989), pp. 14-15.

9. Except when noted otherwise, the information on Restif is taken from Mark

Poster, *The Utopian Thought of Restif de la Bretonne* (New York: New York University Press, 1971).

10. Charles A. Porter, *Restif's Novels, or An Autobiography in search of an Author* (New Haven: Yale University Press, 1967), pp. 385-86.

11. Darnton, *Mesmerism*, pp. 132-34; Viatte, *Les Sources Occultes*, I: 208; II: 255.

12. Poster, *Restif*, p. 39.

13. Johnson, *Birth of the Modern*, p. 476.

14. It is interesting to note, however, that aspects of his work were prized by such literary giants as Schiller and Goethe: Porter, *Restif's Novels*, pp. 4-5.

15. Unless otherwise noted, this discussion of Fourier is based on Manuel, *Prophets of Paris*, and Jonathan Beecher, *Charles Fourier: The Visionary and his World* (Berkeley: University of California Press, 1986).

16. Beecher, *Fourier*, p. 341.

17. Darnton, *Mesmerism*, pp. 143-47; see also Ian Dowbiggin, "Alfred Maury and the Politics of the Unconscious in Nineteenth-Century France," *History of Psychiatry* 1 (1990): 277.

18. Beecher, *Fourier*, p. 84.

19. S. Joan Moon, "Feminism and Socialism: The Utopian Synthesis of Flora Tristan," in *Socialist Women: European Socialist Feminism in the Nineteenth and Early Twentieth Centuries*, eds. Marilyn J. Boxer and Jean H. Quataert (New York: Elsevier, 1978), p. 45n.1.

20. Quoted in Beecher, *Fourier*, p. 208.

21. Moon, "Feminism and Socialism," p. 28.

22. Beecher, *Fourier*, pp. 491-95.

23. Beecher, *Fourier*, pp. 497-502 and plate 29.

24. This discussion of Saint-Simon is based on Talmon, *Romanticism and Revolt*, pp. 61-63; *Political Messianism*, pp. 35-70; and Manuel, *Prophets of Paris*, pp. 105-48.

25. The information on the Saint-Simonians, unless otherwise noted, is taken from Talmon, *Political Messianism*, pp. 70-124; Manuel, *Prophets of Paris*, pp. 149-93; and E. M. Butler, *The Saint-Simonian Religion in Germany: A Study of the Young German Movement* (New York: Howard Fertig, 1968), pp. 11-50. The quotations are from Butler, with emphasis in original.

26. Frank E. Manuel and Fritzie P. Manuel, *French Utopias: An Anthology of Ideal Societies* (New York: Free Press, 1966), pp. 296-97.

27. Talmon, *Political Messianism*, p. 71.

28. Jean Baelen, *La Vie de Flora Tristan: Socialisme et Féminisme au XIXe Siècle* (Paris: Editions du Seuil, 1972), p. 122.

29. Eliphas Lévi in his *History of Magic*, quoted in Christopher McIntosh, *Eliphas Lévi and the French Occult Revival* (London: Rider & Co., 1972), pp. 85-86.

30. In addition to Baelen, see Manuel, *Prophets of Paris*, pp. 4-5.

31. The information on Tristan is taken from Baelen, *La Vie de Flora Tristan*, and Moon, "Feminism and Socialism." Tristan's involvement with Saint-Simonism is noted in Butler, *Saint-Simonian Religion*, p. 32.

32. William Darr, "Foreword," in *Flora Tristan's London Journal,* trans. Dennis Palmer and Giselle Pincetl (Charlestown, Mass.: Charles River, 1980).

33. Baelen, *La Vie de Flora Tristan,* p.106; Moon, "Feminism and Socialism," p.23.

34. Moon, "Feminism and Socialism," p. 31.

35. Unless otherwise noted, the information on Constant is taken from Thomas A. Williams, *Eliphas Lévi: Master of Occultism* (Tuscaloosa, Ala.: University of Alabama Press, 1975), and McIntosh, *Eliphas Lévi.*

36. Francis King, *Ritual Magic in England: 1887 to the Present Day* (London: Neville Spearman, 1970), p. 23.

37. Constant, *La Mère de Dieu* (Paris: Gosselin, 1844), pp. 159-63, translated and quoted in Williams, *Lévi,* p. 28.

38. Constant, *L'Assomption de la femme* (Paris: Le Gallois, 1841), pp. 57-58, translated and quoted in Williams, *Lévi,* pp. 23-24.

39. See Willams, *Lévi,* pp. 29-32.

40. Christopher Johnson, *Utopian Communism in France: Cabet and the Icarians, 1839-1851* (Ithaca: Cornell University Press, 1974), pp. 70-71.

41. Flora Tristan, *L'Emancipation de la femme, ou le Testament de la paria* (Paris, 1845); cited in Beecher, *Fourier,* p. 537n.40. See also Williams, *Lévi,* pp. 20, 33; McIntosh, *Lévi,* pp. 84-90. Baelen and Moon are among the writers on Tristan who never mention Constant at all.

42. See, e.g., Arthur Mitzman, *Michelet, Historian: Rebirth and Romanticism in Nineteenth-Century France* (New Haven: Yale University Press, 1990), p. xiv.

43. David Pinkney, *Decisive Years in France: 1840-1847* (Princeton: Princeton University Press, 1986), pp. 92-104.

44. See Lise Vogel, *Marxism and the Oppression of Women: Toward a Unitary Theory* (New Brunswick, N.J.: Rutgers University Press, 1983), pp. 81-92.

45. Except where otherwise noted, the information on Comte is taken from Arline Reilein Standley, *Auguste Comte,* Twayne's World Authors Series no. 625 (Boston: Twayne, 1981), and Manuel, *Prophets,* pp. 249-96.

46. Comte, *System of Positive Polity,* I, pp. 198, 200; cited in Standley, *Comte,* p. 112.

47. Standley, *Comte,* p. 28.

48. The biographical material on Michelet is taken from Oscar A. Haac, *Jules Michelet,* Twayne's World Author Series no.638 (Boston: Twayne, 1982), and Mitzman, *Michelet,* except where otherwise noted.

49. Mitzman, *Michelet,* p. 31.

50. Ibid., pp. 30, 47.

51. Ibid., p. 59.

52. Ibid., p. 94.

53. Ibid., pp. 93, 102.

54. Michelet, *The People,* trans. John P. MacKay (Urbana: University of Illinois Press, 1973), p. 192.

55. Mitzman, *Michelet*, p. 276.

56. Edward K. Kaplan, *Michelet's Poetic Vision: A Romantic Philosophy of Nature, Man, & Woman* (Amherst: University of Massachusetts Press, 1977), p. 88; see also Linda Orr, *Jules Michelet: Nature, History, and Language* (Ithaca: Cornell University Press, 1976), pp. 78-79.

57. Michelet, *La Femme* (Paris: Flammarion, 1981), p. 119.

58. Ibid., p. 149.

59. Orr, *Jules Michelet*, p. 85.

60. See, e.g., Thérèse Moreau's preface to the Flammarion edition of *La Femme*.

9 *The European Occult Revival*

1. Talmon, *Romanticism and Revolt*, pp. 166-96.

2. Again, the information on Constant/Lévi is taken from Williams, *Lévi*, and McIntosh, *Lévi*, unless otherwise noted.

3. Williams, *Lévi*, p. 153.

4. Ibid, p. 22.

5. Quoted in McIntosh, *Lévi*, p. 99.

6. Quoted in Williams, *Lévi*, p. 68.

7. Quoted in McIntosh, *Lévi*, p. 149.

8. Ibid., p. 150.

9. Eliphas Lévi, *The Mysteries of the Qabalah, or The Occult Agreement of the Two Testaments*, Studies in Hermetic Tradition, no.2 (Wellingborough, Northamptonshire: Thorsons, 1974), p. 121.

10. Ibid., pp. 279-80.

11. Ibid., pp. 16, 111, 142, 262.

12. Ibid., pp. 190-94.

13. Ibid., p. 235.

14. Lévi, *Dogme et Rituel*, pp. 132-35, translated and quoted in Williams, *Lévi*, p. 92. The account is also given in McIntosh, *Lévi*, pp. 101-04.

15 Quoted in Williams, *Lévi*, p. 93.

16. From an article by Mackenzie in *Occult Review* (December 1921), quoted in King, *Ritual Magic*, p. 30.

17. From an article in *Initiation* (August 1890), quoted in Williams, *Lévi*, p. 155.

18. King, *Ritual Magic*, p. 22.

19. Except where otherwise noted, the information on de Guaita and Péladan is taken from McIntosh, *Rosicrucians*, pp. 105-08, and Cavendish, *History of Magic*, pp. 140-42.

20. Waite, *Brotherhood*, p. 586.

21. See W. N. Schors's Foreword to Papus, *The Qabalah*, Studies in Hermetic Tradition, no.4 (Wellingborough: Thorsons, 1977), pp. 13-18.

22. There are now many biographies of Blavatsky available. Unless otherwise noted, the information here is taken from Marion Meade, *Madame Blavatsky: The*

Woman Behind the Myth (New York: G. P. Putnam's Sons, 1980). The most recent critical study is Peter Washington, *Madame Blavatsky's Baboon: A History of the Mystics, Mediums, and Misfits Who Brought Spiritualism to America* (New York: Schocken, 1995); at the time of writing, it has been inaccessible to me for most of a year, and I know it only through the review article by Frederick Crews, "The Consolation of Theosophy," Part I, *New York Review of Books* (September 1996): 26-30, and Part II (October 1996): 38-44.

23. Meade, *Blavatsky*, p. 29.

24. Ibid., pp. 16, 48; K. Paul Johnson, *The Masters Revealed: Madame Blavatsky and the Myth of the Great White Lodge* (Albany: State University of New York Press, 1994), pp. 19-20.

25. Meade, *Blavatsky*, pp. 41, 47.

26. Ibid., p. 55.

27. A useful account of the origins and history of Spiritualism can be found in Geoffrey K. Nelson, *Spiritualism and Society* (London: Routledge & Kegan Paul, 1969). For a well-known believer's version of the same events, see Arthur Conan Doyle, *The History of Spiritualism*, vol. I (New York: George H. Doran, 1926).

28. H. P. Blavatsky, *Isis Unveiled* (Pasadena: Theosophical University Press, 1988), p. vii.

29. A. T. Barker, ed., *The Mahatma Letters: To A. P. Sinnett from the Mahatmas M. & K. H.* (London: Rider & Co., 1923).

30. Meade, *Blavatsky*, pp. 319-20.

31. Ibid., pp. 343, 458.

32. Ibid., p. 362.

33. Arthur E. Nethercot, *The First Five Lives of Annie Besant* (Chicago: University of Chicago Press, 1960), p. 80; Meade, *Blavatsky*, p. 423.

34. Nethercot, *First Five Lives*, pp. 105-06.

35. Quoted in Ibid., p. 150.

36. Ronald Florence, *Marx's Daughters* (New York: Dial, 1975), p. 73.

37. Meade, *Blavatsky*, p. 429, citing Annie Besant, *Annie Besant: An Autobiography* (Philadelphia: Henry Altemus, 1893), pp. 342-43.

38. Ernest Wood, *A "Secret Doctrine" Digest* (Adyar: Theosophical Publishing House, 1956).

39. Blavatsky, *The Secret Doctrine*, I (Pasadena: Theosophical University Press, 1988), p. viii.

40. Ibid., p. 273; emphasis in original.

41. Ibid., p. 274; emphasis in original.

42. Blavatsky, *Secret Doctrine*, II, p. 69.

43. Ibid., p. 780.

44. Wood, *Digest*, p. 374.

45. Blavatsky, *Secret Doctrine*, II, pp. 99-101.

46. Thus T. M. Francis, *Blavatsky, Besant & Co.: The Story of A Great Anti-Christian Fraud* (St. Paul, Minnesota: Library Service Guild, 1939), p. 28.

47. The original exposé of Blavatsky's sources in *Isis Unveiled* was that of William Emmette Coleman, "The Sources of Madame Blavatsky's Writings," in Vsevolod Solovyov, *A Modern Priestess of Isis*, tr. Walter Leaf (London: Longmans, Green & Co., 1895).

48. Jay G. Williams, "What's So Secret about *The Secret Doctrine?*" *Gnosis* 12 (Summer 1989): 63.

49. Quoted in Meade, *Blavatsky*, pp. 160-61.

50. Meade, *Blavatsky*, pp. 379-80.

51. Johnson, "Imaginary Mahatmas," *Gnosis* 28 (Summer 1993): 24-30; *The Masters Revealed*; Stephan Hoeller, "Wise Men from the East. The Myth of the Hierarchy of Adepts," *Gnosis* 36 (Summer 1995): 18-22.

52. The most detailed accounts of Besant's life and career are Nethercot's *First Five Lives* and its sequel, *The Last Four Lives of Annie Besant* (Chicago: University of Chicago Press, 1963).

53. Gregory Tillett, *The Elder Brother: A Biography of Charles Webster Leadbeater* (London: Routledge & Kegan Paul, 1982), p. 168.

54. See Tillett, *Elder Brother*, especially pp. 77-83, 281-85.

55. Meade, *Blavatsky*, p. 460; Tillett, *Elder Brother*, pp. 103-04, 145-61, 234-39. A full account of the Krishnamurti story is available in Nethercot, *Last Four Lives*.

56. Nethercot, *Last Four Lives*, pp. 402-06; Tillett, *Elder Brother*, pp. 230-32.

57. See Nethercot, *Last Four Lives*, especially pp. 56-61, 435-36.

58. Nicholas Goodrick-Clarke, *The Occult Roots of Nazism: The Ariosophists of Austria and Germany, 1890-1935* (Wellingborough: Aquarian, 1985), pp. 24-27.

59. Cavendish, *History of Magic*, pp. 151-53; Goodrick-Clarke, *Occult Roots*, pp. 26-30, 221.

60. The information on List and Lanz is taken from Goodrick-Clarke, *Occult Roots*.

10 *Sex, Gender, and Modern Magic*

1. Talmon, *Romanticism and Revolt*, pp. 27-29, 76-81.

2. Talmon, *Romanticism and Revolt*, p.157.

3. Cavendish, *History of Magic*, p. 134; Hutton, *Pagan Religions*, pp. 139-41, 320.

4. E. M. Butler, *The Myth of the Magus* (Cambridge: Cambridge University Press, 1948), pp. 243, 245; Cavendish, *History of Magic*, pp. 133, 139. Cavendish treats Barrett's magic school as a fact, while Butler expresses some doubt.

5. Marie Roberts, *Gothic Immortals: The Fiction of the Brotherhood of the Rosy Cross* (London: Routledge, 1989), pp. 1-18.

6. Ibid., p. 25.

7. Ibid., pp. 69, 71.

8. Ibid., p. 99.

9. Ibid., pp. 131-38.

10. Ibid., p. 34.

11. Ibid., pp. 166-67.

12. Ibid., pp. 168, 172-73.

13. Ibid., p. 159.

14. Ibid., p. 169, quoting a letter from Lytton to John Forster cited in Robert Bulwer-Lytton, *The Life of Edward Bulwer, First Lord Lytton by His Grandson* (London: 1913), p. 48.

15. Ibid, citing Robert Bulwer-Lytton, *Life*, p. 41.

16. Butler, *Myth of the Magus*, p. 245, citing Barker, *Mahatma Letters*, pp. 209-10.

17. In a letter to Hargrave Jennings in the early 1870s, Lytton claimed that he knew of some actual Rosicrucians who did not, in fact, go by that name in public; those who did presume to call themselves Rosicrucians (the s ri a?) were not the real thing (Roberts, *Gothic Immortals*, pp. 157-58). The Scottish occultist Kenneth Mackenzie, on the other hand, judged Lytton's knowledge of Rosicrucianism to be at the neophyte or pre-admission stage—in other words, almost worthless (McIntosh, *Rosicrucians*, p. 110). Mackenzie's own account of Rosicrucianism, however, was described as "one of recurring mendacity" by A. E. Waite (*Brotherhood*, p. 566); Waite's work, in turn, was characterized as "a pompous, turgid rigmarole of bombastic platitudes" by Aleister Crowley (*The Confessions of Aleister Crowley: An Autohagiography*, eds. John Symonds and Kenneth Grant [London: Arkana, 1989], p. 197).

18. Roberts, *Gothic Immortals*, pp. 164-165.

19. Ibid., p. 185.

20. Ellic Howe, *The Magicians of the Golden Dawn: A Documentary History of a Magical Order 1887-1923* (London: Routledge & Kegan Paul, 1972), pp. 26-27.

21. McIntosh, *Rosicrucians*, p. 110.

22. Ibid., pp. 110-11.

23. Greer, *Women of the Golden Dawn*, p. 1.

24. Waite, *Brotherhood*, pp. 549-54.

25. There are, of course, debates over whether alchemical sexual symbolism was purely symbolic or not; see, for example, Robert Anton Wilson, "Sexual Alchemy," *Gnosis* 8 (Summer 1988), 28-32. The more conventional view is expressed in Cavendish, *Magical Arts*, pp. 160-73.

26. For a general account of Tantrism in India, see Ajit Mookerjee and Madha Khamma, *The Tantric Way: Art, Science, Ritual* (London: Thames & Hudson, 1977).

27. Cavendish, *History of Magic*, pp. 150-51.

28. Robert North, "Introduction to the Life and Work of Pascal Beverly Randolph," in Randolph, *Sexual Magic* (New York: Magickal Childe, 1988), p. xxii; McIntosh, *Rosicrucians*, p. 130.

29. Randolph, *Sexual Magic*, p. 14.

30. Ibid., pp. 46-53.

31. North, "Introduction to Randolph," pp. xxv-xxviii.

32. Randolph, *Eulis! The History of Love* (Toledo, Ohio: 1874), cited in McIntosh, *Rosicrucians*, p. 130; emphasis in original.

33. Howe, *Magicians of the Golden Dawn*, p. 31; Cavendish, *History of Magic*, p. 138; McIntosh, *Rosicrucians*, p. 125.

34. McIntosh, *Rosicrucians*, pp. 110, 125.

35. The information presented here on Anna Kingsford is taken from Meade, *Blavatsky*, and Greer, *Women of the Golden Dawn*. They both draw on Edward Maitland's first-hand account, *Anna Kingsford: Her Life, Letters, Diary and Work* (London: George Redway, 1896).

36. Greer, *Women of the Golden Dawn*, p. 54.

37. Unless otherwise noted, this account of the Golden Dawn is based on Howe, *Magicians of the Golden Dawn*, and Greer, *Women of the Golden Dawn*.

38. Howe, *Magicians of the Golden Dawn*, p. 33.

39. Ibid., p. 11.

40. Ibid., pp. 8-12; Greer, *Women of the Golden Dawn*, p. 47.

41. Howe, *Magicians of the Golden Dawn*, pp. 11-12.

42. From an obituary of Mathers in *Occult Review* (April 1919), quoted and attributed to Waite by Howe, *Magicians of the Golden Dawn*, pp. 41-42.

43. Moina Mathers, preface to fourth edition of Mathers's *Kabbalah Unveiled*, quoted in Howe, *Magicians of the Golden Dawn*, p. 38.

44. Howe, *Magicians of the Golden Dawn*, p. 40; Cavendish, *History of Magic*, p. 143; Greer, *Women of the Golden Dawn*, p. 54.

45. Greer, *Women of the Golden Dawn*, p. 57.

46. Ibid., p. 352. Case left the Order soon afterwards to found his own occult movement, Builders of the Adytum, which is still operating.

47. John Michael Greer and Carl Hood Jr., "A Mystery of Sex," *Gnosis* 43 (Spring 1997): 20-27.

48. An interesting attempt to explain the effectiveness of the GD rituals by appealing to Jungian psychology is presented by Cris Monnastre and David Griffin in "Israel Regardie, the Golden Dawn, and Psychotherapy," *Gnosis* 37 (Fall 1995): 36-42. As we shall see in Chapter 12, however, Jung drew many of his central ideas from the same occult sources as did the Golden Dawn; consequently, it is almost a case of circular reasoning to validate the GD by appealing to Jung.

49. Howe, *Magicians of the Golden Dawn*, p. 49.

50. Ibid., pp. 209-11.

51. Quoted in Ibid., pp. 69-70.

52. Greer, *Women of the Golden Dawn*, p. 41.

53. Ibid., p. 55.

54. Ibid., pp. 350-58.

55. Ibid., p. 28.

56. Howe, *Magicians of the Golden Dawn*, p. 251.

57. Greer, *Women of the Golden Dawn*, p. 349.

58. Ibid., pp. 271, 343.

59. A sympathetic telling of Dion Fortune's story is available in Alan Richardson,

The Magical Life of Dion Fortune: Priestess of the 20th Century (London: Aquarian, 1987).

60. Richardson, *Dion Fortune*, pp. 118-20.

61. See Richardson, *Dancers to the Gods*.

62. Frederic Lees, "Isis Worship in Paris: Conversations with the Hierophant Rameses and the High Priestess Anari," *The Humanitarian* 16:2 (1900), cited in Greer, *Women of the Golden Dawn*, pp. 227-28.

63. There is now a vast literature by and about Crowley. The main sources used here are Symonds, *Confessions*; King, *Magical World*; and Colin Wilson, *Aleister Crowley. The Nature of the Beast* (Wellingborough: Aquarian, 1987).

64. Wilson, *Crowley*, pp. 76-79.

65. Symonds, *Confessions*, p. 35n.

66. King, *Magical World*, p. 28; Symonds, *Confessions*, p. 18.

67. King, *Magical World*, pp. 113-14, 136.

68. Ibid., pp. 135-36, 144.

69. Aleister Crowley, *Magick in Theory and Practice* (Secaucus, N.J.: Castle, 1991), p. xxii.

70. Ibid., pp. xii-xvi.

71. Crowley, *The Law Is for All. An Extended Commentary on the Book of the Law* (St. Paul: Llewellyn, 1975), pp. 98-117.

72. Ibid. The "fiercest of feminists" claim is made in Symonds, *Confessions*, p. 696.

73. Symonds, *Confessions*, pp. 96, 113, 142.

74. Quoted in Cavendish, *History of Magic*, p. 159.

75. Antoinette Lafarge and Robert Allen, "The Best of the Beast: How Do You Sort the Gold from the Dross in Aleister Crowley's Work?" *Gnosis* 24 (Summer 1992): 33, 35.

11 *Bachofen's Theory of Matriarchy*

1. Karl Meuli, "Bachofens Leben," in Johann Jakob Bachofen, *Gesammelte Werke*, III, ed. Karl Meuli (Basel: Benno Schwabe, 1948), p. 1067; Meuli, "Entstehung, Wesen und Nachwirkung des 'Mutterrechts'", in Bachofen, *Gesammelte Werke*, III, p. 1097; Wesel, *Mythos*, p. 10; Henri F. Ellenberger, *The Discovery of the Unconscious: The History and Evolution of Dynamic Psychiatry* (London: Penguin, 1970), p. 221; Stella Georgoudi, "Creating a Myth of Matriarchy," in *A History of Women in the West*, ed. Pauline Schmitt Pantel, trans. by Arthur Goldhammer, I (Cambridge, Mass.: The Belknap Press of Harvard University Press, 1992), p. 451.

2. Johann Jakob Bachofen, *Myth, Religion, and Mother Right*, trans. Ralph Manheim, Bollingen Series no. LXXXIV (Princeton: Princeton University Press, 1967), p. 120; Georgoudi, "Creating a Myth," p. 450.

3. Davis, *First Sex*, pp. 19, 36; Stone, *When God was a Woman*, p. 33; Eisler, *Sacred*

Pleasure, p. 87; Gadon, *Once and Future Goddess*, pp. 226-27; Sjöö and Mor, *Great Cosmic Mother*, p. 13; Adler, *Drawing Down the Moon*, pp. 46, 65, 174, 193.

4. Summaries of Bachofen's theory are available in many places, including George Boas's preface to Bachofen, *Myth, Religion, and Mother Right*, pp. xvi-xx; Ellenberger, *Discovery of the Unconscious*, pp. 219-23; Georgoudi, "Creating a Myth," pp. 450-56. In the following discussion, for convenience, I shall rely primarily on the excerpts from *Mutterrecht* in *Myth, Religion, and Mother Right*, pp. 69-207, and supplement it from the German original as necessary.

5. Bachofen, *Myth, Religion, and Mother Right*, p. 143.

6. Ibid., p. 94.

7. Ibid., p. 105.

8. Ibid., pp. 85-86.

9. Ibid., p. 132.

10. Ibid., pp. 143-44.

11. Ibid., p. 151.

12. Ibid., p. 146; see also pp. 91-92, 109.

13. Ibid., pp. 100-04.

14. Ibid., pp. 157-61.

15. Ibid., pp. 117-18, 147.

16. Ibid., p. 119.

17. Ibid., pp. 114-15.

18. Ibid., pp. 110-11.

19. Meuli, "Bachofens Leben," p. 1077.

20. Bachofen, *Myth, Religion, and Mother Right*, p. 171.

21. Ibid., p. 80.

22. Ibid., p. 84.

23. Georgoudi, "Creating a Myth," p. 457.

24. Bachofen, *Versuch über die Gräbersymbolik der Alten* (original edition Basel, 1859). *Myth, Religion, and Mother Right* contains excerpts in translation from this work as well.

25. Bachofen, *Das Mutterrecht. Eine Untersuchung über die Gynaikokratie der alten Welt nach ihrer religiösen und rechtlichen Natur* (Stuttgart: Krais & Hoffmann, 1861); Bachofen's notes on the illustrations are on pp. 421-24, and the line drawings themselves follow on unnumbered pages.

26. As Meuli notes, Bachofen does not even cite Ranke to acknowledge the profound effect of the latter's ideas on his own thinking: "Bachofens Leben," p. 1031.

27. Bachofen, *Mutterrecht*, v; *Myth, Religion, and Mother Right*, p.69.

28. Bachofen, *Myth, Religion, and Mother Right*, pp. 72, 73, 75.

29. Ibid., p. 199.

30. Bachofen, "My Life in Retrospect," in ibid., pp. 11-12.

31. Bachofen, *Mutterrecht*, pp. 58-62. This is a section of the original chapter on Athens which was not included in the English translation. Bachofen lists various

mythic associations of the number seven with his patriarchal champions like Orestes and Apollo, whereas five is linked to goddesses like Isis and Minerva. Athena, the goddess who sides with Orestes, is connected to both five and seven, and to six as sign of transition.

32. Bachofen, *Myth, Religion, and Mother Right*, pp. 72–73.

33. Ellenberger, *Discovery of the Unconscious*, p. 218.

34. Campbell, Introduction to *Myth, Religion, and Mother Right*, p. xli.

35. Homer, *Iliad* 6:155–202.

36. Bachofen, *Myth, Religion, and Mother Right*, p. 123.

37. Ibid.

38. Wesel, *Mythos*, p. 39; Georgoudi, "Creating a Myth," p. 462.

39. Wesel, *Mythos*, pp. 37–40.

40. Bachofen, *Myth, Religion, and Mother Right*, p. 16.

41. Campbell, Introduction to *Myth, Religion, and Mother Right*, p. xxv.

42. The basic facts on Bachofen's life are taken from Meuli, "Bachofens Leben"; Ellenberger, *Discovery of the Unconscious*, pp. 218-19; and Wesel, *Mythos*, pp. 9-12.

43. Campbell, Introduction to *Myth, Religion, and Mother Right*, p. xxxiv.

44. Meuli, "Bachofens Leben," pp. 1032, 1067; "Entstehung," pp. 1105-6.

45. Bachofen, *Myth, Religion, and Mother Right*, p. 227; see Campbell, Introduction to *Myth, Religion, and Mother Right*, p. xlvi; Georgoudi, "Creating a Myth," p. 456; contrast Boas, Preface to *Myth, Religion, and Mother Right*, p. xix.

46. Butler, *Saint-Simonian Religion in Germany*, pp. 84-86.

47. Bachofen, *Myth, Religion and Mother Right*, pp. 4-5.

48. Ibid., p. 6.

49. Wesel, *Mythos*, pp. 9-10.

50. Bachofen, *Myth, Religion, and Mother Right*, pp. 14-15.

51. Wesel, *Mythos*, p. 10.

52. Adler, *Drawing Down the Moon*, p. 174.

53. Bachofen, *Myth, Religion, and Mother Right*, pp. 22-23.

54. Campbell, Introduction to *Myth, Religion, and Mother Right*, p. xlii.

55. Bachofen, *Myth, Religion, and Mother Right*, p. 80.

56. Ibid., p. 86.

57. Ibid., p. 85.

58. Ibid., p. 87.

59. Bachofen, *Mutterrecht*, p. 390. The translation is my own. In the original those lines read as follows: "Daraus schöpfe ich die lohnende Zuversicht, dass die jetzt zu ihrem Ende gelangte Untersuchung für das Verständniss des Alterthums überhaupt fordemd und auch für die tiefere Kenntniss des Entwicklungsgangs der heutigen Welt, welcher französiche Schriftsteller die Rückkehr zu dem Isis-prinzip und zu der Naturwahrheit des Mutterrechts als alleiniges Heilmittel anempfehlen (Michelet, la femme p. 240 ff.; Girardin, égalité des enfants devant la mère p. 7 ff.), nicht ohne Frucht sein wird." In Meuli's edition, the references to Michelet and Girardin have

been removed from the text and placed in a footnote (Bachofen, *Gesammelte Werke*, III, p. 927).

60. Michelet, *La Femme*, pp. 252–54. In the original: "La femme règne . . . Le grand dieu, c'est une mère . . . L'amoureuse Afrique, de son profond désir, a suscité l'object le plus touchant des religions de la terre . . . Quel? La réalité vivante, une bonne et féconde femme."

61. Bachofen, *Mutterrecht*, pp. 14–15; *Myth, Religion, and Mother Right*, p. 139.

62. See Orr, *Michelet*, p. 78, and Kaplan, *Michelet's Poetic Vision*, pp. 84–88; the quotation from *The Insect* is from Kaplan, p. 87.

63. Bachofen, *Mutterrecht*, pp. 389–90. Wohin wir blicken, überall tritt uns die gleiche Wahrheit entgegen: keinem Volke, dessen religiöse Anschauung in dem Stoffe wurzelt, ist es gelungen, den Sieg der rein geistigen Paternität zu erringen und der Menschheit dauernd zu sichern. Auf der Zertrümmerung, nicht auf der Entwicklung und stufenweisen Reinigung des Materialismus ruht der Spiritualismus des einheitlich-väterlichen Gottes.

64. Bachofen, *Myth, Religion, and Mother Right*, p. 230.

65. Ibid., p. 237.

12 *Spreading the Theory of Matriarchy*

1. Boas, Preface to *Myth, Religion, and Mother Right*, p. xi.

2. Georgoudi gives a useful survey of the positive and negative reactions of various scholars to Bachofen's work; see "Creating a Myth," pp. 457–62.

3. Edward Westermarck, *The History of Human Marriage*, I (London: MacMillan & Co., 1921), pp. 275–98. See Georgoudi, note 2 above, for more examples.

4. Lewis Henry Morgan, *Ancient Society, or Researches in the Lines of Human Progress from Savagery through Barbarism to Civilization* (New York: Macmillan, 1877), cited in Ellenberger, *Discovery of the Unconscious*, p. 250n.; see also Campbell, Introduction to *Myth, Religion, and Mother Right*, p. lii.

5. Vogel, *Marxism*, pp. 75–79.

6. John B. Vickery, *The Literary Impact of the Golden Bough* (Princeton: Princeton University Press, 1973), pp. 20–24.

7. Sir James Frazer, *The Golden Bough: The Roots of Religion and Folklore*, I (1st edition, in two volumes; London: Macmillan, 1890; reprint New York: Avenel, 1981), p. 226n.

8. Jane E. Harrison, *Prolegomena to the Study of Greek Religion* (Cleveland & New York: World Publishing Company, 1959).

9. Sandra J. Peacock, "An Awful Warmth About Her Heart: The Personal in Jane Harrison's Ideas on Religion," in *The Cambridge Ritualists Reconsidered: Proceedings of the First Oldfather Conference, held on the campus of the Univeristy of Illinois at Urbana-Champaign April 27–30, 1989*, ed. William M. Calder III (Atlanta: Scholars, 1989), p. 168.

10. Harrison, *Prolegomena*, p. 131; see also Renate Schlesier, "Prolegomena to Jane Harrison's Interpretation of Ancient Greek Religion," in Calder, *Cambridge Ritualists*, p. 213.

11. Harrison, *Prolegomena*, p. 262n1.

12. Schlesier, "Prolegomena," p. 216n.107.

13. Harrison, *Prolegomena*, 261 and n.3.

14. Frazer, *The Magic Art and the Evolution of Kings*, 2:1 *The Golden Bough*, 3rd ed. (New York: St. Martin's Press, 1966), pp. 271-72; *Spirits of the Corn and of the Wild*, 1:7 *The Golden Bough*, 3rd ed., pp. 35-91, 113-213.

15. Frazer, *Adonis, Attis, Osiris*, 1:4 *The Golden Bough*, 3rd. ed., pp. 44-46.

16. Frazer, *Adonis, Attis, Osiris*, II, pp. 209-10.

17. Frazer, *Magic Art*, II, p. 313n.1.

18. Peacock, "Awful Warmth," p. 182. Here, as throughout, Peacock explains Harrison's shifting opinions entirely in terms of her personal life and relationships. For an interpretation which takes a more straightforward approach to Harrison's intellectual development, see Mary Lefkowitz, "Jane Made Unplain," *American Scholar* (1989), 464-68.

19. Harrison, *Epilegomena to the Study of Greek Religion and Themis* (New Hyde Park, New York: University Books, 1962), p. 494.

20. Harrison, *Themis*, p. 495.

21. Harrison, *Epilegomena*, pp. xxxii-xxxiv.

22. David M. Schneider, "Rivers and Kroeber in the Study of Kinship," W. H. R. Rivers, *Kinship and Social Organization*, London School of Economics Monographs on Social Anthropology, no.34 (London: Athlone, 1968), p.9.

23. W. H. R. Rivers, *The History of Melanesian Society*, vol. 2 (Oosterhout, Netherlands: Anthropological Publications, 1968), pp. 68, 102, 185, 188, 319.

24. Schneider, "Rivers and Kroeber," p. 15.

25. Vogel, *Marxism*, pp. 81-92; Tong, *Feminist Thought*, pp. 47-51. Tong mistakenly assigns the 1845 date of *The Holy Family* to Engels's *Origin*.

26. August Bebel, *Der Frau und der Sozialismus* (Stuttgart: Dietz, 1879); cited in Ellenberger, *Discovery of the Unconscious*, p. 222.

27. Sjöö, *Great Cosmic Mother*, pp. 13-17; Gadon, *Once and Future Goddess*, p. 227.

28. Matilda Joslyn Gage, *Woman, Church and State* (New York: Arno, 1972). Daly emphasized Gage's nine million victims of the witch hunts, and accused those who let *Woman, Church and State* go out of print of committing "mind-rape" against women. (*Gyn/Ecology*, p. 217.)

29. The accusation was made in a letter to the editor of *Academic Questions* (7:4 Fall 1994): 5, over the name of Rev. Ms. Aradia Gynette Apfelbaum, Chaplain of the Lesbian Liberation Army PLC, based in "Womyn House, Glastonbury, British Islands." She demanded "international laws to outlaw such antifemitism [*sic*]."

30. Campbell, Introduction to *Myth, Religion, and Mother Right*, p. xxv.

31. Claude David, *Von Richard Wagner zu Bertolt Brecht: Eine Geschichte der neueren*

deutschen Literatur, translated from French into German by Hermann Stiehl (Frankfurt/Hamburg: Fischer Bücherei, 1964), pp. 24, 121.

32. Richard Noll, *The Jung Cult: Origins of a Charismatic Movement* (Princeton: Princeton University Press, 1994), p. 167.

33. Ibid.

34. Otto Friedrich, *Before the Deluge: A Portrait of Berlin in the 1920's* (New York: Avon, 1972), p. 224; Alan Bullock, *Hitler and Stalin: Parallel Lives* (Toronto: McLelland & Stewart 1993), p. 834.

35. Alastair Reid, "Remembering Robert Graves," *New Yorker* (September 1995), 70–73. Rivers's later books included *Mind and Medicine* and *Instinct and the Unconscious*, both dated 1920.

36. John B. Vickery, *Robert Graves and the White Goddess* (Lincoln: University of Nebraska Press, 1972), pp. 2, 5, 32. The possibility that Graves actually read Bachofen himself is rejected in Martin Seymour-Smith, *Robert Graves: His Life and Work* (New York: Holt, Rinehart and Winston, 1983), pp. 233, 287.

37. Vickery, *Graves*, pp. 29, 47.

38. Ibid., pp. 82–86.

39. Hutton, *Pagan Religions*, p. 320.

40. Douglas Day, *Swifter than Reason: The Poetry and Criticism of Robert Graves* (Chapel Hill: University of North Carolina Press, 1963), pp. 165–67; Vickery, *Graves*, pp. ix–x; Seymour-Smith, *Graves*, pp. 386–88.

41. Reid, "Remembering Robert Graves," pp. 79–80.

42. Graves, "Postscript 1960," in *The White Goddess: A Historical Grammar of Poetic Myth* (New York: Farrar, Straus & Giroux, 1966), p. 488; and "Witches in 1964," *Virginia Quarterly Review* 40 (1964), 550–59.

43. Ellenberger, *Discovery of the Unconscious*, p. 222; on Freud, pp. 222–23, 542; on Adler, pp. 223, 611, 629; on Jung, pp. 223, 660, 727, 729.

44. See, for example, Frederick C. Crews, *Skeptical Engagements* (New York: Oxford University Press, 1986); E. Michael Jones, *Degenerate Moderns: Modernity as Rationalized Sexual Misbehavior* (Ignatius: San Francisco, 1993); John Kerr, *A Most Dangerous Method: The Story of Jung, Freud, and Sabina Spielrein* (New York: Vintage, 1993); and Noll, *Jung Cult*, as well as my review article, "The Swiss Maharishi: Discovering the Real Carl Jung & His Legacy Today," *Touchstone* 9:2 (Spring 1996), 10–14.

45. See Ellenberger, *Discovery of the Unconscious*, pp. 705–719; Noll, *Jung Cult*, pp. 218–233.

46. C. G. Jung, Foreword to "Phénomènes Occultes," in *Psychology and the Occult*, trans. R. F. C. Hull, Bollingen Series no.20 (Princeton: Princeton University Press, 1977), p. 3.

47. Jung, Foreword to Anelia Jaffé, "Apparitions and Precognition," in *Psychology and the Occult*, p. 153.

48. Noll, *Jung Cult*, pp. 121, 126, 181–82.

49. Erich Neumann, *The Great Mother* (Princeton: Princeton University Press, 1955); Gadon, *Once and Future Goddess*, p. 229.

50. Ellenberger, *Discovery of the Unconscious*, p. 660.

51. Kerr, *Most Dangerous Method*, p. 9.

52. For Freud's general views, see Ernest Jones, *Sigmund Freud: Life and Work* III (London: Hogarth Press, 1957), Chapter 13, "Religion," and Chapter 14, "Occultism."

53. Kerr, *Most Dangerous Method*, p. 446.

54. Ellenberger, *Discovery of the Unconscious*, p. 661.

55. Jung, *Memories, Dreams, Reflections*, recorded and edited by Aniela Jaffé, translated by Richard and Clara Winston (New York: Pantheon, 1963), pp. 87, 59; cited in Jones, *Degenerate Moderns*, pp. 201-02.

56. Ellenberger, *Discovery of the Unconscious*, pp. 661, 689-691.

57. Noll, *Jung Cult*, pp. 70-72.

58. Jung, *Psychology and the Occult*, p. vii.

59. Ellenberger, *Discovery of the Unconscious*, p. 665.

60. The story of Jung's encounter with Gross is told in Noll, *Jung Cult*, pp. 152-60, and Kerr, *Most Dangerous Method*, pp. 186-92.

61. Ellenberger, *Discovery of the Unconscious*, p. 729; Noll, *Jung Cult*, pp. 202-204; Kerr, *Most Dangerous Method*, pp. 502-507.

62. Jones, *Degenerate Moderns*, p. 194, quoting *The Freud/Jung Letters: The Correspondence Between Sigmund Freud and C. G. Jung*, ed. McGuire, trans. Ralph Manheim and R. F. C. Hull (Cambridge, Mass.: Harvard University Press, 1988), p. 289.

63. Jung, *Memories, Dreams, Reflections*, pp. 181-185.

64. *Analytical Psychology: Notes of the Seminar Given in 1925 by C. G. Jung*, ed. William McGuire, ed. (Princeton: Princeton University Press, 1989). This particular vision is described in Noll, *Jung Cult*, pp. 211-15; Kerr, *Most Dangerous Method*, p. 469.

65. Quoted in Noll, *Jung Cult*, p. 213. Noll also reproduces the Mithras statue on p. 215.

66. Noll reports that Jung recorded Honegger's role in his *Wandlung und Symbole der Libido* (1912), but that Honegger's name disappears in Jung's later discussions of the case (*Jung Cult*, pp. 181-83). Ellenberger, however, was aware in 1970 of Honegger's involvement (*Discovery of the Unconscious*, p. 705).

67. Friedrich Creuzer, *Symbolik und Mythologie der alten Völker, besonders der Griechen*, 4 vols. (Leipzig & Darmstadt: Leske, 1810-1812); Bachofen, *Myth, Religion, and Mother Right*, p. 114. The comment on Jung's interest in Creuzer is from Ellenberger, *Discovery of the Unconscious*, p. 729.

68. See, for example, Scott Heller, "Flare-Up over Jung," *Chronicle of Higher Education* (June 1995): A10, A16; Noll's reply in a letter to the editor, *Chronicle of Higher Education*, September, 1995; and James Gardner, "Jung at Heart," *National Review* (July 10, 1995): 60-63.

69. See McGuire, *Bollingen: An Adventure in Collecting the Past*, Bollingen Series (Princeton: Princeton University Press, 1982), especially pp. 173-74.

70. Stephen and Robin Larsen, *A Fire in the Mind: The Life of Joseph Campbell* (New York: Doubleday, 1991), p. 414, cited in Craig Payne, "True Lies: The Real Power of Myth," *Touchstone* 8:2 (Spring 1995): 19-23.

71. Jung, *Memories, Dreams, Reflections*, p. 39.

72. See the detailed discussion paper by Rev. Ed Hird, "Carl Jung, Neo-Gnosticism, & the MBTI," available from ARM's national office, 8 Withrow Avenue, Nepean, Ontario, Canada, K2G 2H6.

73. See, for instance, June Singer, "A Necessary Heresy: Jung's Gnosticism and Contemporary Gnosis," *Gnosis* 4 (Spring/Summer 1987): 11-19; and the entire issue of *Gnosis* 10 (Winter 1989), dedicated to the theme "Jung and the Unconscious."

13 *Michelet's Reinvention of Witchcraft*

1. Norman Cohn, *Europe's Inner Demons: An Enquiry Inspired by the Great Witch-Hunt* (London: Sussex University Press, 1975), pp. 211-13.

2. Ronald Holmes, *Witchcraft in British History* (London: Tandem, 1976), pp. 44-46; Elliot Rose, *A Razor for a Goat: A Discussion of Certain Problems in the History of Witchcraft and Diabolism* (Toronto: University of Toronto Press, 1989), p. 195.

3. See Diane Purkiss, *The Witch in History. Early Modern and Twentieth-Century Representations* (London and New York: Routledge, 1996), p. 28n23 and the sources cited there.

4. For this particular terminology, see M. J. Kephart, "Rationalists and Romantics among Scholars of Witchcraft," in ed. Max Marwick, *Witchcraft and Sorcery: Selected Readings* (New York: Penguin, 1970), pp. 326-42.

5. Rose, *A Razor for a Goat*, esp. pp. 152-77.

6. Cohn, *Inner Demons*, pp. 54-59, 99-125.

7. Purkiss, *The Witch in History*, pp. 7-88.

8. Ibid., p. 35.

9. Cohn, *Inner Demons*, pp. 103-04, citing Karl-Ernst Järcke, "Ein Hexenprozess," *Annalen der deutschen und ausländischen Criminal-Rechts-Pflege*, I (Berlin, 1828), esp. 450.

10. Orr, *Michelet*, p. 95.

11. Michelet, *Satanism and Witchcraft: A Study in Medieval Superstition*, trans. A. R. Allison (Secaucus, NJ: Citadel, 1939), p. 326.

12. Ibid., p. viii.

13. Cohn, *Inner Demons*, p. 107.

14. Thus ibid., pp. 105-07.

15. Michelet, *Satanism and Witchcraft*, p. viii.

16. Ibid., p. 73.

17. Ibid., pp. xii, xvii, 4, 19.

18. Ibid., p. xiv.

19. Ibid., pp. 5, 27, 58, 80.

20. Ibid., pp. 106-07.

21. Cohn, *Inner Demons*, p. 106.

22. Michelet, *Satanism and Witchcraft*, pp. 120-21, 163.

23. Ibid., p. 310.

24. Purkiss, *The Witch in History*, pp. 7–8.

25. The main sources on Leland's life are his own *Memoirs*, 2 vols. (London: William Heinemann, 1893), and the biography by his niece, Elizabeth Robins Pennell, *Charles Godfrey Leland: A Biography*, 2 vols. (Boston: Houghton, Mifflin & Co., 1906).

26. Leland, *Memoirs*, 72–73.

27. Ibid., p. 53; Pennell, *Leland*, 1:29.

28. Leland, *Memoirs*, 1:103.

29. Ibid., pp. 98–99.

30. Pennell, *Leland*, 1:63.

31. Ellenberger, *Discovery of the Unconscious*, pp. 79–81.

32. Pennell, *Leland*, 1:184–95.

33. Ibid., pp. 278, 288–89.

34. Pennell, *Leland*, 2:12.

35. Ibid., pp. 214–18.

36. Ibid., pp. 299, 408–09.

37. See Charles Godfrey Leland, *The Algonquin Legends of New England or Myths and Folk Lore of the Micmac, Passamaquoddy, and Penobscot Tribes* (Boston: Houghton, Mifflin & Co., 1884).

38. Thomas Parkhill, "'Of Glooskap's Birth, and of His Brother Malsum, the Wolf': The Story of Charles Godfrey Leland's 'Purely American Creation,'" *American Indian Culture and Research Journal* 16:1 (1992): 45–69.

39. Ibid., pp. 57–58.

40. Ibid., pp. 55.

41. Ibid., p. 63n.6.

42. Leland, *Aradia: Gospel of the Witches* (Custer, Washington: Phoenix, 1990), p. 101.

43. Pennell, *Leland*, II.

44. Leland, *Aradia*, p. 14.

45. Ibid., pp. 4–5.

46. Ibid., pp. 111–12.

47. Rose, *A Razor for a Goat*, pp. 216–18.

48. Leland, *Aradia*, p. 102.

49. Margaret Murray, *The Witch-Cult in Western Europe* (Oxford: Clarendon, 1962), p. 178.

50. Ibid., p. 159.

51. Ibid., pp. 13–14.

52. Cohn, *Inner Demons*, pp. 110–15.

53. Ibid., pp. 107–108; Rose, *Razor for a Goat*, pp. 14–15.

14 *Gardner and the Goddess*

1. Hutton, *Pagan Religions*, p. 331.

2. Aidan A. Kelly, *Crafting the Art of Magic, Book I: A History of Modern Witchcraft, 1939–1964* (St. Paul: Llewellyn, 1991), p. 44.

3. Ibid., pp. 21–26.

4. Several of the contributions to Marwick, *Witchcraft and Sorcery*, deal with this issue.

5. Chas S. Clifton, "A Goddess Arrives: The Novels of Dion Fortune and the Development of Gardnerian Witchcraft," *Gnosis* 9 (Fall 1988), 20–28.

6. Richardson, *Dancers to the Gods*, p. 84.

7. Ibid., pp. 113, 116.

8. Quoted in Kelly, *Crafting the Art*, p. 19.

9. Richardson, *Dancers to the Gods*, p. 175.

10. Kelly, *Crafting the Art*, pp. 19–20.

11. Most of the basic biographical information on Gardner comes from Jack L. Bracelin, *Gerald Gardner: Witch* (London: Octagon, 1960). Bracelin was a member of Gardner's coven (see Kelly, *Crafting the Art*, p. xviii); the book was written during Gardner's lifetime and it contains several factual errors. Insiders, including Doreen Valiente, do not seem to believe that Bracelin was the actual author; see her *The Rebirth of Witchcraft* (Custer, Washington: Phoenix, 1989), p. 69. Kelly (p. 185) was told by another member that Bracelin's name went on the book when Idries Shah, the true author, thought better of it all.

12. Bracelin, *Gardner*, p. 26.

13. Valiente, *Rebirth*, p. 42.

14. Kelly, *Crafting the Art*, pp. 27–28.

15. This list of Gardner's activities and affiliations is compiled from Bracelin, *Gardner*; Valiente, *Rebirth*; and Kelly, *Crafting the Art*. Some of the connections are also reported in Cavendish, *History of Magic*, and King, *Ritual Magic in England*.

16. There are some rather confused recollections regarding Mrs. Besant-Scott. She had been raised under her father's supervision, thanks to Annie Besant's conviction on the charge of distributing "obscene" birth-control information (see Chapter 9) but reestablished relations with her mother in her adulthood. Kelly (*Crafting the Art*, p. 20) suggests that Annie turned her interests towards Co-Masonry after losing to Leadbeater in the struggle to succeed HPB. As we saw, however, Annie Besant's rival at that point was William Quan Judge; it was she who raised Leadbeater to prominence and kept him there, to her own cost. Bracelin has a similar story, possibly from Gardner himself, to the effect that it was Mabel who resorted to Co-Masonry after being defeated by Leadbeater in the contest to succeed Annie (Bracelin, *Gardner*, p. 163). This story has problems too, since neither Leadbeater nor Mabel is named as a candidate for the Presidency in Leadbeater's own biography (see Tillett, *Elder Brother*, p. 250) or in Besant's (Nethercot, *Last Four Lives*, p. 456). Leadbeater died within a few months of Annie Besant in any case.

17. Kelly, *Crafting the Art*, p. 33–38.

18. E.g., Cavendish, *History of Magic*, p. 159; see Valiente, *Rebirth*, p. 57.

19. Adler, *Drawing Down the Moon*, pp. 101, 140.

20. Valiente, *Rebirth*, pp. 51-52.

21. Kelly, *Crafting the Art*, pp. 50-71.

22. Gerald B. Gardner, *Witchcraft Today* (New York: Magickal Childe, 1991), p. 18.

23. Ibid., pp. 102, 151-54, 158.

24. Ibid., p. 41.

25. Kelly, *Crafting the Art*, p. 112.

26. Gardner, *The Meaning of Witchcraft* (New York: Magickal Childe, 1991).

27. Valiente, *Rebirth*, pp. 27-29; Kelly, *Crafting the Art*, pp. 179-80; Clifton, "A Goddess Arrives."

28. Kelly, *Crafting the Art*, pp. 183.

29. Adler, *Drawing Down the Moon*, p. 93.

30. See Valiente, *Rebirth*, pp. 163-77.

31. Janet and Stewart Farrar, *The Witches' Goddess: The Feminine Principle of Divinity* (Custer, Washington: Phoenix, 1987).

32. Starhawk, *Spiral Dance*, pp. 204-05.

33. Budapest, *Holy Book*, p. 306.

34. Adler, *Drawing Down the Moon*, p. 77.

Conclusion

1. See, for example, the discussion in Morris Berman, *The Reenchantment of the World* (Ithaca: Cornell University Press, 1981), especially pp. 289-91.

2. Henry Ashby Turner, Jr., "Peter Novick and the 'Objectivity Question' in History," *Academic Questions* 8:3 (Summer 1995): 19.

3. For the quotation, see *Rama Prasada's Devotional Songs: The Cult of Shakti*, trans. Jadunath Sinha (Calcutta: Sinha Publishing House, 1966), p. 27. For general information on the Hindu goddesses, see David R. Kinsley, *The Sword and the Flute* (Berkeley: University of California Press, 1975), pp. 81-149; *Hindu Goddesses: Visions of the Divine Feminine in the Hindu Religious Tradition* (Berkeley: University of California Press, 1988), pp. 95-105, 116-31; *The Goddesses' Mirror: Visions of the Divine from East and West* (Albany: SUNY Press, 1989), pp. 3-14. Kinsley concluded (*Hindu Goddesses*, p. 132) that the notion of a single Great Goddess in Hinduism is late rather than early and represents the gradual synthesis of many distinct goddesses—exactly the reverse of the process asserted by devotees of the Western Goddess.

4. Sandra P. Robinson, "Hindu Paradigms of Women: Images and Values," in *Women, Religion, and Social Change*, eds. Yvonne Yazbek Haddad and Ellison Banks Findly, (Albany: SUNY Press, 1985), pp. 181-215; Lou Ratté, "Goddesses, Mothers, and Heroines: Hindu Women and the Feminine in the Early Nationalist Movement," in *Women, Religion, and Social Change*, pp. 351-76; Jan Myrdal, *India Waits* (Chicago: Lake View, 1986), pp. 266-76; Katherine K. Young, "Hinduism," in *Women in World Religions*, ed. Arvind Sharma (Albany: SUNY Press, 1987), pp. 59-103.

5. Conrad Schirokauer, *A Brief History of Chinese and Japanese Civilizations* (New York: Harcourt Brace Jovanovich, 1978), pp. 298-99, 535; Kinsley, *Goddesses' Mirror*, pp. 78-79; Nicholas Bornoff, *Pink Samurai: Love, Marriage & Sex in Contemporary Japan* (New York: Pocket Books, 1991), pp. 455-79.

6. For general discussions of feminist epistemology, see *Women, Knowledge, and Reality: Explorations in Feminist Philosophy*, eds. Ann Garry and Marilyn Pearsall, (Boston: Unwin Hyman, 1989), especially the contributions by Caroline Whitbeck, "A Different Reality: Feminist Ontology," pp. 51-76, and Genevieve Lloyd, "The Man of Reason," pp. 111-28. For a more popular introduction, see Gray, *Patriarchy as a Conceptual Trap*, pp. 52-62, 120-25. For an "equity feminist" critique of this approach, see Sommers, *Who Stole Feminism?*, especially pp. 74-78.

7. See Alison Jaggar, "Love and Knowledge: Emotion in Feminist Epistemology," in *Women, Knowledge and Reality*, pp.129-156; Hilary Rose, "Beyond Masculinist Realities: A Feminist Epistemology for the Sciences," in *Feminist Approaches to Science*, ed. Ruth Bleier (Oxford: Pergamon, 1986), pp. 57-76; Margaret Whitford, "Luce Irigaray's Critique of Rationality," in *Feminist Perspectives in Philosophy*, eds. Morwenna Griffiths, and Margaret Whitford (Bloomington and Indianapolis: Indiana University Press, 1988), p. 109-30; and Morwenna Griffiths "Feminism, Feelings and Philosophy," in *Feminist Perspectives*, pp. 131-51.

8. Sandra Walker Ramisch made this claim while discussing her paper "Buried Treasure: A Feminist Historical Reconstruction of Associations of Ascetic Christian Women Before 300 C.E."

9. John M. Ellis, "Feminist Theory's Wrong Turn," *Academic Questions* 7:4 (Fall 1994): 42-50.

10. Jerry L. Martin, "The University as Agent of Social Transformation: The Postmodern Argument Considered," *Academic Questions* 6:3 (Summer 1993): 55-72.

11. In addition to Martin, "University as Agent," see Peter Shaw, "Radicalizing the College Classroom," *Academic Questions* 8:3 (Summer 1995): 67-72.

12. The *Bulletin* is published by CAUT, 308-294 Albert St., Ottawa, Ontario, Canada, K1P 6E6.

13. See Philip G. Davis, "Educational Equity and Its Intellectual Baggage: CAUT Bulletin Supplement On The Status Of Women," *Society for Academic Freedom and Scholarship Newsletter* (December 1993): 3-6. For an American account of similar matters, see Martin, "The University as Agent."

14. John Fekete, *Moral Panic: Biopolitics Rising* (Montreal/Toronto: Robert Davies, 1994), p. 316.

15. The statement was attributed to Catherine Comins, Assistant Dean of Student Life at Vassar College, in Nancy Gibbs, "When Is It Rape?" *Time*, June 1991, 52; cited in Warren Farrell, *The Myth of Male Power: Why Men Are the Disposable Sex* (New York: Simon & Shuster, 1993), p. 309.

16. I am grateful to Dr. Patai for providing me with a copy of the "Vision 2000" document and with an advance copy of her review article, "Women's Studies and the

Future: 'Vision 2000' or 1984?" which is to appear in a January 1998 issue of *Chronicles of Higher Education*; this is the source of the quotation.

17. Tong, *Feminist Thought*, pp. 95-138.

18. Farrell, *Myth of Male Power*, pp. 321-30; Fekete, *Moral Panic*, pp. 54-57.

19. Fekete, *Moral Panic*, pp. 147-152. See also Sommers, *Who Stole Feminism?*, pp. 207-21.

20. See Farrell, *Myth of Male Power*, p. 219.

21. Farrell, *Myth of Male Power*, pp. 214-15 and the sources cited there.

22. Significant studies include Murray A. Straus, Richard J. Gelles, and Suzanne K. Steinmetz, *Behind Closed Doors: Violence in the American Family* (New York: Doubleday/Anchor, 1980); Straus and Gelles, "Societal Change and Change in Family Violence from 1975 to 1985 as Revealed by Two National Surveys," *Journal of Marriage and Family* 48 (1986), 465-80; Merlin B. Brinkerhoff and Eugen Lupri, "Interspousal Violence," *Canadian Journal of Sociology* 13:4 (1988), 407-31; Straus and Gelles, *Physical Violence in American Families* (New Brunswick NJ: Transaction, 1990); and R. L. McNeely and Gloria Robinson-Simpson, "The Truth about Violence: A Falsely Framed Issue," in *Gender Sanity*, ed. Nicholas Davidson (New York: University Press of America, 1989), pp. 163-76. See also the discussions in William D. Gairdner, *The War Against the Family* (Toronto: Stoddart, 1992), pp. 343-49; Sommers, *Who Stole Feminism?*, pp. 188-208; and Patricia Pearson, "Women Behaving Badly," *Saturday Night* 112:7 (September 1997): 90-100. The last-named article is excerpted from Pearson's forthcoming book, *When She was Bad: Women and the Myth of Innocence* (Toronto: Random House of Canada).

23. Fekete, *Moral Panic*, pp. 60-61, 75-80; Pearson, "Women Behaving Badly," 96. Both Fekete and Pearson report DeKeseredy's reluctance to release the figures on female violence. DeKeseredy responded to Pearson with a letter to the editor in *Saturday Night* 112:9 (November 1997): 11, reporting the publication of his article with Saunders, Schwartz and Shahid Alvi in *Sociological Spectrum* 17 (November 1997): 199-222. This article is so recent that I have not been able to obtain it by the time of writing.

24. Farrell, *Myth of Male Power*, p. 216; Fekete, *Moral Panic*, pp. 30-31.

Index of Names

Abrahamson, Valerie, 34
Adler, Alfred, 293, 302
Adler, Margot, 48, 88, 260, 338-39, 354
Agrippa, Heinrich Cornelius, 129, 158, 200, 231, 316, 345
Aldworth, Elizabeth (née St. Leger), 236
Alighieri, Dante, 161, 166, 188
Anderson, Victor, 339-340
Andreae, Johann Valentin, 134-36, 142
Apollonius of Tyana, 204, 233
Ashmole, Elias, 140-41
Atwood, Mary Anne, 236
Austen, Hallie Inglehart, 50
Aveling, Edward, 216

Bachofen, Johann Jakob, 43, 167, 259, 342-43, 351;
  and Freud, 293
  in Goddess literature, 43, 71, 341-42, 354
  and Jung, 293-294, 296, 299, 301-03
  life and influences on, 272-20
  methodology, 265-71
  and modem literature, 290-93
  Mortuary Symbolism, 274-75

Das Mutterrecht (Mother-Right), 260-71, 276-279, 281
The Myth of Tanaquil, 274, 279
  and political radicalism, 288-290
  reception of theory, 282-288
Bailey, Alice, 227, 341
Baring, Anne, 50
Barrault, Emile, 179-180
Baffett, Francis, 230, 316
Bazard, Amand, 178
Bebel, August, 289
Bergasse, Nicolas, 147, 149, 175
Besant, Annie (née Wood), 215-216, 222-223, 235, 340, 351, 403n.16
Besant-Scott, Mabel, 215, 332, 351, 403n.16
Blavatsky, Helena Petrovna, "HPB" (née von Hahn), 197, 235, 242, 351
  early life, 208-211
  in Goddess literature, 341
  Isis Unveiled, 213, 215
  Secret Doctrine, 215, 216-21
  and Theosophical Society, 212-16, 222
Boehme, Jakob, 142
Bonaparte, Napoleon, 11, 151, 154, 156, 189

407

Index of Subjects

413

A Note on the Author

Philip G. Davis is a professor of religious studies at the University of Prince Edward Island in Canada. He has published scholarly work on the Gospel of Mark, early Christology, and Western neopaganism. Professor Davis holds undergraduate and doctoral degrees from McMaster University, Ontario, and has written for *Academic Questions*, the *Journal of Theological Studies*, *Sciences Religieuses*, and *Touchstone*, among other journals. He and his wife live in Charlottetown, Prince Edward Island, with their four children, where they serve as foster parents for Queens Region Child and Family Services and consultants to the provincial Health and Community Services Agency.

This book was designed and set into type

by Mitchell S. Muncy,

with cover art by Stephen J. Ott,

and printed and bound

by Quebecor Printing Book Press,

Brattleboro, Vermont.

❦

The text face is Adobe Caslon,

designed by Carol Twombly,

based on faces cut by William Caslon, London, in the 1730s,

and issued in digital form by Adobe Systems,

Mountain View, California, in 1989.

❦

The paper is acid-free and is of archival quality.

9